ART ACTIVISM
FOR AN
ANTICOLONIAL
FUTURE

SUNY series, Praxis: Theory in Action
Nancy A. Naples

ART ACTIVISM

FOR AN

ANTICOLONIAL

FUTURE

CARLOS GARRIDO CASTELLANO

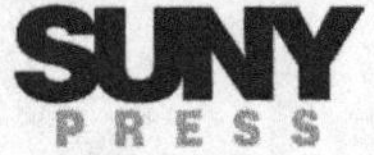

Cover image: Abandoned Beaver Dam at Karukinka, 2016. Image courtesy of Christy Gast.

Published by State University of New York Press, Albany

For information, contact State University of New York Press, Albany, NY
www.sunypress.edu

Library of Congress Cataloging-in-Publication Data

Names: Garrido Castellano, Carlos, author.
Title: Art activism for an anticolonial future / Carlos Garrido Castellano.
Description: Albany : State University of New York Press, [2021] | Series:
    SUNY series, praxis: theory in action | Includes bibliographical
    references and index.
Identifiers: LCCN 2021000579 | ISBN 9781438485737 (hardcover) | ISBN
    9781438485744 (ebook)
Subjects: LCSH: Art—Political aspects. | Art and social action. |
    Decolonization in art.
Classification: LCC N72.P6 G385 2021 | DDC 701/.03—dc23
LC record available at https://lccn.loc.gov/2021000579

10 9 8 7 6 5 4 3 2 1

CONTENTS

PART 4: ENCLOSURES, APERTURES, AND THE PERFORMATIVE

ILLUSTRATIONS

ACKNOWLEDGMENTS

This book owes much to the generosity and determination of cultural activists, scholars and artists all corners of the world. Special thanks to my editors at SUNY, Rebecca Colesworthy and James Peltz, for their continuous support and valuable feedback. Thanks also to the anonymous peer reviewers who contributed to improve the first version of the book. I would like to express my gratitude to: Santi Pérez, Marta Pacheco, Fernanda Gil Costa, Inocência Mata, Magdalena López, Rita Correia, Elsa Peralta, Clara Saraiva, Filipa Rosário, Sofia Pinto, Miguel Amado, Paulo Raposo, Otávio Raposo, Pedro Lapa, Susana Araújo, Everton Machado, Helena Buescu, Ana Nolasco, Ângela Fernandes, Bruno Leitão, Jorge Cabrera Gómez, Lizi Meneses, Adriana Bebiano, Joana Craveiro, António Sousa Ribeiro in Portugal. This book could not have been possible without the supportive atmosphere I found at the University College Cork. Thanks to Helena Buffery, Pedro Nilsson-Fernández, Céire Broderick, Clare Geraghty, Rafa Jaime and all my colleagues at SPLAS; to Chiara Giuliani, Yairen Jerez, James O'Sullivan, Marco Amici, Daragh O'Connell, Pat Crowley, Dónal Hassett, Silvia Ross, Kevin Cawley, Till Weingartner and all my colleagues at CACSSS. Thanks also to Helen Carey and the Firestation Dublin staff, Fiona Kearney and Mary Kelly. I found a perfect space to discuss and improve the chapters of this book in the lectures of the MA in Global Gallery Studies. Thanks to my colleagues Lucy Dubert, Giulia Luciani, Fiona Carey, Kayleigh Falvey, Chloé Griffin, Phoebe Milne, Heather Dorgan, Marie Lynch, and Giulia Priori for providing answers to some of my doubts as well as for arising more productive questions.

My gratitude to the staff of Coffee Dock at the O'Rahilly Building, a place that became my second office in the last stage of writing. Special thanks to Nuala Finnegan for her continuous support and help with the preparation of the final version of this book. In Kampala, thanks to Margaret Nagawa, Lilian Mary Nabulime, Fred Batale, Teesa Bahana, Angelo Kakande and the supportive staff of the art history department at Makerere University and the artistic community of 32° East: Ugandan Arts Trust. Thanks also to Tatiana Neves and the Fundação Amílcar Cabral, to Ceri Dingle, Andrew Smith, Ugochukwu-Smooth Nzewi, Mounira Souliman, Patrick Mudekereza, Alexandros Kioupkiolis, André Mesquita, Denisa Tomkova, Nomusa Makhubu, Jay Koh, Amanda Abi Khalil and the staff of Ashkal Alwan and the American University of Beirut. In Java, special thanks to Agung Jenong, Brigitta Isabella, Wok the Rock, Annie Sloman and the members of Taring Padi, ruangrupa, and the staff of Kunci Cultural Studies Center and the Indonesian Visual Art Archive. In Chile and beyond special thanks to Camila Marambio, Christy Gast and Carla Macchiavello. In the United States, thanks to the *Field Journal* editorial team, Diana Taylor, Suzanne Lacy, Claire Bishop, Brian Holmes, Michaeline Crichlow, Edward J. Sullivan, Terry Smith and all the staff of CUNY, NYU, Duke University and the University of California San Diego who were patient enough to welcome me and help in this research. Special thanks to Grant Kester and Greg Sholette for the feedback provided on specific chapters. This book would not exist without the continuous support of Pat Odber. Finally, my warmest gratitude goes as always to Leonor Oliveira for her infinite patience and support.

It goes without saying that I am the only responsible of all the possible mistakes and lacks of the book. Part of chapter 5 simultaneously appeared in 2018 in *Field: A Journal of Socially Engaged Art* of in California and *Start Journal* in Kampala under the title of "The Boda Moment: Positioning Socially Engaged Art in Contemporary Uganda." Part of chapter 7 previoulsy appeared in 2020 in *Studi Maghrebini* Journal under the title of "Temporary Art Platform and the Reconfiguration of the Public Space in Beirut." A much shorter version of chapter 8 was published in 2019 in *Discipline* Journal under the title of "Utility, Uselessness, and Speculative Study: On Ensayos."

INTRODUCTION

This work, *Art Activism for an Anticolonial Future*, sets out to identify socially engaged artists as active practitioners of decolonization. Conceiving of both socially engaged art and decolonial thought as potentially subversive, praxis-based tools for social transformation, the book argues that there is much to be gained from putting both traditions into dialogue. I believe that both share objectives and can complement and refine each other. Following Cedric Robinson's incisive observation that capitalism is always racial capitalism, and that social inequalities are shaped by (and shape in turn) racial categorizations, *Art Activism for an Anticolonial Future* maintains that art activists and socially engaged artists are equipped with a decades-long experience of challenging the reasoning that lies behind neoliberal capitalism.

In this book, I argue that there exist multiple, alternative genealogies of socially engaged art. This means at least two things: first, that our histories of art and activism and our critical appreciation of those cultural phenomena are incomplete if they fail to explore the transnational articulations (both historical and contemporary) deployed by affirmative, resistant artistic initiatives, many of which have emerged and are emerging from the Global South. Second, and more important, since those histories clarify our present situation, the act of silencing part of them will forcefully imply an erasure and therefore limit and circumscribe the potential that radical, activist artistic practices can still have in the present. Through this book, I excavate the political paradigms at play in socially engaged art in order to see how theories of colonial power relations can explain former, present, and future forms of artistic engagement in which, obviously, different sets of uneven forces and bonds operate. Stressing the relevance of coloniality for the comprehension of socially engaged art does not mean that a decolonial lens (a theory) should be applied to the art projects (a set of creative practices) analyzed in this book. The point is, rather, to look anew at coloniality as a central factor shaping many of the obstacles that socially engaged and activist art have faced in the past and continue to face. However, it is important to determine the extent to which ideas and theories on colonialism and its cultural influence make us more attentive to and more critical of the use and value of art, socially committed or otherwise. Through this double movement, *Art Activism for an Anticolonial Future* will showcase some of the tensions that emerge from this confluence between socially engaged art and coloniality.

It follows from here that recognizing the global currency of socially engaged art does not mean incorporating a few case studies into the well-known list of usual suspects. It is not enough to acknowledge the existence of multiple genealogies of social practice existing under the radar of mainstream academic or artistic backgrounds; nor is it sufficient to point out the relevance of some of these projects as peripheral influences or distant relatives of other commonly discussed practices. On the contrary, *Art Activism for an Anticolonial Future* affirms that it is our whole understanding of the concepts and practices of agency and social transformation that should be expanded and interrogated. Related to this, the universal value of concepts and political constructs, such as civil society and public space, should be interrogated, not just from a theoretical perspective but also when scrutinizing each project. The specificities of context and location are not just additional elements associated with particular creative practices; rather, they urge us to redefine the conceptual apparatus designed to measure the aesthetic and social relevance of artistic creativity.

Critical appreciations of socially engaged art practice have tended to be anchored from within a universalizing conceptual framework, without paying much attention to the spatial dynamics that configure both creative practices and art criticism. Always written in English, the term "socially engaged art" was popularized in the United States and Western Europe around the start of the twenty-first century to refer to a mode of artistic creativity that employed long-term collaboration as a means of achieving certain forms of sociopolitical transformation. The expression "socially engaged" thus competed with many others, including "participatory art," "collaborative art," "useful art," "new-genre public art," and "social practice," among others. Although a specific set of artistic projects and a list of artists' names is associated with each of those concepts, and each has a specific genealogy behind it, they overlap in many ways and their use in scholarly criticism in the art world more widely has increased or decreased over the last two decades. This diglossia notwithstanding, the critical debate over engaged and activist art practices has set aside the debates over which term is most adequate and moved from a debate on terminology to discussions of the many ways in which the strategies and resources of radical creativity can be co-opted and mobilized for conservative and exploitative interests.

Expressed simply, the story of the commodification of socially engaged art is tied to what these specific terms make visible. Some artists operating on the peripheries of the "mainstream art world" realized that the production of material artworks was objectifying, and artists' commitment to separate themselves from other productive forces was ultimately unproductive. In response, they started to collaborate. This artistic collaboration was intended not so much to change what is understood by art but rather to question and explore how the role of art in producing change was both desirable and politically urgent. Then came the backlash. Different forms of creative production were turned into formal arrangements of accommodation to the present, consolidating motionless movement, leading to paralysis. The capacity of artistic collaboration for space making—its ability to redistribute and repurpose agencies, affects, and effects—was placed at the service of institutional desires and predictable, programmed cultural transformation. Emancipatory processes of space making and translatable radical synergies were replaced by the ubiquity of a creative class operating qua the last (the only remaining, the definitive) revolutionary class, of mainstream art institutions choreographing activism, of mutinous experience and local resilience turned into universally applicable know-how. In the last episodes of the story of change that lies at the core of social practice, "change" disappears, becoming commodified ubiquitous inertia.

Although I accept that the global commercial success of socially engaged art (and the concomitant existence of a "social turn" in artistic practice) is linked to the erosion of progressive politics everywhere, I am reluctant to accept the idea of the demise of art's potential for social transformation. In particular, I am skeptical of the idea that the success of this kind of practice implies the consolidation of a modernist form of artistic creativity, one that arose from the context of the Euro-American avant-garde and was later expanded globally.

In opposition to the understanding of socially engaged art as a global trend, this book conceives of socially engaged art projects as a set of located, frequently transgressive actions seeking to challenge visible and not-so-visible forms of coloniality. If the idea of socially engaged art needs to be unpacked before applying it, something similar happens with the critical vocabulary employed to describe, name, and interpret it. Decolonial thought has been essential in dismantling the universalizing nature of the theoretical constellations of Western humanities and social sciences. In this respect, its endeavors have continued, expanding anticolonialism's interest in not only overcoming the culture of the colonizer but also doing so in a way that could equate cultural agency with social change. Decolonial thought and praxis pursue ways of engaging heterogeneous communities existing within national territories in active, radical ways, stressing the urgency of implementing participatory and anti-elitist understandings of cultural practices. In that sense, they attempt to overcome the individualism and the class narrowness of colonial culture, encouraging the emergence of both new cultural forms and new ways of partaking in and expanding them. Conceiving the legacy of decolonial processes as necessarily multiple, complex, and not limited to a specific time frame, this book explores how a decolonial ethos can inform a broader, more effective contemporary socially engaged art aesthetics. In situating "South" socially engaged art projects within a wider framework of progressive, radical action *and* thought, *Art Activism for an Anticolonial Future* aims not so much to contextualize and historicize past and present currents of art activism, but rather proposes to highlight the heterogeneous, productive ways in which these creative currents help us to make sense of our own experience and future expectations. Removed from the urgency of presentism and teleology (explaining current trajectories of social change as being more clever, more effective, and better informed than in the past), the interpretation of socially engaged art presented in this book reframes those questions while also questioning the critical vocabulary used to broach them.

Viewed through a lens focused on coloniality, socially engaged art reveals that critical ideas and appreciations are unintelligible without the experiences and critical traditions emerging in places traditionally left outside of Western and global accounts of contemporary artistic practice. Anticolonial struggles, for example, were essential in materially shaping ideas of collective agency and social transformation throughout the twentieth century. Indeed, anticolonialism was crucial in determining what radical culture looked like in its historical moment, decisively contributing to the configuration of a vocabulary of radical coexistence. When weighing the impact of activist art in the present, it is all the more pressing to evaluate how alive this legacy can be. In this way, the historical indebtedness of Western and Eurocentric philosophy and critical thought to the anticolonial experience (which affects art criticism in similar ways) is aligned with the present blindness of many "global" views that still envision the South as a place of derivative ideas and practices, a place frozen in time, where originality, innovation, and historical relevance have been extirpated and translated elsewhere.

My own engagement with socially engaged art intentionally adopts the experimental, the experience-based impetus channeled by the kind of art projects analyzed here. The second main hypothesis sustained throughout this book is that praxis informs our understanding of cultural processes just as much as theory. When it comes to socially engaged art, the unpredictable process of negotiating a common ground among the multiple actors involved in artistic collaboration becomes a powerful source of critical thought. I am interested, then, in excavating the multiple ways in which radical creativity from postcolonial, non-Western contexts can inform theory. Understanding, in line with Theodore Schatzki (2001: 13), that theory is always practiced and that practice always contains a degree of (collective) thinking, *Art Activism for an Anticolonial Future* envisages the transformative potential of subversive, radical, collaborative artistic creativity for retooling our conceptual repertoire for epistemic and embodied decolonization.

If theory and practice reciprocally inform each other, then it follows that critical conceptualizations of socially engaged art projects should carefully consider the specificities of place and location in which both take place. A short anecdote provides a timely example about the dangers of adopting socially engaged art and activism as a sort of ready-to-use tool susceptible to being applied without context-sensitive awareness. In 2017, during a short period of fieldwork in Hong Kong, former artist Tsang Tak "Kith" Ping shared with me the conclusions he had reached after his experiences of activism and resistance against neoliberalism over the course of several decades: for him, the only effective mode of change was through radical, direct action.[1] Many had tried in the past, he argued, to change Chinese politics. However, only the action of going to Beijing and "poisoning the emperor" (which I took to be a metaphor for the need to locate and know your enemy in order to directly confront it) proved effective. Outside of this radical action, Hong Kong activism, according to Kith, remained a sort of "colonial version of *The Hunger Games*" that the financial elite of the Chinese empire watched with amusement. For him, then, acting was a matter of spatial awareness. The local dimension from which many of the protests and artistic projects were framed was simply not enough for confronting Hong Kong's complex relation with China and the global economy. Kith realized that "local" was not a stable formula ensuring good results; on the contrary, for him "local" stood for the thoroughgoing knowledge that only sustained engagement and experience can provide. Speaking from his situatedness, Kith identified hardcore and soft-core paths to activism. He tried both and, when he thought that it was enough, he partially withdrew from the art world, remaining an educator and a source of motivation for many Hong Kongese artists.[2]

Kith's itinerary should not discourage us. Indeed, I take it to be perfect advice about the importance of conceptualizing and contextualizing space and strategy when producing and analyzing socially engaged art initiatives. Many of the debates on socially engaged art have taken place without enough spatial sensitivity. As a result, the entire scope of practices usually falling under the umbrella term "socially engaged art" have been praised or condemned without taking into consideration the contingent ways in which specific experiments in radical creative imagination nurture specific lexicons of activist intervention. By grounding South radical artistic practices within broader theoretical and cultural ecosystems, *Art Activism for an Anticolonial Future* intends to reverse such shortcomings.

Undisciplining Socially Engaged Art

Operating from a contingent, situated position, the first objective of this book is to excavate canonical and alternative histories of socially engaged art to make them productively unfamiliar. One of this book's main hypotheses can be expressed in a simple way: socially engaged art is much more than an artistic style deriving from the experiments with the artistic collaboration of the Western avant-garde, including historic avant-garde movements in the 1910s and 1920s (futurism, constructivism) and experimental creativity in the 1960s (situationism, Fluxus) (see Bishop 2012). Despite the international success of processes of artistic collaboration and the at least partial consolidation of this kind of creative practice through the interest of mainstream art institutions and the development of master's programs (especially in the United States and Western Europe), the effect and social signification of activist and socially engaged forms of artistic creativity cannot be reduced to any established or canonized phenomenon. Certainly, the canonization of socially engaged art has a decisive influence on the way artists think about and materialize their practices. At the same time, however, I believe that socially engaged art remains a powerful tool for expanding the social relevance of artistic creativity and for addressing pressing socioeconomic concerns. It is from that position that this book argues for redefining socially engaged art as conditioned by its recent success but also still operating as an increasingly disciplined cultural practice that nevertheless remains productively undisciplined.

Throughout the following pages, socially engaged art emerges as both a way of making art (which follows a methodology, reads in a particular way, expresses itself with a particular language, and complies with specific objectives) and a way of understanding art's role within society and emancipative praxis' role within artistic creativity. Socially engaged art has moved from being unrepresented and marginalized within art discussions to being considered and favored by museums (at least in its softer versions). At the same time, however, in the present moment it has also become something far more complex than an artistic trend: a mode of "doing" culture, a powerful tool for despecializing, undisciplining, and unmastering cultural interactions. The consequence of this double conceptualization can also be easily understood: for instance, just as it is impossible to conceive a Western critical tradition without the contributions of Black and non-Western radical thought, it is equally impossible to sketch any history of critical, engaged artistic practice without considering the centrality of insurgent cultural forms produced by individuals and collectivities subjected to multiple forms of colonial domination. Usually confined within local configurations and associated with particular causes, many of the radical movements emerging out of anticolonialism and decolonization were and are concerned with improving humanity and not just the lives of the colonized. This has been made clear recently by movements such as Black Lives Matter and its aspiration to fight to have all human lives valued and respected. When approaching the aesthetic side of what Cedric Robinson (2005) called the "Black Radical Tradition," a different kind of humanity and universalism appears, one based on strategic and contingent alliances. Praxis and engagement are prone to appear with more clarity in contexts subjected to the most brutal forms of racial capitalism, that is, in contexts subjected to the impact of different forms of colonial dominance: first, because cultural models were imposed and therefore cultural renovation could only happen with a social dimension, after expanding the role of culture within society, and second, because in this context cultural struggles take an urgent, political form. When viewed from a peripheral, unfamiliar perspective, socially engaged art can emerge as a resilient force nurturing alternative traditions of partisan aesthetics.

In that sense, without forgetting the consequences deriving from the emergence of activist and socially engaged art as a major art current (even, we would dare to say, as a discipline), *Art Activism for an Anticolonial*

Future resists the idea of defeat. Things would appear differently, I believe, if we conceived of our times as a crossroads where neoconservative forms are being implemented worldwide but also where progressive interventions manifest themselves as a lucid and tenacious force as in few other epochs. Our time of crisis is also, I would suggest, a time of particular social innovation and collective productive coordination. In fact, crisis and progressive response are not just historical stages, advancing or receding forces. Nor can they be universalized. Despite the contradictions surrounding socially engaged art practice and the critical thought emerging around them, the practitioners appearing in the pages of this book can teach us many lessons concerning the importance of experience and experimentation, the need to find open-ended solutions to shifting problems, the fertile mixing of pragmatism and utopian imagination, and the potential of contingent yet open sites of radical struggle. In the context of this book, socially engaged art is conceived of as a set of practices pursuing practical, real objectives related to social transformation and emancipative action. At the same time, in those practices it is possible to recognize an exercise in grounding and materializing ideas on those very topics, in turning theory into practice and exploring the potential of practice to think our present, and to engage it in radical, subversive ways.

Practicing Decolonialization

This issue is that of the genre of the human, the issue whose target of abolition is the ongoing collective production of our present ethnoclass mode of being human, Man: above all, its overrepresentation of its well-being as that of the human species as a whole, rather than as it is veridically: that of the Western and westernized (or conversely) global middle classes

> —Sylvia Wynter, "Unsettling the Coloniality
> of Being/Power/Truth/Freedom"

Central to Sylvia Wynter's epigraph above about the struggle between Western rationality and its universalizing pretensions (that is to say, Man) and alternative "genres of the human" is the idea that Western supremacy was sustained by the drawing of binaries between human and rational, political and apolitical, corporeal ontologies. In her view, the expansion of a colonizing ethnoclass conception of the human came paired with a normative and restrictive understanding of human action. The answer to this limiting situation lies in embracing the invention and imagination of alternative agencies and conceptions of the human, in voicing productively impure approximations to the self and the other, capable of becoming as "isomorphic with the being of being human itself, in its multiple self-inscripting, auto-instituting modalities" (Wynter 2003: 330).

Socially engaged art has often been described as potentially colonizing. Thinking through Wynter, however, I believe that many socially engaged art practices can be read as exercises in radical imagination attempting to invent different categories of the human and of human acting and interrelating. Still talking from the prehistory of the discipline (that is, from its fertile, undisciplined babbling), the curator and art critic Miwon Kwon (2004: 6) launched a warning against the multiple ways in which "new genre public art can exacerbate uneven power relations, remarginalize (even colonize) already disenfranchised groups, depoliticize and remythify the artistic process, and finally further the separation of art and life (despite claims to the contrary)." The many issues at play in this formulation will be discussed throughout this book. What interests me now is how a supposedly emancipatory creative practice can be associated (more or less straightforwardly) with colonialism and colonization. According to Kwon's view, (socially engaged) art not only modulates affects and energies but does so in a teleological way, in which the *ends* of each project are defined by artists and materialized through (collective) means. Following that formula, the collective agency of communities can be appropriated and colonized by well-intentioned artists. Since art "lies" (claims to do something positive but ends up doing the opposite), its criticism must fall under the detective-like task of fault finding. Kwon's words, to be sure, hold some degree of truth: as anyone familiar with the story of socially engaged art will know, socially engaged art can be and has been *used in such a way* that it reinforces capitalist power relations, foregrounds urban exclusion, makes disenfranchised groups more invisible, conceals the causes of social marginalization, and delays public intervention. To assume that this is all that socially engaged art *does*, that this is the whole story, however, is a totally different matter.

What does it mean to conceive socially engaged art's transformative potential as *potentially* (and not necessarily) colonizing? What comes of accepting the existence of alternative options emerging before and within the process of institutionalization of those artistic practices? If the danger of institutionalization overwhelms the materialization and the critical thought about this kind of practice, why is it that colonialism is often left out the main discussions about art activism and socially engaged art? If art is becoming a colonizing tool, to what extent can we ignore the complexities of ongoing forms of coloniality? Would we not advance in our understanding of (social) practice if we conceived of the fraught art initiatives depicted by Kwon as extractive enterprises sucking people's bodies and agencies out and transforming the result into artistic income (and therefore as not just, or only, "socially engaged art")?

Following Sylvia Wynter, I will argue that our appreciation of what socially engaged art can do would appear quite different if we looked at the many ways in which this kind of creative practice has been used as a testing ground for alternative social and cultural relations. There is much to be gained from addressing radical artistic practices from a decolonial optic. With decolonial thinking, this book shares the situatedness of knowledge, the conceptualization of coloniality as an underside of modernity. In this sense, it compels us to understand decolonization as an ongoing, unfinished project, with the emphasis on the racial matrix permeating the capitalist expansion. The book also poses the need to speak about the imposition of racial/racist epistemic categorizations through the *longue durée* of the modern/capitalist system throughout modernity and contemporaneity, thus underscoring the supposed neutrality and placelessness of Western thought (see Dussel 1973; Castro-Gómez 2005; Quijano 2007; Wallerstein 2004) and the need to pay close attention to non-Western "geopolitics of knowledge" (Grosfóguel 2011) while relativizing the European modernist and postmodernist canon. By taking "theory from the South" seriously as a fertile source of intellectual renovation that keeps expanding and transforming subversive critical and creative interventions, a decolonial view of socially engaged art would reveal its non-Western origins and, more importantly, the active potential of its contemporary configurations when emerging in close contact with activist initiatives from the Global South.

At the same time, the focus on experience and long-term collaboration of socially engaged art practices allows us to better understand the provincialization of theory and critical thought: to present decolonization as a collective, practice-led activity. By paying attention to the multiple ways in which art practitioners tackle the presence of coloniality in their everyday reality, *Art Activism for an Anticolonial Future* argues that the efficiency and the critical relevance of decolonization have to emerge from the specificities of practice. Crucial to the arguments of this book is to understand decolonization as something more than an abstract episteme decoupled from practice and applicable to any given situation. Decolonial thought is not a magic wand that reveals the true side of reality when waved. The alternative, eccentric locus of enunciation claimed by decolonial thinkers as a replacement for the modern-colonial geopolitics is the result of previously untested, unforeseen actions developed by many individuals and communities around the globe. By highlighting the performative and active nature of decolonization, by identifying it as a produced and productive mo(ve)ment rather than as an alternative theoretical framework, I attempt to measure the impact of specific decolonial artistic gestures in opening up spaces for discussion and negotiation.

Although artistic practice originally did not constitute the main focus of decolonial analysis, it is increasingly becoming a central area in the debates around this epistemic perspective. Decolonial artists and thinkers, including Guillermo Gómez-Peña, Pedro Lasch, Gloria E. Anzaldúa, Emma Pérez, Alanna Lockward, Mladina Tlostanova, and Macarena Gómez-Barris, to name just a few, are highlighting the importance of creativity in the materialization of decolonial futures. Whereas culture and cultural production was already an important concern in the systemic focus of the initial conversations of the decolonial group, the relevance of the visual was only later recognized. In the Decolonial Aesthetics manifesto that was signed by a group of scholars including Walter Mignolo and Nelson Maldonado-Torres and practitioners such as Tanja Ostojić, Marina Grzinic, Pedro Lasch, and Raúl Moarquech Ferrera-Balanquet, art and visual production is identified as a nodal point through which coloniality is both reproduced and challenged. According to the group, "The creativity of visual and aural artists, thinkers, curators and artifices of the written word have affirmed the existence of multiple and transnational identities, reaffirming themselves in their confrontation with global imperial tendencies to homogenize and to erase differences" (Transnational Decolonial Institute 2011). Central to the group's intentions is criticizing the ways in which artistic views of globalization and multiculturalism lay the ground for a continuation of coloniality's desire for universalism. While some of the prerogatives of the manifesto are not made sufficiently explicit (take, for example, this fragment: "Decolonial transmodern aesthetics is intercultural, inter-epistemic, inter-political, inter-aesthetical and inter-spiritual but always from perspectives of the global south and the former-Eastern Europe"), the document was effective in identifying art as a fundamental battleground where colonizing and decolonial worldviews are opposed.[3]

Adding to that identification, I believe that socially engaged art exemplifies the relevance of the visual for decolonial knowledge-power, while also revealing the main fracture lines where coloniality and the decolonial, Man and alternative modes of being human (to paraphrase Wynter once again), meet and clash. Three main features made socially engaged art a particularly suitable observatory of the colonizing and decolonial potential of visual creativity: its mistrust of representational concerns and its emphasis on direct engagement and active, long-term social collaboration; its allergy to predefined aesthetic models and its interest in unpredicted, unforeseen social interrelation; and its direct (and certainly not conflict-free) engagement with capitalism's interest in commodifying everything, social experiences and do-good informal interactions included (see N. Thompson 2015, 2017).

It may well be that our contemporary art world works as a symptom of our social incapacity to envisage ways of reenergizing and regenerating alternative activist horizons. But although the expansion of NGO capitalism can be directly associated with the vanishing of utopian, emancipative ideals, I believe that the contemporary relevance of decolonization cannot be measured from the narrow rationality through which the praxis of anticolonial struggle is often perceived. I have some reservations concerning the criticism of anticolonial thought and postcolonial theory defended by many decolonial authors. As Anne Ring Petersen affirmed, "Care should be taken therefore not to validate neo-essentialist notions of a particular postcolonial or decolonial aesthetics, and promote the illusion of the singularity and detachment of postcolonial or decolonial art" (2017: 124). First, and concerning postcolonial criticism, it is crucial to relativize the history of its academic canonization and its appropriation by US and European university departments. Decolonial thought not only ignores the heterogeneity of postcolonialism but also overlooks the (more or less effective) self-criticism taking place within the body of postcolonial thought itself (see Spivak 1999; Melas 2007; Sethi 2011; Cheah 2016). Countering the image of postcolonial studies as a disciplined body of thought primarily concerned with cultural or representational manifestations (with discourse analysis), *Art Activism for an Anticolonial Future* reveals the strong component of active and subversive imagination at play in the postcolonial critical project. In this I follow the materialist and agency turns of postcolonial studies, which I identify as fertile theoretical configurations to address the continuities in the present of the colonial episteme. Postcolonial studies, Rumina Sethi argues, are "at variance with social change and uninformed by activism" (2011: 18). By exploring "South" artistic practices invested in social transformation, this book's focus shares Sethi's claim that "unless abstract theory translates itself into action and real events, and is productively employed in materialist history, postcolonial studies cannot claim to be political" (59). Accepting this challenge, in this book I see in many "South" examples of socially engaged art the here and now of radical struggles against neoliberalism and ongoing forms of colonialism that were once at the core of the transformative project postcolonial criticism sought to represent. Being aware of the differences between the postcolonial and the decolonial critical projects, in this book I am more interested in exploring the fertile crisscrossing of both theoretical and practical configurations manifested in the bold, out-of-the-box body of work of a group of heterogeneous thinkers such as Boaventura de Sousa Santos, Denise Ferreira da Silva, Silvia Rivera Cusicanqui, Rumina Sethi, Jean and John Comaroff, Asef Bayat, Talal Asad, Achille Mbembe, and Aníbal Quijano, among others.

Furthermore, I would question the idea that the process of decolonization that brought freedom to many African and Asian territories between the 1940s and 1960s can be reducible to a "mythology" by which a straightforward colonial power matrix was replaced by indirect forms of coloniality (although that also happened). The successes and failures of decolonization cannot be subsumed under the contingent histories of postcolonial nationalism. Rather, it is crucial to understand their impact on a broader, global-yet-located humanist scale, as reverberating and contagious processes whose expiry date is not determined by the particular demise of national emancipative expectations. Besides making a claim for understanding postcolonialism as a heterogeneous, still useful body of work, in this book I am interested in redefining anticolonialism as a particularly productive project whose future potential still informs our present.

Anticolonial struggles advanced many of the aesthetic experiments taking place worldwide after the 1960s. They gave material shape to thinking on community, emancipation, and agency in ways that remain innovative when looked at from our contemporary perspective. Any history of radical creativity would be incomplete without the decisive influence of Fanonian thought, Third Cinema, US Black radicalism (and the international networks of solidarity that shaped it and that it helped to shape), the Bandung conference, and a long list of etceteras. Recent approximations to anticolonialism are rethinking it in the long run as a political and cultural project that largely surpassed the creation of postcolonial nation-states. From multiple perspectives, the work of Partha Chatterjee, Natalie Melas, Nelson Maldonado-Torres, Nikhil Singh, David Scott, Pal Ahluwalia, Vijay Prashad, Hamid Dabashi, Maia Ramnath, and Gary Wilder informs an alternative understanding of anticolonial thought and praxis that highlights its relevance in the configuration of subversive transnational alliances and modes of creative resistance. As viewed by those authors, anticolonialism is no longer charged with being politically naive by framing cultural and social emancipation within the framework of postcolonial nationalism. Rather, they read anticolonial thinkers such as Frantz Fanon, Aimé Césaire, C. L. R. James, and Sylvia Wynter from a broader and more complex perspective aligned to their global, humanist implications. This turn has particular consequences for the configuration of alternative genealogies of socially engaged creativity. The anticolonial enterprise was concerned with exploring the emancipative potential of collective mobilization. Their leaders were aware of the need not only to overcome the culture of the colonizer but also to do so in a way that could equate cultural agency with social change. They pursued ways of engaging the heterogeneous communities existing within national territories in active, radical ways, stressing the urgency of implementing participatory and anti-elitist understandings of cultural practices. In that sense, they attempted to overcome the individualism and class narrowness of colonial culture, encouraging the emergence both of new cultural forms and new ways of participating in and expanding them. Through this lens, anticolonialism appears not so much as a distant, foreclosed past but rather as a fertile proving ground where the "social" of socially engaged art was continuously reinvented and materialized. Adopting that perspective, *Art Activism for an Anticolonial Future* hypothesizes what a decolonized activism and radical agency might look like.

Homegrown Theory

Another main objective of this book is to decenter and deneutralize the conceptual grounds and the vocabulary surrounding socially engaged art. If it is easy to agree that socially engaged art has become a global phenomenon, it seems to me that the consequences of this process have not yet been fully addressed. Despite the success of social practice worldwide (or perhaps because of it), the critical vocabulary that has been developed in the last fifteen years does not fully succeed in describing the diversity of artistic initiatives and situations that emerge in the present day. This is not a problem of numbers. Approaching the expanded, global field of social practice today could not, must not, mean incorporating a few case studies from the South into the existing list of well-known initiatives. Rather, a whole new set of questions and points of confrontation appear if we defamiliarize and look at that field anew, not as a global phenomenon or as a state of things linked to movements such as Occupy Wall Street but as a series of interlinked yet homegrown processes of experimentation.

If we accept that practice informs thinking, the next step should be to understand how our vocabulary on social transformation reads when shaped by heterogeneous practical initiatives. Concepts such as community, agency, culture, people, common, etcetera, are often framed as universal values, as if their mere mention will recall a clear image in everyone's mind. Despite the fact that many socially engaged artistic practices from all over the world are being discussed in international forums, those are often analyzed through a Western prism, with little or no reference to "homegrown theory." As I demonstrate in chapter 2, this also applies to one of the epicenters of socially engaged art, the United States. Socially engaged art began to be theorized at a particular time when issues of social exclusion and racialized stories of persisting violence were being brought to the fore of US debates. At the same time, however, the debates on social practice tended to forget that the same issues those artistic practices were targeting were being theorized *from within*. Gloria E. Anzaldúa, for example, already made the claim about the active role of mestizo collective identity in the 1980s. Why is it, then, that the debates over community art involving Latino communities in the United States preferred to borrow from Jean-Luc Nancy's idea of inoperative community (to mention just one example) and not from Anzaldúa? There is nothing intrinsically bad about Nancy; rather, the question has to do with the supposed universal validity of Western (radical) thought and the confinement of "theory from the South" (Comaroff and Comaroff 2012) to a restricted, circumstantial operativity.

We arrive therefore at a paradoxical and unproductive situation: the aesthetic appreciation of collaborative artistic practices such as those examined in this book is often measured by its capacity to have an impact on civil society, to enact individual and collective agencies or to challenge normative and exclusionary uses of the public sphere. At the same time, however, those practices are aesthetically categorized through a standardized vocabulary that understands civil society, agency, and public sphere as neutral and universal realities. As a result, the emancipatory potential of artistic practice is neutralized by the modernist assumption that there is only one way of measuring its impact. A movement to provincialize those concepts would not only assert that it is only through the contingencies of practice that those ideas come to mind and become thinkable; the provincialization and decolonization of theory will reveal that what sometimes appears to be a dead end might look otherwise when viewed from a different perspective.

Therefore, the use of "grounded" and situated theory is pursued here not just as a way of provincializing the debates on art activism and social transformation. Examining socially engaged art practices directly embedded in anticolonial and decolonial resistance, I attempt to explore how the connection between ideas of social practice and decolonization can be mutually influential. Socially engaged art is grounded in a political vocabulary that was practiced intensely (both in the sense of being materialized and in a more musical sense of tuning, exercising) during decolonization. Anticolonialism initiated a radical experimentation with sociopolitical categories, many of which are central to the public role socially engaged art claims to play. Thinkers from the Global South have been and still are highly successful in experimenting with radical forms of cultural creativity. They have taken to their limit central issues, among them the limitations of representation and poststructural negativity, which nowadays inform our shared cultural and artistic vocabulary. Conversely, socially engaged art has proved particularly efficient at challenging the continuities of colonialism. What we have witnessed within the last two decades is the intensification of coloniality within sociality, at every stage of human reality, both in countries that were former colonies and in former metropolitan societies. Internal colonialism, environmental racism, or slow violence are part of the coloniality of being in our present. Although socially engaged art is not alone in confronting this legacy, its aesthetics and ethics are closely tied to those of decolonization, in many respects. Socially engaged art has been shown to be particularly appropriate for tackling ongoing, not-so-visible forms of epistemic and systemic violence, many of which are the direct consequences of coloniality. Furthermore, socially engaged art's focus on action and social interrelations has successfully revised the role of individual authorship in the configuration of art histories, expanding art's public presence and taking its social relevance to new limits. Through its interest in artistic collaboration and the privileging of process over results, the kind of artistic practices analyzed in this book challenge mainstream ideas of artistic mastery, offering instead a myriad of bottom-up possibilities that are the direct result of experimentation and situated know-how (see Singh 2018).

Chapter Outline

An Indonesian collective that reconstructs an old site of anticolonial resistance as its operating ground; a Chilean group siding with scientists to mobilize human and natural agencies within a supposedly "useless" territory; a Lebanese collective attempting to redefine the rules of the game of public art in postwar Beirut; a transnational Latin American group categorizing colonial and neocolonial exploitation as an enduring error—and reacting against it: these are some of the stories discussed in *Art Activism for an Anticolonial Future.* All these projects belong to the common imaginary of "social practice." Yet they are also something else. Through a direct engagement with the continuities of coloniality in their home societies, these initiatives rearticulate and repurpose former collaborative experiences. Linked to pressing social and economic matters in the present day, these initiatives also react against the legacies of colonialism. In this sense, they cannot be explained in general terms, nor can we interpret them as part of a recent international art trend. Rather, they constitute the latest version of locally grounded, globally connected processes of resistance.

This book is divided into four parts. Part 1 contains two chapters and outlines the main ideas of the book by discussing the configuration of a lexicon for socially engaged art (particularly in the United States), presenting the shortcomings of universalist approaches to social transformation and the restricted view of artistic postcolonialism when it is viewed only from the perspective of art biennials. Chapter 1 deals with the first two questions, hypothesizing how an alternative, race-attentive genealogy of US socially engaged art might look. Underscoring that the concerns about art's interest in the collective and more generally its turn into the field of social relations took place in parallel with the 1980s "wars" on multiculturalism, this first chapter reads US art criticism differently. If socially engaged art emerged in the United States as a consequence of Reaganomics and the dismantling of the country's public cultural infrastructure, then it will be essential to look at how racialized subjects were made visible or invisible through multiple means, including art. Here I draw on the work of Gregory Sholette, Lucy Lippard, Suzanne Lacy, and Grant Kester, all pivotal references in the configuration of avant la lettre theoretical conceptualizations on art activism and artistic collaboration. If the work of these authors is often associated with the main critical lineaments nowadays common in socially engaged art criticism, I suggest that a close reading of their early texts reveals a much more nuanced panorama, one in which the artistic interventions of racialized subjects arise as fundamental for the definition of a critical vocabulary for social practice. When viewed from the point of view of racialization, the US genealogy of socially engaged art looks unfamiliarly productive. Following Sholette's question "How might our narrative about social practice art collectivism be imagined differently?" (2017: 230), chapter 1 decenters and provincializes art criticism, turning past artistic experiences to a conflicting but fertile soil where alternative emancipative horizons can emerge. The main focus of chapter 2 is art biennials and their role in configuring a "postcolonial artistic constellation." Theories on global and world art rely on the impact of the biennial format, a transnational forum endlessly replicated and adapted in every corner of the globe. Biennials have been essential in decentering the Western-centered contemporary art canon and in challenging the influence of the European art museum. At the same time, however, they are the underside of art's articulation with global capital. Instead of criticizing biennials, in this chapter I turn to two less-explored questions: Are art biennials and exhibition making the only vehicles of artistic postcolonialism? And then, more broadly, might it be the case that both art biennials and postcolonial criticism are suffering the same illnesses, experiencing a similar backlash? Comparing art biennials and postcolonial studies as two areas subjected to a parallel process of politicization, I argue for collective, agency-informed genealogies of postcolonial visual creativity that could point to alternative (art) worlds.

Part 2 moves back in time to engage with the transformative project of decolonization. The two chapters comprising this part engage with the thought and praxis of Amílcar Cabral (the anticolonial leader of Cape Verde and Guinea-Bissau) and C. L. R. James (the Trinidadian intellectual who approached the masses to identify in them an active voice and a productive collaborative aesthetics), reading them as precursors of a collective, socially led aesthetics. If the definition *and production* of a radical, emancipated culture was for anticolonial intellectuals tantamount to the creation of a new society and a new humanism, it is surprising that the influence of decolonization is often removed from the genealogies of art activism and social practice. In chapters 3 and 4, I contend that this absence can be attributed to two main factors: a narrow understanding of decolonization as a fraught enterprise whose collapse is self-evident when looking at the failure of postcolonial nation-states, and a critical incapacity to identify in anticolonial thought any sign of coevality, any potential to make sense of contemporary situations. Challenging both assumptions and claiming Cabral's and James's thought *and action* as relevant in our present, this part identifies in anticolonialism an indispensable ally for decolonizing socially engaged art's genealogies and futures.

Chapter 3 reads Cabral's ideas on culture and the land as a precedent of a situated and difference-attentive theory of cultural agency arising from praxis. Having studied agronomy in the Portuguese Instituto Superior de Agronomia, Cabral was well aware of the ways in which "cultural particularities" affected the use of land and conditioned individual and collective responses to colonialism. When shifting from colonial intellectual educated in the metropolis to anticolonial leader, Cabral applied his vast knowledge acquired on the ground in Guinea to developing a cultural theory that shares many of the main concerns of present-day socially led creativity. Cabral criticized essentialism, and mistrusted bourgeois aesthetics for its capacity to master the language of the colonizer, in such way delaying and uncovering the urgency of a deep aesthetic transformation, and finally asked for popular participation and collaborative creativity as the only way to overcome the cultural legacies of colonialism. By identifying in Cabral's thought *and praxis* a cultural theory both bigger and smaller than the nation-state, I underscore the extent to which his criticism can emerge as an appealing source of renovation of radical criticism. Chapter 4, however, begins with an impossible conversation in the 1940s to reconstruct how much the positive consideration of popular culture and the active role of the masses owe to postcolonial voices such as C. L. R. James's. Following his journey across the Americas, Africa, and Europe, in this chapter I claim that James's is the most relevant voice in the postwar period, concerned with expanding the field of cultural production and aesthetically engaging the appetites and expectations of the masses. Highlighting how, by the time James wrote his best-known essays on popular culture in the 1940s and 1950s, the layers of aesthetic modernism were being established in the United States, I argue here that his work presents a valuable mixture of realism and utopian imagination, as well as an interest in curating peripheral subjects and identities *into* critical analysis.

The last two parts of this book shift from theoretical speculation and historical excavations to discussions of specific case studies. The three chapters included in part 3 revolve around the transformative potential of former cases of artistic activism and collaboration. Conceiving these as active forces that "haunt" and illuminate ways of acting in the present, especially in contexts where systemic violence does not appear as evident, this part examines contemporary socially engaged art practices from the point of view of the continuities between colonial and postcolonial times and agencies. The socially engaged art projects included in this part had to confront the difficulties of living in the "post": they emerge in the aftermath of civil conflict, unfinished processes of democratization, and unconcluded postcolonial nationalism. Operating in such terrain might prove challenging, to say the least. For if the "enemy" could appear clearly defined during decolonization, when it comes to the overlapping of coloniality and neoliberalism in officially declared "post" moments, knowing what to do and who the "enemy" is present a serious challenge.

Chapter 5 approaches two Ugandan community-based art projects, Lilian Mary Nabulime's HIV/AIDS social sculpture and the Disability Art Project Uganda (DAPU), to discuss issues of alternative institutionalism, humanitarian colonialism, and informal artistic networks. Both artistic projects are analyzed against the backdrop of the anticolonial legacy of

Makerere University in Kampala, its pivotal role in the configuration of Ugandan art history, and its current negotiations within the neoliberal and privatized panorama of higher education in Uganda. Avoiding a simplistic identification of Nabulime's social sculpture and DAPU action-based dialogical aesthetics as a continuation of "the Makerere moment," this chapter locates in Ugandan socially engaged art many of the most pressing concerns that determine the debates on artistic autonomy, deskilling, and collective agency in East Africa.

Chapter 6 presents the work of an anarchist collective, an informal artist-managed institution, and a cultural studies center in post-Reformasi Indonesia. In 1998, Indonesia put an end to more than three decades of dictatorship, inaugurating a new, democratic period. Indonesian artists did not believe the hype, but rather rose to the challenge of responding to the quandaries emerging as a result of the continuity of coloniality and state violence. Examining the work of Taring Padi, ruangrupa, and Kunci, in this chapter I argue that the experiments with artistic collaboration at play in those three collective endeavors can teach us the importance of tailored, trial-and-error responses to the pervasive, continuously shifting project that is coloniality. Finally, closing this part, chapter 7 moves to postwar Beirut and the Temporary Art Platform (TAP), an artistic collective that in 2014 produced a guide for artists wishing to produce public art works. While a great deal of discussion on the possibilities and limitations of public art does exist, in this case it was necessary to spell out the nonwritten norms deriving from sectarian politics and bureaucratic stagnation so that Lebanese artists could be aware of the terrain in which they were operating. Borrowing from Talal Asad's superb work on the secular and Asef Bayat's impressive defense of popular politics as a radical source of renovation in the Arab world, in this chapter I question the idea of public and socially engaged art as universal tools that can be applied just anywhere. For TAP, as for many other Lebanese artists, the postwar period (itself a continuation of internecine violence, regional instability, and international meddling) made them aware of the need to define the language of public engagement from scratch. By approaching one response to this situation, I identify in socially engaged art a tool for expanding and defamiliarizing public, shared spaces.

The last part of this book moves from the importance of legacy to the pivotal influence of affects and emotions in art activism. Reading, with Sara Ahmed, affect and emotion as culturally produced, the three chapters comprising this last part analyze how the feelings of love, hate, fear, or anger at play in movements such as Black Lives Matter can be better understood when framed in complex genealogies emerging from colonial power relations. Chapter 8 addresses a collaborative project located in a so-called useless space. Exploring Ensayos Tierra del Fuego in Chile in relation to the notions of utility proposed by Tania Bruguera, one of the leading voices in the debates on art activism and socially engaged creativity, I identify in this a call to decolonize notions of purposefulness and purposelessness and alternative definitions of the human and interspecies solidarity in response to the threat of extractive colonialism. The example of Ensayos provides a useful platform for broaching the main debates on *arte útil* (useful art, see Bruguera 2012) while establishing a critical distance from some of the premises of its canonical formulation.

Borrowing from the previous discussion, in chapter 9 I argue that rethinking our radical vocabulary is mandatory in claiming an emancipative horizon for progressive politics and poetics. In the last months of 2017, two public performances concerned with the defense of national identity and the repudiation of supposed threats to that identity by artists and critical thinkers were orchestrated in Brazil and Portugal. Dealing with these events, which included an attack on Judith Butler during her last stay in Brazil and the "defense" of the sculpture of Padre António Vieira in Lisbon by a far-right group, this chapter examines how conservative politics have claimed legitimacy by occupying public spaces and appropriating the strategies and methodology of progressive activism. It also discusses issues of violence, racial citizenship, place of speech, collective ownership, and coloniality in two Portuguese-speaking spaces linked by a colonial relationship.

The book finishes with a speculative journey that has at its center the idea of contributive activism and the digital. Borrowing loosely from the critical theorization of Black Lives Matter, a final coda highlights the importance of video and image sharing, and more specifically of militant visual (and virtual) research, in the articulation of responses against state violence and racial dehumanization. I use this closing chapter to stress the importance of practical and strategic uses and circulation of information in the configuration of subversive public spheres.

◆ ◆ ◆

Before we start our task of decolonizing social practice, two considerations are in order. The most important one concerns my own position as a male, southern European–born, Spanish- and Portuguese-speaking, and European-based scholar doing research on, and in, the Global South. While all the analysis included in this book derives from sustained engagement with the work of activists, artists, cultural practitioners, and thinkers from many South (and some North) contexts, what is offered is only a personal interpretation of the analyzed artistic practices. In any case, I am the only one responsible for all the potential errors of interpretation contained in this book. Whereas my original academic background in Caribbean and Latin American studies has been useful in exploring case studies in the Americas, in no way does it make me more fit to "speak for" or on behalf of any group or individual. Rather, what I try to offer here is an incomplete approximation that owes all potentially positive elements to the generous insights that many activists and artists shared with me during the last five years.

A word is also needed concerning the choice of the specific case studies included in this book. In my last monograph, I explored the role of art in the creation of public spaces for discussion and social transformation in the Caribbean. Between 2015 and 2018 I had the opportunity to teach and do research in various places, including Colombia, the Lebanon, Hong Kong, Indonesia, Uganda, and Kenya. I also engaged with the work of activists and radical thinkers in the Americas, which derived from conversations with Brazilian, Argentinian, and Chilean radical practitioners. In one way, *Art Activism for an Anticolonial Future* is the result of the personal process of learning from brilliant individuals such as André Mesquita, Camila Marambio, Nancy Garin, Margaret Nagawa, and Jay Koh (this list should be much longer). At the same time, however, I am fully aware that the ten chapters that comprise the book are the result of a necessarily limited, personal selection. I have attempted to reflect on the importance of these collective conversations and my own sustained engagement with artists and scholars in my approach to each context. It is for the reader to judge whether the book is successful in that goal.

◆ ◆ ◆

Part One

UNDISCIPLINING SOCIALLY ENGAGED ART

1

◆ ◆ ◆

ART BIENNIALS AND POSTCOLONIALISM'S POLITICS OF DISCOURSE

Poesis is replacing politics everywhere as the retreat position in the international art world.

—*Terry Smith, Thinking Contemporary Curating*

A first step in exploring why "South" histories of socially engaged art are very much still unacknowledged relates to questioning the specific artistic forms through which "South" art histories are constructed. This involves, unavoidably, dealing with mega-exhibitions and biennials. Before undertaking this journey, I want to clarify that my concern is not so much with the functioning of exhibitions but rather with their political economy within global art histories, with their rationale. I am not interested in adding anything to the criticism of biennials as spectacularized platforms of neoliberal exchange, nor in categorizing the possibilities for transnational interaction offered by long-term socially engaged initiatives as better or in any way different from those provided by biennials. This chapter will map how the latter were normalized at the expense of many alternative ways of understanding art making, as well as the consequences of this process of normalization for our understanding of how art works on a global scale.

In his decades-long attempt to define the contemporary (see epigraph above), Terry Smith categorizes artistic contemporaneity as an amalgam of different tendencies of artistic and curatorial creation. For Smith, contemporary art is not art from the present but rather art "capable

25

of calibrating several distinct but related ways of being *in* or *with* time, even of being, simultaneously, *in* and *apart* from time" (T. Smith 2019: 254. See also T. Smith 2009, 2011, 2016). Smith identifies three main currents among these: continuing modernism, transnational transitionality, and relational aesthetics (which Smith defines in a far more complex way than Nicolas Bourriaud's classical approach).[1] The second current, transnational transitionality, would mainly encompass the art produced in relation to the ongoing legacies of colonialism and imperialism. What is important in this categorization, beyond the identification of several forms of contemporaneity, is that Smith associates each current with a specific form of curating and art making. Under this logic, the second trend would be linked to biennials and temporary exhibitions.[2] It follows from here that the history of artistic postcolonialism is linked to the history of those particular curatorial formats.[3]

It is true that, for Smith, none of those currents is conceived of as an isolated container; on the contrary, contamination and crisscrossing are the norm. Museums, collectors, and the market also play a central role in the definition of artistic postcolonialism,[4] their action being indissolubly linked to the history of biennials. I share much of Smith's analysis of artistic contemporaneity as a multifaceted project, one that becomes materialized differently according to the specific history of each context. Smith provides excellent evidence for discussing the emergence of biennials and the consolidation of mainstream postcolonial debates together. There are particular consequences that result from considering biennials and temporary exhibitions as one of the main (but not the only) driving engines of "postcolonial" contemporaneity. Those consequences raise important questions, among them how exhibition making became the privileged form of postcolonial artistic contemporaneity, and also how this preeminence disavowed alternative forms of artistic agency, both historical and present. Responding to those two questions is the main objective of this chapter.

Undertaking this path entails, first of all, historicizing the rise of biennials around the globe during the 1990s as a process running in parallel with the expansion of neoliberal economies. In the second place, it also pertains to the relativization of the weight of exhibition making as just one form of artistic creativity among many others. The critique of biennials and globalization often implicitly carries a negative appraisal of postcolonialism.[5] When biennials are recognized as the main place where artistic transnational expression takes place, postcolonialism is often in the background as the main target in the negative balance of those events. Although some of the criticism directed both at biennials and postcolonial thought is justified, a more careful analysis is needed to avoid confusing both realities or rejecting them out of hand. There is no doubt that biennials and temporary exhibitions have been essential in shaping how contemporary art looks now, and they have done so in many positive ways.[6] I contend that the importance of mega-exhibitions has come at the expense of limiting the visibility of creative forms such as socially engaged art, art activism, and alternative institutionalism, where issues of cultural labor and cultural capital are particularly evident. The problem has, then, nothing to do with biennials or postcolonial criticism per se. Rather, the problem appears when biennials are naturalized as the main space where art becomes global, where local and transnational art interactions are negotiated.

This naturalization, the belief in "the centrality of *reading* as the appropriate form of politics" (Ahmad 1992: 3), is linked to the global success of a mode of artistic practice in which artists undertake research at multiple locations, presenting the results of their local interactions with communities around the world in a rather unified language oriented to its consumption and circulation with little variation in the biennial map. This strategy ties together art's postcolonial aspirations and the exhibition form, and ultimately comprises a sort of lingua franca. This is based firstly on the ubiquitous placelessness of artistic experience (through artistic investigation in particular contexts that are afterward translated and narrated at the exhibition's space) and secondly on negativity (through the process by which contemporary artists critically reveal the hidden ideological rules behind reality), replacing modernist forms and tropes.

My first step in dealing with this set of questions involves the recognition that this lingua franca that we find so often in artistic biennials and the transnational art market is just one possibility among others, and that transnational artistic negotiations occur in multiple ways through heterogeneous creative strategies. It also necessitates an exploration of the way that biennials and temporary exhibitions became the privileged forum with which anyone interested in exploring postcolonial issues in relation to art would expect to deal. Whereas both art emerging from the "social turn" and biennials are identified as markers of the main avenues through which art is nowadays evolving, it seems to me that their relationship remains largely unexplored. In line with the presiding interest of this book, this chapter suggests that the dialogue between postcolonialism and contemporary art cannot be reduced merely to the history of transnational biennials. Simply put, our contemporary art worlds are the result of the interaction between different forms of artistic creation. The history of those interactions, then, would also include decisive exercises in alternative institutionalization, art activism, the creation of South-South synergies, and, in more general terms, active processes of artistic collaboration taking place to a large extent outside the space of the art institution and the temporary exhibition.

If postcolonial criticism is to remain a valuable tool for explaining contemporary ways of being in the world (especially at a time when it runs the risk of being dissolved into less political configurations described as "world" and "global"), then reconstructing its complete history, including experiments with artistic collaboration, might provide a positive step toward this end. Accepting that postcolonialism inspires a variety of artistic forms, including critical, socially engaged artistic practices, could help determine what remains of the colonial within the global and in which ways (artistic) globalization is retooling and repurposing colonial power relations.

It should be clear that what is at stake is far more important than a simple criticism of artistic biennials per se (as if a single image of what biennials might be could be extracted). Nor is the point to affirm that any form of artistic creativity linked to biennials is intrinsically ineffective. More useful and more decisive, I think, is to address how both biennials and postcolonial art in its more accepted form gained prominence simultaneously, becoming the "default" vehicle of artistic research and postcolonial-infused art criticism.

If there is no possible history of art exhibitions without addressing the colonial roots of the act of exhibiting itself, then it is also true that postcolonialism compellingly determines the economics of present-day global art networks. It is evident at several levels that a mainstream and simplified understanding of postcolonialism informs our current understanding of contemporary art, from the adoption of a vocabulary that celebrates ideas of hybridity, transnational mobility, and global positionality to the proliferation of art centers in contexts traditionally excluded from art historical narratives. There is no doubt that this process has had a positive impact in decentering the art world and creating a truly global configuration beyond traditional Euro-American art venues. Yet far less attention has been paid to the ways in which postcolonial concerns are articulated within a spectacularized, transnational art world, ultimately determining what is seen as acceptable and what is not. To what extent can we read the critical crisis of our art world (or its apparently successful other side of the coin, which comes in the form of art turned into global neoliberal finance[7]) in terms of the collapse of a mode of artistic contemporaneity grounded on the same principles (flexibility, transit, hybridity . . .) that once constituted postcolonialism's main critical aspiration? Is what we are witnessing through the current crisis of contemporary art the collapse of transnational connectivity? Does a history of artistic contemporaneity qua the history of transnational biennials leave us with no possible response to the appropriation by neoliberal capitalism of the values of mobility and heterogeneity? Finally, what kind of rationale would follow from a direct excavation of those alternative forms of artistic postcoloniality (including alternative institutionalism or art activism) outlined below? What happens, in more simple terms, when we adopt long-term, noncuratorial, socially engaged artistic strategies as a model to understand international and regional articulations and the continuities of colonial power.

In order to broach these questions, I begin by producing an analysis of postcolonial theory in the fields of artistic production and art criticism. The chapter then explores how postcolonial discourse evolved so as to privilege models of negative criticism—something, I argue, that made possible the naturalization of certain kinds of artistic and curatorial strategies. The chapter ends by addressing some potential alternatives to biennial-based mode(l)s of postcolonial creativity.

Postcolonialism Dematerialized (I): Biennialism and the Contemporary

In recent discussions of contemporary art, biennials still emerge as the main cultural and discursive formation of artistic postcoloniality. In this sense, even the idea of an exhausted postcolonialism, of postcolonialism as a critical model in crisis, is mobilized through transnational biennials (see, for example, the "Farewell to Postcolonialism" proposed by the Guangzhou Triennial in 2008, which will be analyzed in further detail below). The problem is that biennial-based histories mainly highlight the South as a set of enclaves where nothing happens from biennial to biennial, replicating old colonial patterns of misrepresentation and emptying of the territories to be colonized. Although in the current panorama "Western reason" can be exchanged for "the global economy of attention," or more simply "global capital," the image remains similar when "South" artistic contexts are made to appear as a by-product of globalized curatorial attention in a "post–*Magiciens de la terre*" moment. This view not only divests those contexts of any previous history of experimentation with modernity and contemporaneity; it also condemns them to express themselves through the spectacular, internationally intelligible framework of the biennial, and normalizes a certain time and space as the most suitable platform for artistic dialogue.

The success of mega-exhibitions and biennials after 1989 operated as a master narrative that presented exhibitionary practices as the locus par excellence of global exchanges, occasionally naturalizing the process by which biennials acquired that predominance, normalizing their modes of operation, and condemning alternative forms to oblivion. Among those forms are socially engaged and activist art. Indeed, this book's main idea—that socially engaged forms of art linked to anticolonial and decolonial causes present a complex and decades-old genealogy, whose evolution informs an alternative history of global artistic interactions—is directly affected by the consolidation of large-scale exhibitions as the privileged ground for transnational exchanges.

The consolidation of large-scale mega-exhibitions as one of the main markers of artistic contemporaneity came as part of a complex amalgam of social, political, and economic processes, among which the decline of "traditional" art institutions such as the museum, the boom of the art market in the 1980s, the globalization of the art market, the expansion of the curatorial to any facet of creativity (within and outside the field of art), and the cultural geopolitics arising by the end of the Cold War can be described as highly significant though not unique events. Undoubtedly, the success of the biennial form cannot be separated from the creation of a global artistic landscape, in which curators and artists from all continents interacted in shifting, transient scenarios across the globe. Still, these processes are in many cases the result of more durable regional and intercontinental exchanges and collaborations between artists and institutions.

How could the biennial format become so normalized as to hide those alternative forms and appear as the main platform for transnational, difference-based artistic configurations? Answering this question is no easy task. Whereas recent criticism has focused on the logic of the exhibition's form, the way that form relates to alternative modes of contemporary artistic creativity has been much less discussed. The idea that the "contemporariness" of an artwork and of an artist are defined and arbitrated in international biennials is nowadays a common assumption, but one that simply does not take account of the steps leading to such a conclusion. Biennials are not just privileged contact points of exchange between the national, the transnational, and the regional. They also function simultaneously as spaces of transnational capitalism's symbolic value, and as leverage tools of a particular kind of artistic discourse. Seen as a zone of translatability, biennials are also accepted as the main arbiters of local contemporaneities. Their role consists not just in displaying artworks or acting as transnational nodes; more importantly, they also refashion local modernities, modulating their access to global artistic configurations. Their capacity for penetrating and regulating local art ecosystems is often overlooked in favor of biennials' most spectacularized side.

Carlos Basualdo (2010) sees in biennials intrinsically subversive spaces that have been traditionally discredited by academic criticism, which recognizes in them an epiphenomenon of global capitalism. Although acknowledging that biennials have emerged "in tune with the transformation of neoliberalism and global finance," Basualdo nevertheless identifies in the biennial form a capacity for challenging the primacy of museums and the Western values associated with them, thus "perform[ing] an insistent de-centering of both the canon and artistic modernity" (60). For Basualdo, "[biennials imply] the articulation of a reflection capable of linking forms of local culture and history with the horizon of internationalism that appears as a founding element in these events" (59).

From a more skeptical perspective, Angela Dimitrikaki and Terry Smith insert biennials into larger economies of cultural production. Dimitrikaki argues that, despite being autonomous fields of artistic expression, biennials are very much bounded by the relational capacity of capitalism to concatenate different forms of labor and production under the same logic. She recognizes that biennials often offer the perfect location for displaying art (including participatory art and art claiming social relevance) for a reduced, privileged audience: "This is the normally socially privileged constituency who exert their right to have access to art, even by means of documentation of an art that first does its work elsewhere, often outside the institutions that privilege the exhibition form. The document is the means by which even project art ends up as an exhibit, re-establishing the links to representation and, arguably, reinstating the role of the critic-mediator who must now explain to the art community in what ways 'this' is art" (Dimitrikaki 2012: 314). From this perspective, biennials appear not so much as antithetical to the strategies and intentions of socially engaged art, but rather as mechanisms that can be used for restaging "old" aesthetic privileges even for such art overtly opposed to them. Dimitrikaki dismantles the apparent innocence behind the adoption of a documentary form oriented toward a secondary audience, thus allowing for an impression of art's global relevance: the dominance and ubiquity of the exhibition form does not just play a central role in launching art as commodity. Above and beyond this, it is commensurate with a service and experience economy that reduces the aesthetic to an outcome of affective labor to which only a privileged constituency can afford access. Under this logic, art's potential for political and social transformation remains untouched as biennials become "the social sites for [. . .] intervention" (Dimitrikaki 2012: 137).[8] As she masterfully puts it, "On the one hand, the document is essential for an art striving to articulate a politics of knowledge (of the social) and on the other hand, the document permits the continuation of the exhibition form, thus reproducing representation" (314).[9]

For his part, Smith recognizes a certain erosion, and wonders whether biennials should constitute the main object of curatorial thought: "If I am right that the biennial has become structural, then this recent history might indicate a certain ossification of the large-scale mega-exhibition, a lowering of its subversive potential. [. . .] Perhaps it also presumes that the biennial is perfectible, singular, when the success of the format as a vehicle of transitionality has for decades depended precisely on its node-like structure; its easily imitated parameters; and, on the local level, its unique (for the art-institutional ensemble) mix of flexibility, regularity, and reliable unpredictability" (T. Smith 2012: 98). Smith and Dimitrikaki do not simply criticize biennials. Instead, they problematize the position of biennials vis-à-vis a larger economy of production and circulation of artistic contemporaneity. Luckily enough, the rationality of mega-exhibitions is starting to be theorized and historicized. Elena Filipovic (2005: 64) acknowledges that the problem with biennials is not biennials themselves but "the proliferation of a *form*" that owes much to the modernist form par excellence, the white cube. If this form conditioned how art *looks* when inserted into a museum, it also applies its "halo of inevitability, of fate" when transferred to worldwide biennials. Filipovic's take on the rationality of biennials emphasizes the continuities between modernist and international artistic configurations. More specifically, she addresses the way in which modernist strategies of display and the regimes of visibility and visualization associated with those regimes are transposed to a supposedly global platform. A paradox thus emerges between the globalization of the white cube and the localist aspirations of each biennial, attempting to put on a global map the specificities of locales, yet "globally replicating" for that purpose a homogenized form.

Perhaps one of the most interesting takes on those questions comes from Caroline Jones's analysis of biennials as part of a longer tradition of Western display beginning with nineteenth-century art fairs. If we agree with Jones that biennials represent a deeper genealogy going back to nineteenth-century international exhibitions and world fairs, then the link I am trying to establish between the crisis of a spectacularized art world and the proliferation of postcolonial discourses appears clearer. For Jones (2017), biennials are part of a deeper "epistemic shift" in which art is repurposed to produce local nodes with an appearance of cosmopolitanism. Linked to that process is the configuration of a particular aesthetic that becomes the norm.

Because of their long links to event structures, tourism, and apparatuses of knowledge production, biennials have produced and participated in a more enduring epistemic shift. Beginning in the world's fairs and gradually transforming the art world, this shift forces an acknowledgment that the placement of an art object within a world picture determines the significance of both the picture and the object. The central question then becomes: what are the conditions of possibility for the global work of art? And more specifically, in the structures of world expositions leading up to the biennial form, what were the prerequisites such that a work of art could be said to have *international* (now global) purchase, and how does the contemporary aesthetics of experience propel this same claim? (Jones 2010: 70).

Three central elements can be deduced from here. First, biennials are not new, nor is the kind of art they promote. Second, the impact of that kind of art goes far beyond the space and time of the biennial itself, directly conditioning what Jones calls "the global work of art" and having an impact on taste, tourism, and consumption. Finally, and this is crucial, the aesthetic resulting from biennials will not be determined so much by objects as by experience. In this light, biennials condition how we see and understand art, what we demand and expect of an artistic project, and they do so through generalizing a kind of experience of consuming and enjoying art. This has important consequences for our understanding of collaborative and participative art. Jones imagines the "experience turn" of contemporary art as a biennial or exhibition-based long process based on getting audiences accustomed to visiting different venues around the world. In this sense, biennials have been central in "the seductive marketing of experience," being there where "his taste has been cultivated, and its aesthetics codified and defined" (Jones 2017: 82, 86). This means that both the appetite for participatory and experiential enjoyment of art that was categorized as a "social turn" *and* the more conventional image of postcolonial art, where artists move from one country to the next, displaying their works in biennials and engaging communities around the globe for short periods of time, must be inserted into a broader narrative where tourism, urban planning, and artistic world-picturing come together. At the same time, however, recognizing that this form is oriented toward experience does not mean that alternative forms of experience (such as those at play in the socially engaged art project) have also shaped our understanding of artistic contemporaneity. These alternative forms have been fundamental in globalizing and networking their participants in ways other than those at play in the biennial.

I have argued elsewhere (Garrido Castellano 2019) that postcolonial and global art have been articulated through what, following Tony Bennett (1996), I called a "postcolonial exhibitionary complex." By this idea, I sought to understand the ways in which institutions exercise control and impose authority, not by concealing but by exhibiting.[10] For Bennett, the institutions of confinement and the institutions of display constitute coexisting and intertwined forces determining, through self-regulation, the gap between individuals and institutions. The history of cultural institutions would be the history of a specific relationship between audiences and display, as well as one involving the creation of vantage points from which to see the world and to see oneself seeing; they would be "vantage points from which everyone could be seen, thus combining the functions of spectacle and surveillance" (Bennett 1996: 62). Through this passing from conservational and restrictive to the making of exhibition, institutions will be ready to represent and exhibit "society itself—in its constituent parts and as a whole" as spectacle (62). Through the development of the technologies of seeing, Bennett establishes a division between seeing and being seen as full of colonial connotations: "And this power marked out the distinction between the subjects and the objects of power not within the national body but, as organized by the rhetoric of imperialism, between that body and other, 'non-civilized' peoples upon whose bodies the effects of power were unleashed with as much force and theatricality as had been manifest on the scaffold" (64).

According to Bennett, "power" operates in two ways. First, as a matter of difference, a classical "us/them" rhetoric. Second, and more importantly, through the display of that difference by exhibiting in spaces designated for that specific purpose. It involves images as much as audiences and platforms. Power depends not on the external will of an institution that commoditizes and swallows otherness but on the self-regulatory processes of an artistic community. A struggle for visibility and representation within transnational scenarios has blurred the weight that less visible infrastructural practices emerging from different scenarios have in configuring effective and long-lasting public spheres. The commoditization of difference in discursive terms would be symptomatic not only of the continuities of central epistemic and cultural inequalities within our supposedly postcolonial reality; it would also lie behind epistemic and cultural divisions between subjects with institutional and politicized agency and subjects still confined to representation. This division, importantly enough, still holds a geographical appeal. The ways in which the public sphere associated with certain contexts is defined within and beyond the traditional frontiers of artistic practice in uneven ways, limiting curatorial agency to the role of representational exhibition making (which is carried out in many cases by foreign "experts" who exert authority and legislate taste), is what I understand to be the postcolonial exhibitionary complex.

From this perspective, biennials appear more as part of a longer technique of display, representation, and categorization and less as a form of global contemporaneity. The process of dematerialization of postcolonial criticism into cultural and discourse studies can find a parallel in the subsuming of the artistic postcolonial into the global. Recent insights into global and world art have proposed a geographical configuration in which the postcolonial is superseded by recent exchanges and mappings. This, again, does not imply any intrinsic positive or negative appreciation of biennials; it just facilitates a better understanding of their contemporary purchase. How the history of exhibitions became the privileged ground of global art histories is particularly evident in Hans Belting, Andrea Buddensieg, and Peter Weibel's landmark exhibition *The Global Contemporary and the Rise of New Art World* shown in 2011 at ZKM Karlsruhe and the resulting collection of essays concerned with the "globalization of the art world." Weibel sums up very well the main idea of the initiative by documenting how "since the Berlin Wall came down in 1989 and the Soviet Union's implosion, new art worlds have thus been coming into existence in which the Second and Third Worlds play a central role" (Belting, Buddensieg, and Weibel 2013: 23). As a consequence, "new continents and countries, from the Asian to the Arab world, enter the art world" (24). This affirmation is problematic for at least three reasons. It ignores any previous development in those "art worlds"; it maintains a rigid and purely geographical idea of "first, second and third" worlds, and presents their art histories as independent paths crossing only at the present moment; and, finally, it leaves implicit that "non-European countries" can be contemporary only when recognized and filtered through the attentive eye of the curator and the mainstream, Euro-American institution.[11] Global contemporaneity appears, then, as the result of an interest by mainstream institutions in expanding their scope. Significantly, that interest takes the form of an art exhibition.

In the introductory text of *The Global Contemporary and the Rise of New Art Worlds* catalog, Weibel mentions biennials and art exhibitions several times as the terrain where the most important shifts in the art world take place. Belting, Buddensieg, and Weibel reinforce this idea by acknowledging *Magiciens de la terre* as the beginning of a critical concern with "a global production of contemporary art." They also identified the proliferation of biennials across the planet as "a new kind of art, an art that is expanding all over the globe" (2013: 28). For them, contemporary art is equal to a multiplicity of art worlds rejecting the idea of modernism and claiming their "contemporariness." Even more problematically, this expansion implies an automatic erasure of the colonial burden associated with traditional modes of art history and artistic display. "The new art worlds," they argue, "are opposing and replacing the colonial history of world art" (29).

The question that immediately arises is: how? In what way does the recognition of "multiple art worlds" shift issues of connectivity, institutional power, curatorial agency, and economic globalization? Who benefits from the globalization of art, and in what way?[12] And what is the point of distinguishing between one or many "art worlds" if those are equally governed under the same logic of transient spectacularity, if their point of confluence is still identified in the large-scale exhibition (organized, in this case, by a European museum)? The widespread transformation of art into a privileged resource of global finance leaves little room space for optimism in Belting, Buddensieg, and Weibel's idea of leaving colonialism behind. And the increasing "problems in communication," including military interventions, the erection and consolidation of walls, and the privatization of the Internet (reaching the point of its nonexistence as a public space, as the title of a well-known volume [Aranda, Kuan Wood, and Vidokle 2015] by *E-Flux* acknowledges[13]) challenge the very idea of newness behind the existence of multiple art worlds. Leaving aside the anxiety of recognizing something new in the present configuration, as if formerly colonized territories had not played any valuable role in art histories until now, the global contemporary formulation raises many questions related to the distribution of power and influence and, perhaps more importantly, the articulation of alliances, within this "new" world art map.

An interesting alternative to global art approaches has recently been provided by Charles Green and Anthony Gardner through their focus on "South" biennials. Gardner relativizes the "erosion" of postcolonialism and rightfully places the criticism against it in a context of neoliberal globalization and white supremacist and neonationalist backlash. Highly critical of how postcolonialism was dependent on Anglo-American academic privilege and neoliberal globalization, Gardner (2011: 143) envisages in postcolonial-infused art something more than "a mere straitjacket of buzzwords."[14] Together with Green, he argues that "South" biennials "do not sit comfortably within the stereotype of biennials as neoliberal symptom. . . . While they were certainly internationalist in ambition, it was often a socialist, or at least socialist inspired, internationalism that subtended their rhetoric and objects" (Green and Gardner 2016: 100). This point is particularly relevant to our argument here, since it reaches deeper in search of artistic connections across "South" contexts long before globalization. It also compels us to look for the dissimilarities among the seemingly repetitive experience of biennials, recognizing in those a platform where alternative artistic exchanges and collaboration can happen. This perspective also decenters the history of exhibition making, relativizing the dependence of artistic transformations on Euro-American "events" such as the fall of the Berlin Wall. Even more importantly, they recognize "South" artistic processes as leading global transformations.

Biennials and mega-exhibitions within artistic contemporaneity comply with a rationale that goes deeper into the history of modern traditions of display and representation. Those traditions are firmly grounded in Western values, yet they have also evolved into a global form. If the history of exhibition making is deeply rooted in a tradition of modernist and colonial display, as Okwui Enwezor (2008) argues, then the global dimension of biennials and mega-exhibitions owes much to a process of decentralization and provincialization of the contexts in which the contemporary takes shape. In Enwezor's words, "The current artistic context is constelled around the norms of the postcolonial, those based on discontinuous, aleatory forms, on creolization, hybridization, and so forth, all of these tendencies operating with a specific cosmopolitan accent" (2008: 209). The adoption of this accent, he adds, happens within the exhibition space: "It could, in fact, be said that no significant change in the direction of Modern art occurred outside the framework of the public controversies generated by its exhibitions" (209).

Enwezor is right in stating that our contemporary understanding of art owes much to global constellations emerging out of the contradictions of several processes of decolonization. Enwezor's definition of the contemporary as a constellation allows us to transcend the specific space and time of the exhibition and delve into a broad articulation of practices and knowledges that cannot be subsumed under the exhibition form. Enwezor's landmark curatorial projects, including *The Short Century*, the second edition of the Johannesburg Biennial, or *Documenta 11*, were much more than exhibitions, as they examined the complexities of artistic production in Africa and the rest of the world. From the perspective of these projects, Enwezor's nuanced engagement with the genealogies of exhibition making allows us to question whether the primacy of exhibitional platforms as the places where contemporaneity happens leaves aside alternative practices and has been partially normalized as biennials have become "a structural part of the art system" (T. Smith 2012: 91). This normalization derives from a particular rationale, whose consequences we have explored in this section. Recognizing that the histories of contemporary curating and postcolonialism are bound together has important consequences for our understanding of contemporary art. The most positive side of this process is that the idea that Western modernity represented the only mode of modernist innovation is being challenged, along with Eurocentrism and its supposedly universal value. This logic, however, also disregards alternative expressive strategies, which are often considered more local and remain outside the scope of global art historical and critical configurations.[15] The rationality of exhibitions regulates critical discourses dealing with the diverse forms through which postcolonial concerns are expressed. Furthermore, artistic forms outside the exhibition space are not recognized as contemporary to the same extent as exhibitions, while the power structure upon which relations are negotiated privileges the figures of the curator and the artist because of their higher capacity for traveling.

Postcolonialism Dematerialized (II): Theoretical Limitations

So far we have seen how the normalization of biennials as sites of postcolonial artistic contemporaneity is dependent on the consolidation of curating and the silencing of alternative artistic exchanges taking place within South contexts. In this section I explore how this process is also linked (although not in direct, causal ways) to the evolution of postcolonial criticism itself. Although that criticism has been widely applied to poststudio, postconceptual art, the success of this kind of art has been linked less frequently to the transformations undergone by postcolonial thought. By looking at the evolution of postcolonial theory in relation to shifts in contemporary art, I attempt to identify how the consolidation of biennial curating matched a dematerialization of postcolonial thought that also influenced postcolonial-infused art criticism. Both levels privileged discourse over engagement, ambivalence over clear ideological positioning, a deconstructive over a constructive lens, and speculative thought or secondhand approaches to reality over direct engagement. It goes without saying that postcolonial theory and artistic biennials are two very different things; I believe, however, that the success of the latter and their role in restaging modernist aesthetic privileges (as Dimitrikaki has argued) are interrelated with the evolution of postcolonialism itself. If both processes are not causally bound, there is no doubt that the "dematerialization" of postcolonialism and its categorization of direct engagement with reality as naive facilitated the identification of the triad "artistic globalism-biennials-deconstructive artistic practices" as the privileged form of global contemporaneity.

As a critical project, postcolonialism shifted its objectives early on, becoming in many ways attached to the task of deciphering the hidden ways in which literary texts conceal colonial configurations of knowledge and power.[16] Postcolonialism's emphasis on individual subjectivity as a terrain marked by the reproduction of colonial power shifts critical attention from the collective to the subjective, abandoning the task of deciphering in which ways colonial rationality conditioned postcolonial acts of resistance and subversion. As Marxist-infused postcolonial theorists such as Benita Parry, Aijaz Ahmad, and Neil Lazarus argue, postcolonialism emerged in an attempt to counter the primacy of Western thought, and to explore the ways in which systems of colonial domination remained alive after the territories subjected to colonial domination achieved political independence.[17]

Its evolution, however, quickly implied a rearticulation "from a theoretical position freed from the categories of political theory, state formation and socio-economic relationships," as Parry (2004: 4) states.[18] For many, postcolonialism then became an obscure critical discipline with a particular language and a discourse-based array of theories, a body of voices and texts with increasingly less connection to the anticolonial ethos of social transformation. Dealing with this transformation, Parry identifies a "vaporizing of conflict" in the exhaustion of postcolonialism as a critical tool to deal with current global processes of social change. Interestingly enough for the argument of this book and for the criticism expounded in this chapter, Parry also warns that the turn to the symbolic at play in mainstream postcolonialism silences not only alternative theoretical approaches to reality but also those practices based on direct engagement: "For where 'the politics of the symbolic order' displaces the more demanding politics operating in real-world situations, and a theoretical commitment to rejecting fixed subject-positions as ontologically faulty and dyadic polarities as epistemologically unsound acts to erase structural conflict, there is no space for anti-colonialist discourses which inscribe irreconcilable contest, or for anti-colonialist practices that were manifestly confrontational" (8).

I hope it is clear by now that at stake here is much more than our contemporary appreciation of anticolonialism or the preeminence of one or another interpretation of postcolonialism. As we will see in the following chapters, the act of erasure Parry identifies regarding anticolonial ideas and practices also extends to present-day creative interventions. Opposing this primacy of discourse, Parry argues that anticolonial critics identified and critically addressed central issues of ideology, hierarchy, and materialist struggles simultaneously, or even prior to many of their European counterparts. In a similar vein, Robert Young acknowledges the weight of anticolonial thought in the configuration of emancipative theory and activist positionings throughout the world. In his historical overview, postcolonial authors are committed to political and social transformation, not as external contributors but rather as inserted in the genealogies of Western Marxism and radical politics (see Robinson 2005; Young 2001). Updating this approach, Ania Loomba (2015) recognizes the primacy of deconstructive analysis as a potential source of ideological escapism,[19] and claims that postcolonialism's own survival is very much dependent on its capacity to grasp the practicalities of social and cultural transformation in the present: "If postcolonial studies is to survive in any meaningful way, it needs to absorb itself far more deeply with the contemporary world, and with the local circumstances within which colonial institutions and ideas are being molded into the disparate cultural and sociological economic practices which define our contemporary 'globality'" (256).

Loomba's words are easily translatable into artistic debates. Would the meaning of the former quotation change much if we were to replace "postcolonial studies" with "artistic biennials"? Does the supposedly excessive attention given by postcolonial studies to self-representation "as a moment of absolute authenticity," to borrow Aijaz Ahmad's words (1995: 16), remind us of the "erosion" of artistic postcolonialism proposed by Gardner or the "old" aesthetic privileges Dimitrikaki finds in some contemporary art claiming social and political relevance? When Ahmad complements the last point by saying that "intercultural hybridity is presented as a transaction of displaced equals which somehow transcends the profound inequalities engendered by colonialism itself" (17), isn't it possible to read those words with the crisis of the biennial system in mind? Doesn't the sense of déjà vu we find in the postcolonial literary criticism I have presented here resemble the current debates in contemporary art with which I began this chapter?

At issue here is how postcolonial agency is conceptualized, and also how the evolution of global art relates to the evolution of postcolonial criticism. From a Deleuzian perspective, Simone Bignall (2010: 3) attempts to "suggest some positive content for this notion of the postcolonial," breaking with the dualism between Marxism and deconstructivism within postcolonial studies. Her idea of agency is based on the belief that "ontology shapes agency, while practice provokes thought" (2–3). Seeking to counter negative criticism (which she identifies both in opposition to deconstructive authors such as Bhabha and Marxist postcolonial theorists such as Parry and Lazarus) and the excessive focus on the discourse of postcolonialism, she situates agency as the central point determining the very survival of the postcolonial project: if postcolonialism remains incapable of providing constructive answers to the continuities of imperial and colonial projects, then its utility as a critical mode of imagining the world is highly questionable. Bignall conceives the postcolonial project as investing in two interrelated but ultimately different domains: counterdiscourse and concrete action.[20] However, she argues, concrete action is always conditioned by the same colonial logic it attempts to counter. Bignall's alternative to the continuities she identifies in critical negativity comes in the form of discontinuity, which "calls for the inauguration of new kinds of difference, and a qualitative difference in the kind of sociability that is practised" (232). Crucial in this inauguration is the creative role given to social interaction and collective imagination. Also important is the valorization of cases of positive social articulation alongside cases of dissensus and social clash. From this articulation, alternative forms of agency can emerge as an alternative to the "negative agency" that she identifies, for example, Homi Bhabha's idea of cultural mimicry or Gayatri Chakravorty Spivak's attention to the discursive formation of the identity of the subaltern. Pivotal in Bignall's approach to postcolonial agency is the way she conceives theory and practice as interrelated dimensions: instead of ascribing to the critic the task of finding responses to colonial configurations, she defines those responses as emerging from the interaction between thought and action. The main consequence of this positioning is the definition of a "concept of transformative agency" investing in and engaging "a collaborative politics of material transformation in order to construct postcolonial institutions and communities of practice with others." Critically, this interpretation points us towards the question "what view of selfhood, of agency, lies at the heart of the transformative theories we currently draw upon to bring about just social change?" (5).

While I am not sure to what extent I share Bignall's idea that Marxist postcolonialism is driven only by negativity (and, driven by the "bad habits" of my academic training, I would almost instinctively seek to historically ground the "immanent virtual possibility" and the "coming communities" that Bignall draws from Gilles Deleuze), I find her alternative to critical negativity compelling. For this alternative can provide a suitable potential parallel for the subversive modes of (artistic) postcolonial sociability I identify in socially engaged art throughout this book. For instance, her last question is particularly useful for the discussion on exhibitionary practices addressed in this chapter. It begs the question of whether the postcolonial excavations presented in biennials are still fueling transformative horizons to colonial configurations. Bignall's notion of postcolonial agency rejects the idea that theory itself, no matter how good it is, can produce any effective social change when detached from practice. Instead, "understanding must be put into action; thought must be put into practice" (2010: 235) Her approach also forces us to explore how alternative practices (such as those offered by socially engaged and activist art) shape different modes of sociability. Finally, it provides a useful critical mode with agency at its center, one rooted in practice and experimentation.

In this section I identified some shared elements (such as the predominance of deconstructive strategies, the weight of negativity, and the rejection of direct action) between the evolution of postcolonial criticism and exhibition-based notions of artistic contemporaneity. Borrowing (although loosely and without "choosing sides") from Marxist postcolonialism, I found the task of tracking the continuities at play in postcolonial criticism to be a relevant tool for understanding the evolution of contemporary art worlds. From that perspective, the idea that biennials are the main arbiters of "South" art histories can be identified as a "selective tradition" (to borrow from Lazarus [1999: 153] once again) that parallels the development of postcolonial studies and the rejection of more directed forms of agency. For the same reasons, the lack of attention paid to "South" genealogies of socially engaged art can also be connected to that theoretical evolution. Finally, art debates could learn much from the thinking in some postcolonial criticism on how ideas of internationalism and globalization have been dematerialized (see Bartolovich 2004: 11). Recognizing the existence of those similarities does not allow us to conflate theory and (artistic) practice; it does, however, open up interesting comparative perspectives. It is not all bad news, in any case: the next sections will be dedicated to exploring potential alternatives to this situation.

Looking for Alternatives (I): Subversive Excavations

The idea that thought becomes more productive in proximity to practice will lead the first exploration on potential alternatives both to the impasse of postcolonialism and to the exhaustion of biennial-based forms of artistic contemporaneity. One way of responding to this situation derives the understanding that postcolonialism was always far more complex than its more accepted artistic and curatorial formulation. An excavation into the alternative forms that marked artistic contemporaneity in contexts shaped by colonialism would, then, complicate our existing genealogies of art making. Simply stated, the first step in attempting to escape from the situation described above consists of looking at histories of "South" artistic practice anew. This would entail the realization that in many Latin American contexts the relationship between conceptualism and poststudio art practice is not detached from activist positionings (see Camnitzer 2007; Giunta 2007; Mosquera 1996); that agency takes multiple forms in contemporary African art, including collective workshops (see Kasfir and Förster 2013), and pan-African festivals;[21] or that Asian art is shaped by regional alliances between visual creators and activists across the continent (see, for example, Kapur 2007; Tomii 2018; Tomii and Yoshimoto 2013; Koh 2015; Vicente and Jee-sook 2008).

Linked to this goal is the belief that artistic processes are very much dependent upon how they are critically and theoretically framed. A look into the conflicting curatorial positioning at work in the third edition of the Guangzhou Triennial may illuminate this point. The Triennial expanded on the work carried out by the Guangdong Museum of Art in Guangzhou (Canton, China) to insert Chinese modern and contemporary art into global trends. The title of the first edition of the triennial, *Reinterpretation: A Decade of Experimental Chinese Art,* encapsulates the spirit of that endeavor. Subsequent editions of the event, including the third one that is being discussed here, further developed the articulation between Chinese art and global artistic tendencies.

At the core of the 2008 Guangzhou Triennial, which sang an elegiac "farewell to the postcolonial," we find the two antithetical views expressed by two of the biennial's curators, Gao Shiming and Sarat Maharaj. Comparing them and understanding that this farewell reads quite differently depending on their divergent curators' perspectives, reveals the flexibility of curatorial projects while also leaving open the consequences of those events. Referring to the Guangzhou Triennial, Charles Green and Anthony Gardner (2016: 250) identify in the event's first edition of 2002 "a Chinese affair [but also] a very significant, even landmark exhibition, internationalizing the south of China with no need of North Atlantic validation." Since its creation, the triennial's experimental tone has had to cope with censorship by the Chinese government, negotiating "the shifting boundaries created by the often-bizarre conjunction of official civil opportunism and unofficial artistic license" (250). It also strove to find its place amid the overcrowded panorama of twenty-first-century Asian biennials, many of which were concerned with mixing artistic experimentation with the production of spectacular experiences directed toward to large audiences.

Within this particular context, Shiming's position arises from accepting that by 2008, postcolonialism had become a sort of politically correct lingua franca emptied of much of its subversive potential. Even more problematically, he argues that postcolonialism has "over-politicized" art. Under this interpretation, postcolonialism would operate as an ideology of the worst kind, putting artists into boxes, neutralizing criticism, and determining the creative production of artworks beforehand. Shiming highlights how the term itself had been routinely used to the point of fatigue. For him, responding to that fatigue would mean "escap[ing] from over-politicised international art sites" (2008: 50).

It is easy to identify elements similar to Marxist criticism of postcolonial theory in this view. It is striking in this case, however, that those elements are mobilized here for opposite reasons, against any kind of politicization of artistic practice. From this viewpoint, any beneficial aspect of postcolonialism is turned against itself. This is the case of difference and tolerance, which Shiming (2008: 43) quite apocalyptically mistakes for "cultural relativism, or even cynicism in value, thus constituting the emasculation of the cultural ideal." In the case of agency, things are even more problematic: Shiming depicts postcolonialism as an invisible ideological net capturing any subversive reaction, with the notable exception of the artwork practices included in *his* biennial made by "the lucky survivors who managed to escape the post-colonial grasp." Those survivors, he adds, operate "[within] the area where popular discourses on post-colonialism and multiculturalism cannot reach" (44).

It is crucial to understand where Shiming is arguing from here. A great deal of his introductory text is dedicated to explaining how postcolonialism entered the realm of Chinese art in the 1980s, consolidating its critical purchase in the 1990s, at a moment when China occupied the main position in the international art market. Shiming's rejection of postcolonialism thus occasions a rejection of affirmations of nativist and indigenist identity that could be manipulated by the interests of Western markets to insert artistic production into heterogeneous niches of "political art made by global others." As he puts it, "Post-colonial discourse has 'anti-oppression' connotations in the European and American intellectual world, but becomes an enemy of the cultural left in China, a country with a century's history of the left" (47).

The problem with that reasoning is that it overlooks two fundamental elements in its task of imagining an "after postcolonialism": the role of Chinese artists and art institutions in expanding the scope of the art market to the hyperbolic levels attained in the 1990s, and China's own tradition of *colonizing* spaces. At some stage, Shiming mentions a flight to Hong Kong made by the Chinese artist Wu Shanzhuan as an example of the blurred transitoriness the "post" to postcolonialism might represent under his view. The fact of taking Hong Kong as the example of airport-shaped globalization ("Let's forget our destination!," claims Shiming [2008: 57] in a moment of intellectual euphoria) reinforces even more the odd sense that his criticism of identity and postcolonialism brings with it an equally problematic view of market-driven globalization. To be sure, the mention of Hong Kong is joined in the essay by a questioning of how a "post-postcolonial" Hong Kong identity might look. However, recognizing the context of that transition to the city-state as an existence "outside of boundaries" (62) remains all the more problematic. Viewed from the perspective of those two absences, then, Shiming's criticism of the "overpoliticization" of postcolonial artistic contemporaneity appears different. His identification of difference as "a personal, existential thought experiment, a solo march towards strange new realms" seems less a criticism of postcolonialism's dematerialization than a confirmation of the dehistoricized image of globality, the blurring of "the line between the domestic and international" (53).

Sarat Maharaj's confrontation of what a farewell to postcolonialism might look like diverges substantially from Shiming's idea. Maharaj pointed to experience and action and possible ways forward. Around the same time, protests arose in many parts of the world, with a developing belief in praxis and optimism. Suicide protestors in Tunisia, the handover of Hong Kong, and radical movements in Indonesia and India are the examples used on this occasion. Maharaj's concern is with how the renovative potential of globalization is transformed into yet another turn of the art market and the art institution, thus being incorporated and commoditized into the global circuit of difference. Yet his movement is not one of defeat; on the contrary, he urges a reconsideration and insurgent application of a radical genealogy of Third World practices concerned with politicizing cultural practices, with not accepting their enclosure within the invisible hand of the market or its most visible equivalent of global cultural institutions. In rejecting the fuzziness of transnational exchanges, Maharaj urges "a frank turn to the 'raw empirical'. I mean a plunge into quotidian experience—into sounding the everyday rub-up of 'mainstream/marginal', of self/other, in their rounds of communicative endeavour beyond the uncrossables of language" (2008: 72). The challenge contained in these words, I believe, means taking this aspiration further in order to recognize the weight of activist and socially committed art practices as one of the best allies of quotidian experience. It would also mean expanding on "the uncrossables of language" to rethink and to historicize how radicalism was deployed, incorporated into a discursive logic, and consolidated as a global trend. To follow Maharaj's movement the task would be that of recovering the paths that coupled artistic globalism with effective social change beyond institutional inclusiveness, questioning not only, and not so much, the preeminence of the West in museums and biennials as the lack of agency that *both ideological and material* processes of commodification and exoticization conferred on what is rather vaguely called the Global South. This task, therefore, would enact a double movement by examining the impact of that deployment on the configuration of global and postcolonial art views, and yet do so by expanding insurgent artistic forms, both present and historical.

The divergent positions of Maharaj and Shiming did not impede them from creating a single exhibition, a fact worth further consideration in itself. In any case, I find more interesting in the comparison between Maharaj's and Shiming's "farewells" how, in Maharaj's conceptualization, extradisciplinary experience *outside the realms of art* remains the most influential source of artistic renovation. This argument recalls the extent to which postcolonial art stories are dependent on strategies of adaptation and negotiation of elementary conditions of living in difficult situations. In many cases, those strategies have led to subversive forms of collaboration that, paradoxically, are often dismissed and excluded from the official histories of artistic postcolonialism. Rasheed Araeen, one of the most quoted names in those histories, is a telling example of this phenomenon.

Araeen's radicalized artistic practice in the 1970s and his role in the definition of a Black British art are already well known, but a quick reminder will be helpful for my arguments here. After arriving in England in 1964 from Karachi (Pakistan), Araeen gave up a successful career as a minimalist sculptor in favor of more engaged forms of artistic production. After rejecting his minimalist practice as "limiting," he famously proposed a strategic alliance between nonwhite people living in the United Kingdom as *Blacks*. This implied participating in art collectives integrated by "nonwhite" artists such as Cecilia Vicuña or David Medalla (C. Martin 2010: 110). In the 1970s Araeen joined art collectives such as S.P.A.C.E. and Artists for Democracy, while radicalizing his own practice through experimenting with political performance. In 1978 he created *Black Phoenix,* a short-lived magazine that focused on activist forms of creativity developed by nonwhite creators in Britain. One decade later,

Black Phoenix was relaunched as *Third Text*, a journal that Stephen Wright (2013a) rightly places in the category of "art-beyond-art." *Third Text* then became one of the leading platforms ("a global platform for what we consider to be a continuing struggle against colonial structures," in Araeen's own words) for critical thought on radical artistic practice linked to the Global South.[22] Almost simultaneously, Araeen curated *The Other Story* at the Hayward Gallery, a show that Jean Fisher (2009) considers to be "a major breakthrough in 'de-imperialising' the institutional mind."

Araeen interests me here because his story epitomizes how the "turn to the raw empirical" can be tracked down historically as a central piece in South art histories. His idea of practice is directly shaped by his personal experience of racism and exclusion in London, which he addresses by weaving together "a narrative of labor, immigration, and violence" (C. Martin 2010: 112). His self-identification as a Black artist brings together the situation of migrating creators, the weight of Western aesthetics, and the degraded public space of London against the backdrop of increasing repressive politics (suffice it to remember that *Black Phoenix* precedes Thatcherism by only one year). For Araeen, identity was a strategic way to develop subversive alliances, and make space where it did not previously exist. Collaboration, in this sense, was essential in Araeen's strategic practice within the London art scene of the 1970s and 1980s. Although Araeen was concerned with countering the racism and exclusionist politics of the British cultural scene, his alternative was also a constructive one, based on establishing bonds of internationalist solidarity with other "Third World" artistic locations.[23]

Araeen's idea of art's political agency bears a close relation to the main hypothesis of this book, namely that collaborative art has played a central role in the configuration of South modes of artistic contemporaneity. His approach to collaboration arises as one of the most interesting (and most largely ignored) definitions of the concept. For Araeen, there exists an identification between institutional power and ideological determinants (including objecthood and spectacle as privileged platforms for artistic innovation). He understands the struggle of artists against colonialism as a collective enterprise of challenging modernist cultural assumptions, claiming their central place in modernism. In this sense, he argues that "their story is therefore the story of struggle between what these artists wanted to do and what was denied them by the dominant culture" (Araeen 2000: 6). For him, that struggle is shaped by the multiple ways in which the center controls the admission of artists from peripheral contexts in its center: "The real issue is the way others are accepted and accommodated by the dominant culture" (6).

From this strategic position, art becomes a platform for achieving things that mere politics cannot.[24] For Araeen there is a deep division between bourgeois aesthetics and artistic collaboration. The first builds its own position through shaping the concepts and ideas that are used to categorize artistic processes, creating a realm "within which everything becomes trapped and reified" (2010: 62). In his opinion, this "everything" includes many Third World artists, who adopted a rhetoric of political radicalism while replicating Western modernist patterns of authorship and display. This appropriation, Araeen suggests, is part of the capacity of bourgeois institutions to engulf any criticism directed against them by establishing a separation between artistic production and everyday life. At the same time, however, art can adopt any particular form and channel a process of transformation, becoming socially relevant for a given community. This means that it is not artistic collaboration per se that is silenced by mainstream art histories but rather the multiple, strategic uses of the potential of practices of collaboration. Importantly enough, this potential does not depend on the individual signature of the artist; as Araeen argues (82), "The result may or may not be recognizable as a work of art; in fact, it is important that what is conceived of as art remains an everyday object or phenomenon in order to function as part of life." This goal, finally, can be achieved only through collaboration.

Araeen's notion of collaboration should be understood as a social projection directly embedded in practice. It should also transcend the specialized forums of contemporary art, rejecting individual ownership, living a "double life": "On the one hand, it is a conceptual artwork but, on the other, its material form must become independent of whether it is a work of art or not" (Araeen 2010: 82). Collaboration, in other words, is something that must be achieved in real life, through projecting the critical *and constructive* potential of artistic practice into different realms of reality.[25] In those terms, what matters is not what final shape an artistic experience adopts but the multiple and often contradictory positionings that experience adopts until reaching its final expression.

Although *Third Text* and Araeen's own artwork are often considered a central part of a "postcolonial art canon" (due to his participation in *Magiciens de la terre*, for example) the everydayness of his subversive reaction against the exclusivist aesthetic regime of postwar Britain (which can be felt both in practice and thought), and the way that everydayness was associated with a more ambitious project of social transformation, are still often overlooked. Looking at Araeen's project of radical aesthetics, it remains impossible to think theory and ideas beyond or outside practice. The strategic concurrence of both levels in Araeen's creative and intellectual practice opens up "raw empirical" alternatives to the idea that art exhibitions by themselves are behind global art histories. His experience also debunks the idea of "South" or postcolonial art histories beginning with the curatorial interest in operation in exhibitions such as *Magiciens*. Finally, Araeen's position represents the best example of how internationalism and locality, identity and tactics, constructive activism and ferocious anticanonization can be brought together and applied in the construction of alternative (art) histories and in the process of thinking through contemporary artistic practices.

Looking for Alternatives (II): Critical Regionalism

Regionalism offers a second valuable alternative to the primacy of exhibition making in postcolonial art histories. In many contexts, the evolution of contemporary art forms is inseparable from the establishment of long-lasting alliances between artists and alternative institutions. Often those alliances are the result of the "condensed" temporality and spatiality of biennials, yet in many cases their consequences go far beyond the time and space of mega-exhibitions. In many cases, also, regional alliances oppose the interests of official national museums and art centers, focusing more on the search for regional synergies across kindred artistic initiatives. Those initiatives challenge both the central role often played by former metropolitan territories in the circulation and display of regional contemporaneity, and the market-oriented impulse of art fairs.

The Caribbean provides good examples of this. While doing research for my PhD dissertation between 2009 and 2013, I spent several years doing fieldwork research in art institutions in Trinidad, Jamaica, Martinique, Guadeloupe, Cuba, Puerto Rico, the Dominican Republic, Haiti, and Panama. I have recently dealt with the importance of Caribbean socially engaged and alternative institutional practices elsewhere.[26] However, I believe that the Caribbean provides excellent examples of how regional articulations can derive from nonexhibitional practices, so allow me a short semibiographical digression to exemplify this second point.

"What is Caribbean art?" emerges as one of the main recurring questions for anyone doing research in the region. The issue here is to determine what glues together the artistic production of a region as varied as few others in the world might be. This question is indissolubly linked to that of defining what stands for Caribbean identities, a topic that has concerned authors such as Stuart Hall, Édouard Glissant, and Antonio Benítez-Rojo, some of the most well-known theorists emerging from the region. They all have striven to categorize Caribbean identities as fluid and diverse yet solidly grounded in the locality of displacements and entanglements of Caribbean communities. In the field of contemporary art, the question of Caribbean identity is linked to processes of postcolonial national affirmation, where museums and other national institutions seek to determine what stands for each "national culture"; to regional alliances (the Havana or the Caribbean Biennials,[27] two major forums where Caribbean artists from insular and continental territories tend to meet); and to international attention toward the region (as, for example, exemplified by the many blockbuster exhibitions organized in the United States and Europe).[28] What we call "Caribbean art" is therefore regulated through the continuities and discontinuities and the articulation between the local, the national, and the international.

Having said that, it is also true that only recently have participatory and collaborative forms of artistic creativity been analyzed as adding something to that articulation. The focus on audiences and engagement stands in stark contrast to the image that comes to mind when trying to represent contemporary Caribbean art, frequently likened to that of individual artworks or externally curated, large-scale exhibitions. Nevertheless, collaborative projects are fundamental for explaining how Caribbean communities have related to each other without the mediation of mainstream Euro-American art institutions. In cases such as Trinidad, collective practices like those promoted by CCA7, Galvanize, and Alice Yard have also fulfilled some of the important functions that national institutions sought to provide, including support for Trinidadian artists participating in international events, workshop space for Caribbean artists, educational initiatives (of many kinds, not only artistic), and spaces for critical dialogue. Alice Yard, the family home of one of the project's founders since 1953, is located at 80 Roberts Street, at the center of Woodbrook neighborhood, a major financial and recreational area in downtown Port of Spain. The initiative attempted to transfer the relaxed atmosphere already existing in the house's yard to the local cultural field. Trinidadian yards are spaces for hospitality and conviviality, where many people gather and share ideas and thoughts on relevant and ordinary issues. On Carnival days, they become neighborhood headquarters where all the arrangements are discussed, agreed, and finally made. The backyards were (and are) private spaces made public, places where authority is recognized, and tradition is respected, but also where knowledge circulates freely as a common good.

Initiatives like Alice Yard can be found throughout the Caribbean.[29] They channel collective enthusiasm to a process of place making, challenging the ongoing privatization of many Caribbean cities. They also counter the selective traditions displayed by national museums, which are still authorized to speak for postcolonial Caribbean societies. Instead of promoting individual creativity, they have been decisive in developing intraregional processes of dialogue and apprenticeship. If the artistic milieu of Port of Spain is dominated by art galleries that provide conservative collectors with a full array of "the national picturesque," with landscapes, thematic paintings, and still lifes being the favorites, spaces such as Alice Yard have set out to give art a whole different public use.

Viewed from the perspective of long-term collaborative platforms like Alice Yard, the articulation of the local, the regional, and the international in Caribbean art acquires a totally different shape. When the focus is displaced from spectacularized large-scale exhibitions to under-the-radar collectivism, an alternative history emerges. Caribbean art history is to a great extent a history of exhibitions and individual artworks. Less attention is paid to the ways in which artists organize themselves creatively. Yet, without that organization, the former would not exist.

Looking for Alternatives (III):
Curated and Noncurated Collaboration

A third and final possibility for readdressing the dimension of curatorial practices derives from an exploration of the multiple ways in which curating can approach collaborative practices. Issues of collaboration and social transformation are a key factor in curatorial debates. They play a central role in the redefinition of curating proposed by Maria Lind in "The Curatorial," with curators rethinking their role in terms of "frictions" with other agencies and "mobiliz[ing] an entire system of variables and contexts" (2009: 103).[30] Lind (2007) has also been influential in identifying a "collaborative turn" in contemporary curating. More recently, South African curator Nkule Mabaso coordinated a special issue in *OnCurating* on collaboration and activism and contemporary art biennials, revealing that the articulation of long-term collaborative dynamics and biennials in Africa is not always easy (see Pinther, Nzewi, and Fischer 2015). (For the record, the same journal has paid increasing attention to curatorial thought and practice outside the exhibition space, touching on institutional dynamics and public art.[31])

How can we make sense of this turn toward collaborative strategies in contemporary curatorial criticism and more broadly in contemporary curating? For decades, curating has tried to find its own place vis-à-vis art history and art criticism. Several authors, including Terry Smith, Robert Storr, Alex Farquharson, Paul O'Neill, and Reesa Greenberg investigated the specificities of curating in search of what makes it different from other forms of artistic expression. Those voices avoided essential categorizations but at the same time were attentive to the distinct features that could define curating as a specific field of artistic creativity. That anxiety attempted to respond to a double situation, marked by the expansion of curating to many facets of our everyday life, and the influential role that the figure of the independent curator was acquiring worldwide, a centrality taking place at the expense of other figures, such as the art critic, the art historian, or the artist himself or herself. In this expanded moment, "curating" became a much-repeated word that nevertheless hardly can be reduced to its more recognizable practice: that of integrating several artistic discourses into art exhibitions within a transnational framework. On the contrary, for the abovementioned authors, dealing with the specifics of curating implies dealing with a variety of practices and ideas, including infrastructural practices, artistic interventions, educational initiatives, artist-curated shows, etcetera.

That long list of etceteras included, of course, art activism and socially engaged art. Some of the examples of those attempts to "curate" movements include the seventh Berlin Biennale, Claire Tancons's staged carnivals, Nato Thompson's *The Interventionist* and *Living as Form*,[32] the Former West program in Europe, or the Greek-driven responses to 2017 documenta. A first consideration is in order: highly heterogeneous as they are, these initiatives challenge the economic and artistic rationale of biennial and institutional-based curating, even when their organizers operate as curators. Discussing possible initiatives under the banner of an expanded notion of curating, they do not hesitate when it comes to avoiding the specifics of curating. At the same time, even when they take the form of the exhibition, those initiatives displace the centrality of the figure of the curator from the critical scope, while repurposing the space of the exhibition through a temporality different from that of the exhibition. At issue here is much more than a defense or a criticism of those projects or a simple discussion about whether curating is harmful or beneficial when allied to (or interested in) activist, interventional art forms. It would be more productive to think about the frequency with which those alliances emerge and take them as a starting point for further questions: How is curatorial thought and practice remodeling past, present, and future forms of art activism? Inversely, how are collaborative and collectivist processes revisiting issues of curatorial labor, authorship, and spectatorship? What effects are the long-term collaborative strategies associated with socially engaged art having on more "traditional" forms of artistic curating? To what extent is the transformative potential of collectivist practices co-opted when curators intervene? As both curating and socially engaged art operate within an increasingly expanded and diversified framework, these questions must be addressed as shared challenges overcoming protective disciplinary boundaries.

Yet the question remains: what is to be gained from adopting a critical viewpoint that pays heed to those contaminations? Coming back to Mabaso's special issue might be useful here. Even when we acknowledge the importance of collaborative processes in shaping African artistic modernity and contemporaneity, one wonders how those processes successfully challenge the historical weight of art exhibitions produced more often than not outside of the continent. Doesn't the fact that this discussion takes place in a curatorial forum reveal how far the primacy of curatorial practice is normalized over other creative, collaborative forms? How do hierarchies between and within collaborative art projects operate when a curator forms part of "self-instituting strategies" (Mabaso 2016)? If those strategies are rightfully recognized as a driving engine of innovation within African contemporaneity, can art biennials still be identified as the space par excellence where the relationship between the local and the global is negotiated? In this sense, Mabaso rightfully deems biennials as not completely addressing the needs of African art ecosystems: "Here in Africa, as with other similar contexts, biennials mark the sites of productive tensions between the projection and transposing of universalizing aesthetics, the articulation of critique, and the attempt to arrive at self-realization after traditional modes of institutions have been largely accepted as not being able to support, nor meet the demands of localized contemporary practices in many African countries." She adds that "the normalization of major art events in countries and states with problematic governments and policies is a double-edged sword that could be productive and perform criticism of social institutions and politics while functioning within them" (Mabaso 2016).

Much less discussed is how artistic collaboration can operate as an alternative model removed from the limitations of biennials. The way that art biennials normalize critical and creative models is also often overlooked. If African art histories were built through the passing from a colonial genealogy of forms and formats (including the mega-exhibition, art collections, and nation-based representations in international events) to a postcolonial, biennial-based configuration, how can we measure the challenge of the initiatives mentioned by Mabaso in curatorial terms? If many of those examples displace the figure of the curator from their center, shouldn't the turn toward infrastructural and bottom-up practices in Africa be read as opposing, instead of holding a dialogue with, curating?

If those examples operate beyond or even in response to biennials, how are their models of collaboration to be compared with those of biennials?

The difficulty of that comparison is well demonstrated by artistic projects created in response to the economies and ecosystems of transnational biennials. That is the case, for example, of Lubumbashi-based Centre d'art Waza (formerly known as Rencontres Picha), which operates outside the Lubumbashi Biennial. Waza conceives artistic practice as part of broader, long-term dynamics attempting to encourage democratic participation in the Lubumbashi public sphere. Although Waza organizes art exhibitions, these are seen as part of a diversified program that also includes public spectacles, artistic research, and public interventions in the urban space. Used for both small-scale visual art organizations (Bilbao 2019) and biennials, and acknowledging the influence that biennials can have on grassroots art structures, Waza curator Patrick Mudekereza also argues that both models often fulfill quite distinct functions and operate differently at a local level. Mudekereza was involved in the first editions of the Lubumbashi Biennale, which was created as a collaborative project arising from local synergies between artists and writers.[33] After three editions that involved collaboration with international curators Simon Njami and Elvira Dyangani Ose, Picha detached from the biennial, which followed an independent path. In this case, although Mudekereza recognizes that the biennial played a central role in the definition of Picha/Waza, ultimately both models ended up following different aspirations. This separation also entails different understandings of the role of the curator and spectatorship: although events are also curated in Waza, they rely on a vast network of pan-African artistic solidarities that only occasionally take the form of contemporary art exhibitions. To what extent can this separation be addressed? Shall we read it as part of the history of African or "South" biennials? Can both Waza and the Lubumbashi Biennial be framed under the same model of art historical and critical interpretation?

There are two ways of answering these questions. The first has to do with an increasing concern on the part of African curators concerning issues of funding, autonomous institutionalism, and sustainability, as shown by Koyo Kouoh's (2013) superb survey on alternative institutionalism in Africa organized through the Dakar-based Raw Material Company.[34] The second, already revealed in the Lubumbashi example, involves observing that those questions are being equally addressed by African curators, cultural managers, and art activists alike. In this way, even curators who are enthusiastic about their work are exploring alternative forms of pan-African articulation beyond the biennial format and its temporality.

For instance, Mudekereza is one of the founders of PAN!C (Pan African Network of Independent Contemporaneity), a cluster of alternative institutional and collaborative initiatives that challenges the primacy of large exhibitions in the configurations of histories of contemporary art in Africa.[35] PAN!C's focus on providing research and educational resources to a pan-African community counters the temporal and locational logic of African biennials, proposing an alternative articulation of small-scale artistic projects whose modes of social interaction also differ from those of the most common exhibition practices.

Conclusion

This chapter has examined the role of exhibition making in the configuration of postcolonial and global art worlds. My conviction is that the overvisibility of large-scale exhibitions and biennials has overshadowed the importance of many other practices, among them collaborative art (such as those analyzed in all the remaining sections of this book) in the making of those (art) worlds. Postcolonial artistic investigations taking place in biennials are still granted a higher degree of critical value than long-term, collaborative creative initiatives. In this sense, their "criticality" is largely assumed as being more political and less attached to market imperatives than artworks displayed in art fairs or even museums. Despite the increasing recognition of alternative creative strategies, the image of a transient artist going from biennial to biennial and interacting with "local people" to make sense of a specific problem or situation at that place still prevails among us as the most common, and also the most politicized, mode of critically dealing with the world through art. And although there is nothing bad about it, this mode of understanding contemporaneity should be historicized and contextualized as one among many other possibilities.

The successive attempts by postcolonial intellectuals and artists, and even decolonial thinkers and practitioners, to break with the issues of universalism and privilege that persist in global artistic configurations often keep on privileging exhibitional forms over other modes of artistic creativity. Decolonized or not, global art histories are still very much the history of exhibition making, this centrality of the curatorial being another symptom both of how enduring modernist exhibitional patterns are, and how they reproduce and evolve in unacknowledged ways.

Attempting to counter this symptom, this chapter has examined our contemporary art world(s) in order to pose the question of how different artistic practices, including mega-exhibitions and socially engaged art, relate to other forms of artistic production and display, especially at a moment when almost all art claims to embody social and political relevance. In doing this, my objective was not to classify some artistic practices as being better or worse than others. Rather, I sought to answer this question in two different ways: first, by showing how certain forms of contemporary art and criticism replicate and normalize universalist views of modernity, and second, by looking into alternatives to those views as a way to challenge the supposed "crisis" of postcolonialism. Two main goals lay behind this critical exercise. The first was to insert socially engaged art into the broader artistic framework of the multiple modes of artistic contemporaneity that form our art world(s). Whereas Claire Bishop (2012: 13) is right that socially engaged art should be compared to other artistic forms, it is no less true that this comparison also has to consider the rationality of each of those forms, so that the process of normalization of any of them, and, linked to it, the multiple ways in which some others are silenced, emerges from the main landscape of this comparison. The second goal is far simpler, and reinforces this book's main idea: through excavating "postcolonial" art histories, it becomes impossible to identify socially engaged art as a recent phenomenon, and the idea of this kind of art as an outcome of Western art histories is also called into question.

Fortunately, the panorama is already changing. We can see the recent interest in problematizing the historical dimension of neoliberalism as part of an "economic turn" in cultural criticism. The work of Wendy Brown, Jamie Peck, Stephen Shapiro, Sharae Deckard, and Mathias Nilges has continued David Harvey and Fredric Jameson's insightful engagement with the concept in order to directly question the extent to which culture plays a central part in the production (and not just in the representation) of neoliberal reasoning. If the recent interest in exploring the relationship between neoliberalism and culture is motivated by the series of economic crises that have shaped the first decades of the twenty-first century, it is also certainly linked to the emergence of conservative and alt-right movements around the globe (more about this in chapter 9; see also Traverso 2019; Nilges 2019). The increasing interest in exploring the structural aspect of the multiple forms in which contemporary art is made can be linked to this trend. From this perspective, understanding the logic behind each of these forms (including socially engaged art) becomes a central task if we want to understand how the collapse of certain art worlds preceded and propitiated situations of crisis. The next chapter continues these debates by critically exploring the US genealogy of socially engaged art.

2

◆ ◆ ◆

THE LEXICON OF SOCIAL PRACTICE AND SOCIALLY ENGAGED ART'S FUTURES

Consider the following two quotes:

In setting a curriculum for socially engaged art, mere art history and theory won't do: while they are critical to providing a historical and contextual framework of the practice, socially engaged art is a form of performance in the expanded field, and as such it must break away, at least temporarily, from self-referentiality. (Helguera 2011: x)

In a kind of historical displacement, contemporary art was suddenly thrown into relief as a distant prefiguration or prophecy of what was now happening in real time, too close for the comfort of the exhibitions, conferences, and catalogs within which the radical aspirations of contemporary art had sought refuge. As an historiographical provocation, one that admittedly borders on the eschatological, it might be said that this moment of passage represents the *end of socially engaged art*. (McKee 2016: 80–81)

These excerpts are taken from key pieces of recent socially engaged art criticism produced in the last ten years. When viewed together, they show the evolution of social practice, from its marginalization from mainstream debates and media to its inclusion in museums and art institutions worldwide, ending in a particular situation in which the specificity of socially engaged art can be abolished. Pablo Helguera's *Education for Socially Engaged Art* proceeded from the artist's involvement with museum education departments in Mexico and the United States. It is aimed at art students in the numerous masters programs on offer in the United States. Arising out of direct, sustained involvement in Occupy Wall Street, Yates McKee's appreciation of the New York movement as the end of socially engaged art was intended to address the increasing success of the term and its incorporation into mainstream artistic debates. Both authors take the success of socially engaged artists into account, but they also track the interest of curators and art institutions and the increasing popularity of the concept and the idea of "social practice" within and beyond the art world. Altogether, they create a narrative of expansion and exhaustion that has profound consequences not only for our critical understanding of those artistic practices but also in the very way they are produced. Of course, none of them considers socially engaged art as a homogeneous field. On the contrary, Helguera's pedagogical tool originates from the belief that "theory won't do" in explaining the multiplicity of practices and experiments encompassed under the term. And McKee's thought-provoking statement is the result of direct observation of the contrast between Nato Thompson's *Living as Form* landmark exhibition at Creative Time and the "real" events of Occupy Wall Street.

McKee's affirmation is also provocative for other reasons: it preserves the mythical notion of New York City as the epicenter of artistic modernity and aesthetic experimentation, reading a single, located episode as an event of global repercussion. Helguera's interest in creating a curriculum to teach socially engaged art in the museum and the academy will unavoidably lead to pressing questions: Which practices are worth teaching? How should we teach them? Does teaching those practices mean turning them into canonical examples? Noting these concerns does not mean rejecting the praiseworthy task that both Helguera and McKee have undertaken (although I am somewhat skeptical about *Strike Art*'s New York–centric "provincialism"). Rather, what they reveal is that, successful or not, socially engaged art nowadays continues to pose challenging questions about our social interactions inside and outside artistic venues.

It is undeniable that a vast corpus of discourses and ideas emerging within the last twenty years both within and outside of academia has popularized this way of making art in the United States and elsewhere. This chapter deals with this evolution, or more specifically, with one of the most common interpretations of this evolution. It attempts to define the critical and transformative capacity of socially engaged art after the "social turn." I wonder which kind of image would emerge if we tried to relativize the narration offered at the beginning of the chapter. Put more simply, in this chapter I try to think how past forms and processes of activist art reverberate in our present in alternative ways, and ask what is to be done to retain the transformative potential of social practice after its (partial) institutionalization and commodification.

It goes without saying that by doing so I do not attempt to solve all the problems of socially engaged art altogether. My contribution is rather more limited and has to do with attempting two synchronized movements. The first one detaches this kind of practice from its univocal history of global success (or failure). The second, related to the first, points to the urgent need to provincialize and decolonize the words we use to approach this history, rendering them partisan and yet untamable. For example, in *One Place after Another,* Miwon Kwon (2004: 92) identifies "do-good community-based public art" as a symptom of "the context of early 1990s multiculturalist identity politics and political correctness debates." Why, then, did that framework often disappear from both the positive and negative critical evaluations of social practice? To what extent is Kwon's mistrust of "do-good community-based public art" informed by a mistrust of (or a specific reading of) "early 1990s multiculturalist identity politics"?

Related to those questions and central to our interests in this chapter is a conceptualization of socially engaged art as a field in which words and concepts also have a strong say. Socially engaged art can be defined as both a way of making art, and a culturally mediated space of practice and thought that nowadays exists in tension with the instrumental-izing forces of art institutions, governments, and NGOs. Not that this situation is new: from the early 2000s socially engaged art criticism began to realize the dangers that could come from its co-optation (see Kester 2011). However, the way in which socially engaged art is commonly appropriated not only at the level of practice but also, and more problematically, in art education and institutional praxis makes the problem particularly urgent nowadays. This instrumentalization and institutionalization has deep consequences in art theory, for if we understand socially engaged art as a kind of experience-based, "undisciplined," and subversive practice, then its disciplining implies a decisive shift in the way we leverage the political and social saliency of creative practices. In its disciplined form, socially engaged art can be transformed into a "curriculum," a body of well-known names, concepts, and organizations. This reduction involves a historicist view that not only reduces the productive impureness of collaborative praxis but also functions in an exemplary way, in which certain practices are, at best, offered as models and, at worst, read as recipes able to be extrapolated to any other context and to determine beforehand what works and what doesn't. When this is the case, when practices are applied or read as formulas, "peripheral" or new practices are extracted from their contingent here and now. They also appear as provincial replicas, derivatives operating in an art world that despite its claims of global social relevance strives to maintain a narrow, Western geography as its field of operation.[1]

The Lexicon of Social Practice

Given those circumstances, I propose to "retool" our critical vocabulary employed to tackle socially engaged art criticism. This chapter will look for hidden potential lying behind normalized uses of words and concepts such as "social emancipation," "collectivism," and "engagement." Exploring that potential involves conceptualizing our use of those words as both located ("historicized," to borrow Dipesh Chakrabarty's lucid formulation[2]) and universally applied. The objective, therefore, is not to eschew any particular genealogy of social practice as "less productive" than any other; the task this chapter pursues is far simpler, and has to do with questioning the extent to which our own appreciation of the success or failure of socially engaged art depends on an inherited way of looking at it, in other words, on a normalized lexicon.

The word "lexicon" seems to be at odds with the fertility and flexibility of the term "socially engaged art" (or, for this purpose, with any other expression we could substitute for it, including "collaborative art," "collectivist art," or "social change"; not that all these terms are the same, but they are often used to encompass practices that are frequently discussed together). A certain way of thinking *through* contemporary practices that could fall into these categories, however, has become more common with the years; nowadays expressions such as "relational aesthetics" and "collaborative art" that shaped European aesthetic debates on these matters during the 1990s and 2000s have become a ubiquitous—if contested—presence in the vocabulary of any art critic (see Billig, Lind, and Nilsson 2007; Lind 2007; Bishop 2012; Galimberti 2017).

One effect of this popularization has been its uncritical use. Another is to understand that some values associated with collaborative practices are self-evident and therefore measurable according to a single set of critical values, no matter whence these artistic practices emerge. What is the purchase of activist or socially engaged art when the number of practices claiming the social relevance traditionally associated with these practices is growing exponentially? Can we understand it in its global expansion as something "both indispensable and inadequate," to draw again from Chakrabarty's formulation?[3]

In dealing with these questions, it is important to acknowledge how normalized theoretical production works. Dealing with how race was erased from generic theorizations of liberalism, Charles Mills analyzes the formations of what he calls "ideal theory." The difference between ideal theory and any other kind of theorization, Mills posits (2017: 75), is the former's "reliance on idealization to the exclusion, or at least marginalization, of the actual." Related to this, he recognizes an established tradition of forgetting, operating at many levels, among them that of "cognitive spheres." For Mills, an idealized cognitive sphere would have the following effect: "As a corollary of the general ignoring of oppression, the consequences of oppression for the social cognition of these agents, both the advantaged and the disadvantaged, will typically not be recognized, let alone theorized. A general social transparency will be presumed, with cognitive obstacles minimized by being limited to biases of self-interest or the intrinsic difficulties of understanding the world, while little or no attention is paid to the distinctive role of hegemonic ideologies and group-specific experience in distorting our perceptions and conceptions of the social order" (76). Mills's words can be easily applied to the knowledge produced on socially engaged art. Consider, for example, the accepted use of notions of civil society and poststructuralism in the critical debates on art and politics. In the context of civil society, what distinguishes socially engaged art from other modes of art making seeking political and social relevance is the impact the former has on civil society and the public sphere. No matter which strategies of collaboration are set in motion, or which notion of community is implicit in the art project, what constitutes the grounds on which socially engaged art distinguishes itself from other creative practices is precisely having an impact outside the art world, beyond discourse. It remains to be seen which image of civil society is assumed by socially engaged art practices, and how the specificities of postcolonial civil societies affect these practices.

Mahmood Mamdani (1996) has argued that postcolonial civil societies are the result of a troublesome evolution from a restricted group of people in colonial times to a broader national public sphere. In many cases, however, he warns that postcolonial civil society is fraught with important political and economic limitations: access to and participation in a public sphere is limited by instabilities. This turns civil society into a fragile arena where inclusion cannot ever be taken for granted and exclusion is the norm. Far, then, from the Habermasian universalist notion of public sphere, postcolonial civil society is a particularly delicate ecosystem fraught with the uncertainty of collapse. This, of course, affects and conditions the artistic practices operating within it.

Something similar happens with poststructuralism, a term that is often referred to in socially engaged art in relation to European critical theory. In *Out of Africa,* Pal Ahluwalia points out how colonialism was maintained by keeping the promise and the lure of modernity and modernization alive for the colonizers, in a process of perpetual deferral grounded on a promise of transformation that was never supposed to fully materialize.[4] Ahluwalia borrows here from Robert Young's (1990: 1) sharp grounding of poststructuralism: "If 'so-called post-structuralism' is the product of a single historical moment, then that moment is probably not May 1968 but rather the Algerian War of Independence." The "African roots" of poststructuralism are part of a transcontinental, ghostly intellectual history. Crucially, Ahluwalia's "bigger picture" of that history reassess the relationship between poststructural theory and political action in order to acknowledge that Third World revolutionary movements are part of poststructuralism's geopolitics.

Socially engaged art criticism assumed the universal value of some of its analytical categories, among them a restricted understanding of the sites of political transformation. This is obvious in relation to arguments about the lack of a "political horizon" for the Left after the fall of the Berlin Wall, arguments that would appear differently if poststructuralism's expanded geography were acknowledged. Attempting to historicize the universalization of a certain way of understanding criticism, Ahluwalia argues that colonialism constituted the located *realpolitik* of French theory: "It is in Algeria that we find the most radical disjuncture between the promise of European modernity and the reality, which demonstrated the very pitfalls of the universality of those ideas" (2010: 14). This recognition, he adds, would help to think modernist categories otherwise: "Surely, it is more plausible that the questions that have become so much a part of the post-structuralist canon—otherness, difference, irony, mimicry, parody, the lamenting of modernity and the deconstruction of the grand narratives of European cultures arising out of the Enlightenment tradition—are possible *because* of their postcolonial connection" (2).

This has enormous consequences where social practice is concerned. It means that one of the pillars defining this kind of artistic practice—a certain fear of direct action and the deferral of social transformation for a future always to be—might arise from (or at least be in touch with) the contingent everyday of decolonization. The consequences deriving from here are obvious: the success of poststructuralism and its withdrawal from the impurities of direct intervention,[5] which contemporary aesthetics of radical collaboration attempted to subvert, happened at the expense of another coeval modernity, that implicit in the universalist-yet-located agenda of decolonization (think of Sartre "explaining" Fanon in the preface of *Les damnés de la terre*). Inversely, the novelty of social practice, erected in direct opposition to poststructuralism, can be maintained only if the anticolonial project is seen as a fraught initiative deactivated and turned into "history," to borrow from Chakrabarty's apt term once again. How productive the encounter between the engagement-based modernist project of anticolonialism and contemporary forms of artistic collaboration would be is yet to be seen. In any case, I believe that the emphasis on locating thought, of acknowledging that critical theory works only when located, serves as a kindred agenda pursued by both postcolonial studies and social practice.

Dealing with Socially Engaged Art's Master Narratives

In coping with the institutional success (or failure in its goal of social relevance) of socially engaged art, it might be useful to see how the master narrative of the "social turn" actually works. Among other effects, it produces an image of a normalized present in which the potential arising from the "impurities" of practices is beforehand co-opted by the institution in its physical form or disguised as the market. Furthermore, the narrative consisting of the global success of socially engaged art also implies the adoption of a language that originally emerged out of specific and located practices. Despite this fact, the endless repetitions in recent art criticism of the main terms composing that language take no account of the fact that these concepts never aimed to represent universal values. On the contrary, they were conceived through a close engagement with a particular set of practices. Ideas and concepts are by definition tools that can be used in many contexts; at the same time, however, delving into their located genealogies also preempts any uncritical application of them in different cases and circumstances. Besides determining the newness and coevality of certain socially engaged art practices, their institutionalization also operates by fixing and canonizing their aesthetic value according to a specific interpretation of their failure or success. If socially engaged art depends on affecting the realm of the social beyond representational means, measuring this impact teleologically (as if the results of each action should be reduced to one particular aesthetic and social judgment) removes a great part of the translational potential of these practices. As I have argued elsewhere, a good way of measuring the health of activist and socially engaged art practices is to focus on their persistence, their capacity to transcend the here and now of the event, and, consequently, to reassess the immediate lure of both pessimism and euphoria (Garrido Castellano 2018). After all, if (art) objects and processes have their own life, they might also have several future projections.

As we will see throughout this book, one of the main features of any process of subversive and radical imagination is its resilience. As Ngugi wa Thiong'o (1993: 4) has pointed out, our world is shaped by the more or less evident continuities of imperial and other forms of domination, as much as by those of acts of resistance. Applying this example to our current interests is to recognize a stubbornly irreducible diglossia,[6] and a capacity for generating echoes that must be fully taken into consideration when measuring the aesthetic and social impact of socially engaged art practices.

Socially engaged art thus faces a complicated situation whose consequences go far beyond the commoditization of an art "ism."[7] To survive, or at least to remain meaningful, socially engaged art has to be aware of its own success if it still wants to be identified as a more valid tool for social transformation. The so-called institutionalization of socially engaged art works in a paradoxical way, by infusing social relevance into notions abstracted from particular situations of collective praxis. In this way, praxis (always imperfect and projected onto the future, always arising from particular expectations, is frozen into the exemplarity of the norm, as if these expectations could be immediately transferred to other processes of artistic action. What was never supposed to be exemplary becomes the norm. In the "crisis" of social practice it is not simply a matter of mainstream museums and art institutions being entitled, or not, to produce social transformation through art. The real problem involves the political dimension of socially engaged art practices after this confinement within the museum's walls.[8] The question that should be asked of socially engaged art praxis and criticism is whether it is still stretching the categories of political engagement and social transformation in ways that can be described as radical and unpredictable even to the concept of socially engaged art itself. Turned into a question, the point will be, as Gregory Sholette indicates (2017: 230), "How might our narrative about social practice art collectivism be imagined differently?"[9]

Taking this issue as a point of departure, in the following section I examine the United States' genealogy of socially engaged art. Contrary to the other chapters comprising this book, my focus here will be on the more "canonical" European and North American critical discussions of the matter. By engaging with this critical tradition, I seek both to dismantle the idea of it as a closed and homogeneous corpus of knowledge, and to recognize in it voices and alignments concerned with "space matters," issues of diversity, cultural identity, and racialized perceptions of inequities and exclusions.

Before undertaking the task of finding potential ways of "thinking differently" about those critical genealogies, a preliminary consideration is in order. After all, we might wonder, why do words matter when social transformation is at stake? If activist and socially engaged art projects are to be judged on their failure or success, how important is any critical reappraisal of their consequences anyway? Doesn't a focus on the lexicon of social practice betray its original detachment from representational and postconceptual art practices? Words certainly do not condition practice. But they do normalize certain attitudes toward it. At a moment of increasing institutionalization of social practice (the appearance of curricula and strict guidelines for scholarships or grants), we run the risk of losing alternative imaginings. By narrowing down and fixing social practice's past, we also fix and preempt its future.

Birth of a Discipline

Therefore the stringing together [of new genre art and public art] was meant deliberately to bring together both the public nature of the work as well as the non-traditional nature, to introduce the idea of public performance as a form of both performance and public art, and to suggest that public art was not simply murals or sculpture.

—Email exchange with Suzanne Lacy, in the context of the translation of a chapter of *Mapping the Terrain* into Portuguese

In *Death of a Discipline,* Gayatri Chakravorty Spivak investigated potential ways out of the ossification that in the early 1990s affected comparative literature. Spivak was concerned with recovering the social relevance of critical thought, and also with provincializing a discipline strongly connected to the project of European imperialism. As disparate as this insight might appear from a "ready-for-action" field of socially engaged art, I believe that there is something to be learned from Spivak's interest in searching for a "displaced" and undisciplined field of comparative literary criticism. This is notably the case when Spivak (2003: 10) urges that "engag[ing] with the idiom of the global other(s) in the Southern Hemisphere, uninstitutionalized in the Euro–U.S. university structure except via the objectifying, discontinuous, transcoding tourist gaze of anthropology and oral history, is our lesson on displacing the discipline." The task of displacing institutionalized forms of knowledge also requires us to challenge what Natalie Melas (2007: 24), from a perspective germane to Spivak's, calls the "transparent knowability [of] the empirical object": the idea that reality always appears as a neat document awaiting the lucid glance of the critic to be decoded. Sharing Spivak's and Melas's concerns about the task of criticism, I argue that unfamiliar voices and bodies operating in the field of socially engaged art have the virtue of making us unlearn the common ground of our critical appreciation, rendering our interiorized assumptions over engagement and sociality "both indispensable and inadequate," to go back to Chakrabarty once again.

Socially engaged and collaborative art were consolidated in the late 1980s and early 1990s. It was then that a certain group of collaborative artistic projects gained international critical attention, and were thus mobilized to define positions on collaborative aesthetics, agglutinating heterogeneous debates on public art, site-specificity, and activist art, and defining much of the vocabulary that is still used today to approach similar practices. However, as important as this period was as a moment of consolidation, critical debates in that moment also nurtured useful alternatives to the current impasse condensed under the expression "social turn." Through the focus on the evolution of conceptual and public art forms in the context of an unprecedented expansion of the art market during the 1980s, a history of social intervention art operating *on*, instead of *made by*, underprivileged individuals and communities still prevails. Moreover, for many critics not sympathetic to collaborative art, those individuals and communities are seen as agency-less, socially disenfranchised constituents in need of the intervention of an artist to gain voice and express themselves in the public sphere. Through an analysis of the role played by race in the constitution of genealogies of socially engaged art, in this chapter I hope to demonstrate that both assumptions are false. First, the history of the field is far from the "disciplined" image of a tamed practice developed by white, middle-class, male artists in search of "authentic" engagement with groups. Those groups, in turn, are not always socially disenfranchised; as I hope to show, they hold a complex relation with modernity and the nation, one shaped not only by disjointed and ambivalent experiences of exclusion and infrastructural violence but also by the active participation of racialized communities in the making of the civic. Socially engaged art, I will suggest, is part of this process of making, but it is also essential in transforming and challenging the experiences of exclusion that operate on racial and gendered principles.

A first step in pursuing this line of criticism must expose the relationship between socially engaged art and the Western avant-garde. In *Artificial Hells,* Claire Bishop (2012: 5) connects her exploration of participatory art projects in "the legacy of the historic avant-garde." Previously, she stressed that contemporary forms of artistic participation operate without any link to political causes, and are paradigmatically the result of the demise of utopian horizons after the fall of the Berlin Wall: "Participatory art today stands without a relation to an existing political project (only to a loosely defined anti-capitalism) and presents itself as oppositional to visual art by trying to side-step the question of visuality. As a consequence, these artists have internalized a huge amount of pressure to bear the burden of devising new models of social and political organisations" (284). Earlier on, in the much-quoted article "The Social Turn: Collaboration and Its Discontents," Bishop reinforces this view by arguing, "It is tempting to date the rise in visibility of [social turn] practices to the early 1990s, when the fall of Communism deprived the Left of the last vestiges of the revolution that had once linked political and aesthetic radicalism" (2006a, 179).

In her work, Claire Bishop famously denounced a mode of critical judgment in which "nonart" elements determine how good the collaboration between the artist and the community is (2006a, 181). She went on to develop the consequences of this argument in further, equally widely discussed texts (2004, 2006b): the ubiquitousness of collaborative practices would numb our capacity to judge their aesthetic side, pushing ethical principles to the forefront of critical judgment. In Bishop's words, "The social turn in contemporary art has prompted an ethical turn in art criticism" (2006b: 180), which in her view represents a continuation of humanist and Christian ethics. Against this use of collaboration as a tool, she proposed reading participative art practices as art (that is, in close relation with the "historical tradition of the avant-garde"). Following Chantal Mouffe and Jacques Rancière, she also advocated agnostic, dissensus-based participatory practices or "artificial hells," art projects that make the relation between artistic creation and active spectatorship sufficiently uncomfortable to raise the audience's awareness of issues such as labor exploitation and police violence.[10] Acknowledging that nowadays "participation in the West . . . has more to do with the populist agendas of neoliberal governments" (2012: 277), she criticizes projects that seek consensus-based agreement, stressing that the collaboration between artists and communities often ends up in the instrumentalization of the latter by the former. In response, "artificial hells" conceive participation as a provocative experience that unsettles the normalized and ritualized consumption of contemporary art by shocking the audience.

Bishop's ideas on participatory art have been widely discussed in recent years, therefore I will not pursue this analytical approach. What interests me here is that her positioning depends on an aesthetic judgment grounded on avant-gardist traditions. Her mistrust of "do-good" collaborative projects and her attacks on relational artists and collaborative groups such as Oda Projesi comes from the recognition of the primacy of that avant-gardist tradition. This recognition poses, I believe, a contradiction with the experimental confluence of traditions and genealogies at play in the first steps of what we nowadays call socially engaged art. In this sense, we can argue that the birth of social practice is inextricably linked to the creation of what Rosalind Krauss cleverly identified as early as 1979 as an "expanded field," in which traditional categories related to the idea of "medium" were extended and gradually rendered unfamiliar. It is worth noting that in the same essay, Krauss prophetically notes a "rage to historicize" and tame this versatility of artistic practice, acknowledging the pernicious role that art criticism would play in "historicizing that history" (1979: 30). It is also highly revealing that Krauss makes sculpture peripheral ("sculpture is rather only one term on the periphery of a field in which there are other, differently structured possibilities") by tracing its evolution from the history of the Western avant-garde (38). In any case, the same peripherality of art within itself arises out of the Beuysian notion of social sculpture, famously recovered by Claire Doherty (2004) and Maria Lind (2007) in their analysis of socially engaged and participative projects such as Oda Projesi and Thomas Hirschhorn's *Bataille Monument*.

The relevance of alternative understandings of artistic collaboration and participation is derived from different readings of the multiple genealogies converging into 1990s practices. Shannon Jackson recognizes that the term "social practice" is "imprecise," and that this imprecision is felt in the "very different kinds of socially engaged artists" gathered in the events organized under that umbrella term (Jackson 2011: 13). She also points out that the ways in which "we understand the social in socially engaged art" may differ widely (21). We can only agree with this view.

However, Jackson finds in the field of performance an alternative to the primacy of contemporary visual arts in the genealogies of social practice. I wonder whether substituting one avant-gardist tradition for another might work.

To end this section, I propose a different approach to the genealogies of socially engaged art. Going back to the voices of three theorists who contributed decisively to defining the field back in the 1980s, we can see how issues of racial difference and cultural identity were at the core of artistic collaboration. For them, diversity was not a material appropriable by artists operating in the "expanded field"; instead, it took the form of political positionality infusing experiments of social transformation. While I am foregrounding the critical voices of Suzanne Lacy and Nina Felshin, I do not intend to read their understanding of artistic collaboration as being better or worse than anyone else's. Instead, I want to explore how "unfamiliar" our understanding of US history of socially engaged art would look when placed under scrutiny, demonstrating that even the most examined and analyzed genealogy of social practice can be read in alternative, productive ways.

A common assumption explaining the emergence of socially engaged art consists of affirming that it palliates and complements the eroded surface of democracy under the rampant rise of neoliberalism in the 1980s. The association between the consolidation of activist art and Reaganomics (or Thatcherism for that matter) came along with a redefinition of "poor" and "poverty" in which disenfranchised individuals and groups were themselves blamed for their underprivileged social position. The consequences of neoliberal regularization in the art field included not only a flexibilization of corporate power (as argued by Boltanski and Chiapello [2005, especially 419–83]) but also an essentialization and racialization of poverty, a "there is no way out, stick to it" that paralleled the "there is no alternative" master narrative. In this context, racial difference was not only stigmatized alongside economic underprivilege; it was also stigmatized as class difference. It is symptomatic that many art projects arising in these years (both in representational and nonrepresentational forms; this includes Pepón Osorio, Glenn Ligon, Jimmie Durham, Fred Wilson, and Renée Green) challenged this paradigm.[11] Whereas some "difference-based" manifestations in the late 1980s and 1990s adopted positions close to self-referentiality and institutional critique, other projects advocated site-specific, contextual, community-based collaboration. That included the collective work of many self-sustained groups, and also bottom-up initiatives operating voluntarily on the fringes of mainstream art worlds.

Despite the weight that those assumptions still hold in contemporary debates on socially engaged art, there have always been many voices claiming more comprehensive, transnational histories. Central to those histories is the exploration of the links between socially engaged and activist art and difference. For example, Julia Bryan-Wilson has investigated quite brilliantly how antiwar ideologies and concerns with cultural transnational solidarity were articulated with issues of class, gender, and racial difference as specific demands on artistic labor. This included interventions in spaces such as MoMA, and also the creation of "provisional" and heterogeneous artistic alliances, as in the case of the Art Workers' Coalition (Bryan-Wilson 2011: 14). The agenda of this coalition involved not only issues of institutional representation and accessibility but also "mundane" issues of cultural work. This slippage of pacifist ideologies, professional claims, and active criticism of institutional dynamics through artistic means laid the groundwork for future art activist interventions.[12]

The connections drawn by Bryan-Wilson are not exclusive to recent art criticism. Suzanne Lacy's *Mapping the Terrain: New Genre Public Art*, a book rightfully recognized as one of the initiators of the debates on the social relevance of public art,[13] offers a similar perspective. *Mapping the Terrain* contains a final section in which hundreds of politically committed collaborative works are discussed. It is surprising to look back more than twenty years and see how few of these projects have been critically addressed. The success of socially engaged art has taken place despite, or, more precisely, because of the erasure of the complexity and heterogeneity of a spectrum of ideas and experiments put into practice. In her analysis Lacy introduces two politically charged concepts, engagement and social intervention. The term she coined to address the emergence of a new kind of art practice, "new genre public art," stands not so much as a definition of a way of making art as a way of stretching both extremes of the equation (new genre art and public art) in order to deliberately redefine the role of artistic experimentation.

Lacy's early theorization of socially engaged art is key to her recognition of competing histories of art in the public sphere. For Lacy, the mainstream narratives of public art emphasized the sculptural interventions of avant-garde artists in public places, which implied that community and activist art received much less critical attention. The barometer of criticism, she argues—anticipating the debates of the following decade—was social transformation: any art "that claims to 'do' something" (Lacy 1995: 20) was demeaned as utilitarian reformism.

By acknowledging the relevance of projects often remaining outside the discussions of public and site-specific art, Lacy recognizes that "an alternative reading of the history of the past thirty years results in a different interpretation of these same present concerns" (1995: 25). For her, that reading cannot be detached from the intersections between "Marxist," feminist," and "ethnic" artists and an interest in popular culture already present in Allan Kaprow's 1950s happenings. No matter how different these approaches to artistic creativity might be, they share (in Lacy's view) a desire to push artistic experimentation and medium renovation further as tools of social change. Unlike state- or corporate-sponsored public art, artists committed to social transformation use art to develop effective cooperation with multiple sectors of civil society. What separates the different initiatives nowadays included in the vague term "social practice" would be not only whether they are based on consensus rather than dissensus; for Lacy, a deeper fracture operates at the levels of conceptualization and collaboration. Between "art in public places" (i.e., the authorial, sculptural intervention in public space that resizes only a studio-based, avant-gardist object) and "art in the public interest" (collaborative art whose aesthetic premises arise out of politically informed interventions into the social realm) there is much more than divergent understandings of artistic collaboration. These two models belong to two opposing definitions of what art might be, and although they can be found side by side in generic views of the field of social practice based on formal values (on the use of collaboration as a means), they represent competing trajectories whose effects are very much felt in contemporary critical and artistic initiatives.

Mapping the Terrain adds something fundamental to critical appreciation of difference in the history of socially engaged art. For Lacy, that history takes heed of the role of "particularly marginalized [artists and activists]" in repurposing and "re-politicizing" site-specific experimentation (1995: 25). Drawing on Chicano cultural referents, namely feminist artist Judy Baca's artistic and pedagogical interventions in the 1960s, Lacy argues that "activist art grew out of the general militancy of the era, and identity politics was part of it" (26). This means that many of the examples we find in the prehistory of socially engaged art were produced outside the boundaries of the US historical avant-garde by subjects peripherally related to the art world. In many of those cases, "site" was not a strategy of formalist innovation but a logical imperative. Those projects, finally, were not *about* difference, but rather about the potential of artistic practice outside mainstream art worlds to intervene in the social fractures operating at the heart of US society. They did not constitute peripheral acts of social bettering; in many cases, their relationship with national and art institutional politics was at best tangential. Nevertheless, Lacy argues, they laid the foundation of our critical vocabulary on the social potential of artistic creativity. "For this," Lacy adds, "they were called 'community artists,' and critics refused to take their work seriously" (27). It is surprising how this lack of attention has persisted for half a decade.

This focus on bottom-up, activist-infused creativity would counter the primacy of top-to-bottom approaches (namely, the history of the National Endowment for the Arts) in discussions over art's public relevance. Of course, this is not to say that those approaches are not aesthetically or critically interesting. Rather, I infer from Lacy's contraposition of mode(l)s of public art that the price of forgetting the experiences of (often racialized) artists becomes apparent when the potentiality of their innovative investigations from current-day artistic (and social) imagination is eschewed. This has enormous consequences for the debates on the exhaustion of the "social turn." To begin with, it is worth noting that the portion of that history that has been "disciplined" is the one that Lacy calls "art in public places." "Art in the public interest" does remains not only partially unexplored; it also remains untamed.

Nina Felshin's edited volume of essays *But This Is Art? The Spirit of Art as Activism* was also published in 1995. Felshin categorizes art activism as a kind of art operating "with one foot in the art world and the other in the world of political activism and community organizing," which produces an innovative use of the public space and challenges the autonomy of the art field and its so-called independence from "real life" (1995: 9). As an inclusive practice, it tends to exceed the boundaries of the art space, demanding public participation and "expanding art's boundaries and audience and redefining the role of the artist" (13). Felshin also identifies participation with "an act of self-expression or self-representation by the entire community" (12). Although this optimistic view of audience participation and artistic authorship will be nuanced in the following years (notably by Grant Kester, Shannon Jackson, Rosalyn Deutsche, Miwon Kwon, and Claire Bishop), it is worth noting that it belonged to an early moment of emergence, when the interest of mainstream institutions in these practices was beginning to stand out. It is revealing that she ends the book's introductory text with a short section called "regarding the future."

Like *Mapping the Terrain, But This Is Art?* belonged to a moment of transition and therefore was shaped by multiple, contradictory alternatives, only a few of which were consolidated in the following years. As with Lacy's volume, here we also find art activism and "new public art" related to heterogeneous artistic and nonartistic genealogies. A book's chapter discusses issues of gentrification along with migration and coloniality in San Diego in relation to art interventions made by David Avalos, Louis Hock, and Elizabeth Sisco. Jan Cohen-Cruz's analysis of the American Festival Project also explores racial difference and the legacies of racism in the neoliberal United States. (Felshin links this experience to the civil rights movement through the previous experience of one of its founders, John O'Neal, in experimental theater [1995: 23].) *But This Is Art?* also included a revision of the trajectory of Guerrilla Girls by Elizabeth Hess. It is symptomatic that, as with *Mapping the Terrain,* the first voices (*pace* Lucy Lippard and Gregory Sholette) attempting to systematize socially engaged art and activism adopted the form of collective works. It is also telling that both books contain a wide range of practices and practitioners, out of which only a few (Lacy, Mierle Laderman Ukeles, Gran Fury, ACT UP, Mary Jane Jacob / *Culture in Action*) have contributed to "canonical" debates in the field.

Lacy's and Felshin's early contributions are remarkable because they cannot be associated with multicultural views of racialized communities as impoverished and socially disenfranchised groups seeking the state's attention. No matter whether or not we agree with their definitions of new genre public art and art activism, they force us to conceive the US genealogy of social practice as emerging out of a vast diversity of artistic traditions and positionalities, in which "the historical avant-garde" is just one more example.

Looking Anew: Racializing the "US" Genealogy of Socially Engaged Art

Consider now the following story, retold by Shiera el-Malik and Isaac Kamola in a recent book. The Burkinabe anticolonial leader Thomas Sankara was visiting an art exhibition and delivered a speech in Harlem on October 2, 1984. In this speech, Sankara urged his audience to consider art as a socially meaningful tool of future making. "We want," he argued, "to be left free to give our art and culture its full significance" (el-Malik and Kamola 2007: 79). One day later, Sankara addressed an audience of more than five hundred people at the Harriet Tubman School in Harlem. In a short speech titled "Our White House Is in Black Harlem," Sankara acknowledged the role of Harlem in developing an aesthetics of solidarity and anti-imperialism. In his words, "The singers, dancers, and musicians have also told us what the revolution should be" (81). In this speech, references to the Burkinabe revolution were made alongside personal conversations held with Maurice Bishop after the latter's assassination in 1983,[14] and the role played by Black communities in building alternative futures in the United States and Africa. At the most heated points, Sankara pulled out a gun, which the audience greatly applauded and cheered with shouts against imperialism. Dealing with the social significance of this event for an anticolonial archive, el-Malik and Kamola offer the following interpretation: "This speech contained many themes of African anticolonial thought, including a critique of colonialism and imperialism, a vision of an alternative world not limited to Western capitalism or Soviet-style communism, an articulation of a politics premised on emancipation and liberation, as well as the existence of dense networks of collaboration and solidarity among different groups, parties, independent states and organizations" (2017: 2). To this we should add that these networks had a complex, multifaceted notion of art's social relevance attached to them; these networks included but were by no means centered in 1980s New York. The visit of Thomas Sankara to the United States a few years prior to his murder offers four attractive points of comparison: being performative and resembling a gathering any person familiar with the "social turn" will easily recognize, it nevertheless belongs to a different realm. It connects critical appreciation, spontaneous mobilization, and a choreographed occupation of the public space; it is deeply rooted in a tradition of assembly and radical use of the public space running through the veins of African American art history; and at the same time, it arises from transnational solidarities, and as such its repercussions are not centered nor can be contained within the borders of the United States.[15] From these four points, an unfamiliar image of what creative collaboration could bring emerges.

Keeping this action in mind, in this section I am interested in defamiliarizing well-known histories of socially engaged art approaches in the US context to ask if its canonical genealogy could be read in different ways. More specifically, I attempt to see what happens when we introduce a lens focused on race and racial difference into the equation, not as an objective reality informing the artists' and communities' identities but as a complex set of relations with deep implications for the way that social engagement takes place. If it is true that socially engaged art's genealogies are closely linked to a group of artists and critics working in the United States, I hope I can demonstrate that their actions cannot be reduced either to a narrow corpus of artistic projects nor a single country. In other words, I believe that many of the initiatives that are now familiar to anyone interested in the "social turn" can be read otherwise, often through a race-based, transnational prism. Although there are plenty of examples of socially engaged art projects developed by racialized artists[16]—suffice it to mention the names of Rick Lowe, Ricardo Domínguez, Theaster Gates, and Paul Chan—I argue that the specifics of operating within racialized registers have been obscured in favor of a more general estimation of the US social reality. Something similar happens with the voice of Black critics and intellectuals vis-à-vis race-based controversies, such as those revolving around *The Nigger Drawings'* exhibition at Artists Space New York in 1979, Kara Walker's *A Subtlety or the Marvelous Sugar Baby* at Creative Time in 2014, and Yams Collective's withdrawal from that year's edition of the Whitney Biennial.[17] As a result, it has often been forgotten that issues such as urban exclusion or marginalization, among the main focuses of social practice, function as pernicious threats particularly affecting racialized communities. An explanation of such art projects as relating to the general consequences of neoliberalism and deregulation is certainly critically productive. However, at the same time it does not fully capture the delicate racial dynamics at play in such creative collaborative initiatives. Capitalism and regularization have no problems at all in operating across different races and communities (and art worlds), but it is also true that they do not affect all individuals and groups in the same way. Addressing how race works in socially engaged art and criticism entails acknowledging the important role (our assumptions on) racial difference plays in human interrelations, including artistic collaboration, and also assuming that US society never was a unique social continuum undergoing a similar experience.

Disregarding the fact that race played a central role in the US genealogies of activist and socially engaged art brings with it two dangers: the first involves curating a central part of the country's most radical and subversive artistic tradition outside of the general narrative on social practice. As a consequence, the presence of white, male, middle-class, university-educated artists is not just foregrounded but also taken for granted, and the importance of recent examples is overemphasized, while previous experiments are condemned to disappear from memories of the field.[18] "Amnesia attacks," writes Lucy Lippard, "and ongoing reinventions of the wheel are two things that have plagued social activist art and the left for as long as I can remember" (2017: xvii). As the history of science teaches us, "reinventions of the wheel" often take the form of uncanny voices and narratives being silenced and cast out of main master narratives. A third dimension related to this process of "curating" has to do with downplaying the value intrinsically associated with some forms of public art and privileging others. Mural art, which played a decisive role in the United States as tool of racial affirmation, from Diego Rivera to the Public Works of Art Project up to 1980s California, is a good example of this. The experiences of community engagement led by Puerto Rican and Nuyorican artists could provide another significant parcel of a repressed part of US genealogies of activist art:[19] the experiments with public action developed by Papo Colo; the politicized poetry of Reverend Pedro Pietri and Tato Laviera; the creation of a Puerto Rican embassy by Eduardo Figueroa; the creation and dissemination of Puerto Rican passports by Adál Maldonado; the founding in 1969 of the Museo del Barrio linked to the pedagogical work of Ralph Montañez Ortiz and created in solidarity with the Nuyorican and the civil rights movement;[20] and even the (nowadays unthinkable) "conceptual artwork" produced in 1979 by Carlos Irizarry consisting of hijacking an airplane to demand the liberation of Puerto Rican independence activists by the Carter administration (Irizarry was totally unarmed).[21] All these moments belong as much to the history of US radical aesthetics as they do to a history of Puerto Rican engaged creativity.[22] They anticipate much of the ground that wealthier, whiter creators will break one decade later. They were highly political yet many of them were also based on consensual processes of collective identification. Those projects, however, would not fall under the master narrative of the "social turn," nor can they be easily incorporated into canonical views of a US-centric artistic or critical discipline. More than this, that narrative works only when and if such experiences are relegated to a marginal place or forgotten altogether.

The second major danger is more subtle and operates on the level of criticism. It produces the effect of deracializing socially engaged art practices where racial difference plays a central role in their main motivation. It involves downplaying the "particularities" implicit in the racialized identity of artists and communities and dissolving them into generic formulas for the definition of community, the role of the artist in that community, and the uses of art within a public sphere. On other occasions, the existence of racial divides in effect in the controversies arising when an artist "represents" a community (whether s/he belongs to that community or not) is epitomized as a guarantee of failure of community-based public art projects, which are accused of "[reassuring] the viewer with an easily shared idea or subject," as in Kwon's *One Place after Another* (2004: 97). While I share Kwon's mistrust of previously defined identities, I also believe that the recognition of an essential sense of diversity at work in any community does not straightforwardly mean adopting conservative or nostalgic artistic strategies, in the sense of developing public art projects in which a specific group can recognize itself.

Kwon's interpretation of John Ahearn's sculptural project in the South Bronx offers a good case in point. By the mid-eighties, Ahearn was commissioned by the Percent for Art program of the New York City Department of Cultural Affairs to produce a group of sculptures that could oppose negative and stereotypical images of South Bronxites. Ahearn, himself an inhabitant of the neighborhood, developed this goal through active and prolonged collaboration with fellow residents. After encountering local criticism, however, in 1991 he removed the sculptural group. In her book on site-specific art, Kwon compares Ahearn's failure to come to terms with his neighborhood with Richard Serra's *Tilted Arc* controversy. Whereas both cases epitomize opposite ways of understanding collaborative approaches to site and communities (Ahearn's dialogical and constructive approach as opposed to Serra's avant-gardist claims of artistic authorship), for Kwon both initiatives lead to a similar consequence: artists inevitably fail in approaching supposedly cohesive communities, risking instrumentalizing them. Thus, after developing an accurate analysis of the racial dynamics at play in Ahearn's removed public art project, Kwon reads this removal as an example of community art's capacity to appropriate communitarian interests. One of the main conclusions she draws from her examination of Ahearn's work is explained as follows: "Underlying decades of public art discourse is a presumption that the art work—as object, event, or process—can fortify the viewing (now producing) subject by protecting it from the conditions of social alienation, economic fragmentation, and political disenfranchisement that threaten, diminish, exclude, marginalize, contradict, and otherwise 'unsettle' its sense of identity" (Kwon 2004: 97). The problem with this argument is that it leaves no room for positive interactions between artists and communities, identifying any affirmation of coherent racialized identity with a predisposition to uncritically accept artistic manipulation.[23] While cleverly recognizing the deleterious role that community art can play in instrumentalizing collective labor for artistic purposes, this interpretation takes for granted the idea that communities need "well-intentioned artists" to speak on their behalf.

This interpretation constitutes a common example of the role race played in the interpretation of socially engaged and community art projects. There are, however, many other possibilities. I argue that harnessing the potential of artistic collaboration to operate on and across racial divides as a fundamental part of collaborative practices' artistic value has played a central role in the configuration of a field of social practice criticism. Lucy Lippard's *The Lure of the Local* provides a brilliant examination of how artistic collaboration fueled the creativity of "[not] only to those in the know" (Lippard 1997: 263) but also of those directly involved in their production and enjoyment. By exploring art that can produce "alternative relationships to place" (19) and adopting an approach sensitive to class but also racial and gender privilege, *The Lure of the Local* defamiliarizes the US tradition of socially engaged art.[24] Compare, for instance, the following fragment with much of the recent literature about artistic collaboration: "A white middle-class art type without much money will have a different affect and effect on a mostly Latino community with less money than on a mostly white upper-class suburb with more money. S/he remains the same person, and may remain an outsider in both cases, but reciprocal identity is inevitably altered by the place, by the relationship to the place itself and the people who are already there" (6). At issue here is a critical appreciation of how specifics play a central role in defining the context in which artists operate and in modulating the relationship between those artists and the community.

"[Being] already there" means here something other than inhabiting a place. It also implies displaying a particular cultural identity. Forgetting how space is racially mediated or dismissing that identity as some sort of nostalgic particularity largely conditions how artistic collaboration occurs and what critical approaches can be extrapolated from it. Attempting to deal with these two questions, Lippard borrows Judy Baca's words to ask, "Who is the public now that it has changed color? How do we people of different ethnic and class groups use public space differently?" (1997: 273). Besides this interest in acknowledging how race matters affect artistic collaboration, Lippard is clever enough to identify an important point that was already looming over the debates on community art in the 1980s and 1990s: "racialized" artistic collaboration can teach us a valuable lesson about the appetite of mainstream art worlds for difference. Not that "race" brings any intrinsic surplus of critical independence to any art project (to assume this would be naive or even reactionary). In many cases, however, collaborative projects operating under the radar of mainstream art forces incorporate the taste of experience in ways that more spectacular initiatives cannot afford. Lippard's words on this concern are still relevant when read with twenty years of distance: "White, cosmopolitan, and/or art school trained artists could learn something from various other cultural communities, including activists who perceive the mainstream art world as absurdly isolated, incestuous, and irrelevant—out of touch not only with grassroots audiences but with social reality, with its own context" (273–74).[25]

Another example of criticism that takes account of the impact of race in determining sociopolitical configurations can be found in Tom Finkelpearl's approach to socially engaged art from the 1980s. His analysis of collaborative practices is driven by a recognition of the positive role that migration from the Americas and Asia played in revitalizing the civic landscape of US cities. Under this view, the "expanded field" in which socially engaged art operates has nothing to do with mainstream artists helping disenfranchised communities but rather with a decades-long process of bottom-up migrant solidarity that was essential in creating and maintaining public space (Finkelpearl 2013: 35). By acknowledging the importance of this process in exploring alternative paths to social cooperation, Finkelpearl's genealogy challenges the newness of socially engaged art as recognized in recent debates, while at the same time it relativizes the importance of the artistic avant-garde for contemporary forms of activist and collaborative art. This critical shift has the valuable effect of strengthening the link between art activism and political, specifically feminist and race-based causes. We should not forget that the development of social practice in the late 1980s matches a period of intense racial division of the US territory, where centuries-old situations of inequality were recast under the banner of neoliberal "progress" through uneven geographical divisions. It is symptomatic that the emergence of social practice throughout the United States matched the processes of urban decay and the intensification of state-sponsored and state-controlled fluxes of violence targeting underprivileged working-class and racial communities. As Finkelpearl reminds us, Mike Davis's excavations into the history of Los Angeles and the East Coast belong to this moment, as does his superb reconstruction of the role of Latino communities in revitalizing public spaces (Davis 2001).[26] Davis's academic trajectory in this decade captures well, I think, the ups and downs and the wide variety of missed opportunities and achievements that also operated in socially engaged projects from that moment.

A final case of race-attentive criticism can be found in Grant Kester's critical interpretation of Project Row Houses as shown in his book *The One and the Many* and Adrian Piper's *Conversation Pieces*. Kester sees the first initiative as dealing with "questions of spatial sovereignty and the discourse of redevelopment" (2011: 213). He also recognizes in Rick Lowe's interest in preserving shotgun houses a sign of Black affirmation. Kester also emphasizes the influence of John Biggers's politically committed activity before the civil rights movement in the articulation of Lowe's project.[27] In addition to this, Kester identifies in the project an important catalyst for artists to redefine authorship in practical ways.[28] What is important about this interpretation is that it both recognizes Project Row Houses' relevance for contemporary issues (its engagement with issues of gentrification and social imagination) *and* its deep roots in a Black radical tradition of social assistance and community development. That tradition acts as a central element shaping Lowe's practice both socially and aesthetically, and countering racialized, conservative images of poverty as a threat in moral and social terms: "Lowe's effort to link the present-day Third Ward to a set of vital cultural traditions was an essential component of this broader process of resistance" (Kester 2011: 218). In this respect, if several questions can be posed about Lowe's interest in "redeveloping" the Third Ward, acknowledging the dynamics of segregation inherited from the Jim Crow era he attempted to challenge is fundamental to understanding how Project Row Houses works. Concerning Piper, Kester described how her concept-based artistic production was transformed after experiencing sexism and racism in artistic and academic spaces. Her performances and installations attempt to subvert those attitudes by making clear the prejudices and exclusivities that determine access to the art world for certain subjects and bodies. Piper's capacity to challenge our perception of self and others creates, according to Kester, "an opportunity to expand and complicate its cognitive grasp of the world" (Kester 2004: 76). Importantly enough, Piper's interest in deconstructing cognitive models is modulated by a feminist and race-based interest, which rejects generalizations and places difference and its consequences at the center of any dialogical exchange within and outside the art world. This interest reinforces Kester's interest in claiming an experience-based critical framework for analyzing socially engaged art projects, but also compels us to reject universalist approaches to creative practices. Piper's attention to difference is thus both the result of her lived, embodied experiences of social interactions *and* a central part of her artistic production, one that should be taken into account when dealing with the social and aesthetic dimensions of her work.

Through an analysis that takes the "cumulative" effects of former artistic experiments into consideration, Kester confronts Piper and other collaborative artists through their specific positionality at play when enacting collaborative aesthetics. In both cases, Kester identifies positive alternatives to "an ongoing meditation on the ruins of discourse—artworks that are about the artist's inability to achieve the emancipatory communion that is anticipated by the aesthetic" (Kester 2004: 31). But more than this, he also hints at a specific distribution of that meditation, recognizing that the narrow space that art represents within contemporary society operates in different ways according to the position occupied by the artist. In the case of Black artists, this space is even smaller due to the weight of both exclusionary institutional politics (which for many decades have striven to recognize aesthetic quality in Black art, or isolated it within a parallel category) and a centrality of representation (the Black figure) that has overshadowed more material issues of agency, training, and labor. Exploring the influence of former genealogies of Black radical practice in Piper's work, Kester aims for "a more complex understanding of the relationship between historical time and critique" (68). This implies taking into account how dialogical and collaborative works challenge the role of individualism in Black artistic traditions, something with profound consequences for our critical understanding of time and individuality. Concerning time, it is possible to read Piper's excavations as an artistic examination of the consequences of what Michael Hanchard called "racial time." For Hanchard, this concept implies a recognition of "the disjunctive temporalities of both Western and Afro-Modernity" and can be defined by exploring how "unequal relationships between dominant and subordinate groups produce unequal temporal access to institutions, goods, services, resources, power, and knowledge, which members of both groups recognize" (2001: 280–81). Individualism in Black art was never fully assumed or incorporated.[29] As a mark of modernism, it enjoyed an ambivalent relationship with alternative forms of collaborative creativity. For a long time, it was an imposed marker of the contemporary, a way of determining the belatedness of discourses, subjects, and communities. When Piper or Lowe experiment with communal forms, they are not just redefining "old" traditions of communitarian creativity; they are also making a claim against systems of critical judgment where their turn toward the collective allegedly implies losing track of contemporaneity once again.

My point in returning to the debates around artistic autonomy, antagonism, and consensus-based artistic collaboration is not to take sides with any author, or to argue that one model of collaboration is intrinsically better than the other. Rather, what I found interesting in those debates is how their respective choices are justified. In particular, I see in Kester's interest in Project Row Houses and Adrian Piper a critical appreciation of a model of artistic collaboration that does not emerge out of the avant-garde. Whereas both examples can be framed under a well-known tradition of dialogical art practice, they also belong to a genealogy of Black radical creative praxis. The strategies they deploy, the objectives they pursue, the solidarity they generate, can also be explained as part of that tradition that maintains a complex relationship with Western modernism. Through a shared interest in exploring the political potential of certain forms of Black vernacular culture, they can be linked to a project of countercultural imagination as defined by Paul Gilroy.[30] Kester (partially) acknowledges how Lowe's and Piper's practice belongs to a double genealogy, and this has a significant impact on our understanding of his dialogical criticism of socially engaged art. First, placing both actions under the banner of a Black radical aesthetics would refashion both the social dimensions and the artistic content of these projects. From this perspective, artistic collaboration would not (only) be a tool leveraged by neoliberal governments in order to make artists fill out the lacunae left empty by wild capitalist policies. It would also be a set of tools consciously used by artists that in many cases (even after their relative success in the field of socially engaged art) remain outside mainstream art worlds in order to deal with specific manifestations of racial privilege and exclusion at play inside and outside the art world. Concerning the artistic side, then, considering examples such as those two as part of at least two different aesthetic traditions would mean understanding that they operate in the junctures of these traditions. Because of this, their content would appear more ambivalent, resulting not only from an interest in generating socially ameliorative action but also from an interest in redefining and updating the critical potential of Black cultural forms. It is worth remembering in this sense that Lowe arrived at socially engaged art after a "formal" fine arts training.[31] Any aesthetic appreciation of both examples has to start by exploring how they redefine and repurpose the creative strategies of Black creators. Bishop's consideration that Kester's position "constitutes a rejection of any art that might offend or trouble its audience—most notably the historical avant-garde, within whose avant-garde lineage Kester nevertheless wishes to situate social engagement as a radical practice" (Bishop 2006b, 181) overshadows two elements. As the critical appreciation of Lowe and Piper in *Conversation Pieces* and *The One and the Many* demonstrates, Kester's interest in collaborative practices goes beyond accepting or rejecting the "historical avant-garde"; it also foregrounds how Black artists negotiate their own position in touch with, but decisively *beyond*, an avant-gardist artistic tradition.[32]

The history of critical appreciations of socially engaged art in the United States is also the history of a sense of place where aesthetic stakes are negotiated instead of imposed, where the complexities of interracial collaboration are in tune with artistic achievement without overshadowing it, and where belonging results in aesthetic audacity without becoming reactionary (Lippard 1997: 292). "Artists," Lippard continues, "are trained to think of themselves as 'free', and the challenge of public art lies in dealing with other people's freedom as well" (264). She concludes, "The other stuff—most of what fuels public controversy and the mass media's rhetoric on public art—is still private art; no matter how big or exposed or intrusive or hyped it may be" (264). What would it mean, then, to imagine past experiences of socially engaged art in alternative ways? Isn't Lippard's mistrust of "what seems to be public art, but despite that fact remains private" anticipating the recent "crisis" of socially engaged art?[33] What kind of narrative would arise, then, from the kind of categorization proposed by the examples discussed above, which takes form and intention into account but also values the practical materialization of shared, lived experience, especially on the few occasions in which voices from below socioeconomic power are included and heard?

Conclusion

In this chapter I have attempted to frame the US socially engaged art tradition in a racial context. It was my intention to raise further questions about the nature and applicability of socially engaged art as a form of social engineering, questions that demand closer examination of past practices. For now, let us just observe that there is a wealth of difference in rooting contemporary socially engaged art initiatives in multiethnic traditions of radical politics rather than in top-to-bottom "multiculturalist cultural politics." The second choice does not simply misrepresent the stakes at play in many collaborative creative practices; it also fuels a tradition of forgetting, particularly pervasive where the contribution of African Americans in the making of the United States, and of Western modernity more broadly, is concerned.[34] It makes a huge difference to see socially engaged art practices such as *Waiting for Godot in New Orleans* or Project Row Houses as (also) dealing with the legacies of a colonial genealogy of racial violence and categorization. When pinpointing how race is often overlooked in critical interpretations of practices such as these, I am not trying to privilege one reading over others, but rather to fully understand how artistic collaboration addresses multiple aspects of the social from the specificities of place. For example, artistic authority works in a totally different ways when joined by (unnoticed and unrecognized) racial privilege. Recognizing that alterity is always at work within (more or less equal situations of) collaboration does not imply identifying all collaborative projects as restaging the figure of the "ethnographer" proposed by Hal Foster as a new paradigm of artistic practice in the 1990s;[35] however, it reminds us that the link between "economic" and "cultural/ethnic" otherness is never straightforward. Introducing a racially sensitive lens, then, does not obfuscate but rather *complements* other approaches, making us aware of the complex and unpredictable terrains into which collaborative artists often throw themselves and also (I hope) making socially engaged art less familiar, less appropriable, under any "turn."

RADICAL AFFINITIES AND THE HORIZONS OF DECOLONIZATION

3

◆ ◆ ◆

ON EXPERIENCE, LAND USE, AND THE THREATS OF THE BOURGEOISIE

Learning From Amílcar Cabral

The main argument presented in this part is that anticolonial thought and praxis anticipated the interest in exploring communitarian and collectivist practices as potential alternatives to global capitalism. Anticolonialism was a complex political and social project that involved millions of people, not just intellectuals, freedom fighters, and politicians, in the achievement of better conditions of life and the construction of a new society. Its main goal was not merely the creation of new nations but rather a thorough redefinition of the interrelations between human beings. This goal could be accomplished only when the uneven power relations brought about by colonialism were overridden. For anticolonial thinkers and practitioners, decolonization was conceived of as a crossroads where different alternatives to the darker side of postwar politics coexisted and were put into practice. Looking at anticolonial theory afresh and displacing ideas from their original background, I believe that anticolonial thought and praxis can illuminate many of the cultural issues we are facing nowadays. Engaging the cultural production of decolonization as simultaneously historically located *and* translatable, realistic *and* utopian, this part argues that there is still much to learn from anticolonialism.

From early in the twentieth century, many anticolonial thinkers confronted and criticized the claims of criticality of discourse and representation when based only on individual subjectivity. They also underlined the urgent need to ground any emancipative aspiration within the sociopolitical and material contingencies of the here and now. Their

87

anticolonial aesthetics and praxis were permeated by an interest in exploring the process-based, experiential, insurgent, and collaborative potential of culture. This emphasis, I suggest, makes them more than suitable interlocutors to shed light on contemporary concerns around the limits of elitist and market-based art worlds, the agency of collective radical imagination, and the potential of socially led creativity to fuel and channel social transformation. By dealing with the "afterlives of anticolonial political action and cultural imagination" through the specific cases of Amílcar Cabral and C. L. R. James, I believe that the potential of those texts resides in their capacity to illuminate the potential of cultural creativity in radical, unexpected ways (see Elam and Maclean 2014; Busch and Franke 2015).

Prefiguration goes a long way in the context of Marxist and especially anarchist thought. To say that anticolonial aesthetics prefigured many of the creative responses that we see in contemporary forms of cultural activism necessitates our accepting the fact that anticolonialism was concerned with a problem far greater than that of creating new postcolonial nation-states. There is no doubt that anticolonial struggles were revolutionary in their attempt to create a new society and a more democratic future for territories subjected to colonialism. At the same time, they also imagined new uses for cultural production that were supposed to go far beyond the process of independence of specific nation-states. In many cases, although formal independence was not yet achieved, anticolonial practitioners and thinkers advanced radical thinking on art and culture that involved imagining that future while remaining focused on the more "revolutionary" task of ending colonialism.

Literally hinting at the idea of something "coming before" and anticipating what is to happen in the future, in the context of this part "prefiguration" means more than the future happening in the present (now past) of global decolonization. The radical potential of anticolonial aesthetics lies not so much in its capacity to detect something yet to happen, but rather in accepting that what we call the contemporary has to remain a multilayered and multitemporal field of struggle and negotiation. From this perspective, prefiguration implies a radical engagement with the present of decolonization, a present that was inseparable from the active imagination and materialization of futures alternative to the futureless horizon marked by neoliberal's presentism. The understanding of anticolonial aesthetics presented in this part is therefore aligned to recent discussions that highlight the need to contest neoliberal understandings of time and the contemporary that elude the possibility of imagining alternative futures precisely by deeming such imaginings as utopian and naive.[1]

The anticolonial project still constitutes a neglected zone in critical thought. Despite the concern shown by key voices in postcolonial studies such as Robert Young, Benita Parry, Ania Loomba, and Neil Lazarus, more often the focus has been placed on exploring the tensions of empire from a more ambivalent, confusing terrain, stressing the weight of diasporic mappings in the constitution of postcolonial subjectivity. The militant and anticapitalist ethos of anticolonial struggle has been faulted for its political naiveté and ideological myopia concerning the future of postcolonial nationalism, the outcomes and aftermath of that struggle being reductively and permanently bound to the crisis of emancipative alternatives in the South, as if they did not also contain a valuable internationalist, humanist, and anticapitalist dimension. Exploring the persistence and the projection of the anticolonial project in our troubled present, and framing postcolonialism's critical purchase in the light of anticolonial expectations, remains all the more urgent. Anticolonialism constituted the clearest and most sustained experiment produced in the twentieth-century history of grounding radical, revolutionary theory within practice. Anticolonial radical practice and thought were not a concern of left-wing Western theory; rather, they infused and influenced the main currents of radical theory *from within*, contributing decisively to a redefinition of political and insurgent agency beyond colonial soil, in the metropolitan space. In this part, I locate anticolonial thought within the transnational traditions of radical philosophy, recognizing it as constitutive and internal in the expansion of Marxist horizons and solidarities throughout the previous century. Decolonization was not a theme, a variation played by Western radicals, but a center stage on which the potential of transformative action and insurgent theory came together.

Anticolonialism provides a precedent for socially engaged art and art activism's interest in grounding theory, in turning theory into practice and exploring the potential of practice to think our present in order to engage it in radical, subversive ways. The concern of many anticolonial thinkers with the capacity of colonial rule to survive the moment of nationalist independence also carried a cautious warning against "easy victories"—to borrow Cabral's words—that is highly applicable to the transformative aspirations of social practice. Anticolonial thinkers conceived their work simultaneously in dialogue with and as a challenge to a Western body of thought, accomplishing the double task of decentering and provincializing that thought and translating it into effective social change in those parts of the world still subjected to different forms of colonial domination. The authors examined in this part share a desire to go beyond simple theorization and to insert critical theory into a plea for social change and an active, practice-driven redefinition of what it is to be human.

Conceiving the legacy of anticolonialism as necessarily multiple and complex, this part analyzes the usefulness of anticolonial thought in conceptualizing a militant, collective-based idea of agency and cultural praxis. Its objective is not to excavate a non-Western genealogy of radical aesthetics to offer it as an alternative for another, Western-based genealogy. The point is not to substitute one set of authors for another. Exploring the transformative potential of anticolonial aesthetics means much more than rewriting the history of art and aesthetics. It involves two things. First, the range of options we have is conditioned by the lexicon we use. Second, when dealing with radical aesthetics, we will be missing a central piece of the puzzle if we ignore the weight of anticolonialism in challenging the *longue durée* of imperial-neoliberal-extractivist violence, something much greater, albeit not necessarily less material or harmful, than imperialism.

Such an exploration identifies a valid interlocutor for socially engaged creative processes in anticolonial experiences and experiments.[2] Anticolonial intellectuals such as Frantz Fanon, Amílcar Cabral, and C. L. R. James did not write about socially engaged art. They *did*, however, write extensively about community-based praxis, social transformation, and cultural and collective agency. In his seminal *Refashioning Futures: Criticism after Postcoloniality,* David Scott asked what it would mean to approach Fanonian thought as a lens through which to look at our present. Scott constructs his analysis around the question of whether Fanonian action still constituted a valuable and usable conceptual tool. Since Fanon's understanding of action cannot be detached from the legitimation of violence exerted in the struggle for decolonization, Scott wonders about the futurity of Fanonian revolutionary praxis in light of his turbulent postcolonial Jamaica. The point, in this context, is to "discern whether these Fanonian questions (whatever their adequacy for the problem-space within which they originally emerged) continue to be the questions in relation to which the limits of *our own* postcolonial present ought to be addressed" (1999: 194; emphasis in the original). By counterposing the aspirations of socially engaged art in the present against the cultural and political mo(ve)ments of anticolonial thinkers and practitioners who set out to revisit the relevance and transformative potential of culture, I seek to provide answers to this and other similar questions, among them: What do decolonization and our present have in common? What can the former bring to the latter? From what position should we approach the legacies of a project largely disavowed for being supposedly essentialist and limited to its modernist liberational teleology, according to some postcolonial thinkers? Finally, anticolonial thought was a practical thinking, based on a very specific, pragmatic experience: that of decolonization. Would its use in the present risk trivializing or misunderstanding it? How easy is to *relativize* and detach that thought from its original experience?

In dealing with these questions, a first element to be stressed relates to the inherent difficulties of translating a past cultural and political project into a contemporary key. In making sense of anticolonial thought, we must problematize our relationship with our anticolonial past and its postcolonial expectations (which, it is crucial to note, do not follow the guidelines of our present). It is worth remembering that this relationship does not respond to a neutral, objective continuity. Regardless of the weight of the continuities, the influence of that legacy, asking the anticolonial question would make sense only if we addressed the contradictions and radical heterogeneity of past, present, and future expectations. In other words, a past utopia presupposes updating and sharpening our questions, rather than incorporating anachronical sets of answers. At the same time, however, in assuming the "strategic selfishness" of any process of remembrance, it is also crucial to acknowledge the heterogeneity of the anticolonial inheritance. For the purposes of this part, this challenge would imply discarding untested solutions, but also accepting that those solutions could work even when not specifically designed to that end. The anticolonial legacy should be looked at as multiple and contested, recognizing the perils of romanticizing agency but also accepting that this same agency is not, indeed never was, fixed to a single particular agenda, not even that of nation building. Here I am proposing an exercise in stretching anticolonial theory, which is different from relativizing and universalizing the connection between that theory and its particular spatial-temporal coordinates. Anticolonial leaders have often been accused by their postcolonial predecessors of being essentialist, of reducing the horizon of change to the constitution of the nation-state. This part counters that assumption by locating anticolonial futures (that is, the concatenation between the present of action and its postcolonial future envisaged by freedom movements) as complex and multilayered. If that complexity does not in itself justify the critical return to the anticolonial enterprise, at least it helps to make alternative linkages of past and present emancipation possible.

This chapter will read the political and cultural thought developed by Amílcar Cabral (1924–1973) as a valuable resource for an expanded genealogy of radical aesthetics. Cabral was the leader of the anticolonial movement in Cape Verde and Guinea-Bissau, a clever thinker, and a practical man. The contemporary assessment and recovery of his influence, and the current dimension of futures inspired by Cabralian thought and action, are strongly linked to how we make sense today of the productive way in which Cabral brought together theory and practice. For Cabral, both elements (theory and practice) were inseparable, this confluence being the main conditioning element of any cultural initiative. Cabral's idea of political and cultural agency, as presented in "Nacionalismo e cultura" (Nationalism and culture) and other texts, was strongly shaped by an interest in knowing the surrounding reality from which the act of thinking and planning emerges. For Cabral, culture was simultaneously "both a cultural fact and a factor of culture" (1999: 118; translation mine), a structured and structuring element that echoes Pierre Bourdieu's habitus and that continuously reappears in critical evaluations of contemporary radical creativity. Rejecting any kind of generalization or untested application of existing formulae, Cabral believed that experience and close engagement paved the only possible way toward action. More importantly, aware of the need to build bottom-up solidarities as the only way of making possible a transformative use of culture, he brought together emancipation, social transformation, and culture almost prophetically. This articulation, along with his conception of struggle as the engine of social transformation, makes him one of the most useful resources for any practice- and action-based critical theory, including socially engaged art. For many of the artistic projects this book discusses have one thing in common: their ability to acquaint many people who are not used to interacting with that kind of initiative with contemporary cultural manifestations (see figure 3.1).

What use can we make in the twenty-first century of the ideas of this Guinean/Cape Verdian agronomist-turned-freedom fighter and founder of two nations? What applicability can this legacy have in the context at the center of this book? Asking why Cabral matters today is ultimately equivalent to asking whether or not his conceptualization of cultural agency and militant engagement has any relevance in our present, despite (or beyond) the immediate concatenation of events that followed the assassination of the Guinean leader in 1973. The death of Cabral presented a serious drawback for the anticolonial struggle in Guinea-Bissau and Cape Verde. Although both countries gained independence in 1974, one year after his murder, Cabral's aspirations for a postcolonial reality quickly sundered.[3] His desire to merge both countries in a single national entity soon collapsed due to the differences between the Cape Verdean and Guinean political class and the Portuguese counterinsurgence.[4]

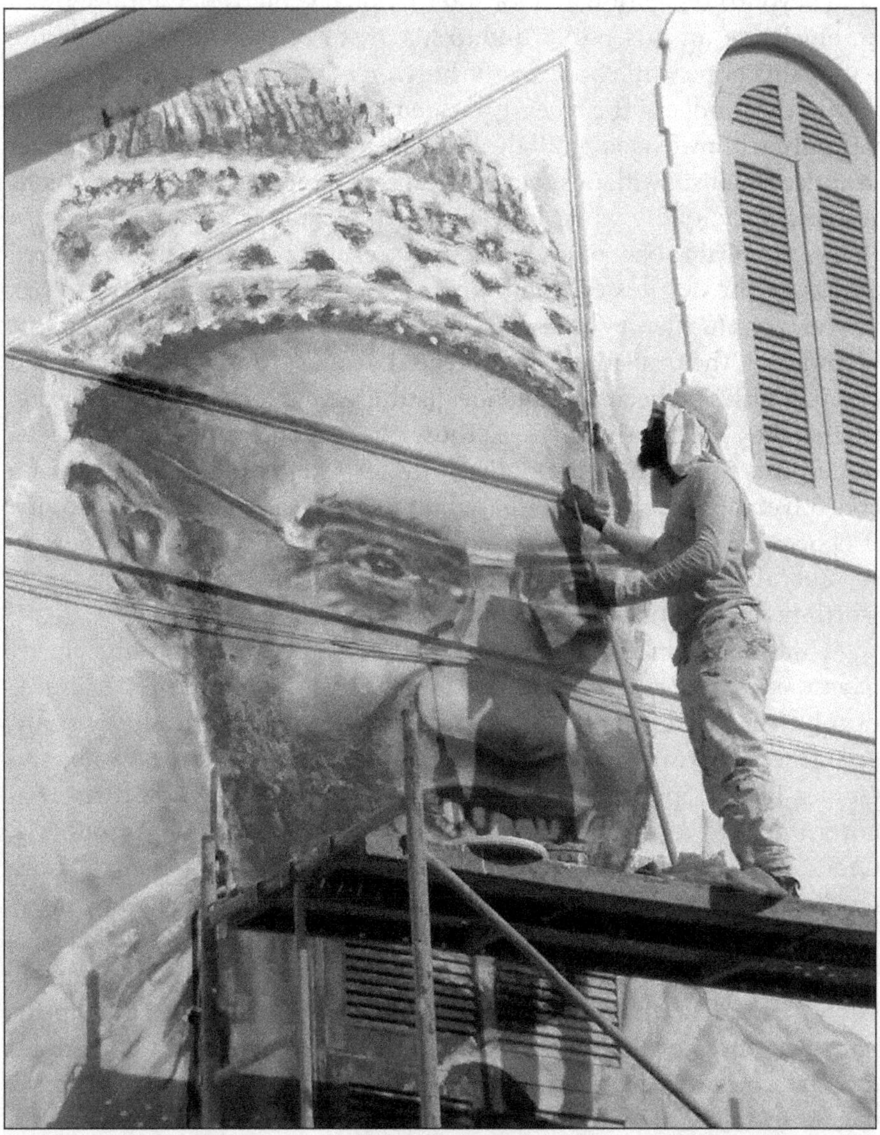

Figure 3.1. Graffiti in honor of Amílcar Cabral. *Source*: Courtesy of the Fundação Amílcar Cabral, Cape Verde.

That chain of events places any reading of Cabral in close relation to the demise of the nationalist promise in Africa, of the idea that the collective endeavor of nationalism would overcome the hindrances brought by colonialism (see figure 3.2).

I argue that the afterlives of Cabralian thought go beyond the medium of nationalism, occasioning important consequences both for "smaller" and "greater" frameworks, that is, both for collective articulations within (and beyond) the nation and for international solidarity. Cabral showed ambivalence on this point, due to his grasp of the limitations of the nationalist hope while framing the horizon of social and political change within the border of the recently created nation-state.[5] This is something partially acknowledged by all the theoreticians who approach the legacies of anticolonialism with positive expectations. However, those expectations resound very loudly when viewed through Cabral's idea of culture. In that sense, Cabral becomes particularly useful today when considered alongside the debates on community-led cultural dynamics. His work provides a valuable way of reassessing the influence of class and economic boundaries, the transformative potential of artists and intellectuals, and the difficulties of discursive and idealistic creative approaches attempting to provoke any effective change. Those elements informed Cabral's idea of culture, something that makes him an interesting antecedent of a collective, radical, and social-based understanding of artistic creativity. It is because of the singularity and appeal of that particular modality of "Cabralian futures" that the experience and the thought of Cabral is worth revisiting in this context.

As was usual among anticolonial leaders, Cabral was not trained in art or aesthetics. He never wrote on collaborative art, for that matter. His ideas of culture derived from his experience gathered through academic study, scientific fieldwork, and militant action in Portugal, Cape Verde, and Guinea-Bissau. Sponsored by a fellowship from the Portuguese dictatorial government to receive training at the Instituto Superior de Agronomia, Cabral studied in Lisbon between 1945 and 1950, where he joined the Casa dos Estudantes do Império, a major cultural center frequented by many of the future leaders of African revolutionary movements.[6] The Casa dos Estudantes do Império was a place of exchange, where Africans (mostly but not uniquely students) living in Lisbon acquired a direct and up-to-date awareness of the political situation in Portugal and the colonies despite António de Oliveira Salazar's censorship.[7] After receiving his degree in 1950 and working for a couple of years in Santarém, Cabral returned to Bissau in 1952 to conduct the first agricultural census of the country. Through this expedition, prior to Cabral's open engagement

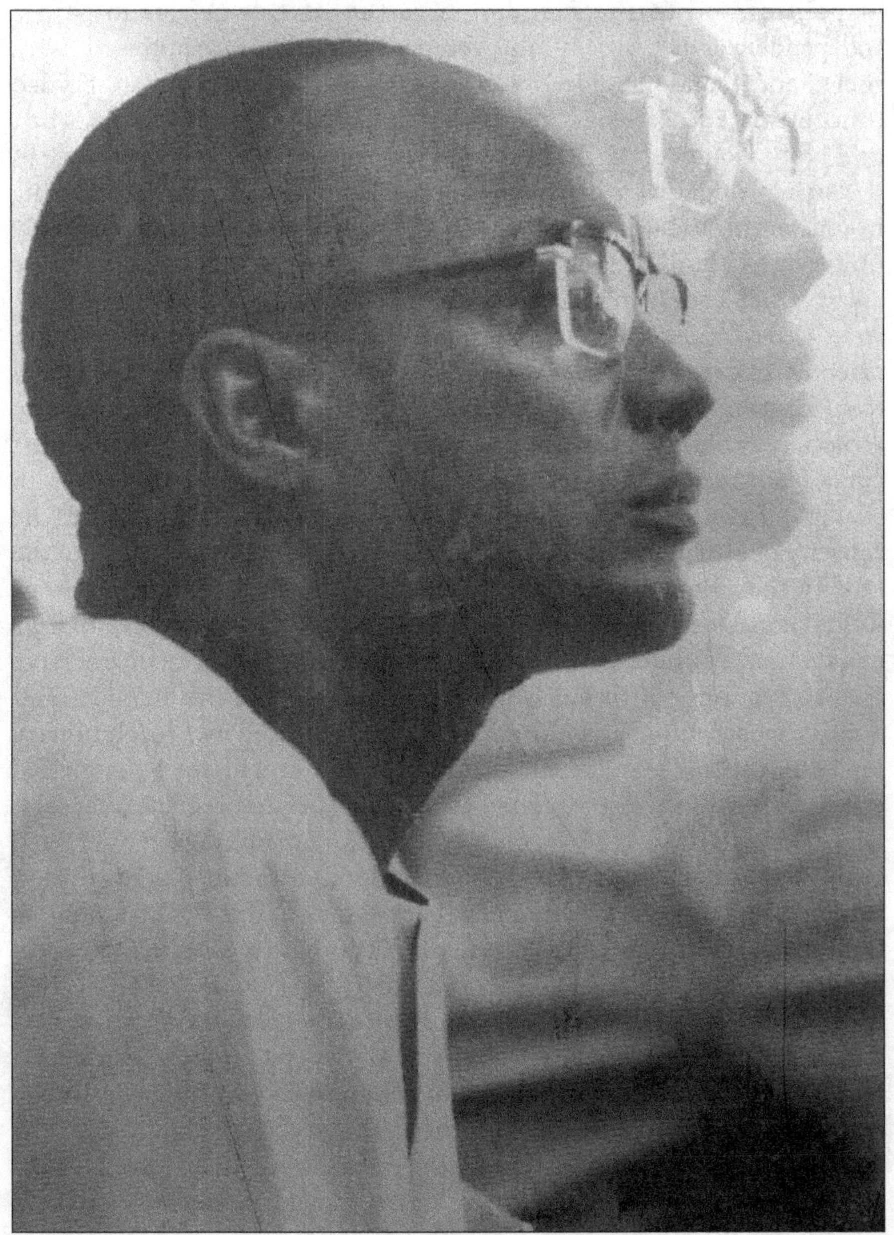

Figure 3.2. Amílcar Cabral. *Source*: Courtesy of the Fundação Amílcar Cabral, Cape Verde.

in politics and to the foundation of the Partido Africano para a Independência da Guiné e Cabo Verde, he became aware of the ethnical, social, and economic diversity of the country, something that afforded him intimate knowledge of the particularities of each region, while providing a body of topographical data that would be of importance in the struggle against Portuguese colonialism.[8] The experience of being in touch with the Guinean peasantry throughout the country strongly influenced Cabral's writings, making him one of the most context-aware anticolonial leaders in all of Africa.

In Cabral's thought, theory follows from practice, and both are oriented toward the achievement of anticolonial liberation and social transformation. Cabral conceded that no simple answer exists to the "colonial problem." On the contrary, both action and theory must come from experiential testing on the specific ground. Succeeding in the fight against Portuguese colonialism was for him a matter of "the capacity of allying, in the transformation of each main factor and of the totality, theory and practice and vice versa" (1999: 69).[9] In the same essay, Cabral conceived the moment of struggle as a moment of collaborative engagement, where sharing the cause brought about a decisive transformation, not so much in the discourses as in the attitudes and political positioning, and also where action is infused by a revolutionary model of theory: "We have to remind those that will see a theoretical character (within the struggle), that each practice impregnates a theory. And also that, if it is true that a revolution can fail even when nourished by perfectly conceived theories, still nobody practiced a revolution successfully without revolutionary theory" (77).[10] This duality counters the idea of Cabral as practice-driven, with little or no interest in theoretical matters beyond the struggle against Portuguese colonialism. Patrick Chabal, author of the first major, in-depth biography of Cabral, depicts him in a well-known passage as a practical man, driven by instrumental reason. For Chabal, he was "a man of action. His political leadership is best understood by looking at what he did rather than what he said. His writings were essentially analyses of the events in which he was involved; they were not theories about, or into, abstract social or political questions. He did not view himself as a political theorist although his writings obviously have theoretical relevance. He was loath to commit himself to any ideology or theory. The majority of his writings are party documents and they reflect the very specific purpose and audience for which they were intended" (Chabal 1983: 167). This image of Cabral as a "man of action," with an understanding of reality exclusively and directly derived from the practical and material needs of the moment, was predominant among the first biographers and theoreticians investigating into Cabral, and has to some extent persisted.[11]

Cabral's practical sense, in any case, must be nuanced. Ultimately, it risks denying the critical saliency and political engagement of Cabral's approximation to reality and to scientific analysis, and also the universal value of his thinking, something especially important if we attempt to frame his value within our contemporaneity. Discussing Chabal's biographical trajectory as well as classical texts on Cabral, such as Mário de Andrade's and Pablo Luke Idahosa's, the Portuguese historian José Neves (2017: 338) writes, "Chabal's interpretation proceeds from an excessively rigid division between science and ideology, as if he replicates the distinction between things and words within the domain of words themselves, assuming that that scientific terminology will turn reality transparent whereas ideological categories will mislead it."[12] Neves's main interest is in recognizing the role of ideology and political engagement within Cabral's notion of science, but in a way that cannot reduce his scientific and methodological positioning to the direct result of a specific political position. By "situating Cabral's scientific works in the context both of a history of science and of a history of political ideologies," Neves acknowledges that in Cabral science and practical analysis were shaped by a sociological and humanist understanding that took account not only of the specific terrain and the flora and fauna of each particular region but also of the heterogeneous ways in which the "particularities" brought into the equation through cultural means have an impact on that conundrum (Neves 2017).[13] This theoretical movement not only elicits Cabral's singular approach to emancipative struggle; it also reinterprets the ideas of Cabral from the perspective of an emancipative and decolonial understanding of science, in which method, experience, and ideology are closely interrelated, a position that anticipates the articulation of theory and practice of much contemporary politically engaged cultural creativity.

Cabral conceived of scientific and social research as committed to human empowerment and liberation. His understanding of those two concepts was grounded on collective action, in which each participant should be accountable for their role within a public endeavor. Cabral conceived of epistemic emancipation as something that could be achieved only through collective effort, therefore demystifying science as an obscure tool to be used only by the colonizers, and also the role of revolutionary leaders and social scientists as isolated experts at the forefront of society. In this sense, his warnings against ivory towers are connected to his interest in basing all knowledge on experience and dialogical exchange. The task of "epistemic decolonization," Lewis Gordon (2013: 142–43) clarifies, "required . . . active participants, active minds, people who took responsibility for what they ought to know." Cabral was the African leader who insisted most on the need to ensure collective leadership as the only way toward effective decolonization. This thought permeates Cabral's political and cultural texts, and remained crucial in Cabral's perception of the national society emerging out of the anticolonial process.

Cabral's mistrust of individualism in cultural matters remains invaluable as part of a genealogy of socially committed cultural production. For Cabral, culture constituted a perfect and necessary platform for turning his idea of emancipatory and political practice into reality. Cabral's idea of cultural agency combined two overlapping elements: the capacity of a people to make sovereign decisions about their own lives, and the incarnation of a body of values simultaneously inherited from tradition and in constant change (Neves 2017). In Cabral, culture is always granted a transformative capacity, an ability to mobilize the various *povos* (people) integrating the nation around a common cause. Like Frantz Fanon and many other anticolonial leaders, Cabral (1979) acknowledges the capacity of cultural praxis to be the "germ of contestation" of national and social struggles. Culture is something that remains latent during colonization, a substratum that can be activated and brought back to life through emancipative action. Here we find that a first element that approaches Cabral's understanding of culture and the emancipative ideals to which socially engaged art aspires concerns the way that both conceive revolutionary transformation as collective engagement (Rabaka 2014: 265). As Cabral puts it, "Our cultural resistance consists of the following: while we struggle against colonial culture and the negative aspects of our own culture, either within our personality or our medium, we have to create a new culture, also grounded in our traditions, but respecting all the conquest of the modern world for the benefit of humankind" (1999: 20).[14] Culture, therefore, is not something monolithic, frozen in time, that must be recovered: on the contrary, it is the result of a collective process of transformation based on the here and now of resistance. This last idea has two main elements attached: it is conceived of as the result of popular organization, and it involves a redefinition of inherited concepts and cultural values. Resisting therefore consists of a selective and critical evaluation of those elements that could provide the basis for creating a modern self.

The first point attempts to counter the elitism and political hesitation of the colonial bourgeoisie. Especially problematic for Cabral was the position of the petite bourgeoisie, whose coordinating capacity was essential to ensuring the success of the anticolonial movement ("the only social stratum capable both of raising awareness about the reality of imperialist domination in the first place, and manipulating the State apparatus inherited from that domination" [Cabral 1999: 93],[15] while at the same time capable of taking advantage of the efforts of the masses). In many Cabralian texts we find an insistence on the need for popular classes to control that segment of the population, stressing the urgency of subjecting it to a process of "cultural reconversion" (24; translation mine). A similar opinion permeates Cabral's understanding of the role of the party within popular movements. Interestingly, this "reconversion" is produced only through sustained engagement with the requirements, imperfections, and conjunction of praxis. The need to construe any approximation to reality from the contingencies of practice provides Cabral's idea of culture with a critical process of self-reflection, able to distinguish within emancipative action "what is essential from what is secondary, the positive from the negative, the progressive from the reactionary, to characterize the master lane of progressive definition of any national culture" (110).[16]

In particular, the comparison drawn between popular culture and the creative manifestations of the bourgeoisie recalls and prefigures key points in the debates on socially engaged art. Grant Kester points to two major pitfalls in contemporary art criticism concerned with socially engaged or activist practices: its use of theory as a kind of "master discourse" overlapped with practice without any interest in seeing whether or not the latter challenges the former; and the claiming that only through a detachment of reality and contingency could aesthetics achieve a critical voice (see Kester 2013). Similarly, in *O papel da cultura na luta pela independência* (The role of culture in the struggle for independence), Cabral notes both elements as characteristic of the petite bourgeoisie's understanding of art and culture, which will be recognizable through their uncritical following of the modernist values imported by colonialists, rejecting a direct commitment to the models of collective and emancipative action promoted by the working class and the peasantry. As a result, even when they aspire to incorporate a transformative avant-gardist element through the defense of African values, this class remains trapped in a marginal and parasitical position that is ultimately unproductive. This marginality, Cabral argues, "constitutes, as much locally as within the bosom of the diasporas implanted in the colonialist metropolis, the sociocultural drama of the colonial elites and the indigenous petite bourgeoisie, lived more or less intensely according to the material circumstances and the level of acculturation, but always at an individual, not a collective, level" (1999: 130).[17]

As we will see in the chapters concerned with African socially engaged art, the relevance of that elitist and individualistic understanding of modernity remains highly present in contemporary African aesthetics, determining how artistic contemporaneity was defined and the kind of agency granted to representational and discursive practices (even when, or especially when, those intend to depict the suffering of subaltern groups without attempting to counter it).[18] In Cabral, that elitism is explained as the result of a failed attempt to pursue an autonomous position of aesthetic avant-gardism, concerned with the affirmation of local and national cultural values, but, as Kester argues, only "addres[sing] the social world second hand" (Kester 2013). One particular passage in *O papel da cultura* explains brilliantly the inefficacy of this secondhand approach to reality: "Part of that minority, integrated into the pre-independence movement, uses foreign cultural data, resorting mainly to literature and the arts, to express more about the discovery of their identity than the aspirations and the suffering of the popular masses serving them as a theme. And because they use precisely the language of the colonial power for that expression, only rarely do they manage to influence the popular masses, in general illiterate and familiar with other forms of artistic expression" (Cabral 1999: 137–38).[19]

Cabral was aware of the fact that the postponement of direct engagement with reality could have terrible consequences in Africa. He recounts how the colonial powers encourage elitist and individualistic manifestations with the objective of developing a structure of cultural clientelism, while curbing bottom-up initiatives. He depicts this system as one of collusion between colonial institutions and the local bourgeoisie, in which the colonial elites sublimate their productive energy toward the securing of privilege instead of transformative agency, and are rewarded with a privileged prominence in the definition of national culture. This results in a double exclusion, that of popular segments of colonized society, and also that of the collective aesthetic forms emerging out of popular solidarity. Cabral understood national emancipation and social justice as inseparable processes. The objective was not to favor those manifestations coming from the masses but rather to ensure that any cultural enterprise could have a direct applicability within the context from which it arose. In a particularly lucid fragment, he warns against "unselective praise; systematic exaltation of virtues without taking account of defects; the blind acceptance of cultural values without considering what is or may be negative, reactionary or regressive; the confusion between what is the expression of an objective and material historical reality and what seems to be a creation of the spirit or the result of a specific nature; the absurd link between artistic creations, be they valid or not, to alleged characteristics of a race" (114).[20] He also depicted the potential of "a collective understanding of culture as a liberalizing and emancipative force, through which the working masses and, especially, the peasants [. . .] lose, in the contact with other classes, the insecurities limiting their relations with other ethnic and social groups; they understand their condition as decisive elements in the struggle; they break the shackles of the universe of the village to become progressively integrated into the country and the world" (117).

Because this depiction cannot be separated from the here and now of anticolonial struggle, its critical value remains all the more relevant, especially when many of the contradictions arising from it are still very much alive in respect to postcolonial societies (see Okeke-Agulu 2010). Cabral's conceptualization of the second element mentioned above, namely the renewing potential of traditional African cultural values, also emerges as up-to-date and acute. There was a general concern among African anticolonial intellectuals about the impact that colonial modernity had in the erasure and commoditization of cultural traditions, and also about whether or not the modern influence brought onto the scene by the colonizers could constitute something appropriable. In many cases, the option of "returning to the source," as Cabral expressed it, was connected to the emergence of oppositional nationalist forces. In a nutshell, the idea of the return to the source argues that European colonialism blocked native cultural identity, affecting both present manifestations (which are resignified, commoditized, or forbidden) and the genealogies behind those (which are labeled belated or backward and emptied of their active, modern creative force). It was therefore the task of anticolonial cultural agents to examine and restore such a traditional core.

In his seminal essay "Cultural Identity and Diaspora," Stuart Hall recognizes the importance of a similar approach "in all the post-colonial struggles which have so profoundly reshaped our world," pan-Africanism and negritude being the major followers (2005: 223). In those cases, an already existing ideal image of the past waits to be recovered and updated in order to emancipate the present, to put an end to the cultural alienation that colonialism imposed. Hall opts for a "second" path that highlights the "becoming" over the "being" and rejects any stable and uniform essence hiding in the past. Nevertheless, he acknowledges how history shapes culture, acting as an "imagined community" and determining the "positioning" and the politics of identity of any cultural practice. What Kwame Anthony Appiah calls "nativism" constitutes, in fact, a diverse body of approximations to the African pasts, many of which relate to the political dimensions of the uses of that past in the present. Although Appiah's warning against the limitations of nativism when it idealizes a mythical, lost African past should not be forgotten, it will be equally necessary to keep in mind how many of those reinterpretations acted as "transcriptions and improvisations of dissent" (Parry 2004: 42), and also how that emancipative potential was acknowledged even by the most fervent critics of negritude, including Fanon.[21]

Cabral's view on this matter echoes Fanon's,[22] and lays the foundations for Hall's anti-essentialism. Like the Martinican psychiatrist, he recognized the instrumental and conjunctural value of some revivalist movements in the articulation of a common front against colonialism; like Fanon in *Black Skins, White Masks*, Cabral warns against coupling modernity and colonization, recognizing the value that some returns to the past could have in the present. There are, however, remarkable singularities in Cabralian thought, not least his insistence on introducing class struggle into the equation. Cabral was skeptical of negritude's interest in recovering an unaltered African past, and identified in the colonial petite bourgeoisie an instrumental infatuation with popular culture. In this context, the strategy is one of representation and capitalization of supposedly traditional values. The cultural manifestations emerging out of that particular version of the "return to the source" were for Cabral "the rejection, by the local petite bourgeoisie, of the alleged supremacy of the dominant power's culture over that of the dominated people, with whom they need to identify in order to resolve the sociocultural conflict being waged, looking for an identity" (Cabral 1999: 131).[23] The pitfalls of this position, Cabral believed, are manifold. First, it identifies cultural identity with an untouched essence that is opposed to the European influence in binary terms, something that limited the reach of the return to the moment of emancipation. Secondly, and related to that, it unproblematically conceives the emerging national culture as immune to criticism: since the "enemy" has been rejected, the only thing that remains would be the celebration of the expression of a recovered national ethos. Neither the existence of differences and inassimilable elements within that ethos, nor the idealism with which tradition is identified, are confronted.

Cabral recognized an alternative, critical way of materializing cultural transformation in which the "return to the source" becomes a productive action. When led by the popular classes, the recovery of the past is conceived of as a collective act of positioning directed not only toward the eradication of colonial domination but also toward any backward or individualistic element at play in the culture that might constitute an obstacle to social equality. In that framework, identity emerged as linked to practice and experience, not as a reenactment of something frozen from the past but as an active path for collective agency simultaneously asserting and unfixing racial and class boundaries, and contagiously projecting the echoes of this emancipative action beyond the boundaries of the nation. In Cabral's words,

> When the "return to the sources" overcomes the individual case to express itself through "groups" or "movements," the factors conditioning the political and economic evolution of the society both internally and externally have already reached the level at which that contradiction is transformed into conflict (hidden or overt), anticipating the pre-independence movement or the struggle for liberation from the foreign oppressor. Therefore, the "return to the sources" is only historically consequential if it involves not only a real commitment to the independence struggle, but also a total and definitive identification with the aspirations of the masses, which not only challenge foreign culture but also, globally, foreign domination. (1999: 131)[24]

This second option offers important insights that are relevant for our conceptualization of the potential of collaborative, socially engaged cultural practices. First, it rejects individualistic and "symbolic" forms of cultural identification, recognizing that the instrumental potential of recovering the past becomes critical and effective only when grounded in the specific needs of the present situation. The contemporaneity of the "return to the sources," secondly, must be a process-based action, built out of a trial and error method, in which the integration of elements from the past always takes place with the contemporary reality in mind. That implies relativizing what is remembered and understanding it as a functional resource that transforms the participants throughout the process. For Cabral, something can be revolutionary in one case and reactionary in another, depending on how it is used. Cabral was quite aware of the inadequacy of inherited formulas when not considered critically and adapted. Communities are formed through the act of remembering; the bonds between different groups and individuals depend on the critical potential they have at that stage of the struggle.

In that sense, the practice of remembering entails "stretching" history in order to adapt it to specific experiences and circumstances. As with theory, cultural identity must be continuously tested and derived from practice. Thus, whereas knowing the experience of others is essential, that experience must never be copied or imitated, only taken into account.

For Cabral, all theory, without exception, must be subject to that logic. That includes Marxism.[25] Examining the critical potential of this second path for "returning to the source" and inserting it within a tradition of militant African critical theory, Reyland Rabaka highlights how Cabral's understanding of ideology and of the articulation of historical elements in the present was "concrete and situation-specific" (Rabaka 2014: 260). Rabaka locates the potential of Cabral's approach in two major areas. The first rejects the cultural positioning based on criticizing European colonization without critically weighing the African precolonial past. Cabral, Rabaka argues, was aware of the ways in which "the catch-all concepts and umbrella theories about Africa had a tendency to consistently downplay the many ways in which ethnicity, class, and religion often influenced participation, or non-participation, in decolonization and re-Africanization efforts" (268). The challenges posed by a Cabralian "return to the source" require the pairing "radical political education, social (re)organization, and revolutionary praxis" with productive criticism (269).

It is from the position I have just described that we can begin envisaging how Cabral's ideas of practice can be useful to illuminate socially engaged understandings of culture in our present. The idea that practice is something that cannot be imported, incorporated in an unaltered form from any other context, is a concern shared by many anticolonial leaders. Yet it manifests with a particular intensity in Cabralian thought. Practice emerges as a dialogical and relational tool, counting on continuous dialogue with all the people involved in the process of social transformation. For Cabral, this dialogical and relational understanding of action leads to the active and continuous exchange of opinions and information channeled through a process of testing different solutions to pressing collective issues and perfecting them. Furthermore, he reminds us that "national liberation and social revolution are not export goods. They are (and they will become more and more so) a local—national—crafted product [. . .] determined and conditioned essentially by the historical reality of each people, and ensured only by the victory or the adequate resolution of the internal contradictions of diverse kinds characterizing that reality" (Cabral 1976: 202).[26] The interest in finding an "adequate resolution" to any internal contradiction goes along with the need to emphasize "the increasing participation of the population in the management of their lives" (Cabral 1999: 143).

Let us recapitulate. We have seen so far how Cabral's understanding of culture and practice can lay the ground for an engaged and collective-based critical theory. In the first case, we have outlined several elements that very much inspire socially engaged art's approach to artistic creativity and social engineering. Concerning practice, Cabral's interest in experience-based research and collaborative knowledge makes him a precursor of many of the projects and initiatives this book analyzes. After acknowledging that prefigurative potential, it remains for us to determine how that critical theory can be detached from the historical confluence of the process of nation building. Nationalism was the sphere of action where Cabral envisaged the materialization of his ideas, the domain where praxis and revolutionary experience ought to be located. Consequently, both issues are strongly linked to and determined by that national framework, something that raises the unavoidable question of the sense and value of the insights I have already presented after the demise of Cabral's nationalist utopia. Engaging that question, the Angolan anthropologist António Tomás also criticizes the lack of specificity of many of the approaches to Cabral. Tomás warns about the fact that, in many instances, "Cabral's thoughts and ideals are discussed in a void, as theoretical interventions with no practical importance" (Tomás 2016: 24). This applies on two different levels: through a lack of awareness of the particularities of every specific context and, equally significant, through a disinterest in the consequences and continuities elicited by anticolonial action, as if the (then) postcolonial futures were decoupled from the historical processes that produced them. Tomás frames Cabral's actions "not only as answers to the very particular problems imposed by the colonial situation. [. . .] Cabral's interventions, however, themselves became questions that elicited other answers" (23). In Tomás's view, nationalism acted in Cabral as a factor of cultural uniformization; it functioned as "a kind of filter, a way to solve the many contradictions posed by diversity, by eliminating differences, and re-organizing a new totality" (29). Tomás links the possibility of Portuguese counterinsurgence to the disarticulation between Cabral's ideas of nationalism and its practical realization.[27] Although Tomás's idea of postcolonial nationalism as being present and entangled with the anticolonial imaginary is relevant, the correlation he draws between the pitfalls of nationalism in Cape Verde and Guinea-Bissau and Cabral's miscalculation of the importance of ethnic plurality over monolithic nationalism can be revised. Furthermore, identifying Portuguese counterinsurgence as elicited by Cabral's failure, as the answer provoked by Cabral's "nationalist" question, he frames his legacy within a somewhat teleological position, in which its potential is equated with the direct concatenation of events revolving around Cabral's assassination and its aftermath.[28]

Against this position, it is worth recalling that Cabral was always conscious of the multiple dimensions in which anticolonial struggle ought to be implemented. Part of the appeal of Cabral's anticolonial nationalism is that it comes along with both socialist and humanist elements concerning its own formation. Regarding the first element, whereas an all-inclusive image of nation building as a collective endeavor emerges in his speeches, Cabral is also aware of the need to focus not only on the inclusions but also the exclusions and marginalization that the making of nationalism could leave behind.[29] In Cabral, nationalism is a force of collective mobilization, the practical instance through which anticolonial struggle should materialize. But it also entails at least three other dimensions. The most important one for our purposes is that the nation should never eradicate or unify cultural difference. Tomás points out that Cabral mistook the way by choosing to focus on nationalism in lieu of ethnic pluralism. However, Cabral conceptualized nationalism as an amalgam of plural popular manifestations was always subject to change and evolution. Whereas in Cabral, culture belongs to the realm of national politics and to the specific here and now of anticolonial nationalism, it also leaves ample room for collective agency not completely attuned within it, for scales "smaller and larger than the nation," to borrow Fredrick Cooper's keen formulation (1994: 1519).

It is precisely this capacity to envisage collective agency committed to a multiplicity of causes under the umbrella of revolutionary nationalism that makes Cabral's ideas of praxis and experience so useful for understanding contemporary socially engaged creative practices. Apart from encompassing difference and class struggle within the process of nation building, Cabral also contemplated the shortcomings of national liberation if it is not linked to African emancipation and universal social justice.[30] From that position, we can envisage the potential of Cabralian thought in conceiving collective cultural agency in a present haunted by the persistence of multiple, not always evident, forms of colonial domination.

4

⬥ ⬥ ⬥

ART, ENGAGEMENT, AND POPULAR IMAGINATION

Around the "Missed Encounter"
between Theodor Adorno and C. L. R. James

Paul Buhle, who produced one of the most exhaustive biographies of the Trinidadian activist, writer, and anticolonial intellectual C. L. R. James, mentions a much-repeated anecdote about an encounter between James and Theodor Adorno during their stay in New York. The short paragraph Buhle dedicates to this enigmatic exchange reads as follows: "The same James would just as easily (although not with the same degree of pleasure) stop off for coffee in the New School with Theodor Adorno and the Frankfurt School exiles. They hardly knew what to make of the Black man who shared their enthusiasm for Hegel. He found them interesting, but by no means compelling. They dwelt upon the collapse of the West. James sought the fragments of redemption" (2017: 106). Four elements structure the enigmatic encounter narrated by Buhle: the fact that James shared the space of mid-twentieth century Manhattan with the exiled intellectuals of the Frankfurt School; the fact that Adorno and James were concerned with similar preoccupations; the fact that, despite their common interests, they were moving in opposite directions, understanding culture and the legacies of modernity in ways so different as to make one another, if not unintelligible, quite diverse, or, as Buhle says, "by no means compelling." Finally, Buhle recognizes in James a potential way forward from the impasse that struck Adorno concerning popular manifestations; whereas the German philosopher will understand US capitalism as the greater manifestation of an aesthetics of administration, James will interpret in this same landscape latent signs of social transformation, creative "fragments of redemption" giving birth to something radically new.

The discrepancies between Adorno and James have been framed differently according to each commentator on James who has reproduced the anecdote. Overall, a general sense of a missed encounter prevails.[1] In fact, their conversations represent a missed opportunity for both thinkers to tap into common interests: James breaking Adorno's Eurocentric vision of historical development and modernity; the latter reinforcing James's Marxist-infused cultural criticism of postcolonial nationalisms and Third Worldism. Echoing this line of argumentation, Enzo Traverso (2016: 193) recently asked, "What could have produced a fruitful, rather than a missed, encounter between Adorno and James?," speculating that this trade of ideas would have enriched both the traditions of the Frankfurt School and Black Marxism. In fact, he attempts to resolve that speculation by proposing a hypothesis worth quoting at length: "The Frankfurt School would have overcome its Eurocentric boundaries and the colonial revolutions would have approached the question of development with different paradigms. . . . The second generation of the Frankfurt School would not have exclusively focused on topics such as public space and communicative action, but also on the critique of capitalism and globalization. Postcolonial studies, on their own, would not have reduced Marxism to a simple Eurocentric worldview and would have been more than a 'critical discourse' founded on textual rather than historical bases" (Traverso 2016: 193). In describing the "missed encounter" between Adorno and James from the point of view of what each of them could have gained from the other side of the equation, Traverso addresses the figure of James from an interesting perspective, identifying him as a "Black Marxist" and a "Trotskyist" (192). Framed in those terms, the speculation on a fruitful encounter between Adorno and James, between Western and Black Marxism, also has some limitations that are relevant here. For this assumption involves recognizing in Western Marxism the "first generation of critical theory," and consequently identifying cultural criticism as the element lacking to "Black Marxists" like James. This approach does have limitations. On a basic level, it encapsulates Jamesian thought under the label of Black Marxism, something that, as we will see, the versatility and originality of James's political and cultural understanding simply does not allow.[2] Secondly, this view still identifies Adorno as *the* authoritative voice in aesthetics, recognizing in James an interesting voice in exploring new forms of collective agency, yet one lacking the sharp critical tools at the disposal of the German philosopher.

The paths of James and Adorno might, after all, have crossed in the United States during the 1940s. And Traverso is right in identifying a deeper significance in this convergence, despite the specific details of the encounter. However, I believe this significance can also be understood in different terms. The consequences of that encounter, what it reveals, are at the core of the debate.

The main objective of this chapter is not to compare James and Adorno, nor to explore the latter's well analyzed American period. Rather, what interests me here is the frame that makes the figure of James less thinkable as a valuable precedent for the debates about collaborative aesthetics in the Americas. When viewed through the lens of the canonization of an aesthetics of disengagement and autonomy, the missed encounter between Adorno and James appears illuminating in a different way. It becomes relevant as much as for what it represented—two opposite but related ways of coping with the crisis of modernity in the postwar world—as for what it anticipated: a recognition of collaborative aesthetics as a decisive field of social transformation. But it should be noted that a limited interpretative framework overshadows James's importance as precursor of an engaged, collaborative, and practice-based aesthetics in the context of mid-twentieth century debates on modernism and mass culture.

Both James and Adorno experienced the United States as exiles, in the context of the rise of Nazism in Germany and the military crescendo that would lead to the Second World War. Adorno arrived in New York in 1937 following an invitation from Max Horkheimer, at the end of a productive experience in Oxford that lasted four years. After some comings and goings, the German philosopher settled in the country in February of the following year. Also coming from Britain, James arrived in the States in 1938, establishing his residency in the country after a short trip to meet Trotsky in Coyoacán, Mexico, in 1939. Adorno left the United States in 1949 to join Frankfurt University, where he would work until his death in 1969. James was deported in 1953 after being denied an extension of his visa, moving then to Britain until 1958, when he returned to his native Trinidad.

Their periods of residence in the United States marked a turning point for both Adorno and James. The former refined the basis of his critique of mass culture as instrument of mass deception. The latter wrote two central pieces, the essay later published as *The American Civilization* and *Mariners, Renegades, and Castaways*, a critical analysis of Herman Melville's *Moby Dick* produced while on Ellis Island, waiting to be deported, when the tensions of the beginning of the Cold War were about to be felt in US intellectual and cultural circles. In this period, James also wrote at length on cinema, comic strips, and sports.

When the "missed encounter" between Adorno and James took place, the latter was defining an aesthetics that had at its center the creative potential of collective subjects.[3] This aesthetics emphasized the role that individuals play in the definition of new cultural forms and, more broadly, in the articulation of emancipative horizons. With regard to Adorno, his mistrust of mass culture would inform an aesthetic based on individualism and autonomy from social and political causes. In Adorno, the potential of cultural massification and any possible political engagement is overshadowed by the risks brought by the Nazi instrumentalization of culture, whereas in James, this threat does not impede the recognition of the potential of spontaneous actions of creativity as a mean of collective self-fulfillment. This, it is important to note, does not imply a blind celebration of popular qua populist agency, but a critical assessment going "beyond the staple fare of economic analysis on the one hand, and elite cultural criticism on the other," as Andrew Ross (1996: 83) categorizes it.[4]

Nothing new so far. The audacity of James's approach to cultural creativity has paved the way for several disciplines and positionings claiming his intellectual inheritance. There is, however, a recurring missing element in the commentators of the missed encounter between James and the Frankfurt School. This element is the influence of Adornean and Jamesian aesthetics in subsequent decades and its relation to postwar aesthetic metanarratives. From this perspective, the main point of separation between Adorno and James was not simply a matter of discrepant interpretations of how instrumental reason provoked a definitive rupture in the way modernity appeared in the mid-twentieth century through contributing to the rise of totalitarianism. It was more a question of two alternative and opposite ways of understanding the "world they live in" (to paraphrase James in *Mariners*), and this discrepancy opened a fracture in contemporary aesthetics whose consequences have persisted to the present day (see Høgsbjerg 2006b). This is crucial, because the division has featured extensively in recent debates on socially engaged art and aesthetics.

By the time James wrote his best-known essays on popular culture in the 1940s and 1950s, the layers of aesthetic modernism were being established in the United States. His stay in the country has to be interpreted in relation to a shifting landscape in which the democratizing goals of the New Deal were collapsing.[5] Whereas James never wrote about socially engaged or public art in terms we can identify with our current take on both topics, recognizing a public dimension in cultural forms such as cricket was central to his conceptualization of culture. In turn, James's proximity with US workers, his close firsthand knowledge about rank-and-file desires and expectations, and the way this knowledge affected his own activity as an intellectual, were directly shaped by the doors opened by the New Deal. As for Adorno, his mistrust of direct engagement laid the foundations, as Grant Kester points out, of an aesthetics in which spontaneous action would be seen as naiveté and art's autonomy should be preserved "only by refusing to debase itself through any direct involvement with social resistance or activism" (Kester 2015). In further works, Kester goes on to explain how mistrust of immediate action turned into *the* mainstream form of critical analysis, not only working as a specific form of cultural criticism in competition with many others, but also becoming "master discourse," monological thinking (Kester 2013). From this perspective, he argues, "contemporary art can maintain its purity and autonomy only by confining its critical powers to a virtualized field of resistance" (8). Resistance, ironically, appears as a gift unavoidably coming from the active side of the thinker (or the artist-intellectual) to that of the passive audience.

By now it goes without saying that this vision of cultural production as an autonomous field is radically opposite to James's understanding of art and creativity as shared and lived cultural phenomena. The question I want to pose in this chapter, however, is different. If James represented a valuable alternative for those critics seeking to recognize the centrality of activist aesthetics in the configuration of cultural debates in the United States, why then is James obliterated from the debates on socially engaged aesthetics? If he almost embodies the opposite model criticized by Kester, why is James hardly credited in the genealogies of collective, radical creativity?

Borrowing from Raymond Williams, Neil Lazarus (1999: 151) argues that the invisibility of James in modern aesthetics is part of a broader act of modernist erasure in which genealogies become naturalized as unique paths: "Modernism recast, rewrote, and rearranged cultural history, producing a selective tradition whose selectivity was invisible to it." Lazarus goes further by saying that the opposition between high and mass culture curtails a further critique of how that dichotomy is in itself produced by modernism: "High Culture *or* Mass Culture: this 'or' is the dominant conjunction through which, in the bourgeois world at least, the politics of cultural production in the twentieth century have tended to be conceptualized. Of course, the opposition is in itself a modernist construction, what we might in fact call an *ideologeme* of modernism" (151). What is the basis of Jamesian aesthetics? From where does it emerge? James's insights on cinema, popular magazines, and comic strips arise out of the ruins of the experiments in social transformation at play in the New Deal. In the United States, James saw a world in transformation, in which individualism and cultural industries were all-encompassing. In this context, however, he glimpsed spaces for collective self-fulfillment and radical social transformation. As we will see, these spaces were not just "cultural forms"; as James makes clear in his analysis of cricket, creative manifestations play a decisive role in modulating affects. They are not vehicles for indirect or representative forms of politics; rather, they are political by themselves. To be sure, James's trajectory in the country was not related to art activism; indeed, it belonged to a moment when such a thing was not even discussed. The fourteen years he spent before being deported from Ellis Island, however, were devoted to three elements, radical intellectual commitment, bottom-up creativity, and political activism, which form the backbone of what has been recognized as the main genealogy of progressive, socially engaged artistic practices.

In this chapter, I argue that James's writings on collective creativity constitute one of the most vibrant challenges to establishing a model of modernist aesthetics based on autonomy and individualism. I believe that his eradication from the genealogies of US radical aesthetics is part of the process of naturalization that both Kester and Lazarus deal with in different ways. Contrary to this silence, I will argue that the Jamesian aesthetic arises directly out of the acknowledgment of emergent forms of collective creativity that will also initiate any aesthetics of collaboration and social engagement. The missed encounter between Adorno and James would hide, then, a deeper fracture, that of James and socially engaged criticism in the Americas. It is only through this fracture that genealogies of US activist aesthetics can begin in the 1960s. The banishment of James from these genealogies has profound consequences: it silences a moment in which social cooperation was still paired with a sharp, Marxist-infused criticism of the role of the intellectual as commentator of cultural forms.[6] This criticism also tends to forget that James never conceived of himself only as an intellectual; on the contrary, he developed his work as an adamant defender of anticolonial and antiracist causes.[7] He also produced many of his works collaboratively, stressing the importance of militant research. The emphasis on collective agency and radical social transformation infusing James's aesthetics thus appears as a nuanced and timely model. What I seek to explain here is how this emphasis could nurture present and future forms of radical creativity.

Jamesian Aesthetics

The aesthetic thought developed by C. L. R. James is complex and interesting enough to stand on its own merits, without need of any comparison. Throughout his career, James produced a solid body of criticism dealing with disparate cultural phenomena, including cinema, literature, visual arts, and, of course, cricket. James addressed each of these manifestations carefully, recognizing the specific characteristics of each modality of creative expression, and avoiding any simplistic generalization.

Jamesian aesthetics were built around two major nodes: the importance of popular collective agency in shaping creative responses to cultural phenomena, and the attention given to form and, related to it, the space given to improvisation and performance. By reinforcing the importance of these two elements, James anticipated many of the methodological and disciplinary debates concerning contemporary collaborative art. Placed together, these two elements constitute an aesthetic positioning emerging out of the turning points of the mid-twentieth century, a moment, as I will explain later, when the transformative capacity of politicized cultural forms was giving way to a mistrust of close engagement and collective imagination, as represented by Adorno in the conversation that opened this chapter.

Before looking at these two nodes in detail, some questions are in order. Does the word "aesthetics" encompass the multiplicity of cultural forms addressed by James? Does it not betray his refusal of literary criticism and bourgeois intellectualism, against whose ivory towers James set the passions and interests of ordinary men?[8] If we conceive Jamesian aesthetics in collective terms, how should we interpret his interest in the individual expression of artistic genius?

Each of these questions is worth considering closely. To begin addressing the first two, we must consider whether it is possible to detach a single critical interpretation from the interest James expressed in a vast range of cultural forms. If James's cultural criticism centered on such heterogeneous objectives, would it be possible to read any common pattern among these expressions of aesthetic judgment? Could we read James's insights on sports, fine arts, literature, or cinema as infused by a single way of looking at cultural manifestations? In a famous passage of *Beyond a Boundary,* James warned against categorization and specialization, "that division of the human personality" which he considered a by-product of bourgeois culture and "the greatest curse of our time" (James 1990: 191). This frequently quoted fragment is part of chapter 16, "What Is Art?," in which James famously asserts the artistic nature of cricket, which is to be compared to any form of artistic expression in its own right, "not a bastard or a poor relation, but a full member of the community" (192). Here the singularity and the aesthetic value of cricket are claimed in comparative terms, stating that "cricket is first and foremost a dramatic spectacle. It belongs with the theatre, ballet, opera and the dance" (192).[9]

Although possessing a unique code, cricket emerges as a form of creative expression comparable to others. As we will see in the next section, something similar happens when James deals with art and literature. It is important to note that James did not attempt to replace these two forms of cultural expression with cricket or any other popular manifestation. He granted each of them its own singularity and, unlike Adorno, avoided any classification or consideration of a specific domain as particularly uncontaminated by mass consumerism and therefore more prone to being transformed into a culture industry. At the same time, he conceived of the value of each field contextually. In effect, his writing on cricket was not about cricket because he considered the game superior to any other in essential terms (although, interestingly, James praised it for the role played by the audience). On the contrary, his interest in the game arose from historical (biographical) interests. This awareness of both the historical relevance of each artistic medium and its specificities lends coherence to Jamesian aesthetics.

The second question has already been partially answered above. The capacity of popular forms of creativity to channel collective engagement acts as a common thread throughout the manifold interests that occupied James throughout his life. From cricket to cinema, from his analysis of the Haitian Revolution to his reading of *Moby Dick*, creativity is always associated with the spontaneous activity of groups of individuals. This does not mean, however, that Jamesian criticism was not infused with aesthetic appreciation. Andrew Smith acknowledges that he was "always alert to the subtleties, nuances and ambiguities of cultural expression" (2010: 2).[10] Smith describes James as the twentieth-century intellectual best placed for dealing with popular culture, race, and colonialism together. More than this, he acknowledges in James a rare and original flexible talent capable of treating with rigor a wide range of sociopolitical issues and cultural manifestations. This talent emerges from a genuine comprehension of the specific rules determining each artistic and cultural form. Rejecting a separation of the cultural and the political writing of James, Smith argues that the interest in cultural forms constitutes a field through which James looked at reality, a field, is important to note, with its own rules and particularities.[11] In this, he recognizes in James a precursor of Pierre Bourdieu, since both thinkers clearly knew that the seeming neutrality of cultural and artistic fields hides "a disillusioning exposure of the field's ethic of disinterested participation" (A. Smith 2006b: 100).[12]

For Smith, the originality of the Trinidadian thinker lies in recognizing that cultural fields in James operate as autonomous spaces of expression.

These spaces, however, are meaningful not according to an abstract or supranatural logic but rather by their being embedded in everyday actions ("cultural practices and objects are those things 'about' which we argue and around which we are arrayed"; A. Smith 2010: 62), by being opened to historical contingence, to what Smith calls "a willful vulnerability to his thinking . . . , an openness to the changing lessons of historical context" (62). From this viewpoint, Smith concludes that "James developed a view of historical progress, not as a metaphysical juggernaut, but as something with which we are intimate, something which we look for in the only place that it is possible to look for it: the here-and-now" (63).

From here, a first parallel with socially engaged art and socially engaged criticism can be drawn. The crucial possibility opened by recognizing cultural forms as autonomous fields of contingent expression is that this recognition allows certain articulations of social aspirations to be channeled through them, while also being attentive to individual genius.[13] James was very much aware of the role that some key figures play in stirring the passions of the crowd. He also acknowledged that the position of each player would never be the same; because of this, he never disparaged the agency of the participants in sports or cinema. At the same time, however, the audience does not stand here as a passive entity. Its relationship with these actors is fluid and bidirectional.

Looking at sports from ancient Greece to the mid-twentieth century, James recognized the role they played in bringing individuals and cities together around a critical vision of shared citizenry. At the same time, however, James recognized that the link between audience participation in sports and cultural events and radical, democratic aspirations was neither obvious nor straightforward. Both historically and in his examination of the present, James is aware of the dangers hiding behind the economic and political forces seeking to control each game and to turn it into a spectacle. Despite this lack of direct correlation, he acknowledged a potential for social transformation deriving from the gathering of masses and the imperfections of practice-based creative activity. That potential, James argued, was what made it possible to confer aesthetic value on sports and popular cultural manifestations. In other words, it is only through the collective transference of emotions, of fears and happiness, that these activities are considered art.

As Smith argues, when James acknowledged a "significant form" in cultural expressions such as cricket, he was attempting to describe "the way in which cultural practices become expressive of historical contradictions and social possibilities precisely because they are practices that are contingent and time-bound. Of course, the phrase draws attention to the relationship between such practices and their audiences, which is, after all, the only way in which anything cultural can be said to have significance. But it draws attention also to the fact that what matters to an audience, matters because it meets them in the specificity of when and where they are, and speaks to them in ways that they find worthy of attention" (Smith 2010: 56). In Jamesian criticism, actions and passions, effects and affects, always move back and forth. Moreover, creative genius is always dependent on the historical forms of expression available in each epoch, of opportunities collectively seized to express itself.

Let us now move on to the two major elements of Jamesian aesthetics. Concerning the first point (the importance of collective agency), we could begin by pointing out that James knew the masses firsthand . His heterodox position within Left politics, and more specifically within Trotskyism, was largely motivated by his rejection of the idea of party leadership in revolutionary processes and by his disappointment in the Stalinist Soviet Union. He engaged with bottom-up social and creative movements in the Caribbean, Europe, the United States, and Africa. He wrote extensively on the role of popular creativity in channeling the social imagination. More than any other twentieth-century thinker, he anticipated the appearance of new revolutionary subjects within the transitional moment of the beginning of the Cold War, paying attention to feminism and anticolonial emancipation as driving forces in shaping the then near future. Nowhere is this clearer than in *American Civilization,* the long manuscript James wrote in the early 1950s, at a time, as Anna Grimshaw observes, "which he felt was critical for the future of human society" (1993: 1). *American Civilization,* which Bill Schwarz goes as far as to categorize as James's "*Grundrisse,*" summarized the theoretical drift of his "American years" (2005: 18). This book, which marked the moment of consolidation of James's mature writing, is also the result of direct and almost daily engagement with and consumption of US culture. In this regard, it is important to note two elements concerning expression and objectives. The first point is concerned with how *American Civilization* is written and with the deliberate adoption of the language of liberalism. It is surprising to find the "Marxist James" expressing himself in terms such as "freedom," "equality," "happiness," etcetera. Grimshaw explains that this gesture "enabled James to engage his subject and audience directly" (1993: 19) while also sidestepping some of the major pitfalls of the intellectual Cold War climate. The second point relates to the way that critical analysis and the everyday experiences of ordinary people are framed together in *American Civilization*. As will happen in *Beyond a Boundary*, also the result of direct and engaged observation, the personal dimension of James the enthusiast of cinema or noir literature overlaps with the theoretical view of these manifestations.

The letters James wrote to his second wife, Constance Webb, provide a good example of this. On September 1, 1943, he acknowledges the importance of daily experience in artistic creativity: "You write, 'I read every book I could find on acting' and, again, 'I was a monomaniac about acting'. Sister, that is life and living and finding yourself. Stick to it and squeeze it dry. The feelings that surge and must be expressed are the pulsations of a life within you more powerful than in the average person. All people have it. Capitalism stifles it. But with some it is so powerful that it breaks through" (James 1992: 128). A similar celebration of life appears in his insights on cinema,[14] which James consumed almost compulsively:

> The movies, even the most absurd Hollywood movies, are an expression of life, and being made for people who pay their money, they express what the people need—that is, what the people miss in their own lives. That explains a great deal I think. Why the popularity of the Western? Because young people who sit cramped in buses and tied to assembly lines terribly wish they could be elsewhere. . . . Like all art, but more than most, the movies are not merely a reflection, but an extension of the actual—an extension along the lines which people feel are lacking and possible in the actual. (James 1992: 129).

Without relinquishing authorial voice, the point of enunciation from which the book is written incorporates this subjective dimension as a positive contribution, not as a burden. This point separates James from other critics of mass culture in the mid-twentieth century, including Adorno, who considered that adopting a critical distance was essential in dealing with popular creativity. In *American Civilization,* the masses are not a simple theoretical problem to be solved; their presence in the text is far more complex: they inform the book's audience, they were James's interlocutors through the process of writing, and, ultimately, they are conceived of as carrying the responsibility of social transformation.

American Civilization is not simply a celebratory book on popular, collective creativity. Everyday Americans mattered to James only because of their role in the sociopolitical transformations the United States was undergoing in the 1950s. This role was seen not as an essential condition but rather as a historical state of things in which mass production and self-organization were deeply redefining the values of modernity worldwide. James saw in the American masses the agent in shaping what he considered to be the main values of American society: freedom, equality, individuality, and happiness. In his view, these words were not conceptual abstractions but the lived reality of many Americans: "The Europeans wrote and theorized about freedom in superb writings. Americans lived it" (James 1993: 31).

Popular creativity enters the discussion of *American Civilization* when James explains how Americans enacted these principles in the present. For him, film and comic strips were quintessential realms of American expression, not burdened by the weight of European culture. More than this, for James modern aesthetics were inconceivable without the global revolution brought by mass consumption that he epitomized in the United States as universal values ("the vast successes of these specifically national productions are truly universal for our age" [1993: 37]). It is worth quoting James here at length:

> During the last thirty years, *mass production* has created a vast populace, literate, technically trained, conscious of itself and of its inherent right to enjoy all the possibilities of the society to the extent of its means. No such social force has existed in any society with such ideas and aspirations since the citizens of Athens and the farmers around trooped into the city to see the plays of Euripides, Sophocles, and Aeschylus and decide on the prize-winners by their votes. The modern populace decides not by votes but by the tickets it buys and the money it pays. The result has been a new extension of aesthetic premises. The popular film, the radio, the gramophone, the comic strip, the popular daily paper and far more the popular periodical constitute a form of art and media of social communication which through mass production and the type of audience produced in the United States as the art of printing in the fifteenth. (James 1993: 36)

This fragment anticipates important debates in modern aesthetics, and particularly any critical appreciation of artist collaboration, on several points. The social significance of any art form derives from its closeness to human reality and its capacity to respond to collective needs and demands; consequently, artistic mediums are not valuable per se, but for the relevance they could acquire at any particular historical moment. This democratization of cultural consumerism decisively affects both artistic production and modern aesthetics, and the impact is not necessarily negative. James does not reject individual genius and originality, but rather closely couples them with collective critical responses. For James the popular arts are a unique terrain of social expression and social transformation, yet one haunted by the very contradictions surrounding US society and humankind at large. In recognizing this dimension, he envisaged cultural consumption as a political arena, directly linked to the sphere of social action. In this sense, the prolific space dedicated to the masses in *American Civilization* responds to the need to explain a broader transformation in the uses and potentialities of culture that James recognized as a decisive turning point affecting all societies at the crossroads of the twentieth century.

Despite recognizing this potentiality, James never forgot the coercive weight of the culture industries in modulating and conditioning creative agency. The identification of latent contradictions within the success of popular cinema is part of his belief—shared with Adorno and the émigrés of the Frankfurt School—that totalitarianism cannot be reduced to its manifestation in Nazi Germany (or the Stalinist Soviet Union, as James made the case) (Schwarz 2005: 20). "The essential conflict," James writes, "is between these ideals, hopes, aspirations, [and] needs, which are still the essential part of the tradition, and the economic and social realities of present-day America" (1993: 31). This conflict derives from an articulation never before achieved to such a degree between the public and the private and between labor and leisure, which made US citizens (and especially Black citizens) active participants in the construction of a social whole. This aspiration to totality, to a merging of art into life, as Schwarz affirms, is "what made private and civic relations political as never before" (2005: 39). Inversely, he adds, intellectuals were increasingly detaching themselves from direct engagement with the sociopolitical consequences of the cultural transformations of the moment (31). Instead of confronting how different creative forms were fueling social transformation, they were contributing to the managerial control of the masses by introducing specialization and by deferring the moment of action.

Concerning the second dimension mentioned above, the importance of form, nowhere is James's position clearer than in his writing on cricket. In *Beyond a Boundary*, cricket emerges as both an inherited colonial burden and a space for emancipative individual and collective expression. Mastering the disciplined field of the wicket implied, in the contested ground of the pre-emancipation West Indies, opening up spaces for collective insubordination unattainable through political means. As many readers of James have affirmed, learning the ceremonious and repetitive code of cricket, being disciplined through this code, meant also giving way to the unpredictable possibility of emancipative contagion. Early on in the book, James declares, "Two people live in me: one, the rebel against all family and school discipline and order; the other, a Puritan who would have cut off a finger sooner than do anything contrary to the ethics of the game" (James 1990: 37). The key point here is that, when coming to the cricket field, both persons were one and the same. Playing by the rules was the only possibility of subversion, since cricket, like any other sport, works as a cultural performance that modulates collective affects. James saw cricket as a partially independent cultural arena full of possibilities. He was aware that cricket and sports could serve to control the masses, but at the same time he rejected the possibility of that control being so encompassing as to annul any possible subversive response. Instead of conceiving of the game as an instrument of colonial governability, he saw cricket as a complex platform for social and political issues. For him, those issues were something that the critic must discover and make evident. It is in this sense that James's warning to the readers of his book goes: "The reader is here invited to make up his mind. If for him all this is 'not cricket', then he should take friendly warning and go in peace (or in wrath)" (57).

In this game, more important than the result was the expression of outstanding singularity emerging out of repetition. The episode in which James criticizes fixed college basketball games in the United States is a good case in point. The shock James felt was twofold: first, because this attitude did not fit into James's sports ethics; second, because of the indifference demonstrated by US audiences, who simply did not care about the games being sold. Andrew Smith makes a good point in this story by stressing that it does not matter whether or not the responses from the audience were correct. The important point here is how sports ethics was assumed by James not as an essentialized code but as a measuring tool regulated on its own terms and determining what is allowed and what is forbidden. In Smith's words, "Far from presenting some unconscious defence of an imperial 'games ethic', *Beyond a Boundary* is the work of someone driven to reflect, by a kind of culture shock, on what might or might not be at stake in the defence of cricket's peculiar boundaries" (2010: 28).

This is especially relevant for any aesthetics of social transformation. In James, moral judgments took second place. Much more important than the act of selling games is the denial of the fortuitous nature of sports performance and the elimination of the unpredictable reverberations a singular action could have when followed by collective responses. When dealing with "the politics and the aesthetics" of cricket, James makes shrewd observations that might sound familiar to any reader of collaborative art: he refuses to conceive of cricket as merely a given set of rules, an instrument used by colonial powers to seize and concentrate the needs of emancipation of the colonized. He recognizes, with Friedrich Schiller, the moment of performance as a moment of potential when human singularity can be constituted. But he also makes that potential conjunctural and dependent on the specificities of the here and now. As Smith argues, "James insisted that even mass-produced cultural forms could become the context in which potentially explosive social contradictions made themselves felt anew" (2010: 139). Cricket would be, then, both a space of social transformation, where change could be brought about ("Here, on the cricket field, if nowhere else, all men in the island are equal . . ." (C. L. R. James quoted in Smith 2010: 30) *and* a space of difference and competition, where each actor expressed himself from quite heterogeneous positions (. . . and we are the best men in the island" (James 1990: 61). By "ground[ing] the autonomy of art," to borrow Jacques Rancière's words (2010: 116), by acknowledging that cricket's expectations are first and foremost linked to cricket's singularity as a field, James produced a nuanced approach to cricket in which the potentiality of cricket was very much grounded in the social and racial divides of colonial and anticolonial Trinidad.

Paying Attention: James as Engaged Critic of Culture

During his stay in the United States, James not only redefined the object of cultural criticism but also refashioned the role of the intellectual in approaching that object. One of the major differences between Adorno and James lies in the fact that when James wrote about culture, his writing mixed and problematized different positions, among them that those the avid spectator and consumer of film and music, the activist, and the militant researcher. James's cultural (and political) criticism has to be read from that complex, flexible position, and this stance can only reinforce the position that James should occupy in any genealogy of radical criticism.

Faced with the lure of consumer culture that the mid-twentieth-century United States offered him, and set against the background of the collapse of European postwar rationalism and belief in modernity,

James decided to immerse himself in mass cultural forms in order to understand whether those forms carried within them a germ of mass deception similar to that of totalitarian Nazism or Stalinism. The burden of lived experiences, nevertheless, did not constrain James: although clear parallels with that close past can be found throughout his thinking, they did not prevent him from looking at the American masses and their participation in cultural creativity as potential agents of social transformation. It is from this perspective that James's insights on culture are important: they do not just focus on popular manifestations that precede the interest of collaborative and socially engaged aesthetics in democratizing art processes; I believe that James himself offers a perfect example of what a critic of these processes might be.

The engaged dimension that cultural criticism must have is presented at its best in James's reading of Herman Melville's *Moby Dick*. Written in 1953, while James was being detained on Ellis Island awaiting deportation, *Mariners, Renegades, and Castaways: The Story of Herman Melville and the World We Live In* projects the conflicts lived on board the *Pequod* on to the mid-twentieth-century United States. More particularly, the book reflects the situation that many diasporic subjects such as James were experiencing at that time. James wrote the book to mobilize support for his citizenship cause as well as to counterbalance the accusations on which his sentence of deportation hinged. The book, therefore, constitutes much more than a piece of literary criticism, and emerges as a plea for social change that extends James's specific situation to the shared condition of fellow migrant subjects (of diverse political ideology[15]) and, more broadly, of the oppressed segments of US society. In his introduction to the first complete reedition of *Mariners*, Donald Pease states, "By reinterpreting this Americanist masterwork from the standpoint of the crew, James had extended into the largest metropolitan nation of the mid-twentieth century a practice of social resistance that he had learned on the colonial cricket field" (2001: xv). Earlier, Pease flags something of particular importance: "The writing practice that James fashioned in [*Mariners*] enabled him to turn relatively discrete questions concerning the interpretation of Melville's novels into reflections on much more significant matters of social change and transformation" (xii). It is therefore not only the Jamesian interpretation of *Moby Dick* that constitutes the innovative part of the book; the way it is written and the objectives it pursues coincide with the identification of transformative potential in the *Pequod*'s crew. That means that in Jamesian criticism, subject is just one of the strategies used to envisage possibilities of social emancipation; the act of writing itself and the importance attributed to cultural forms lie in the fact that cultural criticism and these cultural forms can become sites for collective struggle and emancipation.

This does not imply, as many critical voices have pointed out, that James either accepted or was ignorant of the dangers behind US mass culture. Those who underestimate *Mariners* as a laudatory account of US capitalism might struggle to put aside James's interest in describing the crew of the *Pequod* as a social order determined by labor. At some point, after explaining that the character of Ahab does not appear out of nowhere but rather constitutes the most accomplished result of a deep observation by Melville of the collapse of the world he lived in, James declares that "the crew embodies some type of social order. Their association at work gives them interests, ideas and attitudes that separate them entirely from the rest of society" (2001: 81). Earlier on, he expresses this idea even more emphatically: "Their heroism consists in their everyday doing of their work. The only tragic graces with which Melville endows them are the graces of men associated for common labor" (28). This separation includes, of course, Ahab (and by extension totalitarian individualism), and grants a space for autonomous self-organization. At the end, as we know, the *Pequod* sinks, that tragedy being the result of Ahab's insane obstinacy, which ultimately derives from a voluntary disengagement with the world ("The high purpose in reality is for him alone, not for them," says James [16]). But James foresees that alternative possibilities might emerge out of the spontaneous work done by a crew united round a common purpose. *Mariners* recognizes time and again that this spontaneity did not stand in the way of Ahab's totalitarian aspirations; this recognition, however, does not prevent Melville from asserting the creative potential deriving from the self-organization of common men. The greatest achievement of James's reading of Melville lies precisely in understanding that a social rather than a political definition of freedom was gradually being created. Indeed, James manages to see beyond the point that holds *Mariners* close to mid-twentieth-century intellectuals such as Adorno (or Hannah Arendt, for that matter[16]), that is, "how the society of free individualism would give birth to totalitarianism and be unable to defend itself against it" (54). The crew's creative agency and shared sense of purpose is James's response to this question.

It is worth recalling here that the main achievement James recognizes in Melville is that of seeing ahead of his time, of kindling the possibility of the new amid the old. In these situations, the hesitations of the intellectual lie in choosing between both sides of the equation, as Ishmael, whom he deems an "intellectual Ahab" (41) was more likely to choose Ahab over the crew. This choosing, however, emerges in James as a direct result of social engagement (hence James's emphasis on how Melville perfected the character of Ahab through his previous novels, which were in turn inspired by Melville's own experience) and not of abstract calculations. The character of Ishmael depicted in *Mariners* appears almost as a caricature of the hesitations and discontinuity proposed by Adorno in his *Minima Moralia,* written during the latter's stay in the United States. Edward Said (2012: 57), who draws an image of Adorno as exiled intellectual from this piece of work, describes its structure and tone by saying that "it represents the intellectual's consciousness as unable to be at rest anywhere, constantly on guard against the blandishments of success, which, for the perversely inclined Adorno, means trying consciously *not* to be understood easily and immediately. Nor it is possible to retreat into complete privacy, since . . . the hope of the intellectual is not that he will have an effect on the world, but that someday, somewhere, someone will read what he wrote exactly as he wrote it."[17] The depiction of Ishmael in chapter 2 of *Mariners* seems to replicate word for word this conception of the intellectual. James could not see himself in the skin of Ishmael for several reasons—his precarious situation as a Black alien deprived of the right of citizenship being ultimately the main one. "There is," James writes, "a fatal flaw in his misery and his challenge and defiance. Never for a single moment does it cross his mind to question his relations with the people he works with. Those relations he accepts. . . . He has been trained in the school of individualism and an individualist he remains to the end" (2001: 11). Ishmael is not driven by individual *angst*; James also recognized in him a will to look beyond reality in search of deeper explanations: "For Ishmael[,] who believes in nothing and therefore constantly analyzes all that he sees to find something, everything in the world is appearance, something superficial, put on" (2011: 42). Going even further, James recognized a potential thread in the application of a way of thinking based on discerning the hidden meaning of historical and social processes. He also criticized the attitude of intellectuals who assume the right to speak on behalf of particular communities: "Ishmaels, we say, live in every city block. And they are dangerous, especially when they actually leave their own environment and work among workers or live among them" (James 2001: 40).

Related to this aversion toward the authoritative voice of the critic incapable of acting was James's emphasis on the importance of innovative strategies for creative collaboration. Throughout his career,

James articulated fascinating and innovative ways of breaking with the authoritative voice of the critical intellectual, producing much of his work in close collaboration with others and taking his writing beyond purely intellectual discussion. A clear example of this lies in his involvement with Missouri sharecroppers organizing a strike in 1941. Against the predominant view that conceived of this body of workers as an example of extreme poverty and belatedness, unassimilable within Northern narratives of progress,[18] James adopts an ethnographic approach capable of individualizing the group, and recognizing an element of resilience.[19] To this effect, he argues that "these are men whose spirits have not been broken, who stand ready to fight with every worker against class tyranny" (James, quoted in McLemee 1996: 22). A little later, he concludes that "they know their enemies and they will not yield" (C. L. R. James quoted in McLemee 1996: 22). Christopher Taylor sees James's experience with the sharecroppers as informed by the failure of the New Deal to address racial issues in its attempt to counter social inequality. Taylor positions James's engagement with the Missouri sharecroppers alongside wider debates on the US South, but he also extends the causes and consequences of such episodes as resonating across a wider transnational frame, reaching Trinidad and Ghana.[20] He goes on to say that the recognition of Black sharecroppers' self-determination by James operates in this case as a recognition of the failure of official policies to successfully address the racial dimension of social and economic exclusion both in the South and throughout the country.[21] The excitement James showed in recognizing forms of self-organization in these Black workers, whose economic and social conditions "have driven them far forward in political understanding" (James, quoted in McLemee 1996: 30), so as to put them "among the most advanced in America" (31), is set alongside the lack of interest of official institutions in placing emphasis on disenfranchised Black working communities.

Two elements of relevance to our discussion can be singled out here. The first involves James's position as a researcher engaged in the organization of the strike. Taylor reveals how James established a dynamic of dialogical exchange and collective writing. In a pamphlet titled "Down with Starvation Wages in South-East Missouri," we read,

> The sharecroppers [would] have their own strike. . . . When the time came for us to have a strike, I called some of the leaders together and said: "We have to publish something, for everybody to read about it."

They said yes. So I sat down with my notebook and said, "Well, what shall we say?" So (I used to call myself Williams) they said, "Brother Williams, you know." I said, "I know nothing. This is your strike. You are all doing it, you have to go through it. I have helped you, but this pamphlet has to state what you have to say. Now, have you got something to say about what you think?" And I went through each of them, five or six of them; each said his piece, and I joined them together. Everybody said what he thought was important. I didn't write anything, none of them wrote it. . . . They said what they thought and I put it together. (James, quoted in Taylor 2012: 84–85)

In this fragment, James places himself in a daring and original position. Instead of imposing theory on practice, he joins a group and listens. Any outcome of this conversational research is the result of collective exchange among the participants. This position, however, cannot be confused with an absence of critical appraisal. As the expert in revolutionary politics, James refuses to impose any external model and accepts dialogical exchange as the only way of learning something from the experience of collective self-organization. In this, he anticipates what Staughton Lynd (Lynd and Grubačić 2008: 40) has called "accompaniment," a militant way of conceiving research based on direct, continuous observation of others' organizational strategies, "a homegrown, close-to-the-earth kind of theory that evolved directly from folks' experience in organizing" (Lynd and Grubačić 2008: 40).

The second point worth considering for our purposes here pertains to the context in which the episode takes place. For James, the sharecroppers strike demonstrated the failure of the New Deal program to address racial inequalities. He constructed a typically Jamesian argument in focusing on the organization of a strike whose proponents lacked the support of a so-called national campaign and were unaccounted for and unassimilable into the broader narrative of national optimism and regeneration. Doris Sommer (2014: 44) describes how the New Deal cultural program was concerned with identifying the positive values of US culture, granting quality public education and ensuring aesthetic freedom and artistic innovation. This view, it is important to note, shaped both James's political and creative thought.[22] The New Deal public art program is often acknowledged as playing a pivotal role in the prehistory of social transformation art. Although James shared some of the aspirations of this program, his interest in the particularities of experience led him to explore groups that remained unaffected by those aspirations and to categorize the New Deal as "one of the greatest pieces of humbuggery that you can find" (James, quoted in McLemee 1996: 29). What matters is not whether the New Deal achieved its goals, or whether James was right or wrong in his opinion that matters here. The most interesting lesson to be learned from this episode is that James used his ability to accompany everyday men and women in challenging a bigger picture of national social transformation.

This opinion cannot be considered exceptional. The whole edifice of Jamesian thought rests on his belief in the exhaustion of a mode of criticism based in the privileged capacity of the intellectual to decipher and have the last say on reality. Andrew Smith has argued that James approaches popular creativity in a way that rejects single interpretations made by the critic. His conception of criticism also rejects the possibility of recognizing in the critic an authoritative figure with the exclusive right and capacity to decipher the hidden meaning of films, works of art, or sports. Underlying James's notion of culture, says Smith, "is a more general suspicion of the very idea that a novel or painting was some kind of puzzle that awaited a once-and-for-all solution" (2010: 58).

The repulsion James felt for interpretative models of cultural analysis arose out of his broader conceptualization of mid-twentieth-century historical time, a time, as we have already said, when the authoritative role of cultural criticism was being both asserted and redefined according to the major transformations undertaken by capitalism and mass society. The passages in which James criticizes his fellow historians and social analysts are linked to his ever-present desire to explore the details of cultural manifestations in greater depth, avoiding crude generalizations while also rejecting any specialization or compartmentalization of knowledge and experience.[23]

In a way that not only resembles the paths of many art activist groups in the future but also the interest of Joseph Beuys in recognizing everyday exchanges as an art form (*pace* the fact that we do not find in James any similar interest in proposing his own personality as exemplary, and James's more acute class consciousness throughout his career), James privileged the moment of discussion over the final result of investigative and creative processes. This is evident, for example, when he claims that "appreciation of cricket has little to do with the end, and less still with what are called 'the finer points' of the game" (1990: 194). The comparison with the German artist is not gratuitous. For both, aesthetics lies in the process of work and everyday activity; both merge teaching, learning, and producing; both attribute value to the way that form can become a vehicle for meaningful affirmation; both, finally, consider art and creativity as playing a central role in collective improvement.

More, then, separates James and Adorno than a simple positive or negative appreciation of popular culture. It is James's conception of the intellectual—one deriving to a great extent from his own situation as a Black migrant deprived of citizenship, as an alien—that makes him an innovative voice as early as the 1940s. If, to return once more to Said (2012: 62), "for the intellectual an exilic displacement means being liberated from the usual career," in the case of James that liberation took the form of an opening up to collective creativity not only as a subject but also as profound deep transformation of the practice of thinking itself. It is, therefore, the *how* as much as the *what* that separated both authors. In the mid-twentieth century, James was redefining what ought to be the role of radical intellectuals and practitioners, opening up interesting and still timely paths for criticizing artistic forms.

Creative Forms, Transnational Linkages, and the Militant Avant-Garde

Another aspect of Jamesian criticism of great value for any analysis of radical forms of creativity is his ability to read causes past and present as concatenating and opening into each other across epochs and continents. For James, significant cultural productions emerge out of specific sociopolitical conditions (those of "crisis" or transformation [see James 1977a]) and therefore are not essentially connected to any specific identity or expressive form. Attempts to "regionalize" James through his identification with the British intellectual, the Trinidadian nationalist, or the enthusiastic observer of US mass culture inevitably fail to capture the continuous search for different forms of collective agency and the not always evident ways in which these are perpetuated in different scenarios. Opposing this compartmentalization, in this section I argue that James's emphasis on agency still holds appeal because it allows us to envisage different nexuses of radical solidarity beyond the immediate result of a cultural process, cutting across continents, cultural manifestations, and even history.

James's writing repudiates universalism. He can identify agents of social mobilization and sites of struggle in different cultural forms and in the way that these forms are not only flexible and specific but also mobile and translatable to other contexts and causes. This means that each intervention (practical or theoretical) that James made into collective forms of creative agency was defined alongside a vast range of comparable examples, past and present. It is also what allowed James to reject any image of the future as straightforwardly determined by a unique vanishing cause.[24]

Several examples can be mentioned here. We have seen how *Mariners* was infused with mistrust of European totalitarianism and with the idea that this authoritarian specter was becoming part of US culture. David Scott (2004; see also Forsdick and Høgsbjerg 2017) has finely traced how important the expected future of anticolonial revolutions in Africa was for the writing of *The Black Jacobins.* In his insightful reading of the Haitian Revolution, James recognizes in the Haitian communities of slaves the first subjects of a modern world as well as the precursors of capitalism, acknowledging also their capacity to introduce a crack into the system. During his first stay in Britain, the writing of his history of the Communist International (published only one year prior to his masterpiece on the Haitian Revolution) prepared the ground for recognizing the potential of "US Negroes" to become a source of social transformation in the case of a demise of proletarian strikes in the country. The experiences and experiments with self-organization James went through in the United States led him to recognize the value of workers' assembly in the Hungarian Revolution.[25] This recognition, as well as his experience with South sharecroppers, found echoes in his analysis of Ghanaian peasantry (Taylor 2012: 92).

James maintains this position in respect of "art" forms, which he identified as part of a field whose potential was always dependent on their specific relevance for particular audiences. Take, for example, his readings of Caribbean art and literature expounded in a lecture in 1959 at the University of the West Indies Mona Campus (Jamaica) under the title "The Artist in the Caribbean." The first idea expressed in this lecture had to do with the oft-cited dichotomy between individual genius and social context (see A. Smith 2010). After asserting that creative mastery is influenced by the social medium in which the artist is born, he also remarks that "artistic production is essentially individual and the artistic individual is above all unpredictable" (James 1977c: 185). This individuality, however, is always achieved because an opportunity for outstanding expression is seized through an aperture in a given society. James, as he affirms, "is not chasing masterpieces" (185). Why, then, spend time in dealing with art and literature? Why not focus on reinforcing his appreciation of cricket as a fully valuable aesthetic form?

One potential answer to these questions lies in the expectations James had for Caribbean nations becoming "complete." James's concern is not with "deliver[ing] encomiums or disapprovals of West Indian writers and artists" (James 1977c: 187) but with recognizing that the social transformation West Indian countries were undergoing could make such creative manifestations as literature or art more socially significant than they were before. He then read the fields of art and literature not as impermeable systems of rules but as malleable platforms that could eventually become relevant for a group. Inversely, James states that only through a direct engagement with the audience could such forms acquire any transformative potential. No matter how strongly or how frequently individual genius is expressed through these forms, creative genius will be relevant only insofar as such individual excellence meets popular appreciation. Besides relativizing the (otherwise immense) importance of cricket in James's Caribbean criticism, this last fragment explains how the efficiency of creative forms is conceived of in James as conjunctural and not essential. In James's words, "When our local dramatists and artists can evoke the popular response of a Sparrow, the artists in the Caribbean will have arrived" (1977c: 188).

"The Artist in the Caribbean" is also illuminating for a different reason. Further down the same page we read, "It is inconceivable to me that a national artistic tradition, on which I lay so much stress as an environment in which the artist must begin, it is inconceivable to me that this can be established by writers and artists, however gifted, working for what is essentially a foreign audience. I think I could prove that already their work is adversely affected by it" (James 1977c: 188). This passage lends itself to at least two different interpretations. A first would involve James's emphasis on the national context as a determinant of artistic individuality. However, I believe that James here is writing against the grain of any deterministic servitude toward cultural context. By stating that art and literature can be relevant only when not directed toward foreign audiences, James is not making any chauvinistic claim on the ownership of West Indian creativity by West Indian audiences. Rather, he is rejecting any mode of artistic production based on commenting on a given context to encapsulate and previously export Caribbean experience.

Those familiar with discussion on Caribbean art would recognize this argument. For decades, the Caribbean has been exoticized and objectified according to the expectations of a foreign gaze. When the also Trinidadian artist Christopher Cozier (2011: 8) argues that "the Caribbean artist is always in competition with a long history of expedient labelling of their world and their very selves—externally and also internally," he is alluding to the same problem that James had already detected in 1959. The originality of "The Artist in the Caribbean" comes from identifying art as yet another form of cultural manifestation that could become relevant not by reversing Western expectations of the region but rather by offering potential ways to overcome the specific burdens that might emerge for Caribbean societies. By examining the work of a successful calypso artist such as the Grenadian Mighty Sparrow, James is not attempting to appropriate art for uncritical populist judgments but contending instead that it is impossible to identify in artists any special talent for looking at reality or extracting any hidden meaning. For James, the role art plays in fueling social transformation is conjunctural and, by virtue of this, redefinable in different forms and in different contexts. From this position, it is not aesthetic relativism that follows but a need for continuous critical, affirmative redefinition of art as a field of expression. In this sense, James concludes that "we lack that impulse towards a more advanced stage of existence which sees material obstacles in terms of how to overcome them" (James 1977c: 189). It was this potential that he saw coming at full pace through the sociopolitical transformation taking place during those years.[26]

What "The Artist in the Caribbean" reveals is particularly important for any attempt at provincializing and decolonizing the genealogies of social practice. James's interest in the overlapping of cultural agency and collective forms of social and political mobilization worked by putting American references beside African, European, and Caribbean referents in coeval comparison. For this reason, it is impossible to establish a ground narrative or a categorization of Jamesian cultural interest in which, for example, cricket would stand higher than cinema (as we have seen, even the "suspicious" field of high art and the Hollywood film industry take a big share in the distribution of Jamesian genius and transformative potential). A direct consequence deriving from this argument resulted in the heterogeneity of the Jamesian legacy, as demonstrated by its multiple appropriations. Yet I believe that James's capacity for reading cultural processes that achieved social relevance and led to effective transformation through their translatability (which is not to say their homogeneity) turns him into a highly positive value for any genealogy of socially engaged creativity.

The idea of leadership might sound strange for those familiar with James. Doesn't it approximate too closely the avant-garde that the

Trinidadian author sought so stubbornly to challenge? Isn't his attempt to democratize the notion of art simply incompatible with any idea of leadership? In light of examples such as the 1959 Mona lecture, I believe that James again has much to say on this point. His position advances recent attempts at reading art activism alongside the idea of the avant-garde. Marc James Léger conceives the contemporary avant-garde as subsisting as "the repressed underside of the contemporary forms of extradisciplinary practice" (Léger 2012: 13). This would imply not recognizing themselves formally as avant-garde but rather intervening within the public sphere. Stephen Shukaitis reads avant-gardist practices from an autonomist perspective, recognizing in their most successful models a "living surplus of resistance" that can adopt a plurality of forms, among which what we traditionally used to call art (Shukaitis 2015: 18).

James's malleability in terms of focusing on heterogeneous cultural processes, within and beyond the art domain, quickly comes to mind as prefiguring contemporary reappraisals of the avant-garde such as these. (James would particularly salute Shukaitis's [2015: xi] recognition of artistic practice as a valuable form through which to strategize.) Yet I am not sure whether James's thinking on this matter is in tune with these arguments. To be sure, James was an adamant recognizer of the multiplicity of groups and fields of cultural expression that could lead to radical change. However, he also struggled to explore the coexistence of multiple temporalities within our present, challenging the idea of an all-triumphant capitalism thwarting any possibility of resistance. So, when Shukaitis, following Toni Negri, blurs the space of contemporary avant-garde by saying that "avant-garde practices have no frontline today, precisely because the entirety of the social has been subsumed by strategic vectors of exploitation by capital" (Shukaitis 2015: 7), the Trinidadian writer would probably only agree in part with this argument, pointing out the centrality of "old" forms of cultural production (such as art or cricket) as autonomous fields of social interaction in postcolonial contexts.

Conclusion

In this chapter I wanted to stress how Jamesian aesthetics arises from a profound exploration of collective cultural agency in social transformation. Diachronically, I set out to imagine a Jamesian afterlife infusing current thought on art activism with a concern for radical social transformation. By stressing this side of James, I did not intend to turn him into an activist, nor forget the complex and multilayered variety of critical strategies and positionings he adopted. Rather, I regard him as being preoccupied with many of the central questions that nowadays still persist in debates on politicized art and activism. James identifies four main elements to be broached in dealing with these questions: recognition of mass culture as a contested field in which alternative social imagination can be put into practice; emphasis on the creative potential deriving from the imperfections of experience and praxis; exhaustion of critical appreciation based on the authoritative and exclusive role of the intellectual to delve into hidden meanings of reality; and interest in exploring the adaptability of emancipative action from a transnational perspective based on continuous dialogical exchange.

James's works on culture written after his arrival in the United States coincided with the emergence of heated debates on the public role of arts and the importance of cultural practices in engaging broader segments of the population. It is all the more strange that the scholars who have dealt with either the role of culture in the articulation of the Jamesian idea of agency and the prehistory of socially engaged art in the United States have ignored each other.[27] At a crucial turning point where aesthetics started to be associated with individual acts of self-criticism, James's engagement with the cultural dimension of the masses' activity offered an alternative aesthetic path. This path recognized the possibility of an aesthetics based on collective agency and radical engagement. James acknowledged the importance of common situations for raising new political questions and forming new agents of social transformation, for example understanding Black struggles as a fundamental contribution to cultural and human renovation. His approach to "the Negro question" was, however, as nuanced and multifaceted as James's personal and political trajectory itself (see James 1977b). His collaboration with the Missouri sharecroppers and the continuity of this experience in Ghana would diversify the voices considered in any genealogy of US radical tradition, also challenging ethnocentric views—emerging both within and outside Marxism— that declared non-Westerners as people without history. Contrary to this view, James asserted the leading role of anticolonial struggles in the configuration of the modern world. Because of this, if nowadays, as Kester explained, many of the values deriving from an interpretative tradition (with Adorno as one of its cornerstones) based on the rejection of direct engagement are affecting not just ideas about art but also artistic production itself, looking at Jamesian aesthetics remains useful in trying to confront the exhaustion of that tradition.

James's approach to aesthetics and cultural production during the postwar period complements and also partially challenges this view. His interest in the American working class, and more specifically in the capacity of American workers to produce "new political categories," new fundamental social questions, through their everyday activity (see Bogues 1997), not only challenges Adorno's "aesthetics of detachment"; it also proposes an alternative aesthetics based on collective experience and mass culture. The distance between Adorno's and James's understanding of culture therefore transcends an individual dimension and points toward an alternative aesthetic genealogy in which criticism and social engagement are not separated from one another. Viewed from this perspective, and contraposed in a fairly speculative way, the "missed encounter" between James and Adorno epitomizes a pivotal shift in contemporary aesthetics, where two major strands begin to be defined. On one side, Adorno's mistrust of close engagement and mass culture will lead to an aesthetics privileging representational approaches to political commitment. On the other, James's interest in the mundane aspects of American culture and the everyday reality of the working classes will lead to a celebration of collective creative agency and the productive "impurity" of collaboration. That is not to say that one of these aesthetics is better than the other, nor even that James is better suited to describing our present. The point is, rather, that both emerged from the same crossroads, reacting to a similar set of stimuli. Consequently, if Adorno's thought is seen as marking our relationship with art in the present, no less can be said of James's. Asking about the current relevance of socially engaged art has much to gain from viewing both James and Adorno as synchronous but also multitemporal referents haunting our present.

Recognizing the modernity of Jamesian aesthetics does not only redirect the centrality of the defeatism of the Frankfurt School toward activism and socially engaged creative forms; it also challenges the neutrality with which particular aesthetic interpretations ended up nurturing broader critical traditions. From this perspective, James would be much more than "the colonial unconscious of critical theory" (Traverso 2016: 191), becoming a central voice in the articulation of a subversive and radical transatlantic critical tradition. This means recognizing James's personal experience as transnational and translatable both geographically and temporally. In his critical writing as in his political texts, he approached a variety of subjects from their specificity but with universal human transformation in mind, whether in the United States, Ghana, Trinidad, or Britain. James wrote on culture from a mobile yet situated perspective, attentive to the nuances of the multiple groups of individuals he met along his way. His relentless search for new revolutionary subjects challenges any melancholic approach to the anticolonial past, while he also compels us to provincialize our histories of creative social transformation.

If it is true that it is not easy to fit James in any single critical tradition (this being one of the possible reasons why James has been erased from the accounts on art and social change in the Americas), I also believe that this complexity can only be something positive. That is why recognizing an aesthetics in James's cultural criticism is so important. His aesthetic appreciations were not limited to the passing of emancipative expectations, nor, as Traverso suggests, to the recognition of Third World nationalism as transformative agent. James's reading of culture stands out for being malleable, for rejecting the possibility of applying old solutions to new problems for the single reason that these solutions have worked well in a particular situation.

The main lineaments of Jamesian aesthetics were produced in a moment of profound transformation, when the pillars of modernity were shaken by totalitarianism and the promise of emancipative action embodied in anticolonial struggles were more alive than ever. This moment also featured a deep shift in contemporary aesthetics, one marked by the consolidation of the artist as an autonomous being whose importance lay in deciphering the malaises of society without being contaminated by too much political engagement. James developed his insights on art and popular culture in this context, without being compromised by any ideological alignment (it is worth remembering here that the break with Trotsky was shaped by James's recognition of the creative power of new revolutionary subjects), or being anchored in a single geographical or cultural context. From this perspective, James emerges as one of the main names standing up for a bottom-up, Marxist-inflected, collaborative aesthetics. While James is undeniably important because he preempted many of the concerns that would be developed two decades later in the field of cultural studies, I believe he also stands as an adamant precursor of socially engaged forms of creativity and radical criticism.

◆　◆　◆

In this part I set out to identify some of the main preoccupations of contemporary debates on socially engaged art as emerging out of anticolonial thought and practice. "Practical" intellectuals, such as Amílcar Cabral or C. L. R. James, are useful for envisaging alternatives that can be applied to our postcolonial, postutopian present. Although their understanding of artistic practice included the aesthetic appreciation of a variety of cultural productions that nowadays would seem far from radical creativity, in different ways both Cabral and James infused their understanding of culture with a plea for action and collective experimentation. Certainly, our world is not theirs. The articulation of their thought, the decisions they made, are the fruit of specific predicaments and of the confluence of a specific ideology, that of decolonization and anti-imperialism, and a specific context in which individual and collective freedom, autonomy, and emancipation were battles to be fought and won. At the same time, however, their being-in-the-world (expressed through the articulation of theory and practice) remains eloquent in our present.

Part Three

◆ ◆ ◆

LEGACIES

5

◆　◆　◆

THE BODA MOMENT

Repositioning Socially Engaged Art
in Contemporary Uganda

KLA ART is a biennial festival that has been held in Kampala, Uganda, since 2012. In its first edition, the festival revolved around a public art exhibition called *12 Boxes Moving*, the result of the joint collaboration of seven local institutions.[1] After a call, twelve projects were distributed in an equal number of containers scattered throughout the city.[2] The choosing of the container as artistic venue is highly symbolic in the Ugandan context: containers evoke transitiveness, mobility, and multi-purpose use; they refer to the transit and exchange of goods but also to informal economies within the city landscape, where they are a common sight. The idea behind this choice was to raise public awareness of contemporary art, a phenomenon traditionally associated in Uganda with the academic milieu, largely defined by gallery spaces and government-ruled museums.[3] In this context, using containers meant a big step forward in giving contemporary art public relevance. The degree to which that goal was achieved did vary: some interventions aimed for interactivity and performativity, while others were simply limited to hanging artworks inside the container space. Whereas some criticism on the event focused on the fact that the containers were also "enclosing" art and *containing* it in public spaces already exposed to "cultural forms," the festival did have repercussions in challenging views on art's purpose, ownership, and relevance. It also initiated a lasting dynamic of institutional collaboration linking public and private stakeholders. Katrin Pieters, who recently dedicated a long essay to public art in Uganda, writes that "*KLA ART 012* was a pilot, an experiment in many ways, from the outset with the

139

intention of following editions in two or three-year intervals. The main aims were to create new physical and mental spaces for visual art projects and to interact with new and different audiences. The festival was strictly non-commercial to allow for ideas beyond a direct saleability" (Pieters 2015: 65). She adds that "the festival had a visionary, experimental aspect, attempting to open up a space for new artistic but also curatorial approaches," opposing the long tradition of solo shows mostly motivated by economic ends (66).

Contrary to that process of tagging and highlighting public places, the 2014 edition of KLA ART decided to frame public intervention in a different way. Titled "Unmapped," the festival attempted a more intense projection into the public space. The second edition of the event was coordinated by 32° East, Ugandan Art Trust, and brought interesting novelties to the Ugandan artistic arena. The initiative was split into three interrelated projects: a "conventional" exhibition taking place at the Uganda Railways station in Central Kampala;[4] a series of studio visits highlighting the workplaces of local artists;[5] and a set of public interventions grouped under the Boda Boda Project. The latter, which was not intended to be the nucleus of the event nor the depository of the major part of the funding, outperformed the "regular" gallery exhibition in terms of visitors and critical response. All the local newspapers and cultural journals dedicated a space to the event, and the Contemporary And platform opened with a special focus on Kampala (Peters-Klaphake 2014).

The initiative consisted of a series of collaborations between Ugandan artists and the *boda boda* drivers, whose motorcycles were customized and then used regularly throughout the city. The *boda bodas*, motorbikes providing taxi services, are the most common means of transport in Uganda and East Africa. They also constitute a cornerstone in Kampala's popular culture and informal trade network.[6] Choosing them both as the artistic venue and as the target community to collaborate with acknowledges their role in configuring Kampala's urban landscape and recognizing their legitimacy. At the same time, their use raises questions about the capacity of one-time artistic interventions to raise awareness of regulatory and customary issues. Customizing motorbikes that would have a regular use during and beyond the festival time involved reconsidering the participatory nature of KLA ART in different terms. The interventions varied from project to project, but in this case the terms of the dialogue were now more balanced and horizontal, with each artist interacting with the *boda boda* drivers and owners in a sustained way. The

Boda Boda Project also functioned differently in terms of space, shifting the relatively controlled locations where the containers were installed in KLA ART 012 to the more daring routes traversed by the *boda boda* drivers.

In a recent article, Angelo Kakande has shown how Ugandan artists are increasingly adopting partisan positions concerning the influence of extralegal forms of slow and not-so-visible violence in the definition of the debates on Ugandan public space (Kakande 2016). The projects belonging to the Boda Boda Project made evident that concern. Among the issues raised were everyday violence against marginalized groups (Adonias Ocom Ekuwe, Xenson), the liability of passengers and drivers alike and the lack of respect for passersby (Ronex Ahimbisibwe, Petro, Babirye Leilah Burns), and the invisibility of *boda boda* drivers despite constituting a central sector of Kampala's economy (Kino Musoke, Enock Kalule Kagga, and Sandra Suubi). While many of the interventions came about with a central topic in mind that was supposed to develop into a mobile artwork,[7] the format allowed more complex and more interesting forms of collaboration. The 2014 edition of KLA ART generated mostly positive critical responses (Namakula 2014; Serubiri 2016), being perceived by many of the persons I interviewed in Uganda as the beginning of a "new mood" in contemporary art, more prone to project itself into the public space, but also deepening the terms of the collaborations set in motion.

In this chapter this mood is defined as "the *boda* moment." *Boda bodas* symbolize a whole cultural landscape characterized by the centrality *and invisibility* of the informal sector within the configuration of urban imaginaries. The landscape of informal economies and practices in Kampala has been substantially altered since the creation of the Kampala Capital City Authority, which has developed a modernization campaign encouraging private investment and urban transformation. This has left many informal vendors and agents in a precarious and paradoxical position, for those same individuals still constitute the backbone of the Ugandan economy. By referring to a *"boda moment,"* this chapter alludes to a general concern in contemporary Ugandan artistic practice, one seemingly marked by: (a) the success of collaborative and oppositional practices challenging the privatization of the urban space and the sphere of education and culture; (b) the incorporation of artistic collaboration within the realm of the informal city; (c) linked to that, a certain decentralization of the role played by academia in the definition of Ugandan contemporaneity, motivated by the conjuncture of the irruption of economic neoliberalism and "political stability" in the Museveni era;[8] and, finally, (d) a constant questioning of the possibilities and limitations of artistic interventions operating in that terrain, something manifest in the rejection of "traditional" art audiences and contexts and representative means for political expression, but also in the adoption of an experimental and processual approach to creativity.

||

KLA ART did not crystalize out of nothing. It was the result of a fundamental shift in the Ugandan artistic panorama, something that could be felt on an institutional, curatorial, and representational level. Here I will concentrate on both editions of KLA ART, picking two long-term projects that will be the focus of my discussion here.

One of the containers of the 2012 edition of the festival was occupied by Lilian Mary Nabulime. She filled the space with a series of usable soap-made sculptures alluding to HIV/AIDS, the main concern of her practice since the early 2000s, after going through a direct experience of caring for a relative with HIV/AIDS. In the context of her PhD studies at the University of Newcastle, Nabulime started experimenting with sculpture as a way of generating social awareness of HIV/AIDS among literate and illiterate communities in Uganda. Nabulime had vast experience in artistic collaboration, and for her intervention in 2012 she stood in front of her container, dialoguing with the audience about the meaning of her sculpture and the social relevance of AIDS in Uganda. Years before, she had attempted to develop a research and practical project on "the role of sculptural forms as a communication tool in relation to lives and experiences of women in Sub-Saharan Africa," which focused on a variety of topics confronted from an art historical perspective (Nabulime and McEwan 2011). This was the original PhD dissertation proposal she began at Newcastle University. On this occasion, Nabulime started experimenting with different sculptural techniques. "A key concern," she said, "was the development of a sculptural language which transcended ethnic and cultural divides to reach the greatest possible audience, and elicit interpretation based on individual experience rather than the conditioned response to more familiar sculptural idioms" (Nabulime 2007: 14). Soon, however, her interest turned toward the impact of HIV on Ugandan women.

Sculpture (which Nabulime, after Joseph Beuys, understands as a social practice) was the artistic medium of choice because it sought to break with ethnic and religious boundaries (which constitute a real boundary in the Ugandan context), and also because it presented a desirable balance between abstraction and objecthood. Finally, it allowed interaction, simultaneously triggering and tempering the dialogical elements that lie at the core of the project (see figures 5.1 and 5.2).

When I interviewed Nabulime in 2018, I asked her what role sculpture played in her project. Since conversation and dialogical engagement were her central concern, why was she not getting rid of the "more conventional" process of carving? She replied that the manipulation of objects of daily use was essential for ensuring a degree of confidence, allowing the conversations. Since many of the issues the project raised (such as polygamy or extramarital relations) were taboo, only by relating them to the sharing of "neutral" everyday acts such as cleansing could they be dealt with publicly and critically.

A first experiment, which took place between 2001 and 2002 with Ugandan and African women living in the United Kingdom, barely revealed those conditions. Although some positive results were obtained, the experience was partially unsatisfactory for the artist. At this moment, practice, Nabulime explains, "was informed by imagined ideas of the life experiences of women living with the disease and by personal experiences. Information was gathered by a world-wide review of the literature and practice, drawing on published material and 'grey' literature, web-materials and other communication resources" (Nabulime 2007: 20). Consequently, the targeted audience was not the most suitable one for the artist's interests; additionally, there was a gap between Nabulime's expectations and her awareness of the specificities of context, audience-composition, and interests. As a result of this, not only were the dialogical aspects of the project more a symbolic enactment of the artist's will than an open exchange, but the sculptures were also dominated by an educational, black-and-white tone (women with sad expressions representing victimhood, men with big penises representing a threat, and so on).[9] Nabulime bridged this gap only through a sustained engagement with her audience and curiosity over the following years.

The last stages of the project involved an active collaboration with populations (women and men) in rural and illiterate areas, in which the sculptures are used as triggers for discussion going beyond AIDS to include issues on women rights, patriarchy, social (in)visibility, and polygamy. Well aware of both AIDS art activism and the social use of sculpture in the African context, Nabulime inserted her dialogical practice into contexts traditionally unconnected to contemporary artistic practice.

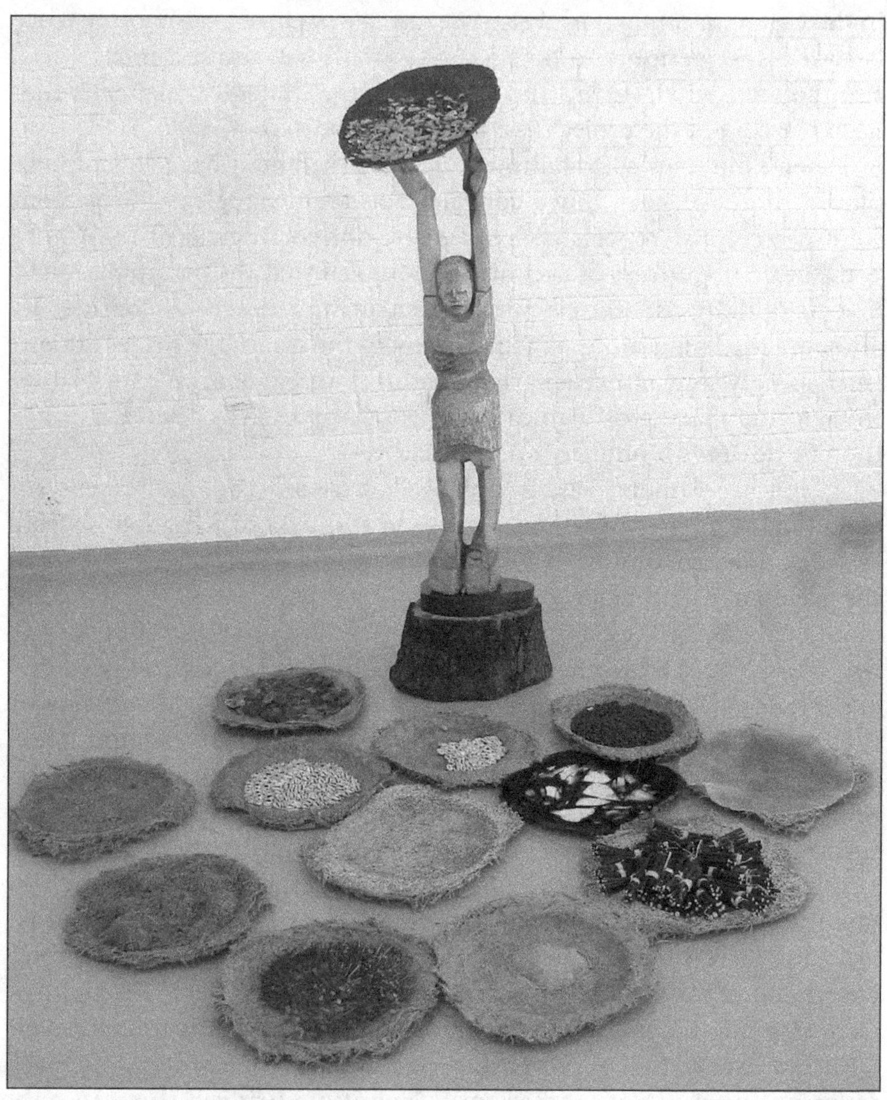

Figure 5.1. Lilian Mary Nabulime, *Winnowing*, 2002–2004. 168 cm. x 125 cm. x 125 cm.; scrim, flat baskets, nails, cowrie shells, wood, beans, ground nuts, latex, glass, wasted tea bags, color. *Source*: Courtesy of Lilian Mary Nabulime.

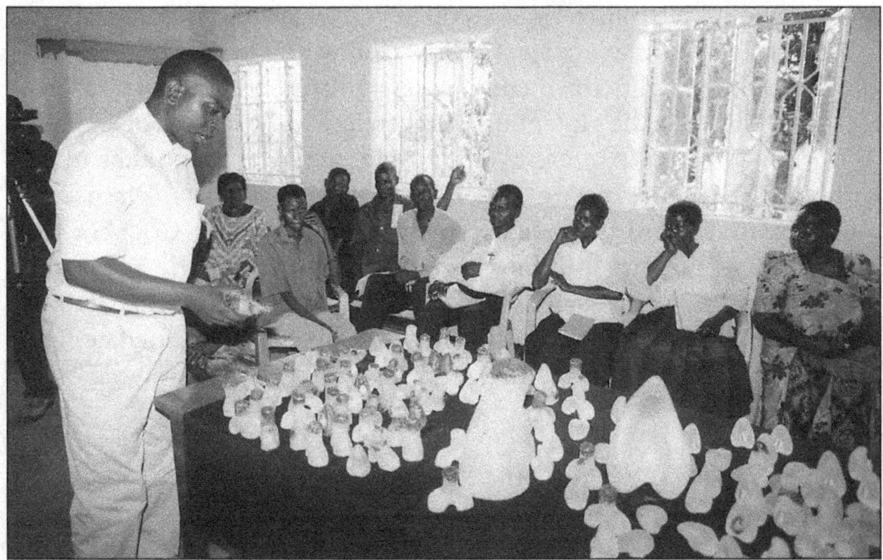

Figure 5.2. Participants in discussion, responding to Lilian Mary Nabulime's collaborative project on HIV/AIDS. *Source*: Courtesy of Lilian Mary Nabulime.

III

Fred Batale, the initiator of our second project, was one of Nabulime's collaborators on the 2012 project. One year later, Batale created the Disability Art Project Uganda (DAPU), which took part in KLA ART's Boda Boda Project in 2014. On that occasion, they modified a *boda boda* so it could carry a person with impaired mobility. *Boda bodas* epitomize neoliberalism in Uganda: they greatly contribute to the country's informal economy and allow rapid mobility, although they are often involved in traffic hazards. They are also a symbol of transnational commerce, with many motorbikes being imported from India. Finally, the efforts invested in the customization of *boda bodas* responds to the quick urban landscape of Kampala, turning these vehicles into a symbol of the city's aesthetics.

Engaging the material side of this symbol, the DAPU project brings together Ugandans with disabilities and explores issues of accessibility, recognition, and self-empowerment. The activities developed by DAPU include a series of practical workshops in design and art aimed at people with disabilities living on the streets; public demonstrations and counseling people with disabilities about practical issues; and pooling people for personalizing their vehicles and prosthesis. The outcomes of those activities are multiple, ranging from "conventional artworks" and individual customizations to open conversations and educational workshops. "We do art projects which lobby and sensitize the public about disability rights to equality, accessibility, among others," affirms DAPU's website. Batale's intention was therefore to develop an open-ended platform in which the interests of multiple participants could be united without the existence of a unique objective or final end. In that sense, the representational means of each activity are collectivized. Collaboration here is framed not just at the level of research but also in the final results of each activity, which remain open to the desire of each participant (figure 5.3). As we will see, those dimensions usually concatenate. How is this achieved? What is the importance of this concatenation?

IV

Now that we know the initiators of both projects, we may ask, Who are the subjects that make up the communities that DAPU and Nabulime work with? How can we approach them? How do both projects shape those communities? And how do those communities shape both projects? In the case of Nabulime, her audience is determined not only by personal or familiar exposure to AIDS; concerns with ethnicity, heteronormativity, and literacy also play a pivotal role in configuring each experience.[10] Whereas the first element was clear from the beginning in the artist's mind, the others emerged as the successive phases unfolded. The variety of reactions, ranging from misunderstanding to denial and active engagement, revealed that complexity. In fact, the heterogeneity of topics and approaches required Nabulime to embrace an ambivalent aesthetics. A common argument in Nabulime's explanation of her own work is that the use of soap as a means to fabricate sculptures and, through that process, to encourage open conversation among groups of women, is related to the necessity of "avoiding many partners and sticking to one" in order to prevent AIDS contagion, as well as the transparency of those who "accept living with AIDS" (Nabulime 2007: 186). The project leaves a margin for nonpredetermined interaction with the soap sculptures, allowing the clinical and emotional appreciation derived from contact with the objects to be derived from each participant's individual experience. This is encouraged by limiting firsthand information on each piece and replacing it with conversational moments with the artist.[11]

Something similar occurs with the Disability Art Project Uganda, which uses the customization of *boda bodas* as a way of encouraging dialogue and raising awareness about the lack of public infrastructure in the Kampala cityscape. Although the participants joining DAPU

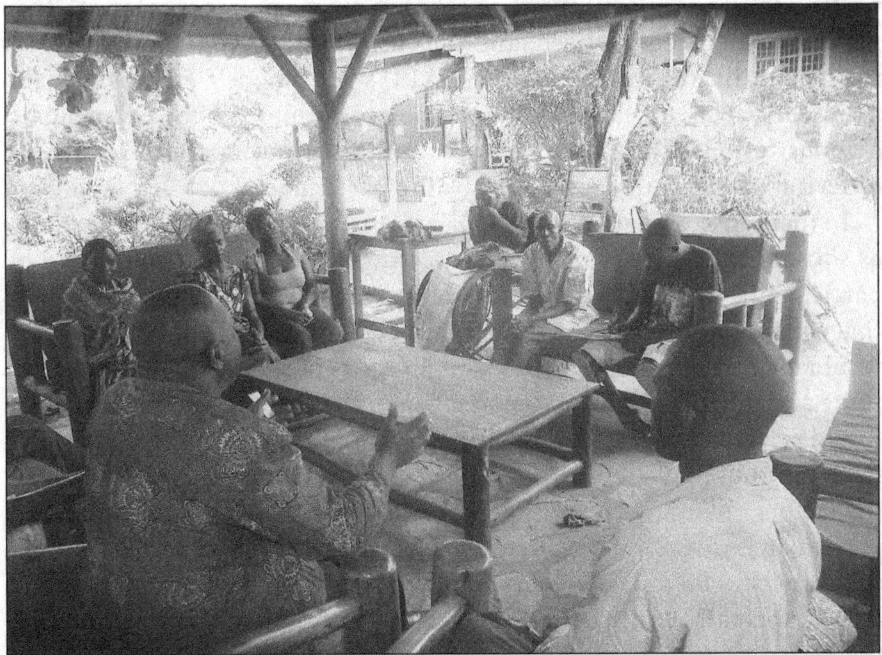

Figure 5.3. Disability Art Project Uganda meeting, 32° East, Ugandan Art Trust, Kampala, Uganda. *Source*: Courtesy of Fred Batale.

could be seen as belonging to an already existing group, the dynamic of the project shows how this point should not be taken for granted. When Batale started his project, he faced many challenges. Many were reluctant to expose themselves in public; many others wanted to be paid for their participation; yet a third group could not understand why art was important as an engine for collective action. Lacking any (artistic) education in many cases and facing a harsh reality, to these participants, design and aesthetics must have seemed remote and abstract—and dispensable—aspirations. Nevertheless, when I spoke to Batale, he insisted on the importance of art in the whole configuration of the project, as well as in the cohesion of the collective agency displayed through DAPU. He outlined that in their practice, creativity is not an ornamental element but rather an instrument inherent to the means of living and the everyday economy of Ugandan people with disabilities. DAPU does not "stand for" any collective; rather, it acts as an artistic platform making possible multivalent approaches and different degrees of engagement. Each initiative frames participation in multiple ways. For example, DAPU sets up an educational platform that produces art objects that can be sold; the outcome of this process gives some of the participants the opportunity to purchase a means of transportation. This purchase can be customized, and the customization of the tricycles is a main asset in the achievement of DAPU's goals of self-encouragement and public awareness. The customization is normally followed by public demonstrations. This chain of events, which can be operated in several different ways, is fully controlled by the participants.

In that sense, although a first look at both projects could identify them as socially engaged art projects addressing a preexisting community of participants, the reality is far more complex and relates to the public role that collaborative creativity often assumes. A first glance at both projects would locate them on the side of tangible acts of solidarity motivated by acute and practical social urgencies. Under that logic, their aesthetic side would be very much based on sharing a biopolitical condition of exclusion from the public sphere. However, that would not take account of many of the factors operating in the specific context in which they take place. In particular, it would fail to understand how the two projects frame both the subjectivity of their participants and the agencies put into play in strategic and performative rather than essentialist terms. Similarly, categorizing them according to a simple "aesthetics versus politics" antithesis would mean losing sight of the existence of complex negotiations—aesthetic as well as social—within the conceptualization and the internal dynamics of both projects. In both initiatives, subjectivity is not something essential (derived from being a person with a disability or experiencing a situation of HIV personally or through a family member or close friend). On the contrary, it implies self-definition, performance, external recognition, and economics.

Interlude I: Locating Socially Engaged Art in Africa

Economics and nonrepresentational artistic agency have always been central concerns in contemporary African art. In the last decade, however, there has been an unprecedented renovation of institutional and collaborative practices. The creation of "power stations" (as Koyo Kouoh [2013: 17] refers to African institutional and collaborative initiatives) is increasingly inserting artistic practice into discussions of elements as important as civil society, autonomy, and urban gentrification. Above all, contemporary African art has shown a coevality with the main concerns of the continent. This causes a rupture with the construction of an external gaze on African reality detached from the contexts of production and engagement. Discussions about the "invented" nature of African art (Mudimbe 1988[12]) and its commoditization (Appiah 1991;

Oguibe and Enwezor 1999) have been central to the development of critical thought and practice on Africa, especially since *Magiciens de la terre*. Projects such as Batale's and Nabulime's show a direct connection with the everyday reality of the participants in both initiatives. Terry Smith identified heterogeneity, collaboration, and coevality as the three major challenges present in contemporaneity. In that sense, he urges us to "picture all of the worlds in which we live in their real relation to each other; work together to create and sustain a viable sense of place for each of us; [and] establish and maintain coeval connectivity between worlds and places" (Smith 2016: 3). In our two projects, those three elements converge: the proximity between artists and participants is not only thematic; rather, it affects engagement and the temporal proximity between process and product.

In 2013, the Equatoguinean curator Elvira Dyangani Ose interrogated the recent emergence of collaborative practices in Africa with a pressing set of questions that supersedes the quest for identity and national relevance. It is worth quoting her at length: "For contemporary artists working today, the questions might now be: What does it mean to produce knowledge from a specific territory? How do artistic experiences produce new forms of counter culture or inform new urban solutions? What determines the success or failure of this kind of project? And, as in many of these cases where continuity and self-sustainability are unachievable outcomes, how does one rally against this to make the temporal experience develop into a permanent structure that at the same time would permit certain African actors to exercise their ability to live simultaneously in multiple temporalities?" (Ose 2013: 118). Also addressing that turn, Euridice Kala characterizes the pioneering production of the Cameroonian artist Goddy Leye as a "reflective and action-prone work in which the artist sprang between intense spaces for reflection—and spaces for action—across widening geographies" (Kala 2014: 8). She adds something crucial: "By acknowledging that African art practice could be an ephemeral continuum of thought, rather than a halted representation of African narratives, Leye may have positioned himself in a space that rendered object-based art a passive way to engage with contemporary ideas, a way which removed the responsibility from the artist to challenge concepts and ideas just by allocating value to the aesthesis. A way, thus, removed from representations of the African narrative" (8).

Ose and Kala's remarks show the centrality of processes of mobility and active transformation within the African space. They also evince the criticality of local operational contexts in the definition of African contemporaneity, something that challenges the role traditionally played by metropolitan art scenes in the definition and commodification of African discourses. The practices grouped here under the umbrella term of the *boda* moment can be seen as directly answering this shift. As we will see, this transformation also introduces an alternative temporal conceptualization of creative practice.

v

Political struggle, Stavros Stavrides argues, is a matter of the everyday (Stavrides 2013, 2016). To a great extent, the transformative potential of the initiatives developed by DAPU and Nabulime is based on social exchanges taking place in that day-to-day dimension. Both projects operate in the realm of the quotidian, on a sustained basis, bringing interesting consequences for their practice. It is precisely through questioning the social pertinence of public artistic practice against the backdrop of increasing marketization and transnational exchanges that initiatives such as DAPU and Nabulime define their "horizon of intelligibility." This permanent concern with central, everyday issues in both projects arises from adapting tactics of activism to the present needs. In a well-known essay, Brian Holmes (2007) writes that "a territory of art appears within widening 'underground' circles, where the aesthetics of everyday practice is considered a political issue." Not that that territory is without conflicts. Speaking from Kenya, Ory Okolloh—herself an entrepreneur—points out the potential dangers of romanticizing cultural entrepreneurship as a response to structural situations of economic instability. For her, the increasing praise of cultural entrepreneurship runs the risk of masking the weight and the violence of neoliberal intervention in the Eastern Africa region; it could also conceal the dependence of local initiatives on transnational capital (Okolloh 2015; C. Thompson 2014). The two projects analyzed in this chapter reject spectacular actions and temporary initiatives, developing long-term collaborations in contrast to (but not in total contradiction with) the nature of cultural festivals. In KLA ART 2014, for example, DAPU was the only part of the *boda boda* exhibition that produced a permanent engagement. The customization of the vehicle also triggered a reaction among the participant members: many who did not participate also began to customize their tricycles. In that sense, the action operated in the fields of "high art," urban creativity, and amateurism, effectively blurring them. This blurring also affects the material results of the gatherings. These include "conventional art objects," public performances, and actions of collective creativity. For example, most people who join DAPU have no education or previous interest in art making. Although the project operates by giving those people skills so that art can contribute effectively to their personal economies, the act of teaching operates here in multiple ways: it is horizontal; it includes experimentation; it does not end with the production of artworks; and its emotional consequences are as important as its economic ones. Skilling is paired with a multidisciplinary approach and paradoxically simultaneously leads to despecialization.[13] Holmes establishes four elements for contemporary social movements. As it is no longer possible to operate in the ivory towers that constituted professions and academic disciplines, those movements, Holmes argues, are forced into an expanded field where critical research, "commitment to both representation and lived experience," networking, and self-organization are framed together (Holmes 2012: 73). Those four elements intertwine effectively in DAPU. Flexibility is opposed to a much reduced artistic milieu frequented by connoisseurs; experience counters the marketable focus of exhibition making, immediacy, and art selling; and skilling and despecializing challenge the restrictions of public academic artistic education, as well as the economic dependence of many cultural projects.

Interlude II: The Makerere Moment

The fieldwork for this chapter was done at a very particular time, marked by the most prolonged strike in recent times at Uganda's (and East Africa's) main educational institution, Makerere University. After years of protests against budget cuts, national oversight of public education, and rigidness in the payment of tuition fees and salary arrears, in April 2016 the demonstrations intensified, resulting in continuous police intervention and student arrests. This situation culminated in November 2016, when President Yoweri Museveni ordered the closure of the university, which was reopened on January 2. In this situation, professors and students were locked up in the university buildings, and classes suspended. It was in this context that I met the Makerere Art School staff in November 2016.

Strikes are common in Makerere's history. The university has been an active platform for social struggles since independence, combining critical thought with a constant review of the potential threat to public education. Founded in 1921 under the Protectorate rule, the University of Makerere soon became East Africa's main institution of higher education. The university was founded for a variety of reasons, among them the consolidation of British power in the region and the fear that the foreign education of Ugandans could bring dangerous ideologies to the territory (Kyeyune 2003: 38). Makerere was essential in fueling the debates on artistic modernity in the context of Uganda and Eastern Africa. Since 1937, when Margaret Trowell founded the first art programs with the intention of bringing "local" ideas and creative expression together, the university was a cauldron of theoretical discussions as well as a locus of artistic creativity. George Kyeyune argues, "[Trowell] believed that Africans had a kind of aesthetic intuition peculiar to themselves: an innate artistic imagination, which was radically different from that of Europe" (2003: 42). It was Makerere's mission, Trowell believed, to adapt this innate potential to the contemporary situation of the territory. The main debates held at the art school therefore revolved around the applicability of modernism to the Ugandan art scene. Whereas Trowell and some of her disciples defended the indigenization of artistic practice, other figures central to the development of Ugandan art, including Cecil Todd (director of the art school since 1958) and Gregory Maloba, argued that only by including modernity in the dialogue would it be possible to engage Uganda's shifting contemporaneity. Those debates were not just a theoretical aesthetical consideration; on the contrary, behind them lay an interest in making artistic practice "meaningful to the African" (Kyeyune 2003: 24). This implied recovering and promoting many nonfigurative and nonrepresentational practices, such as dance, drama, and music, attempting, in Trowell's words, to "[consider] the aesthetic, emotional response to life of ordinary man."[14] The history of Ugandan contemporary art was largely shaped by those debates, which, it should be stressed, were not merely academic discussions. On the contrary, they were directly embedded in the political climate of the moment, marked by the decolonization of Africa, national independence, and the emergence of neocolonialism. *Transition* was a direct consequence of that alliance between critical thinking and political action.

In 1961, Rajat Neogy, then a lecturer at Makerere, founded the journal *Transition* in Kampala. Like other publications emerging around the same time, for example, *Présence Africaine* or *Black Orfeus*, *Transition* emerged out of a belief in the role that culture should play in achieving independence. These, Neogy writes, were times "when idealism and action merge with various degrees of success" (Neogy 1961: 2). This interest in action and anticolonial praxis was present from the inception of the journal, accompanied by a process of "testing intellectual and other preconceptions" as well as "thoughtful and creative contributions in all spheres" (2). Although the project emerges in cultural terms (a preoccupation with "what is an East African culture" closes this introductory remark), in the context of a Kampala at the gates of independence, "culture" could hardly be understood as a contemplative, segregated milieu. The provocative tone of many of the articles published in *Transition* reflected a crucial moment for the configuration of independent Africa.[15] *Transition* was conceived of as an expansive tool, intended to have an impact on the field of politics and anticolonial struggle. Stressing its links with the African political and intellectual avant-garde, Cédric Vincent (2013: 42) demonstrates how figures such as Wole Soyinka, Ngugi wa Thiong'o, Chinua Achebe, and Julius Nyerere were actively involved in the publication, and also emphasizes that *Transition* was identified "as the Black Orpheus of East Africa." Vincent also stresses the journal's interdisciplinary approach to present-day reality, pointing out how "it became capable of providing a broad forum that went against the current of debates on immediate problems and fundamental questions that are almost always confined to communication in a limited, closed circuit of insiders and partisans" (5).

This editorial standpoint, a mixture of commitment to the everyday life of the colonial and postcolonial situation of Uganda and East Africa and an experimental understanding of culture, fermented a critical and noncelebratory questioning of the role that speculative theory should play in the configuration of a postcolonial citizenry and public sphere. *Transition*'s "nuanced commitment" to practice and action remained present in the Ugandan cultural milieu during the 1970s, although it was highly threatened by the violence and censorship enacted during the Obote and Amin regimes. Neogy was incarcerated in 1967 and exiled to Ghana in 1969. In 1972, the project faced a decisive change when it was moved to London, where it was published as *Ch'indaba* under the direction of Wole Soyinka. In Uganda, the situation was marked by censorship and political violence, something especially evident at Makerere during the dictatorship. The 1970s also introduced an interest in experimenting with new materials and creative techniques that, in addition to formal innovation, brought a more nuanced relationship with the local reality, stressing, as George Kyeyune argued, "[a better adaptation] to economies of scarcity" (Kyeyune 2003: 5). The arrival of "political normality" and "stability" after the election of Museveni in 1986 placed Makerere in a new situation, where it would compete with the increasing weight of neoliberal investments and the private educational sector. This was the situation played out in the 2016 strikes.

The history of the university, as well as its centrality in the context of Ugandan civil society, sheds more than a little light on the practices discussed in this chapter. In some respects, the KLA ART festivals, as well as Nabulime's and Batale's collaborative initiatives, represent a continuation of the interest in exploring new methods of dealing with the political in ways that could be relevant to society. At the same time, however, they are a reaction against the consequence of academic education in the configuration of a restricted art environment. They also represent a decisive shift of the spaces in which the political is framed, spaces that go beyond these of the "culturally sanctioned" university and art gallery, therefore affecting the quagmire of the urban day-to-day. The recent strikes have brought back the importance of testing the limits of academia and its impact on society, on this occasion in relation to the loss of relevance of public education against the backdrop of a fierce modernization and the instrumentalization and privatization of culture.[16] In this context, artistic collaboration emerges as a crucial tool for testing how cultural practices can engage the fault lines of economic modernization and political stagnation.

VI

For Lilian Mary Nabulime and Fred Batale, operating on those fault lines involves challenging the locus and unidirectionality of power relations set into motion by the Ugandan cultural milieu. Borrowing the potential of informal chains of knowledge and affect, they also negotiate with "official" frameworks such as art spaces, cultural festivals, and, in the case of Nabulime, health infrastructures and religious institutions. One recurring question arising in my conversations with Nabulime and Batale concerned the suitability of using art to address the concerns they are dealing with. If many of their "audiences" are not familiar with art, why not just engage those communities, and leave artistic creativity aside? Their answers to my question show the utility of artistic collaboration in acting as mediator across different spaces and formal and informal structures. Throughout my conversations with Batale, another recurrent element, in addition to the immediate attainment of pragmatic ends, was the importance of art for achieving a critical self-awareness. DAPU tackles directly issues of precariousness, social and urban exclusion, and marginality. Those issues, importantly enough, exist alongside a challenge to the definition of utility and disposability from a personal and social perspective. DAPU's workshops are intended to develop economic tools of sustainability and improve the participants' self-image in a context where people with disabilities are stigmatized. Such social pressure, however, is not addressed in a referential way, as something that must be denounced; rather it is defined as a decisive field in which the agency of people with disability can function. It is conceived of not as a burden but as a challenge. In the case of Nabulime, we saw how her incursion into "social sculpture" was the result of a process of trial and error in which formal perfection walked hand in hand with an improvement in the intelligibility and communicational capacity of the project. The interconnection of social awareness and personal consciousness is also remarkable here.[17] It is symptomatic that our two projects do not address "nationally-sanctioned important issues" but rather operate in the margins of what is left to one side both by modernization and informal economies. DAPU acts at the fractures of the urban reconfiguration of Kampala developed through both official and informal means.

Similarly, Nabulime challenges the logic of urban space as the only place of struggle, developing a complex field of action. Her HIV/AIDS sculptures disperse the focus of cultural practices in urban spaces and contexts, pointing to the heterogeneity of the population linked to the epidemic. Jean and John Comaroff (2012: 67) used the term "ID-ology" to refer to a similar experience in which "political personhood [is lived as] a fractured, fractal experience,"[18] in tension between an increasingly normative notion of national citizenship (a "grounding of citizenship in the jural" [78]) and an economically conditioned ethnoidentitary condition. Considering the case of South Africa, they argue that this duality is shaping "a new popular politics [that] is catching flame as older struggles—under the signs of class, race and partisan ideology—fade away" (88). Looking at Brazil, João Biehl also pointed at the corrosive character of economic power when channeled into the invisibilization and disposability of segments of the population within the borders of the nation-state. Biehl looks at "the ways in which social destinies of the poorest and the sickest are ordered" (Biehl 2001: 136).[19]

In the case of Uganda, AIDS centers a landscape where foreign economic intervention, ethnic and religious divisions, and uneven modernization have a direct impact on the vulnerability of specific sectors of the population, affecting illiterate women in particular. In deciding to work with those sectors, Nabulime points at the hidden mechanisms (both "official" and "communitarian") reinforcing that segmentation. In both cases, we see how there is a transposition among economies of care, affect, and (self-)recognition in the urban landscape. This introduces a novelty into the political tone of former generations of Ugandan artists, who were traditionally oriented toward the discussion of issues more easily perceived as having "national interest."

Both DAPU and Nabulime are immersed in those debates; but this proximity operates in both cases by expanding the fields of political agency, and by mediating across the instances of community awareness, individual polarization, cultural criticism, and collective decision making.[20] The sphere of action of both projects is located at the crossroads of those four dimensions. The sense of estrangement from the field of "contemporary art" also places both projects closer to the body of Ugandan cultural practices and policies. Indeed, collaborative practices and public art festivals have brought many newcomers to the restricted terrain of the Ugandan art scene. National art history was built mostly from an academic (and, we must add, Makerere-centric) point of view;[21] this was a natural consequence of the country's political and cultural evolution (Kyeyune 2008). The processes analyzed in this chapter challenge that centrality, not just because of their externality vis-à-vis that system but also because of their inassimilable condition, which makes it impossible to characterize any reduction of the collective exchanges triggered by Batale and Nabulime as specific, singularized interventions or artistic creations. Newcomers, Stavros Stavrides argues *through* Jacques Rancière, are "those who were "unaccounted for" (Stavrides 2013: 47). It is symptomatic that the success of the "public" side of KLA ART was not anticipated. Rather, the attention that experiences such as the Boda Boda Project received were the result of an unexpected positive response from an audience that greatly overtook that of exhibitions and other artistic activities. That success was thus very much the result of the multiplicity and the originality of the participants, the audience, and the festivals themselves.

VII

The artistic initiatives developed by Nabulime and Batale reject any deferment of their capacity for action. What is more important, they are resistant to the divorce between the moment of practice, the heterogeneity of the participants involved in that practice, and any later theoretical or representative resolution. It is true that both projects have "a face," a representative side that is articulated in multiple ways when they interact with cultural agents (for example, in their participation in the KLA ART festivals), or when they negotiate their position between the local scenario in which they operate and the transnational arena to which they are linked.[22] We have seen, however, how this translatability does not mean a deferral or a simplification. DAPU's activity can be seen as a concatenation of initiatives and forces working together, sometimes toward a shared end, but also affecting the ways in which each individual conceives their own relationship with the urban environment of Kampala as political. In this sense, the internal tensions within the project reflect not only the malleability of the project's collective agency but also the heterogeneity of the political voice behind those actions. Dealing with the commons in the context of contemporary cities, Stavrides points out that "political subjectivation through communing is characterized by the rise of new collective subjects which are inherently multiple and which escape from the dominant classifications of political actions" (Stavrides 2013: 45). This especially applies here.

In a similar way, the outcome of Nabulime's practice that we can define as "more aesthetical" (e.g., the production of sculptures) is indeed a middle step within a larger chain of actions and consequences that include the production of dialogue, the manufacture of sculptures, their consumption and display (both within and outside the art world), and the insertion of HIV/AIDS awareness into an expanded field of action and discussion. The multiplicity of the effects triggered by the project is as important as the relationality and horizontality of all those aspects. The link between representational issues and behavioral elements is crucial for understanding the potential of social practice in the Ugandan context. In these two examples, artistic production is directly embedded in the intervention of the behavioral. The artists or project coordinators are the facilitators of this intervention but in no way determine it. On the contrary, the role of each project role has more to do with activating a reaction from the participants than with portraying or controlling it.

Equally interesting is the way that both initiatives intervene in a space where the consequences of the continuity of colonial situations of marginalization and political violence are fully felt. Rather than expose "the consequences of" the expulsion of a great part of the citizenry from the public space, they operate from within that excluded citizenry, articulating a dialogue that would otherwise be impossible. This element establishes a link with activist and politically committed forms of insurgence in the past: both *Transition* and Makerere attempted to intervene in the not-so-evident policies of segregation and exclusion in the time of the transition from colony to postcolony; now contemporary Ugandan social practice updates and diversifies this concern. It does so by highlighting the continuities between colonial and postcolonial exclusionary policies; by placing issues of mobility and "factual" difference at the center of the cultural debates; by connecting those issues with more abstract (but not more harmless) issues of gender violence, social acceptance, self-identification, and entitlement to the city; and, finally, by inserting politically charged collective agency into the everydayness of social struggle. Furthermore, both projects evidence how African social practice is transected by the contradictions of the encounters of neoliberalism, modernization, and cultural recognition, in itself not subsumable to a single postcolonial national identity *nor reduced to absolute pluralism and an institutional vacuum.*

A final key dimension for understanding both projects is autonomy. The need for help and development has always been troubling for African artistic initiatives. Working from a difficult position, DAPU turns this around: the project's emphasis is on the capacity of a group of individuals to produce their own means in a sustainable way. Constant engagement and creativity do not conflict with economic self-organization. DAPU achieves its objectives not by applying a recipe, a unique mode of empowerment, but also by offering a broad set of tools from which participants can choose. Each participant can attain individual ways of sustainability and develop their creativity in the ways they want. In that sense, there is a strong component of inspirational influence, of the capacity of "ripple[ing] into extra-artistic institutions and practices," to borrow Doris Sommer's words (Sommer 2014: 7). The project as a whole also pursues this autonomy, unlike NGOs, which normally pursue a cause and work toward achieving a goal. In this case action is conceived of as cyclical and fragmented, and the participants are able to not only join initiatives but develop independent actions and create new solidarities. DAPU's goal is not to "help" individuals but to articulate individual and collective action in effective and innovative ways.

6

◆ ◆ ◆

ART AND POLITICS IN TIMES OF REFORM

The Collective and the Contemporary in Indonesia

In September 1999, the recently appointed Indonesian President Bacharuddin Jusuf Habibie delivered a speech in response to the "unrest" East Timor was then undergoing. The presidential discourse justified the Indonesian occupation of the former Portuguese colony on the grounds of strengthening democracy in the country and consolidating the "rule of law" throughout the Indonesian archipelago. As "stability" is one of the words that appears most frequently in Habibie's speech, the tone and content contrast dramatically with the turbulent situation that the Indonesian military intervention in East Timor would unleash. In addition to this, the tone of the discourse evidences the Reformasi conception of politics, which marked the self-declared entrance of Indonesia into a radically new epoch.

The government of Habibie followed, and in some way continued, the thirty-one-year-long dictatorship of Soeharto, also known as the New Order period. The term "Reformasi" (reform) is used in Indonesia to refer to the years subsequent to Soeharto's removal from power in 1998. Speeches such as the one dealing with East Timor officially sanctioned an image of trust and modernization that would imply an updated notion of national identity, overcoming the burden of colonialism and dictatorship and providing a solution to the complex entanglement of ethnic and cultural identities that constitute modern-day Indonesia. At the same time, however, the similarity between the official call for "stability" and the "rule of law," and the almost clinical neutrality of the terminology justifying the military genocide of the 1980s in East Timor during dictatorial times, when enforced starvation and massive killings were publicized under the banner of "national security" by the dictatorial Soeharto regime, hardly passes unnoticed. When viewed together, the time frame of the Reformasi, its calling for a new democratic present and a future outside colonization and dictatorship, are drastically and dramatically called into question.

Compare this discourse with two visual productions that emerged around the same time in Java. The first, *Multicultural State Hegemony*, is a collectively produced poster. The second represents a public artwork titled *Sakit berlanjut* (Ongoing illness) and consists of satirical cardboard figures publicly displayed. Both images are relevant for their capacity to capture many of the darkest aspects of the Reformasi: the relationship between modernization and militarization; the inability to determine the exact nature of the "illnesses" affecting Indonesian society (despite knowing only too well their effects on everyday life); the continuity of political corruption and nepotism within a democratic, multiparty political system; and the harnessing of religious difference to uncover political and military violence and genocidal politics.[1]

In *Multicultural State Hegemony*, the media appear as a stultifying instrument of propaganda and entertainment leading to the enrichment of the few while the many are condemned to uneven competition within a degraded, modernized, dystopia-like environment. Presiding over the scene, the poster shows the silent approval of international organizations such as the World Monetary Fund. *Multicultural State Hegemony* suggests a sense of continuity and despair, pointing out how three of the main pillars of the Soeharto regime—militarism, the encouragement of foreign investment, and the strategic (mis)use of racial difference and religion as symbols of chaos and unrest—remain alive. On the whole, the message is clear: despite the democratic appearance of the Reformasi, dictatorial and neocolonial power dynamics are far from over. For its part, *Ongoing Illness* depicts the newly rebranded society as one incapable of overcoming the diseases of the past; it not only contradicts the principles of the cultural and political imagination implicit in the discourse inaugurating the Reformasi one by one; it also declares that, despite the image of renovation and reform, the ground upon which colonialism and dictatorship were built remains untouched.[2] Altogether, both artworks declare newness as a distraction silencing the burden of continuing problems. Finally, they make evident the degree to which artistic creativity is itself enmeshed in the continuities between the narrow group of privileged people that would benefit from the so-called democratization of the country, and the configuration of an elitist society that is supposedly open and democratic but is in fact closed for many.

In addition to discussing similar topics, both artistic projects have something else in common: being collaboratively produced. *Ongoing Illness* was the first intervention of the Yogyakarta-based collective Apotik Komic (Comic Pharmacy), created in 1997. *Multicultural State Hegemony* is part of the creative interventions that the collective Taring Padi (Rice Fang), founded in 1998, dedicated to the long-lasting legacy of dictatorship and colonialism in Indonesia. Whereas both examples are significant because of their capacity to highlight the continuities between past and present repressive politics, their singularity resides in their capacity to also repurpose the legacy of progressive action, to adapt this legacy to modern challenges, and, finally, to do it collectively (see figure 6.1).[3]

How to make art in times such as those? What can we learn from those two examples, which seem to state that the worst danger lies in the belief that problems from the past have ended? The Reformasi placed Indonesian artists in a difficult and contradictory situation: on one hand, formal democracy supposedly brought freedom of expression; on the other, it blurred the target of sociopolitical criticism: as the Soeharto dictatorship officially ended, from then on it became more difficult to

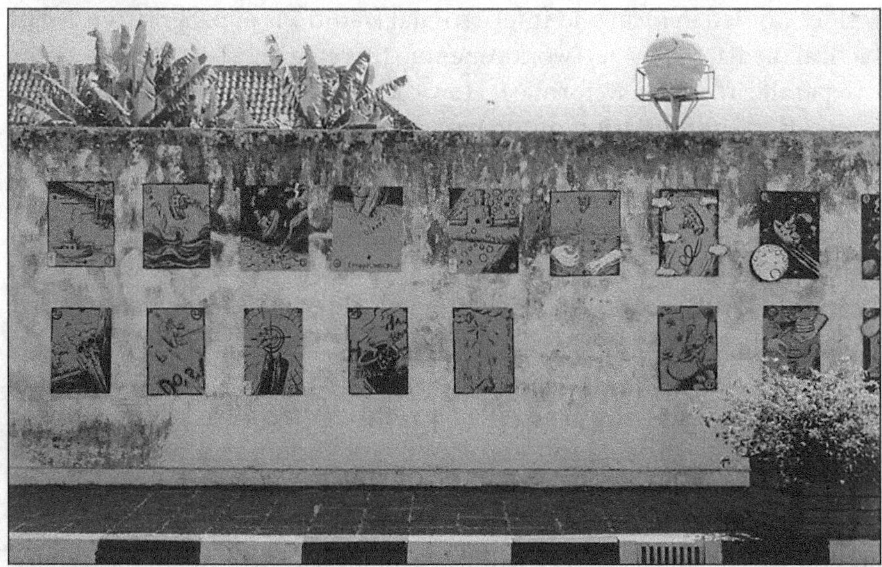

Figure 6.1. Apotik Komik, *Sakit Berlanjut*, 1999. *Source*: Courtesy of Indonesian Visual Arts Archive (IVAA).

identify "the enemy," to track the causes and consequences of political and economic power. The consequences of the economic crises that were felt in Indonesia and in Southeast Asia by the end of the twentieth century in the form of increasing socioeconomic inequalities added an element of uncertainty about the near future, motivating economic and political criticism. At the same time, the expansion of the art market and the internationalization of Indonesian art made it easier than ever to export art that was critical of the country's sociopolitical situation, thus forcing artists to explore alternative paths besides the representation of the political class and the pains and difficulties of subaltern groups.[4] The overabundance of politically charged art and the reintroduction of ideology within art debates matched the consolidation of a market-driven economy and the alleged normalization of democratic governance through a multiparty parliamentary system. To complete the picture, the increasing international attention focused on Indonesia after 1998 permitted the emergence of cultural products ready to be consumed within an international arena, in music and film festivals and artistic biennials, but was also key in the dissemination via television and Internet of global cultural references that would be essential in the establishment of underground networks and groups.[5]

But if the political and cultural imagery that inaugurates the Reformasi can be read in terms of continuities with the past, where does the novelty of collaborative actions, such as the ones behind our early examples, reside? Rooted in local and international traditions of progressive, leftist tactical media, the two artworks opening this chapter are at the same time inseparable from the Reformasi. How then should we interpret them? As a revivalist appropriation of the past to denounce the continuities of its contradictions in the present? As part of an epochal imagination? As a tentative experiment emerging from the threshold that the first years of democracy represented? From where, and more specifically from which temporality, do they confront us?

Indonesian modern and contemporary art has often been explained as particularly affected by sociopolitical criticism. "Political art" is seen by recognized critics and curators such as Jim Supangkat (1997) or Agung Hujatnikajennong (2009, 2014) as a common trend running through the history of modern and contemporary Indonesian art. However, this focus on politics and direct criticism, as Caroline Turner argues, coexisted with a no less intense and persistent principle of freedom and autonomy.[6] In this chapter, I will try to demonstrate how this search for freedom and affirmative action worked side by side with the development of collaborative strategies and the will by many artists to merge artistic activity within the everyday struggles of the Indonesian people, the *rakyat*. In addition to dealing with issues of cultural identity and political criticism, Indonesian modern and contemporary art also employs artistic collaboration to deal with issues of creative labor and class inequalities.[7] This applies equally to the action of collectives such as Taring Padi and Apotik Komic, and to the individual actions of contemporary artists who in the 1990s frequently resorted to collaborative strategies, such as Tisna Sanjaya, Moelyono, Dadang Chrisanto, and Arahmaiani. Those strategies involved practical engagement with the here and now of many communities.[8]

One of the major shifts brought about in the Suharto era consisted in a normalization of a mode of art criticism prioritizing individual artists, aesthetic criteria, and debates on Indonesian national identity over collaborative and participative creative processes (Arbuckle 2000: 9). By looking at collaborative practices, I aim to understand Indonesian artistic collectivism as a long-lasting tradition challenging individualistic, market-oriented creativity and enabling sociopolitical action in fertile, original ways. The aesthetics debates that impelled many Indonesian artists to combat colonialism, elitism, and state oppression were supported by an interest in translating radical positionings (in more or less successful terms) into socially meaningful action; the discussions of style hid dense and complex considerations on how to best serve the interests of the masses of the recently created postcolonial nation. To assess how artistic collaboration and social engagement were increasingly practiced in the difficult context of transition of the late 1990s and early 2000s, I will examine the experience of several cooperative projects, including Taring Padi, ruangrupa, Ruang MES56, and Kunci. Quite different in objectives and strategies, the action of these projects reveals that there was not a unique way of dealing with the sociopolitical configuration that followed the Reformasi period. "Collaboration" means something completely different in each of these cases, and this variety, I would say, arises not so much as a contradiction but rather as a confirmation that when it comes to socially engaged art, practice and trial-and-error strategies are as important as ideas and ideological positioning.

Taring Padi

The People Oriented Culture Taring Padi (Lembaga Budaya Kerakyatan Taring Padi in Bahasa), which is responsible for the poster that opened this chapter, was created in Yogyakarta months before President Soeharto gave up power.[9] A few months later, Taring Padi gained national attention and received increasing requests to include woodcut and cardboard banners such as *Multicultural State Hegemony* in protest campaigns led by human rights, environmental, and anticorruption associations. The result of each of those collaborations is not only a physical piece of public art but also a collective process of production and decision making that includes the discussion of hot political issues and choosing the theme of each poster, as well as design, coloring, and polishing up the final work. Although some steps of this process are produced individually (such as design sketching in the most difficult cases), the outcome is collective. Taring Padi's symbols—a rice sprig, a star, and a cogwheel—are the only marks of authorship the poster bears.[10]

Taring Padi is one of the most original collectives to emerge in late 1990s Indonesia. At the same time, its activity incorporates and redefines elements of the left and anticolonial tradition in Indonesia. This is evident at many ways, including the place Taring Padi uses as its hub. Soon after its creation, the collective occupied the headquarters of the Indonesian Academy of Fine Arts (Akademi Seni Rupa Indonesia, ASRI) in Yogyakarta. ASRI was widely known for being a cauldron of progressive politics and engagement with popular segments of the population. Taring Padi sought to continue this tradition not only through collective art but also by radically transforming the occupied academic campus into a productive pedagogical platform for radical popular democracy. Many of the original members of Taring Padi were young students connected to art and the creative disciplines. For many younger people inside and outside the university, Taring Padi's move into the ASRI campus in Gampingan provided an alternative space for learning and socialization, "a gathering place, an area where one shares a living and forges friendship," in the words of Dolorosa Sinaga (2011: 24). Those gatherings lasted for years, sometimes without a specific purpose, developing an informal and open-to-all dynamic of sharing and "thinking through doing" that attracted a community much larger than that of contemporary art-goers in Yogyakarta.

Heidi Leanne Arbuckle, who has examined the evolution of Taring Padi in detail, depicts the position of the collective within the art panorama of the post-Suharto era as a complex one. She warns about oversimplifying the Indonesian art scene by distinguishing between gallery-oriented and public art (2000: 59). Arbuckle points out that sometimes the collective was often intentionally curated out of exhibitions and cultural programs. In other cases, the reactions were more ambivalent, leading to the invitation of the collective to humanitarian or social events by virtue of its capacity to attract large sectors of the population and provoke massive, spectacular public mobilization. The position the collective occupies in the Indonesian contemporary art scene is thus permeated by the new spirit of democratization brought about by the Reformasi; yet this influence is contradictory and ambivalent. While on some occasions this has led to uncritical (both positive and negative) appreciations of the "radicality" of the collective, Taring Padi's evolution is in fact the result of a subtler ideological negotiation within the supposedly tolerant cultural atmosphere of post-Suharto Indonesia. This ambiguous, sometimes uncomfortable position, Leanne Arbuckle affirms, "is reflective of the contentious position the Left holds within post-Suharto Indonesia. 'Ideology' continues to imbue debates within the art community, and has become a point of contention within the Yogyakarta arts scene" (45).

Taring Padi's first steps clearly indicate the importance of ideology in the supposedly de-ideologized transition of the Reformasi. The collective produced posters and urban interventions announcing that the country's transition into democracy in fact involved a neo-imperialist move through economic control. They differentiated between party electoral democracy, which allowed the continuation of corruption and military violence, and popular democracy, which is understood as an unfinished project to mobilize anticolonial and antiauthoritarian politics and achieve radical equality and social transformation. Under the umbrella of "democratization," Taring Padi argued, popular democracy was once again deferred and excluded from political priorities in spite of the appearance of popular participation and the closure of the dictatorship period.

The commitment to achieving radical, popular democracy is omnipresent in Taring Padi's banners and woodcut posters. If we look, for example, at the series the collective produced on the occasion of the 1999 elections, the first democratic elections to be held after the 1965 coup, Taring Padi's interest in revealing the continuities between the New Order period and the Reformasi becomes evident. The powerful are often represented as animals or skeletons oppressing the *rakyat* through military violence and economic profit. In turn, the *rakyat* is often represented in those works as a diverse and heterogeneous social body. Women and men, old and young, Muslims, Hindus, and Catholics are usually depicted together but differentiated in the demonstrations represented in the posters. Messages of unity and universal humanism are also commonly joined by different religious or ethnic characters.

A first impression those images might give us the idea that Taring Padi simply reproduces well-intentioned messages of global harmony and multicultural understanding among different ethnicities and religions.

However, diversity operates here at a much more intentional level. The messages of unity, humanism, and harmony can be seen as a direct response to the New Order politicization of difference. When dealing with Indonesian identity, it is almost compulsory to refer to the enormous diversity of cultures, religions, and groups populating the archipelago. It goes without saying that this diversity is not easy to handle. However, during the Soeharto regime what came to be known as SARA (an acronym standing for the amalgam of religion, race, ethnicity, and other group-based issues), religion and race became a common excuse for military intervention and authoritarian politics. Even the conflicts of Aceh and East Timor, which took place after the Reformasi, hinted at the logic of SARA. The result was that a blurred and narrow idea of difference was frequently mobilized strategically to prevent public discussion and ensure state control over the Indonesian society. As Myengkyo Seo, dealing with the management of religion and religious issues for political reasons, explains, "Public discussions on issues related to SARA were prohibited in order to prevent clashes sparked by SARA and to suppress any criticism of the government. Successful nation-building, in the eyes of the government, required substantial control of information about SARA, particularly where religion was concerned because of its volatility at the local and national levels" (2013: 20).

Taring Padi's iconography is particularly effective in dismantling SARA ideology. The collective denounced how power in Indonesia depends on an intricate network of local, national, and international interests. For example, in a poster headed by the slogan "Kekerasan adalah fasis" (Violence is fascist), police repression is portrayed as part of a repressive machine opposing worker's rights. Depicted in varied guises, the artwork's main characters emerge in front of a factory where the slogans "Setiap kepala mempunyai hak yang sama" (Everyone has equal rights), "Hentikan perang!" (Drop war!), and "Hentikan kekerasan terhadap buruh!" (Stop violence against workers!) center the collective mobilization. State violence takes the form of a brutal intervention at the workplace; on other occasions, the liaisons between different sources of power and control are subtler. This is the case of *Anti Udang* (Anti-debt), a poster connecting the grief of local politicians (depicted in an animal-like way [see Taring Padi 2011]), the connivance of international organizations such as the World Trade Fund or the International Monetary Fund, and the worsening of environmental conditions through industrial development, all under the acute surveillance of the national military. Posters such as these oppose the official, celebratory narrative of the Reformasi as a radical closure of dictatorial power, revealing the political and economic arrangements that allow the continuation of state violence and social inequality behind a supposedly democratic facade. They also reveal how thin the frontiers between the public and the private became at the moment of "transition" that followed the New Order, when the state invented new ways of oppressing progressive causes through corruption or privatization. A couple of final examples illustrate those connections beyond doubt: the first appeared in Taring Padi's zine *Terompet Rakyat* (People's trumpet) and refers to the intervention of militarized private militias, such as Pancasila, in labor disputes; and the second, *38 Free Seats to Oppress the People*, alludes to the excessive power the military is guaranteed in the democratic Indonesian parliament.

For Taring Padi, however, the masses are not only a recurrent motif appearing in their banners. The collective has also targeted and sided with NGOs, human rights organizations, and specific local communities to protest on issues such as environmental hazard and rampant unemployment. Although Taring Padi frequently helps in organizational matters, operating as a facilitator of dialogue and negotiation, the collective also easily adopts a position of follower and accompanier of dynamics set in motion by third forces. On some occasions, the collective joins strikes called by local workers and farmers' associations. In other cases, it uses its creative force to generate awareness and force dialogue between sectors of the *rakyat* and higher political instances, as in the case of an antipesticide mobilization in 1999, in which the tactical actions of Taring Padi lured a delegate to dialogue with local farmers (Arbuckle 2000: 83). The protest was followed by a festival in which the community created politically charged *memedi sawah*, or scarecrows. In this case, aesthetics and creative decisions were left free to anyone wishing to join the festival, and the entire process was characterized by spontaneous exchanges between the participants. The festival set out to promote the local, receding varieties of rice that are disappearing and being displaced by intensive, industrialized agriculture, but instead of adopting the form of a direct mobilization, it achieved a festive spirit through music, humor, and irony and encouraged self-reflexive creativity through the process of sculpting (see figures 6.2 and 6.3).

Episodes such as these reveal how the category of "neo-imperialism" is conceived of by the collective as much more than a descriptor of a global state of things. Instead, the idea of resisting ongoing and enduring forms of imperialism takes the concrete form of intersubjective alliances between Taring Padi and other organizations. In these cases, rhetoric is left aside in favor of technical agricultural concerns about pesticides or varieties of rice. This way of siding with the people therefore goes beyond the schematic image that a superficial approach to Taring Padi's banners could offer and reveals the collective's will to engage real and ongoing processes of impoverishment and economical intervention affecting rural and urban communities in Central Java.

As in the case of Lilian Mary Nabulime's social practice analyzed in the last chapter, these actions reveal how the rejection of "traditional" spaces of exhibition also imply a reconceptualization of the relationship between urban and rural. Taring Padi's interest in agriculture and alliances with local farmers challenges the work of those artists who take the image of the subaltern and place it in the middle- or upper-class context of the gallery space. Although this approach to rural communities was not exempt from misunderstandings by both sides of the equation, it also attempted to democratize Taring Padi's transformative capacity beyond the comfort zone of Yogyakarta and the reach of urban art audiences. Taking place right after the Reformasi, the Memedi Sawah Festival reveals the limitations of the political and social renovation brought about by the political elections, and demonstrates that many of the problems carried over from colonial to dictatorial times were still present in the form of increasing social disparities and economic disenfranchisement.

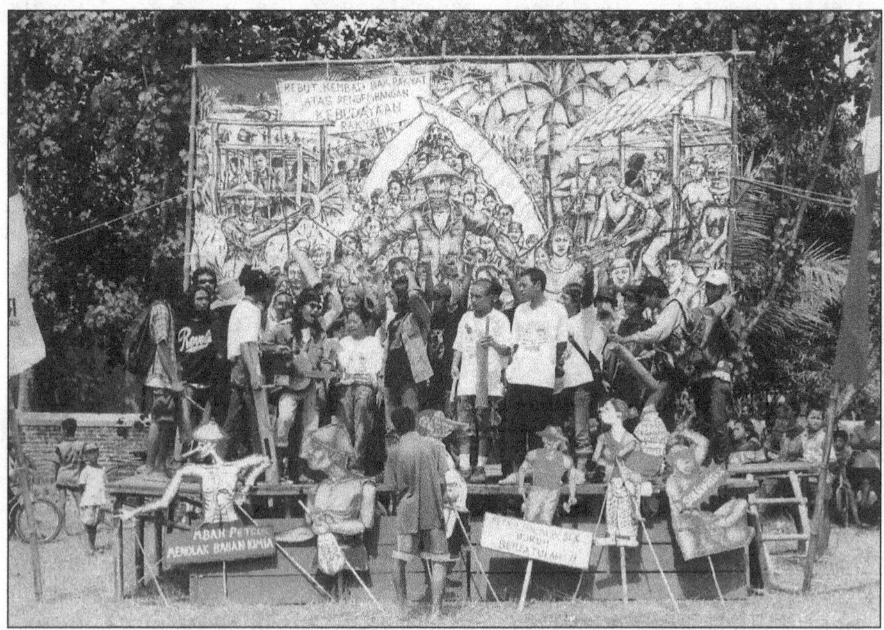

Figure 6.2. Taring Padi, Festival Memedi Sawah. *Source*: Courtesy of Indonesian Visual Arts Archive (IVAA).

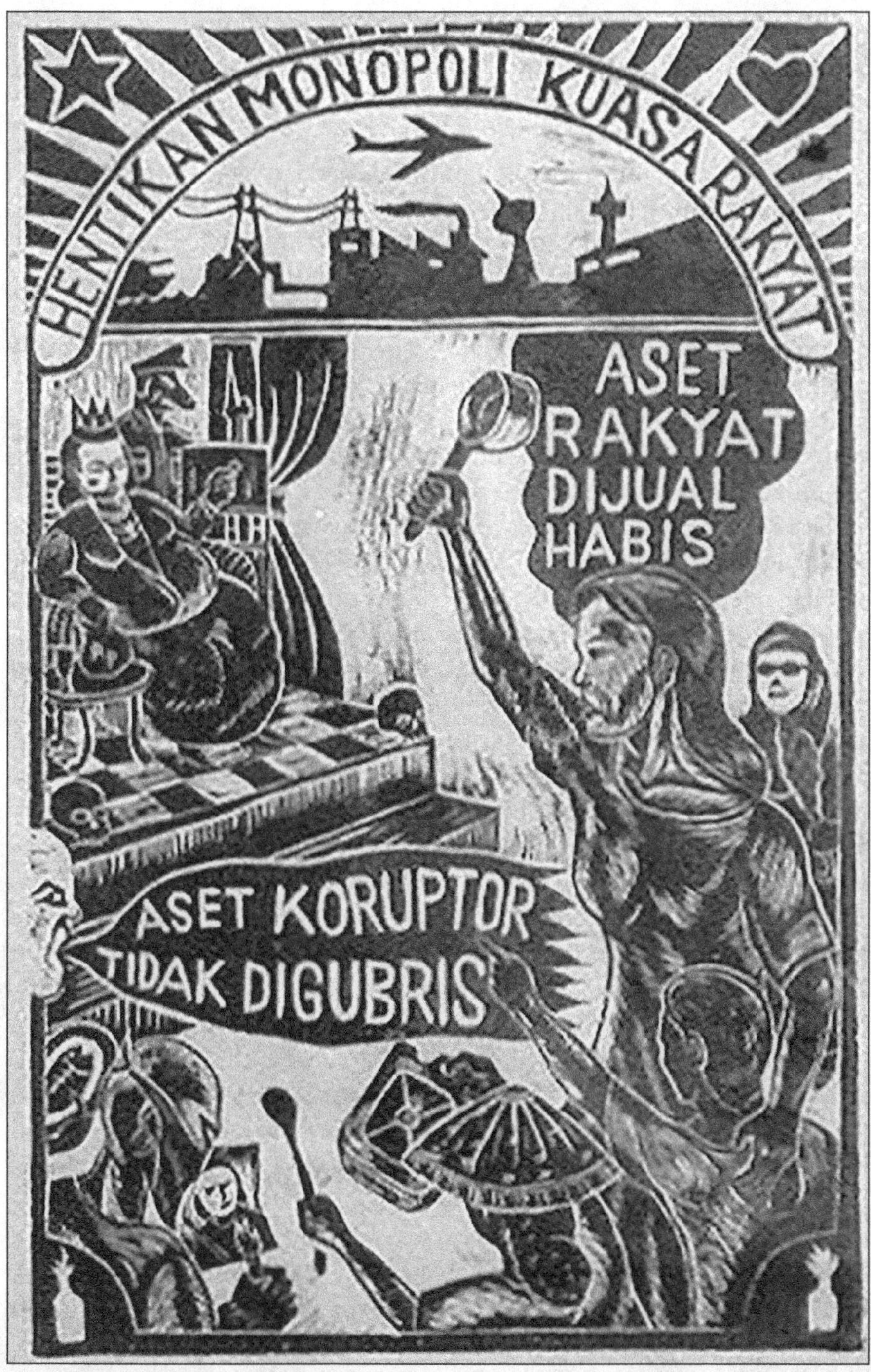

Figure 6.3. Taring Padi, *Aset Koruptor*, 2003. *Source*: Courtesy of Indonesian Visual Arts Archive (IVAA).

The festival also raises important questions about public and private accountability in the aftermath of dictatorial authoritarianism, revealing how not all Indonesians benefited from the freedom and capacity of decision that the post–New Order period supposedly brought. By taking issue with those continuities, Taring Padi made use of both present-day needs and cultural traditions to encourage local awareness of ongoing economic and environmental violence.

Two final features of Taring Padi are worth discussing in relation to the main topics of this book: the way the collective conceives its own position within the Indonesian art scene, and the way it relates to and reactivates an anticolonial ethos present in twentieth-century Indonesian radical (cultural) politics. Both features are related to Taring Padi's understanding of the power and agency of art and artists. Transferring the focus of attention from the state to the way in which it spreads and diversifies its power within private spheres in civil society is part of Taring Padi's understanding of Indonesian politics and, more specifically, of their rejection of the state as the sole framework of politics. Without delimiting the collective's position within the spectrum of Left politics, the group is particularly sympathetic to anarchist, bottom-up approaches to power and collective agency. In this respect, a member of Taring Padi argues, "We don't spend much time finding out ideologically where people come from, the farmers and other people that we work with. If they're independent and want to talk about problems, subjects of interest to us, then okay, we can get together" (Peet 2007: 122). At the same time, however, that member conceded, "I think generally we are more anarchist." This position implies accepting that the construction of a national state is not the best solution to achieve popular democracy. Combined with Taring Padi's zeal for struggling against enduring forms of coloniality, this anarchist spirit is particularly useful for pushing the horizon of the spirit of the unfinished 1945 revolution forward and up to the present, although not in a nationalist way. Taring Padi challenges the common assumption that postcolonial nationalism implied a contradiction and an overcoming of colonialism. Against this idea, the collective's focus has been on pointing out the many continuities within both political forms. In the initial manifesto signed by Taring Padi's members, the bond between nationalism, recolonization, and elitist culture is clear. After the end of colonialism, many of the obstacles for a people-oriented cultural policy remained in play, and consequently "arts development is restricted by ruling class interests" (Taring Padi 1998, quoted in Arbuckle 2000: 103). This restriction appears as an ongoing, not always evident burden that postcolonial nationalism is unable or unwilling to address. As we have seen, many of the actions developed by Taring Padi are oriented toward exposing and challenging this continuity. At the same time, Taring Padi's idea of art for change involves much more than a critique of nationalism, and takes on a positive shape. A plurality of elements and priorities are agglutinated around this view: "The Institute of People Oriented Culture Taring Padi endeavors to develop art and culture by searching for the needs of the people and prioritises: openness, social justice, people's sovereignty, fairness among generations, democracy, respect for human rights without forgoing duty, gender awareness, reformation of global relations and good management of the environment" (Taring Padi 1998, quoted in Arbuckle 2000: 104). Arbuckle directly links Taring Padi's orientation toward social justice with former collectives, such as Lembaga Kebudayaan Rakyat (Institute of People's Culture, more commonly known as LEKRA). LEKRA was an important collective operating in the 1950s in Java. It was from LEKRA that Taring Pari took the idea of *seni kerakyatan* (people-oriented art). Like Taring Padi's, LEKRA's manifesto also emphasized the idea that culture provides fertile ground for ongoing, shifting forms of colonization. It stated that "colonial culture is a weapon of the 'elite' class, which already enjoys the comforts and luxuries which are produced by the blood and sweat of the mass of the People" (LEKRA 1950, quoted in Arbuckle 2000: 100). The counterpart to the privilege of this elite was the silencing and underestimating of popular and collective forms of visual creativity: "In that way, the process of the development of a People's Culture, that is the culture of the mass of the people who represent more than 90% of the whole nation of Indonesia, will be hampered and suppressed" (LEKRA 1950, quoted in Arbuckle 2000: 100). What is important is that, for LEKRA, an elitist cultural and visual art medium (no matter which political form it took) always remains potentially a dangerous ground where new forms of elitist and colonial domination could arise, a space where "an anti-People's culture, a feudal and imperialist culture will once again rampage out of control" (LEKRA 1950, quoted in Arbuckle 2000: 100). Finally, fifty years before Taring Padi, LEKRA also identified popular democracy as the right alternative to colonialism.

Another element shared by both groups can be extrapolated from the negative criticism they received. The attacks on LEKRA categorized left-wing and *seni kerakyatan* art as vulgar (Arbuckle 2000: 42), establishing an aesthetic criterion that operated in two ways: first, those attacks partially silenced parts of the tradition of Indonesian radical and popular creativity, dismissing them as rudimentary artistic forms; second, through this reinterpretation of the past, representational and market-oriented art in the present also appeared as *the* self-evident, unique path toward contemporary art. Similarly, during the Reformasi the standards of "political art" were defined around the cornerstones of humor, irony, smart criticism of the sociopolitical situation, and ambivalence.[11] Other values, such as individual authorship, as well as the status of the artists, remained very much unchanged, something that conditioned the position of groups such as Taring Padi, with strong collaborative dynamics, within the Indonesian art scene.

For Arbuckle, Taring Padi's interest in LEKRA involves a direct criticism of the limitations of the art world during the Reformasi period. She points out that the fostering of the *seni kerakyatan* model by Taring Padi responds to the fact that the group identifies many of the diseases affecting Indonesian democracy within the art scene itself (Arbuckle 2000: 6). The "Reformasi art world," in other words, replicates and is subjected to the same limitations as the movement of reform initiated by President Habibie. Taring Padi, Arbuckle (58) explains, "is critical of 'political art' that adopts visual images of the *rakyat* and their 'anguish', while presenting work in exclusive spaces in an attempt to enlighten complacent middle-class elites and thus capitalising on 'the suffering of the Indonesian people'." The intensification of neoliberal economic policies polarized the Indonesian art scene, delimiting a small group of internationally renowned "critical artists" and a vast mass of visual creators that even lost its capacity to buy basic painting resources such as canvases and paint (hence the use of cardboard and black-and-white imagery by many collectives by the turn of the century).[12]

Taring Padi's approach to ideology also exemplifies the differences between "political art" and socially engaged art, as mentioned in the first part of this book. After Soeharto resigned, many Indonesian artists displayed politically charged work. A common feature in this production was to locate the artists as being critical of, but also complicit with, the troubles the country was experiencing. For instance, artists such as Agung Kurniawan, Heri Dono, and Agus Suwage frequently drew on their own experiences and their identity as artists as mediators between the critical capacity of art and the sociopolitical reality they focused on.[13] The success of self-portraits of Indonesian artists as ambiguously criticizing and benefiting from the chaotic situation of transition the Reformasi represented is indicative of the proliferation of "political" and "critical" art discourses within the Indonesian art scene. In those cases, the figure of the artist is chosen as paradigmatically representing the contradictions of a "dictatorship turned into democracy but not quite." In the case of Taring Padi, however, that "guilt complex" is left aside in favor of active alliances with other local and regional civic groups. Whereas the articulation with those groups often involves important differences and misinterpretations in positioning and strategy, and the collaboration does not always translate into good results, negotiating with social agents outside the art world has been essential in redefining the creative activity of Taring Padi and many other Indonesian collectives. In this case "the political" appears as a process of repurposing art to address the needs and expectations of a society undergoing a difficult process of transition.

As in many other examples analyzed in this book, this gesture reveals how socially engaged art should not be measured by its final, more visible results. Neither does its "originality" come *only* by rejecting representational means over direct experience. Groups such as Taring Padi are singular because they do not opt for a single artistic medium or strategy; rather, they combine many, adapting to the circumstances and also to the needs of those individuals and groups collaborating with the collective. The question of how best to engage with the "praxis" of social transformation is addressed here through multiple means, including the representation of the *rakyat* and of the wealthiest and most corrupt in the banners and *memedi sawah*. Facing a time of individualism and consumerism disguised as democratic reform, Taring Padi invents new ways of articulating progressive agencies in order to make space for discussion and intervention, renewing the strategies of the Indonesian left and using art to provide organizational resources to a wide diversity of marginalized groups. The collective confirms how collaboration and direct engagement with local communities "became one of the approaches to empowering communities affected by New Order de-politicisation and inequitable development" (Arbuckle 2000: 77). More than this, by recovering past revolutionary and anticolonial creative ideas and praxis, Taring Padi radically redefines the possibilities that remain open within the Indonesian political horizon: if the expectations brought about by the Reformasi were grounded on the idea of overcoming the past through the radical difference of the present and the confidence on a future of neoliberal modernization, the collective dismantles the rationality of that temporality, making past forms of insurgence available in the present, although in updated, strategic ways.

Periodizing Indonesian Collectivism

Taring Padi is singular for many reasons, but in no way exceptional. Many other collectives emerged by the last decades of the twentieth century, presenting different solutions to the same issues Taring Padi addressed. Those groups, in any case, should be understood as continuing a decades-long tradition of collaboratively working and living that runs throughout Indonesian cultural history. The country proves exemplary in corroborating one of the main premises of this book, namely the idea that socially engaged art is not a recent phenomenon expanded in times of globalization but rather a central aesthetic resource, a "continuing tradition" employed in many different contexts throughout the twentieth century to challenge restrictive political and cultural policies, and particularly colonialism and its legacy (Moon 2000: 68).

We have already seen how Taring Padi's praxis and thought cannot be fully grasped without our moving back to the unfinished project of democratization and anticolonialism represented by LEKRA and anticolonial cultural policies. Something similar occurs with key features of other collaborative projects emerging in the late 1990s and early 2000s. To understand the importance of these, it is therefore worth revisiting the history of Indonesian collective art, paying particular attention to how notions of collectivism were used at different stages to oppose the individualism and elitism associated with ongoing forms of coercive power inherited from colonial times up to the Suharto regime.

Dealing with visual art in Indonesia always poses the problem of the modern. For a long time, a strong division between performing arts and music on one side, and modern painting and sculpture on the other, has permeated art historical interpretations of the twentieth century. This is the case of one of the most influential surveys of modern Indonesian art to date, Claire Holt's *Art in Indonesia*. Holt (1967: 7) makes a distinction between "living traditions," in which "traditional conceptions of form and content are perpetuated, even though often executed in a new medium," and modern art, which is described as "an urban phenomenon that has developed principally in Java." Besides being perceived as separate "spheres," in Holt's view modern art is conceived of as an emerging manifestation progressively taking a more central role in the definition of Indonesian culture (unlike the first and second spheres, "the heritage" and "living traditions," which correspond to bygone historical eras, in the first case, or are the result of centuries-old evolutional processes, in the second). In the case of modern art, its history would begin, not unproblematically, with the arrival of European colonizers (first the Portuguese, and then the Dutch) and the consolidation of the Mooi Indië (Beautiful Indies), an exoticizing style oriented toward consumption by the Dutch colonial elite and the metropolitan population. Around the 1920s, matching the creation of the first art schools around Java (Holt 1967: 195), Indonesian artists began to question the colonial orientation of painting styles and topics, using local artistic elements and an earlier version of cultural nationalism as a way of countering colonial artistic education.

The problem with this argument is that it traces an evolution exclusively driven by individual genius. Colonial or postcolonial, the institution of artistic authorship passes unquestioned, thus disregarding the many experiences of collaborative creative practices marking twentieth-century Indonesia. If it is true that discussions of national identity—What does it mean to be an Indonesian artist? What counts as Indonesian art? How best to deal with ethnic and cultural diversity?—were recurrent themes throughout the history of modern and contemporary art in the country, it is no less true that in practice, those questions were usually addressed from realistic points of view that took account of the ambivalent role of the artistic class within Indonesian society, as well as to its relation to the *rakyat*.[14]

The history of Indonesian collectivism is the history of the search for better ways of engaging, representing, and/or working side by side with the popular classes. The articulation of collaborative strategies is part of the aesthetic responses to this search, which also involves the use of irony and self-awareness, the criticism of those in power, and the denouncing of colonialism and of any other form of international political or economic interference. What distinguishes collaborative projects from individual actions of sociopolitical criticism is the emphasis placed on understanding art as a center stage for expanding the sphere of politics and democratizing the access to cultural creativity. Collaborative experiences expressed a concern with class and social inequality, which they articulated (though often in problematic ways) by valuing cultural traditions and adopting a practical approach to the process of nation building. This positioning not only counters Western aesthetics based on individualism; it also makes the division between contemporary and traditional culture and between high and popular culture more complicated.

The tension between those values was already present in the first collaborative initiatives emerging in the time of Dutch colonialism. By then, groups such as PERSAGI (Persatuan Ahli-Ahli Gambar Indonesia, Union of Indonesian Artists), created in 1938 by Sudjojono and Agus Djaya, attempted to use collaboration to define an Indonesian approach to art. The activity of the collective, which was essential in shaping the early form of Indonesian cultural nationalism (Sambrani 2016), sought to navigate the binary division of the cultural polemic that split artists, writers, and intellectuals between those in favor of cultural traditions and those in favor of Western aesthetic values. Starting in the early 1940s, many artists joined together in *sanggars*, artistic studios where intellectual and creative meetings were frequent.[15]

The Japanese occupation from 1942 to 1945 that followed Dutch control of the archipelago involved a valuing of local art, but only at the service of the pan-Asian, anti-Western Japanese imperialist project. The *sanggar* tradition was then encouraged, and many artists were grouped under the cultural center, a guild-like structure used by the Japanese for propagandistic ends (Holt 1967: 198). In those three years, however, the social relevance of this Indonesian mode of collaboration was repurposed to be included within the greater narrative justifying the Japanese presence in Indonesia. For artists such as Sudjojono it had became clear that collaboration between artists would not lead to national autonomy. In their view, the dichotomy between local and Western was incomplete, because it allowed the continuation of an imported cultural elitism that seriously restrained art's effectiveness in dealing with the masses. At this time, the question of national identity becomes indissolubly attached to that of social and institutional transformation.[16]

The cultural divisions following independence echoed those of the cultural polemic. Several collectives operated at the beginning of the 1950s, but the most organized and the one that had the most lasting impact was the Institute of People's Culture (LEKRA), mentioned above. LEKRA functioned as an umbrella structure working through branches in many Indonesian provinces, and it was active in the arts, literature, music, and drama. Originally basing its action in the promotion of popular creativity and the appreciation of local creative traditions, LEKRA brought together many of the most renowned figures of Indonesian modernist art, including Affandi and Sudjojono.

Keith Foulcher explains the creation of the group as part of an impulse toward social commitment and public responsibility that runs throughout the history of modern Indonesian art. This impulse, he argues, has to be understood as part of the process of definition of a modern national identity. Crucial here is the fact that the origins of LEKRA, like those of Taring Padi, are linked to a moment of transition from colonial domination to postcolonial national sovereignty. More than this, LEKRA's political positioning is also shaped by a mistrust of the depth of the democratic system inheriting the 1945 revolution, and by a belief that identity and modernity would be meaningful only when aligned with the creative values of the *rakyat*. This meant that the search for cultural identity was directly associated with day-to-day, practical cooperation with disenfranchised sectors of the Indonesian population. In this sense, Foulcher (1987: 84) maintains that "the distinctive place which Lekra was to occupy within it was already being defined as involving not only cultural nationalism as it had already existed in Indonesia, but in some implied, and later much more specific way, a class-based conception of Indonesian social realities." Balancing both sides of the equation, however, would prove to be more difficult than expected. The task of incorporating the diversity of cultural traditions and developing a specific aesthetics based on radical democracy encountered increasing problems in the heated period between 1960 and 1965, when ideological debates intensified. This moment matched LEKRA's "cultural offensive," which involved the banning of opposing cultural views (such as the tradition of "cultural humanism," in which LEKRA identified the persistence of bourgeois aesthetics) and the censorship of cultural productions (such as films from the United States) associated with neoimperialism. However, even at this stage there remained space for aesthetic diversity. In Foulcher's words (93), "This was not a period in which 'politics' totally overwhelmed cultural initiative and creativity."

Although LEKRA's activity allowed room for spontaneous organization, the group also played a central part in Soekarno's politics of friendship. Analyzing LEKRA's role in securing and channeling the politics of cultural diplomacy and internationalization of the Soekarno government, Brigitta Isabella (2018: 95–96) highlights how many LEKRA artists occupied positions of authority in many friendship organizations abroad. At the same time, however, she points out how this participation in cultural policies was far more ambivalent than it may seem: artists were sufficiently autonomous to maneuver within the Cold War climate of cultural influence, taking advantage in divergent ways of the United States and the Soviet Union, and of state- and party-sponsored activities.[17] Although LEKRA defined its role within the Indonesian art scene within the Left, "in practice," Isabella adds, "they interpreted socialist realism loosely, without any homogenous artistic formula. It should be noted that LEKRA had no official statement that strictly rejected modern art or abstract expressionism" (94). This strategic positioning survived in the art collectives of former decades and becomes relevant when trying to establish links between the projects analyzed in this book. Although LEKRA was formally linked to the Indonesian Communist Party (Partai Komunis Indonesia, PKI) and grounded its aspirations of popular democracy in aesthetic realism, on a practical level the group ensured artistic freedom to individual members and managed to adapt Soviet social realism to the circumstances of 1950s Indonesia (Foulcher 1987: 87).[18] Conceiving of cultural influences as ambivalent and allowing the possibility of assessing the strategic capacity of art collectives to repurpose external influences through their practical activities is essential in determining art's capacity to play a transformative social role in highly ideological contexts such as mid-twentieth-century Indonesia.[19]

Understanding LEKRA in the complex context in which the collective arose, and not simply as the cultural branch of Left political forces, or as a "local version" of avant-gardists' social realist aesthetics, sheds light on how important practice can be in determining how each group identifies itself and defines its role within society.[20] At the same time, it also places emphasis on individual and collective agency, though without ignoring the impact of Cold Ward political and economic constraints on the shaping of artistic responses. Isabella argues that "many Indonesian artists were neither passive recipients of artistic styles, nor aesthetic ideologues, due to the sense of nationalism and self-determination in their search for a modern identity" (Isabella 2018: 100), allowing us to focus on the multiple strategies employed by Indonesian artists to challenge static sociopolitical configurations.

Finally, situating LEKRA (along with mid-twentieth-century Indonesian collectivism) within its context requires us to pay attention to the continuities and influences between progressive projects emerging in subsequent decades while also not losing sight of the limitations of each initiative. In an examination of LEKRA's activity within the difficult period preceding the Soeharto Coup, Foulcher (1987: 96) demonstrates how the group's proximity to the modern, postcolonial nation-state stood in the way of articulating closer ways of approaching local popular creativity: "At the level below overt ideological commitment, the common conception of art stood as another indication of *Lekra*'s origins in the modernizing nationalist intelligentsia, rather than in the cultural realities of the masses it championed." In his view, however, this incapacity was not unique to Lekra: "The failure of Lekra's attempt to transform the nature of the modern Indonesian arts between 1950 and 1965 was the failure of the Indonesian revolution as it was conceived by the radical left during this period" (99).

The decades after the 1965 massacre of left-wing intellectuals and artists were marked by market expansion and a progressive "depoliticization" of art.[21] After the communist purge of 1965 and during the 1970s and 1980s, censorship arose as a major concern in the work of many Indonesian artists, who struggled to escape the control of the regime by leveraging the tone of sociopolitical criticism and becoming more ambiguous. Soeharto restricted cultural and political associations, and attempted to encourage the internationalization of Indonesian art. Because of this, in those two decades the art market reinforced its presence within the national art scene and became the main gateway for Indonesian artists to join regional artistic circuits. The rebellion of young students in Yogyakarta and Bandung that led to the configuration of the Gerakan Seni Rupa Baru Indonesia (Indonesian New Art Movement, hereafter GSRBI) arose as a response to this climate. This group, which included artists such as FX Harsono, Bonyong Munni Ardhi, Siti Ardiati, and Ris Purnomo, targeted the stagnation of an increasingly formal and official art system, adopting strategies from Pop Art. The art of Harsono, Munni Ardhi, and other members of this generation adopted an experimental tone that favored installations and ready-mades. Thematically, those works contained a strong dose of political criticism. However, at the same time, this generation started to experience the contradictions affecting many of the projects discussed in this book: aiming to "speak for the poor," on many occasions it was difficult to insert art into the public sphere outside the museum or the academy; moreover, medium innovation posed a challenge to the strategies of social integration sought by the GSRBI. Many of the artists of this generation (among them Harsono, Tisna Sanjaya, and Arahmaniani) produced bold pieces of public art to challenge this limitation, combining artistic experimentation with collaborative installations and performances in public locations. The work of those artists also anticipated a growing concern with globalization, internationalization, and the role of technology that took root in the 1990s, at the same time as curating became more professionalized in the Indonesian context. From this decade onward, like many other Southeast Asian art scenes, Indonesian contemporaneity has been curatorially mediated through participation in events such as the Arts Asia Pacific Triennial or other Asian biennials, with Japan and Australia playing a central (and not unproblematic) role as promoters and mediators of taste, audiences, and connections (Supriyanto 2013: 11). Yet, as we have seen, in many cases art debates are very much indebted to decades-old social and national debates. This takes us back to our starting point and the main topic of this chapter: the emergence of art collectives around the political crossroads of the Reformasi.

Excursus: Collective Sampling/Sampling Collectivism

No matter how complex and varied the history of collective creativity in Indonesia, it does not explain the effervescence of collaborative practices in the post–New Order period. If the political changes brought about by the "democratization" of the country reinforced the orientation toward the market and individualism already present in the Indonesian art scene since the 1980s, why do we find so many collectives emerging at the end of the twentieth century? And why do those collectives take a leading role both locally and internationally, decisively characterizing Indonesian art and reintroducing (although in heterogeneous ways) concerns about the *rakyat* and *seni kerakyatan*?

The first person I interviewed while doing research in Java was the Bandung-based curator and scholar Agung Hujatnikajennong. Hujatnikajennong is responsible for curating important exhibitions of Indonesian art both in the country and abroad, and his work highlights the importance of video technologies in shaping the contemporary Indonesian art scene. In the late 1990s, the proliferation of VHS and personal cameras revolutionized the capacity of regular Indonesians to produce, share, and edit images of everyday subjects.[22] This democratization came along with a radical expansion and depoliticization of television and radio, making room for a wider multiplicity of voices and topics than those accepted during the New Order era.[23] In 2003, Hujatnikajennong curated the first edition of OK Video, the first event dedicated to video art and recording technologies in Indonesia, which also presented for the first time in the country a selection of the Electronic Arts Intermix of New York. The festival was organized by ruangrupa, a collective that will be analyzed in the following section. Drawing now on OK Video, it revolutionized the panorama of fine arts in Jakarta due to its dimension and aspirations. It was conceived as a massive festival occupying the National Gallery of Indonesia in Jakarta. The shock provoked by the festival was related not so much to the attention given to video (instead of painting or sculpture, which are still seen by many in Indonesia as the privileged mediums of artistic creation) but rather to the way artists and curators approached Indonesian media culture and popular creativity. OK Video celebrated the expansion of audiovisual technology as a decisive shift in the country's civil society. The floors of the National Gallery were radically transformed, with screens and DVD players temporarily occupying the space of the national masters. This symbolic movement was unprecedented, because the focus of the festival was placed on popular creativity with artists tasked with following and joining that shift (see figure 6.4).

The most immediate precedent of OK Video can be found in the exhibitions organized by GSRBI in the 1970s. Unlike then, in the early 2000s the figure of the artist as commentator and interpreter of social processes was challenged. This attitude became clearer in the next two editions of OK Video, "Sub/Version" in 2005 and "Militia" in 2007. In the last edition, the festival expanded its spatial scope beyond "traditional" art spaces,[24] and reached twelve different locations within Java. OK Video Militia consisted of practical workshops on video production. These

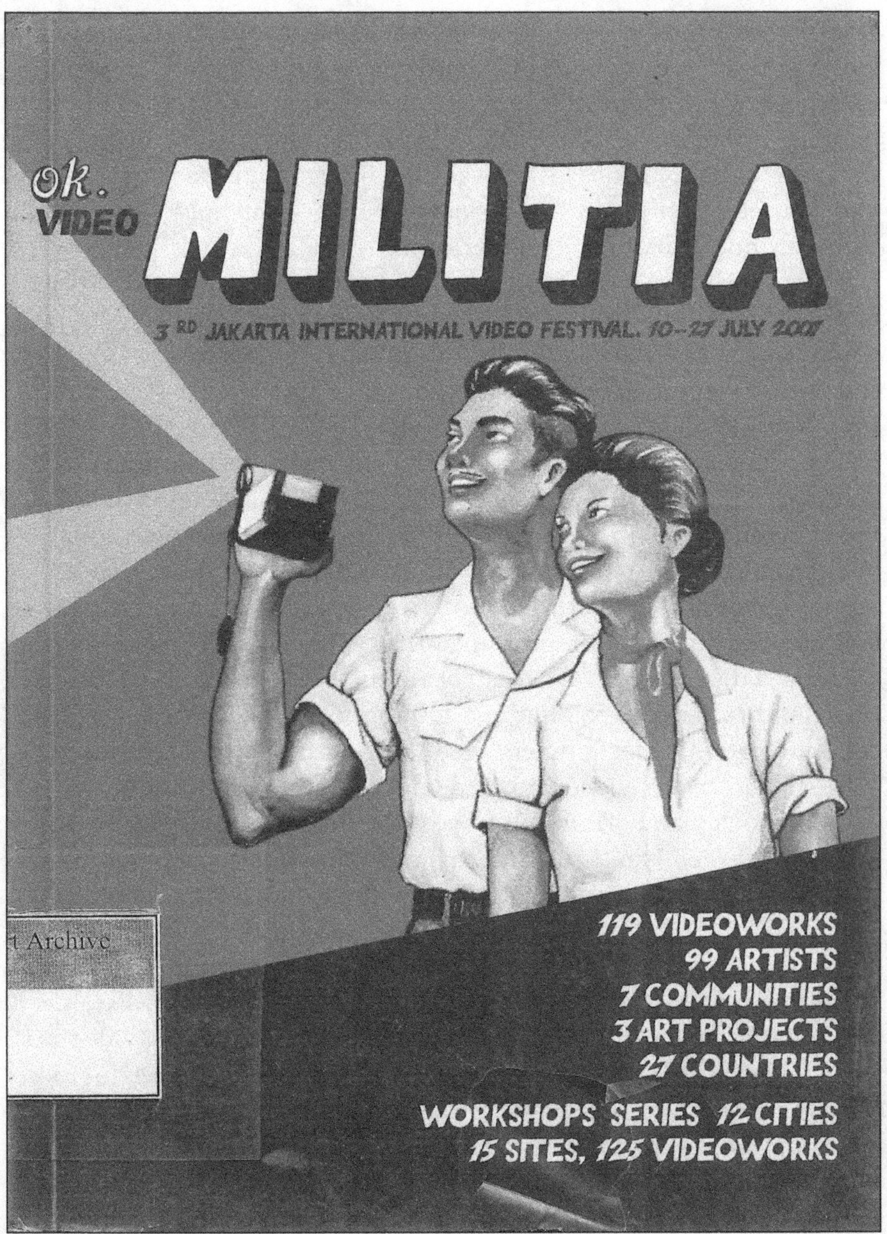

Figure 6.4. OK Video Militia festival poster. *Source*: Courtesy of Indonesian Visual Arts Archive (IVAA).

workshops were offered at a second stage to ask local participants to use video filming as a way of documenting pressing issues. The resulting videos were exhibited in popular cafes, shopping centers, and office buildings. Reinforcing the festival's focus on direct action, the program included collaboration with local and international activist groups and community organizations, such as Forum Lenteng, EngageMedia, Videolab, and Urban Poor Consortium.

Hafiz, the festival's director, conceived of these collaborations as part of an effort to break the elitism of the traditional fine arts medium, while joining the social and cultural transformations of contemporary Indonesia in more effective ways: "In *OK Video Militia—3rd Jakarta International Video Festival 2007* 'to arm' means to give opportunity to the public to use a video (camera) to challenge the hegemony of the audio-visual language. This is connected to the development of the video medium within the society, inviting the people as technology— and media—users to join us in building awareness of social issues that are taking place" (Hujatnikajennong 2007: 26). Adopting a similar position, Hujatnikajennong claimed that video had become a political medium, a device within the reach of almost everyone (in urban settings) that could be used to counter and leverage the top-down industries of communication, entertainment, and political propaganda. In his view, "The shift from 'art videos' toward 'videos' in general must be seen as an effort to shy away from the trap of the high-art hierarchy, which is identical with elitism. I see that this effort has also been based on the wish to make the festival an 'interdisciplinary' activity, observing the importance to signify the existence of the video medium in non-artistic ways, socially and culturally" (Hujatnikajennong 2007: 30).

OK Video confronts us with a theoretical challenge. To what extent can collaborative work operate to reduce the gap between "video art" and "video"? Are (activist-led) festivals more subversive than exhibitions on art activism? Finally, and summarizing both questions, how do mass consumption and social transformation coexist in the different editions of the festival? To begin addressing these questions, it is worth noting that OK Video was more than an exhibition or a festival. It involved long-term collaboration with civil society and activist organizations. These were not merely represented in the exhibition part of the festival but rather conferred enough autonomy to conduct workshops and develop initiatives according to their regular activity. In addition to this, as Hujatnikajennong points out, the festival simply tapped into an omnipresent interest in video technologies in Indonesia, devising fertile ways of using artistic experimentation to deepen (but in no way to create) the social relevance of those technologies as critical tools. Video art scholar Edwin Jürriens, one of the top specialists in digital creativity and media in Indonesia, discusses OK Video as an instance of the connections that video art communities are making with the avant-garde, which include breaking with the autonomy of art, the engagement with the praxis of life, the pursue of utopian goals of social transformation, and the encouragement of aesthetic innovation (Jürriens 2013a: 49). Dealing with the activity of the Yogyakarta-based House of Natural Fiber collective, Jürriens (2013a, 2017) rightfully notes that the main key to evaluating Indonesian collaborative projects lies in their complex relationship with the aesthetics and the temporal logic of the avant-garde. He explains the increasing relevance of video communities as part of an informal creative laboratory based on rhizomatic platforms that facilitate interconnectivity and social engagement. In his view, video art communities differ from individual political art in the sense that they are more integrated into social processes, and give greater importance to praxis than to critical observation. At the same time, they differ from video activism due to "the[ir] stronger emphasis on stimulating people's imagination and promoting aesthetic experimentation" (Jürriens 2015: 109).

Jürriens's depiction of video initiatives as community enterprises in productive tension between their avant-garde aesthetic aspirations and their connection with broader transformations within Indonesian civil society is interesting in the way it portrays art collectives as sampling and repurposing other collaborative processes.[25] Many of the projects we are discussing in this section are political because they seek to merge with already-existing networks such as television or radio production, or to replicate everyday acts such as iPhone picturing, for socially committed ends that often go far beyond the traditional domain of visual artists. During the New Order, the idea of art as a privileged site of cultural discussion prevailed. Among the elements binding together the initiatives arising from the late 1990s onward is the rejection of the idea of visual arts as a cultural field with any specific cultural relevance. This is particularly evident in the work of video communities, not only because they often operate with free content but also because they rely on horizontal and informal means of distribution, on collective documenting of everyday life, and on active ongoing engagement with groups of urban unemployed and youngsters.

Even from the more pessimistic point of view concerning social media and communicational technologies, it is undeniable that they have conditioned the possibilities and limitations of social processes since 1998.[26] This is visible, among other things, in the increasing role that online communities are taking in defining a national public sphere.[27]

In this sense, as Krishna Sen and David Hill have demonstrated, media distribution was key in accumulating and channeling dissent against Soeharto and reporting situations of militarist violence against students in Java and against independence movements in spaces such as East Timor.[28] The ability to record, produce, and sample images directly counters the elite patrimonialism that permeated the relations between state and civil society in the New Order period and that survived the government of Soeharto in the form of political correctness and maintained respect for the state for the sake of national unity. If we agree with Bagoes Wiryomartono (2017) that "the sense of an Indonesian nation-state has been literally established with the use of Indonesian language by press and media since Dutch colonial times," then the centrality of the media also means that some principles of nepotism and patronage were also left untouched. Against the frequent situations of nepotism, corruption, and covert intimidation, the proliferation of amateur video provided many with the right to tell their own version of the story, developing a sort of counterpublic sphere that largely exceeded the narrow sphere of action of traditional visual arts. At the same time, however, video technology has been essential in redirecting the interests and strategies of Indonesian artistic communities. More than this, it has revealed that multimedia experimentation can also provide fertile ground for social transformation.

One last question remains: How does the increasing weight of media and digital activism fit into the general narrative of this chapter? What equal ground exists between the aspirations of video communities and those of groups like Taring Padi? In critical terms, what does the wide spectrum of Indonesian collective practices tell us about the political dimension of social engagement? Certainly, politics seem to be more obviously addressed in groups such as Apotik Komic or Taring Padi than in video festivals such as OK Video. At the same time, however, some common points lead to the conclusion that the three initiatives emerge from a similar historical context. We have seen how the objectives of Taring Padi cannot simply be reduced to political confrontation. In this sense, for instance, the collective's interest in environmental justice and the everyday reality of farmers can be seen as closer to the "everyday politics" involved in the video documentation of local issues that is encouraged by groups such as Tromarama, Forum Lenteng, VideoLab, and the House of Natural Fiber. Finally, viewed from the perspective of the media employed, Taring Padi posters replicated the outburst of multicolored propaganda that broke out on the occasion of the first elections after the New Order, while the video communities did the same with the proliferation of technologies of media production, consumption, and distribution. There are sufficient grounds for comparison, certainly more than a simple view of the physical appearance of each medium would seem to allow.

The popularity of video also speaks of the shifting ground on which socially engaged creators operate. These have appropriated the potential of video in imaginative ways, developing an arena of exchange and imagination that reveals the good health of the Indonesian activist scene. Video activism, indeed, becomes a catchall expression when trying to describe the multiplicity of approaches adopted in Indonesia within the last years of the 1990s and the beginning of the twenty-first century. These include popular festivals, tactical media, politically engaged documentary, hacking and free sharing, video experimentalism, video documentation of political and military violence, grassroots community video, communities of informal sharing, exchanging, etcetera. Although the commitment to praxis and locality still constitutes a cornerstone of the artistic and social aspirations of many groups, in the Indonesian case "locality" has decisively shifted and expanded in order to incorporate a growing online realm. Like many other social agents, Indonesian artists operate across the thin line where the "real" and the digital overlap. In this sense, their actions confirm Ario Seto's idea that digital citizenship in Indonesia often goes back and forth between the online and offline domains, "enlarge[ing] both civic agency and networks of citizens" (2017: 2). But Seto also conceives of digital activism as a task of configuring rather than operating in a previously given medium. Like Indonesian democracy itself, those operating through media (and this includes almost everyone in the country) are navigating unknown waters.

ruangrupa

Operating in those waters often means dealing with organizational matters for which many artists were not initially prepared. The history of ruangrupa, Yakarta's most celebrated art collective and one of the main points of reference of the networked fabric of Southeast Asia's alternative art scene, is one of adaptation and gradual shifting from an informal gathering of students with similar interests to a large creative cluster expanding over areas as disparate as urban planning, cinema and video technologies, comics and graphic design, and essayistic writing, and reaching a wide variety of locations throughout Java. ruangrupa was founded in 2000 by a group of six "creatives": Ade Darmawan, Hafiz, Ronny Agustinus, Oky Arfie Hutabarat, Lilia Nursita, Rithmi. Besides the hyper(activity) that has characterized the existence of ruangrupa since its origin, the search for an alternative place for exchange and dialogue was central to the project members. Hujatnikajennong (2010: 11) argues that ruangrupa was created as a strategy for pursuing creative freedom in the context of the suffocating art medium of Jakarta. Having a space unaffected by the art market and the official bureaucratized cultural scene of the capital city allowed the founders of ruangrupa to support others' cultural production in an informal, friendly way. If Hujatnikajennong is right in pointing out that mediation and collaboration are central to understanding ruangrupa's activity, it is also true that they work differently in each of the initiatives organized or joined by the group.

The first steps of ruangrupa are the result of the hyperactivity of this small group of friends, which achieved the creation of major programs in areas neglected by official institutions in Jakarta: OK Video, ArtLab, and the Jakarta 32° Art Students Biennale. ArtLab is a research-based program focusing on emerging urban practices, youth subcultures, and alternative uses of public space. Begun in 2004, Jakarta 32° encourages artistic experimentation and provides a space for art students to show their early work. In addition to the exhibitional outcome of this last activity, the biennial fostered dialogue among art students, curators, and critics, which was unusual in the Jakartan art scene at that time. In 2003 ruangrupa also organized the Apartment Project, an art residency initiative that involved continuous communication with the inhabitants of Jakarta and the application of social science methodologies to understand the social interactions taking place in the city. The initiative analyzed issues of labor and leisure, and also considered how media technologies were altering the everyday life of Jakartans. Further initiatives such as RuruRadio and Picnic Kit (developed in 2006) continued this observation in a playful way: in the last case, ruangrupa established an observatory of leisure practices, and also organized games and provided tools for collective amusement in public places. These projects are intentionally conceived through the use of popular strategies of social interaction. The fact that they lack the solemn atmosphere of an art event makes them attractive to large segments of the population. At the same time, they depart from the gallery-centered "social experiments" developed by Nicolas Bourriaud's relational aesthetics. Whereas Bourriaud saw art advancing new modes of interaction and communication, ruangrupa goes in the opposite direction, conceiving of art as a way of networking already existing initiatives. This has profound consequences, since it affects how artistic authorship and expertise are conceived. Unlike Relational Art, which granted a small group of well-renowned international artists the capacity to transform social relationships,[29] ruangrupa approaches sociocultural exchange in a more "ecosystemic" way.

A thought on the new paths Indonesian art was taking at the beginning of the twenty-first century was produced through the journal *Karbon* and through *Jarakpandang*, an online initiative focusing on documenting and critically analyzing art initiatives. The first issue of *Karbon*, for example, included a discussion of the recent developments of Taring Padi and Apotik Komik and of the role of similar projects in the shaping of public spheres. This interest is further pursued through shared projects with collectives such as Serrum and Forum Lenteng in Jakarta, Jatiwangi Art Factory in Jatiwangi, or Ruang MES56, and the Indonesian Visual Art Archive and Kunci in Yogyakarta (see figure 6.5).

Despite the enormous amount of activity developed over the course of the more than twenty years that ruangrupa has been active, two elements remain common to all initiatives. The first is informality. On the occasion of the commemoration of fifteen years of existence, ruangrupa's founding members recognized that "since early on, the running of this organization has been designed loosely so that every member can still work individually."[30] They also acknowledged that their original interests were not the same as those of the younger generations approaching and reinvigorating the project: "For the latter flocks, ruangrupa is not only seen as a place to gather but also as part of a career journey, some kind of office, or something official, as well as a learning space, a place to study, and to gain experiences."[31] Being flexible in its structure, ruangrupa relies on spontaneous collaboration with colleagues and "creators" from all around Java, including DJs, music bands, comic producers, performance artists, and graphic designers. On other occasions, ruangrupa has shared the organization of events, providing support to other collectives and expanding the scope of activities to the streets of Jakarta. This is the case of *Poligame*, a performance and interaction with urban spaces co-organized with Asbestos, a Bandung-based performance group. In those cases, ruangrupa acts as an open space, placing its experience and know-how in the coordination of events at the service of those interested in approaching the group. The most dangerous consequence deriving from this spontaneity in alliance making comes from the impermanent sporadic logic of many actions. Since ruangrupa is immersed in such a level of activity, collaborations risk ending with the materialization of particular events. Since the artistic and interdisciplinary alliances ruangrupa joins in are based on specific shared interests with other organizations at particular times, there is a risk of losing sight of those partners whose situation or interests evolve in different directions than ruangrupa's. The group has tried to prevent this situation by sustaining initiatives such as Jakarta 32° and OK Video that run on a regular basis. However, priority is given to fluid interrelation and horizontal networking.

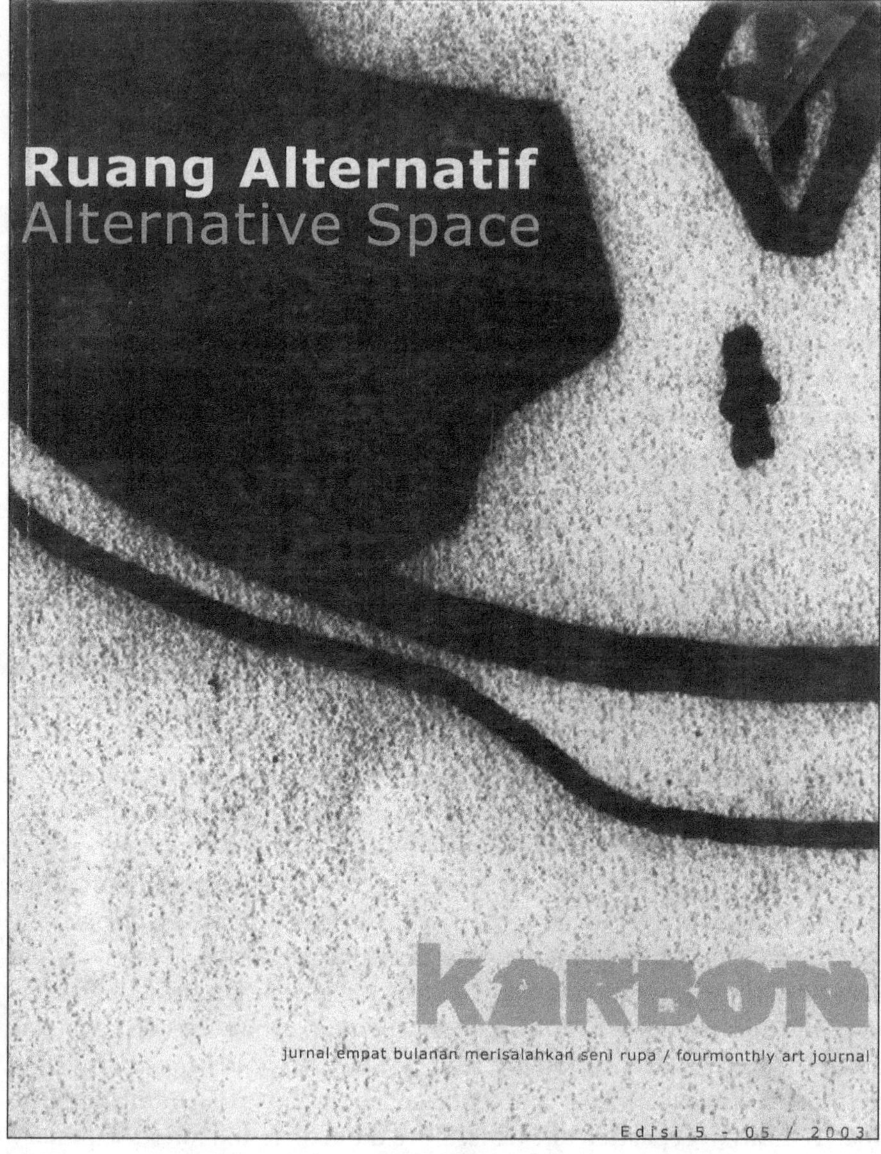

Figure 6.5. ruangrupa, *Karbon* journal cover, 2003. *Source*: Courtesy of Indonesian Visual Arts Archive (IVAA).

The second element common to all ruangrupa initiatives is the public projection of each of the abovementioned activities. Even in the case of the actions directed toward critical writing and curating, we find a direct correlation with the sociopolitical situation of early 2000s Jakarta, where visual arts were largely oriented toward national celebration and the art market. Curating and critical thought were, in other words, missing elements sought after by many young students and creatives of the Jakartan and Javanese cultural scenes. In this sense, the focus of *Karbon*, *Jarakpandang*, and the curatorial training offered by ruangrupa responded to an already existing need, but it did so in an accessible way, rejecting formal academic training and making use of personal bonds and shared interests. It is important to point out that this informal approach to curating and cultural creativity enhanced the operational capacity of attendees without making their activity fall into this or that category. Rather, ruangrupa's educational action was conceived with the objective of "generat[ing] artists, curators, managers, producers, writers—or anything in between." As those roles were being drastically redefined by the early 2000s, ruangrupa was able to act as supplier and intermediary, fulfilling the different needs of each participant without establishing formal models or conditioning creative responses beforehand.

By the mid-2000s, ruangrupa supported partner communities, and by the end of this decade it operated in a quasi-institutional fashion. From the same period onward, ruangrupa took part in important international events such as the Istanbul Biennial and Sonsbeek (Vanhoe 2016: 26). The original group of friends who founded ruangrupa has shifted into a wide variety of young professionals with different backgrounds and creative interests. Recent changes to the structure of ruangrupa, as well as its capacity to articulate with other creative projects throughout Java, raise important questions concerning the potential of socially engaged art and its proximity to other forms of artistic practice. What happens when collective initiatives such as ruangrupa acquire the size and the features of alternative art institutions? How can we evaluate their action in aesthetic terms, when this action consists in articulating bonds with other collaborative groups with differentiated aesthetic values and strategical objectives? To what extent can virtual networking and transnational alliances be developed for existing "local" processes of transformation?[32] How should we measure the impact of projects such as ruangrupa, if its basic role is to act as an umbrella organization for many different initiatives involving different crit groups and leading toward the achievement of specific outcomes?

Although it is true that ruangrupa reinforced its managerial role in the decade following the new millennium, positively affecting the careers of the individuals related to the project, it is not easy to categorize ruangrupa simply as an alternative institution. A first point that should be noted concerning the questions above is the fact that many Indonesian creators belong to different groups. Their participation in art collectives, indeed, replicates a common element of the everyday life of many people in the country. Wok the Rock, coordinator of the Yogyakarta project Ruang MES56 and himself responsible for collaborative initiatives in the underground and punk community of Yogyakarta, affirmed in an interview that collaboration responds to a common, logical habit among communities.[33] Helping neighbors and gathering unexpectedly on noticing that events are taking place in someone's house is a common practice for many in Yogyakarta, one that contemporary collaborative projects simply replicate. In the case of Wok, for example, he used to share space with the Kunci Cultural Studies Center, the last project we will analyze in this chapter. The Ruang MES56 collective, in which Wok collaborates, often produces its activities in partnership with other projects in the city, the establishment of those partnerships being the result of spontaneous, in-the-moment decisions by all parties. A similar logic presides over ruangrupa members, who, besides coming from very different backgrounds, and understanding and defining what ruangrupa means in quite different ways, do not limit their work to engaging in ruangrupa activities. Although this might seem counter to the commitment with specific communities and targeted groups at play in many socially engaged art projects, in reality it has not limited the action of ruangrupa, Ruang MES6, or Kunci. The origin of these three initiatives is linked to students' will to break with the etiquette of public and private museums and formal exhibition spaces. Visiting the (former) space of ruangrupa or the current location of MES56 or Kunci gives the impression of entering into effervescent hubs of informal exchange, where the space allocated to office, library, conversation room, and kitchen happily intermixes. This spatial dynamic partially reflects the origins of each one of these projects, in which students decided to create flexible structures (often located in their own rented apartments) to break with the codes and rules of formal education and artistic creativity. Talking about MES56, Wok revealed that one of the reasons the collective changed its location so many times simply had to do with the fact that, as students, they depend on renting a property.[34]

A second question arising from ruangrupa's hyperactive and diverse action has to do with measuring the social impact of the project as a whole. If the organized activities are so diverse as to address different needs and enroll different collaborators, how can we categorize the role of ruangrupa in the Indonesian cultural scene in critical terms? The first thing that ruangrupa member Farid Rakun told me when I interviewed him was that "you cannot use ruangrupa as being representative of Indonesia."[35] At the same time, however, the immersion of cultural practice in the everyday reality of urban Indonesian youths and the adoption of a flexible, DIY working strategy resemble many of the characteristics of post-Reformasi Indonesia. Paradigmatic in this sense is ruangrupa's interest in some of the radical potential of forms of popular politics, and the way these are located and searched for within processes of everyday urban interaction and media exchange. Dealing with the question of whether ruangrupa's activity is political or not requires analysis of the extent to which ruangrupa manages to grasp the transformation of the Indonesian sociopolitical arena by the late 1990s.

There are at least two levels on which those activities reveal a conscious interest in exploring this transformation. The first involves recognizing the limitations of traditional forms of visual creativity due to the compliance of those forms with the market and the instrumentalization of "political art" for purposes of commodification. The spontaneity of many ruangrupa projects and the flexibility for articulating diverse alliances work in opposition to more formal modes of artistic production and education. The second level relates to ruangrupa's interest in the urban and, more specifically, in the role of media technologies in reshaping processes of urban interaction between Indonesian youngsters and configuring a public sphere after the Reformasi. In this sense, Reinaart Vanhoe (2016: 28) reinforces the relation between ruangrupa and the Indonesian independent music scene, pointing out that "the youth culture consisted to a great extent of people from the 'lower' socio-economic classes, who were not interested in politics or institutional programmes." At the same time, however, he also recognizes that "ruangrupa is fascinated by the realities of the 'lower' socio-economic class, and sincerely identifies with the mentality of this class, particularly its inventiveness and solutions. This is a domain of precarious relationships, self-organisation and ingenuity" (37). The connection with urban youth groups explains the success of ruangrupa, yet I would question whether the apparent purposelessness and immersion in the everyday activities organized by ruangrupa can be really understood in terms of being apolitical. As we have seen, video technologies and digital interaction became so omnipresent in twenty-first-century Indonesia as to evolve into a powerful pillar of national politics. OK Video, for instance, merges into a general interest in using filmic image to reflect on corruption and abuses of power as obstacles to social transformation. Yet at the same time, the practical orientation of the event made it transcend that representational level by literally placing cameras and mobile phones in the hands of young Indonesians. The playful and supportive nature of the ruangrupa space, which even provides a bed for those interested in staying overnight (34), does not imply political or social disinterest; rather it reveals the extent to which collective experimentation, the precariousness of cultural labor, and broader class and social concerns are intertwined in ruangrupa's activity. And although some elements of that activity are directed toward negative aspects of Indonesian and global society, this criticism is channeled through an accumulative, affirmative logic. As David Teh (2012: 112) explains, "ruangrupa has made a profound commitment to Jakarta as both site and subject, to its people as both audience and authors." It is precisely from this last perspective that ruangrupa can add interesting elements to the main issues running through this book.

Expanding the Field

The final project examined in this chapter, the Yogyakarta-based Kunci Cultural Studies Center, reinforces ruangrupa's extradisciplinary approach of collective creativity and networking. A central concern in many of the initiatives organized by Kunci is broadening the popular understanding of artistic practice. Borrowing loosely from the original aspirations of the tradition of cultural studies (Stuart Hall and Raymond Williams appear several times in the collective conversation I had with some Kunci members), Kunci attempts to deal with important but disparate concerns present in the Indonesian visual art medium (political violence, militarism, the inheritance of Bandung, the commons, alternative and flexible institutionalism, Walter Benjamin, and hacking culture) without the pressure to produce any object-based outcome or engage potentially uninterested audiences. As membership is totally free and reversible in Kunci, the group structure has altered several times since its creation in 1999. Brigitta Isabella mentions that this flexibility often translates into different understandings of what Kunci is or what it does. For many of the younger members (who are also students at Yogyakarta), Kunci provides a platform for informal exchange on pressing topics affecting their everyday life outside of the rigid and vertical system of formal academic education.

A first group of activities developed by Kunci focuses on reverting the academized field of knowledge production and dissemination. For instance, Kultur Cell is a Ford Foundation–sponsored, praxis-based research program aiming at understanding how cell phones and digital technologies are shifting the modes of communication and socialization in contemporary Indonesia. Although the project includes an analytical side that is methodologically closer to sociological investigation, it also involves a more creative side of interaction with communities of users in different locations, including places outside Java. The results of the fieldwork research included a booklet but also a series of online clips and abundant visual material.

A more direct approach to collaborative, democratic research was adopted as a result of the After Work Reading Club. In 2015 Kunci was invited to collaborate with Para Site, an alternative space in Hong Kong. Both groups decided to approach Indonesian migrant workers employed at construction sites in Hong Kong. The personal experiences of a part of the global cohort of blue-collar workers that are building Hong Kong's dream of futuristic modernization seemed good enough to test the contemporary acceptance of transnationalism and Third World friendship. The personal documents gathered through active collaboration with Indonesian migrants explain the harsh consequences deriving from the fall of the utopias of modernization in Southeast Asia. Given the contradictions and the uncertainties deriving from the handover, Hong Kong nowadays is facing a similar watershed to that of Indonesia and other neighboring countries in the late 1990s. At the same time, the city-state has become one of the main centers of global art, attracting a large audience from all over the world. Kunci's collaboration with Para Site aimed at finding bridges between both types of mobility: that of global precarious labor and that of art's transnational spectatorship in Hong Kong. While in residency in Para Site, Kunci developed six reading sessions with migrant domestic workers from Indonesia and the Philippines, testing their feeling about the city and also their experiences. The result of those exchanges, significantly, was not ethnographic observation but in-depth creative interaction: many of the contributions were in the form of unguided literary writing. While artists were invited to the sessions, not all the chosen locations were "art spaces"; the popular Victoria Park and an educational facility also hosted conversations. Para Site justifies this modus operandi by claiming collaboration with the community in the following terms:

For Para Site, it is essential to realize this project in close dialogue with the community, avoiding the patronizing attitude of giving a

> voice to or being the vindicators of the struggles of migrant workers, which sometimes happens in art projects with a social dimension. Rather, together with members of the community, with artists from Hong Kong, the Philippines, Indonesia, and from other parts of the world, we would like to tell another crucial story of our city, besides the often heard stories of affluence, dominating the mainstream, and also besides the stories of struggle specific to the Hong Kong Chinese majority. (Kunci and Para Site 2016: 18)

The After Work Reading Club resembles many of the features associated with socially engaged art in this book. The dialogical and democratic nature of the activity is close to C. L. R. James's experience of shared writing in Missouri described in previous chapters. By choosing migrant workers as primary sources of knowledge and opinion, and not international artists with previous experience in producing critical work itinerantly, Kunci was also seeking innovative ways of breaking with the primacy of representation and artistic individuality as the privileged medium for generating sociopolitical knowledge. Finally, the project also shifted the tone from the celebratory narrative of Hong Kong as a global city to the practicalities of precarious migrant labor.

If the two initiatives analyzed seek to dismantle the aura of privilege and the compartmentalization of knowledge encouraged by Indonesian academic institutions, a second body of work by Kunci attempts to do the same with the rigid exclusivism of the country's art world. Space/Scape, for instance, was an initiative on urban spaces and practices of socialization developed by Dina under the umbrella of Kunci. In addition to documenting how different groups make use of plazas, occupy streets, and conceive the city, the project also included public art works (such as *Kamar Gelap* [Dark room], an installation displayed in 2009 in the popular South Square within the Kraton area). Already a place bursting with collective exchange, on this occasion the installation invited passersby to write their impressions of the location inside a cabin. The installation was part of Alun-Alun, an enquiry into the role of *alun-alun* squares, large open spaces like those contained in the Kraton area in Yogyakarta. Three years later, a second group of actions under the general title of Bon Suwung gathered public opinions on the existing and potential uses of wasteland in Yogyakarta.[36] As in the case of Ensayos Tierra del Fuego in Chile, here the project raises important questions about useful and useless spaces, also mapping human interaction with empty spaces. Dealing with the cultural meaning of Bon Suwung, Dina explains:

The etymological meaning of "Bon Suwung" is closer to the "Empty Garden" in the following Javanese language with all its performativity dimensions. The word "garden" here refers to the dimensions of ownership and potential management of a plot of land or land. While "suwung" or empty here is closer to psychological experience, as a mental aspect (e.g., emptiness of the mind), rather than as a physical characteristic, without content. So that as a void of space in Bon Suwung here is interpreted as a condition where empty land has never really separated from its relationship with humans, the local environment, the urban conditions surrounding it and its relation to wider space discourse and practice, in the Indonesian context as well as global.[37]

Also exemplary in this sense is Megamix Militia, a cooperative project supported by Yale University that combined practical research and cultural production and revolved around the idea of creative appropriation and remix. Dealing with the objectives of this project, Kunci members mention three main interrelated elements: "Firstly, it aims at disentangling the complexity of the meaning of authenticity and authorship in the field of cultural production. The second is an attempt to frame the multiplicity of copying practices in local music scenes, ranging from cover-version, remix, repurposing and so forth. And last and not least it seeks to map out the economic and political structures that enable and limits sharing-culture practices in a shifting digital landscape."[38] Beginning in 2011, Kunci organized workshops on video and music sampling that brought together local music bands, fan clubs, law experts, and artists. The outcomes in this case were quite practical and ranged from a CD in the Megamix Militia 2 to a collection of video clips produced by fans with the help of Wok the Rock in Megamix Militia 3. All the audiovisual materials were collected through online voluntary contributions and freely distributed under a Creative Common policy. Megamix Militia was organized around the idea of music tribute, in which replicas of "original" songs are produced by both amateur and renowned musicians.

Conclusion

The evolution of collective practices in post-Reformasi Indonesia holds important lessons concerning the potential and the limitations of socially engaged art to negotiate a transformative role within postcolonial public spheres. The first lesson could be summarized by saying that working collaboratively is not an end but rather a starting point for addressing how art can best be used to involve wider audiences in processes of social transformation. Widely disparate in their intentions, tactics, and ways of conceiving their position within—and beyond—the Indonesian art scene, the activities of Taring Padi, ruangrupa, MES56, and Kunci are driven by a trial-and-error, experimental methodology of work. This methodology not only informed each group's theoretical and ideological approach to the sociopolitical reality of Indonesia; it also adapted and modulated each approach according to the variety of actions and activities each group undertook. This makes it difficult to categorize each collective at the outset, as it is necessary to track how each project modified the group's general structure and initial goals.

Secondly, as in the case of Ugandan, socially engaged and collaborative art from Indonesia provides a good example of the continuities marking processes of cultural and political renovation and evading strict historical categorizations. At the same time, the practical orientation of those projects also warns us about romanticizing the past and avoiding critical thought by identifying the continuity of that past everywhere in the present. Whereas it is easy to find traces of anticolonial and left-wing initiatives such as LEKRA and the *sanggar* tradition in present-day collectives, it is unhelpful and most of all unproductive to look for word-by-word versions of the "Bandung spirit" or of any other anticolonial progressive political project in the analyzed collectives. Indonesian collectives show us that the legacies of anticolonialism can haunt our present just as much as oppressive forces do. At the same, the four examples we examined reveal the potential of socially engaged art creativity to update and revitalize past emancipatory actions in new and unexpected ways.

A third lesson we can learn from looking at Indonesian collaborative art has to do with the complex ways in which the adjective "political" is presented, claimed, and mobilized. In the post-Reformasi context, the label "political art" was used and appropriated for multiple purposes, many of which were alien to the original intentions motivating Indonesian artists to express their anger against sociopolitical injustices. As Jim Supangkat warns, many Yogyakartan "artists entered the art market not despite but because of their social and political social matter" (quoted in Vanhoe 2016: 14). A major difference in the case of collaborative practices is that the varied interpretations of political action are always dependent on proximity to marginalized sectors of the population, with the *rakyat*. This does not mean that by working collaboratively, artists are by definition capable of fusing creativity with the social demands of civil society groups. What collaborative work in the analyzed cases does, however, is reveal the limitations of a mode of critical art based on the representation (no matter how ambivalent) of the *rakyat* and the redundant obsession with the troubled position occupied by visual artists in a moment of sociopolitical transition. In this sense, Indonesia reveals the multiple ways in which socially engaged art can be channeled to address not-so-obvious artistic and political objectives. Through this lens, the fact of many artistic collectives rooting their activity in a nonunified political ideology—the anarchist way in which they maneuver within the Indonesian Left, retooling strategic mo(ve)ments from the past while imagining the future—appears not so much as a disadvantage but rather as a way of responding to the emerging sociopolitical configurations of a country in transition.

The four examples analyzed above, like many other Indonesian collectives, look into future scenarios from the uncertainties deriving from the transition of Indonesia from colony to postcolony and from postcolony into something still unknown. In the contested terrain of post- Reformasi, groups like Taring Padi and initiatives like Kunci and ruangrupa challenge the accusation often leveled against socially engaged artists of being too obvious or too naive in their claims. The activity of those groups involves a difficult negotiation with official entities and political agents but also with different communities and public spheres and with the Indonesian art establishment. That negotiation is often used to attract attention toward issues that are overshadowed by broader national debates (for example, Taring Padi addressing environmental hazards and women's participation in the public sphere while criticizing the limitations of top-down democratization in 1998). Similarly, Kunci appropriates the methodology of cultural studies to criticize both the elitism of an academic system still based on a colonial inheritance of specialization and compartmentalization of knowledge, and a visual art medium often satisfied with publicly voicing its opposition to state oppression.

Indonesian collectivism also illustrates the importance of practice and long-term, trial-and-error processes in social transformation. If the necessity to incorporate the *rakyat* within the body of modernist national culture (and the collaborative answers this problem motivated) was one of the central concerns of Indonesian art throughout the twentieth century, this also meant that the only way of keeping pace with popular transformations was to incorporate sectors of the popular classes as active creators. This strategy, notwithstanding its contradictions, proved to be particularly efficient in times of transition such as the 1950s and the

1990s. Collaborative groups sought to respond to a brief widening of the horizon of progressive politics but also to a feeling of general uncertainty about the future. Practice-based collaboration with the *rakyat* gave Indonesian artists the possibility of inventing and putting into practice more efficient ways of using art to operate within a contested public sphere. Those practices reveal that the contemporary is a ground for experimentation (and not an imported formula or pattern to be followed). The experiments of Indonesian collectives are, in this sense, the result of a complex negotiation with global influences and a home-brewed tradition of social criticism through art spanning across the history of twentieth-century Indonesian politics.

Finally, we cannot end this chapter without leaving some important questions open. To what extent can socially engaged art be different from multimedia creativity and alternative institutionalism? What happens when the defining lines of socially engaged art projects begin to blur, and collaborative actions are the result of the sporadic collaboration of several collectives? What does the proximity of those groups to "official" national institutions (ruangrupa operating in the Jakarta National Gallery, for instance) mean for its original goals and their habitual audiences? Are art collectives more fitted than individuals to decolonize the logic presiding over those institutions? How is the centrality of location and located action altered in the case of collective practices increasingly relying on the digital domain? How are their offline and online sides articulated? How best to criticize the power relations and alliance networks resulting from the back-and-forth modulation between the local and the digital? To be sure, each of these questions is relevant by itself, and, as we have seen, the Indonesian context provides enough examples to address them. For now, however, we will end our exploration of Indonesian collective practices. The next chapter returns to these questions, while offering alternative answers within and outside the art domain.

7

• • •

AGENCY AND (STREET) ART POLITICS IN BEIRUT

On Temporary Art Platform's Guide
for Urban Intervention

The art project examined in this chapter can be seen as different both formally and in its objectives from the main examples examined in previous chapters. It takes the form of a 122-page bilingual guidebook with practical advice for Lebanese artists on how to make public artistic interventions in Beirut. The story begins in 2014, when independent Lebanese curator Amanda Abi Khalil created Temporary Art Platform (TAP). TAP is a curatorial and interventionist collective that focuses on producing and researching public art projects. TAP facilitates site-specific art interventions and mediates between artists and private and public powers. Seeking to understand how public art can become more context-sensitive, the platform also conducts research on legal and practical aspects surrounding existing and ongoing initiatives. Finally, TAP has recently started lobbying for production budgets for public art.

Within a research framework and in collaboration with lawyer Nayla Geagea, TAP decided to gather the expertise of different creative practitioners to set out a roadmap for artists wishing to produce site-specific and public artworks. The first step in constituting the guide came in the form of surveying past public art projects developed in Beirut and other parts of the country. Several elements, including funding, audience responses, and legal requirements, were analyzed and compared. From this survey, it turned out that formal procedures and nonwritten interests were among the trickiest elements Lebanese artists had to cope with.[1] For TAP, the idea of linking the analysis of public art to the preparation of a legal tool kit enabling artists to gauge and

199

attenuate bureaucratic and administrative hazards came as a natural step, one that, as in many of the cases examined in this book, conceived of praxis and shared experience as the best learning methods. The result, a tool kit addressing issues as mundane as fundraising, local legislation on public space use, and pathways for international collaboration, received the pragmatic and straightforward title: *A Few Things You Need to Know When Creating an Art Project in a Public Space in Lebanon.* The manual contains guiding principles, legal advice, and a panoply of examples organized with the intention of helping Lebanese artists to "chart the way," "get the way," or "ease the way" in relation to public and private regulations operating in Beirut. Whereas the formal tone of the guide and its focus on legal questions makes it less appealing than more overt political artworks dealing with equally problematic but catchier topics, such as the legacies of war, collective trauma, or the conflicted memories of conflict, *A Few Things* can actually be read as both a perfect mirror of the main issues postwar Lebanon is facing and a direct response to this book's driving questions (see figures 7.1 and 7.2).

Interestingly, a first standout feature of *A Few Things* hinges on its lack of sectarianism and its ideological neutrality. Within the politically turbulent panorama of postwar Lebanon, the guide adopts no political or religious allegiances. Although the country's political situation is analyzed in the book, we will not find in its pages any critical views on

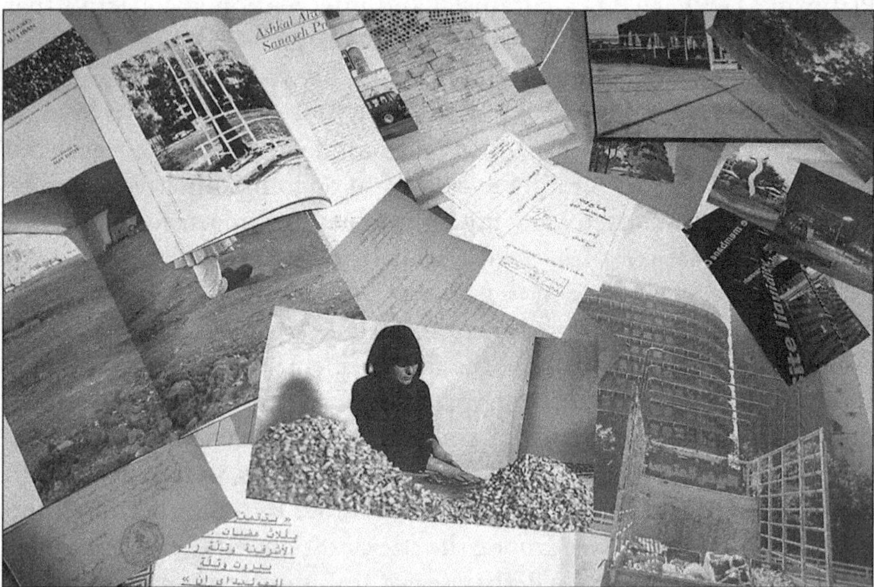

Figure 7.1. Temporary Art Platform, research photos for the database on public art practices, Lebanon. *Source*: Courtesy of Temporary Art Platform.

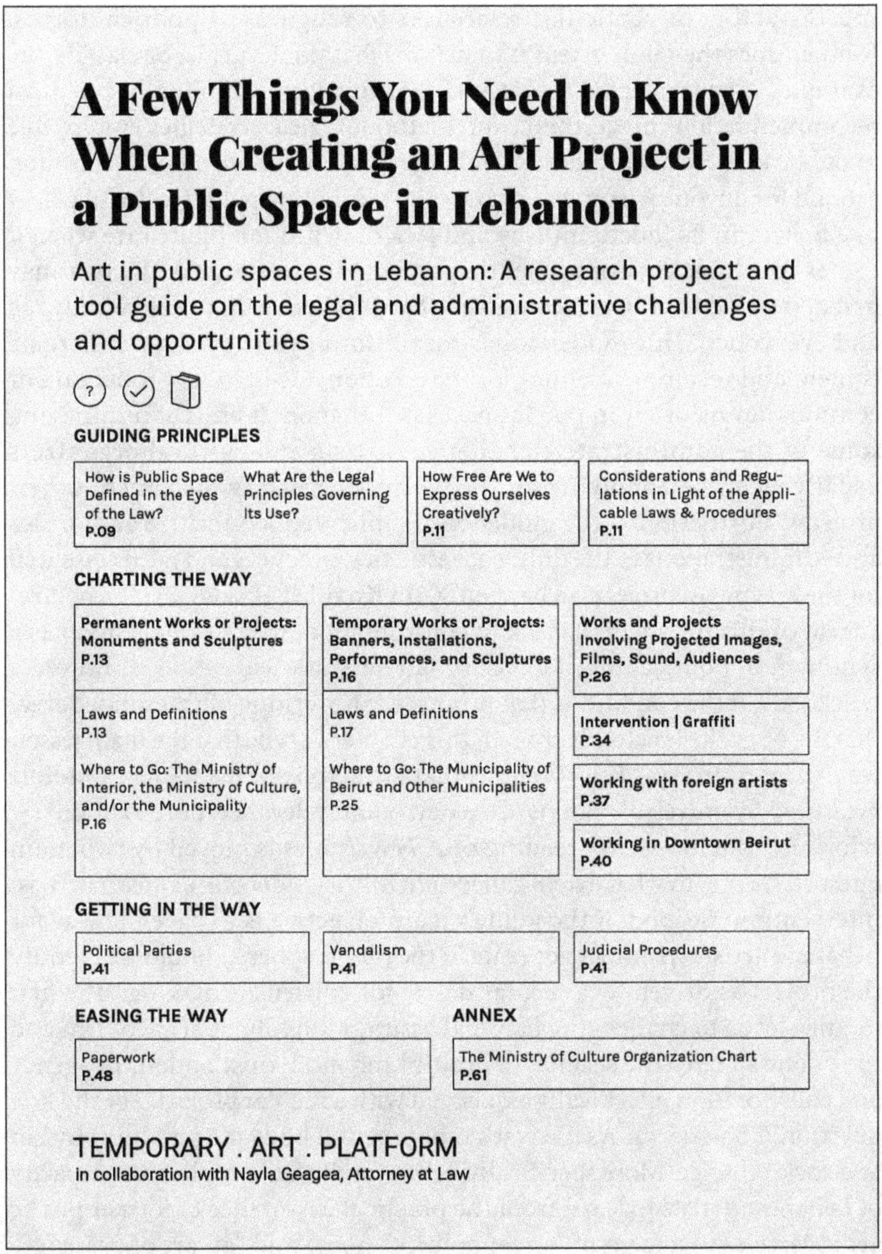

A Few Things You Need to Know When Creating an Art Project in a Public Space in Lebanon

Art in public spaces in Lebanon: A research project and tool guide on the legal and administrative challenges and opportunities

GUIDING PRINCIPLES

| How is Public Space Defined in the Eyes of the Law? P.09 | What Are the Legal Principles Governing Its Use? | How Free Are We to Express Ourselves Creatively? P.11 | Considerations and Regulations in Light of the Applicable Laws & Procedures P.11 |

CHARTING THE WAY

Permanent Works or Projects: Monuments and Sculptures P.13	Temporary Works or Projects: Banners, Installations, Performances, and Sculptures P.16	Works and Projects Involving Projected Images, Films, Sound, Audiences P.26
Laws and Definitions P.13	Laws and Definitions P.17	Intervention | Graffiti P.34
Where to Go: The Ministry of Interior, the Ministry of Culture, and/or the Municipality P.16	Where to Go: The Municipality of Beirut and Other Municipalities P.25	Working with foreign artists P.37
		Working in Downtown Beirut P.40

GETTING IN THE WAY

| Political Parties P.41 | Vandalism P.41 | Judicial Procedures P.41 |

EASING THE WAY

| Paperwork P.48 |

ANNEX

| The Ministry of Culture Organization Chart P.61 |

TEMPORARY . ART . PLATFORM
in collaboration with Nayla Geagea, Attorney at Law

Figure 7.2. Temporary Art Platform, cover page of the tool guide *A Few Things You Need to Know When Creating an Art Project in a Public Space in Lebanon*. *Source*: Courtesy of Temporary Art Platform.

specific actors or particular references to religious or political forces. Neither does the guide attempt to define what public art is, or classify the examples it has collected as successful or unsuccessful. Finally, practical recommendations on aesthetic and methodological strategies employable in public arts are also absent. Rather, the guide is conceived of as common ground for anyone wishing to recover the crumbling public realm of places like Beirut. In its indeterminacy and lack of definition (quite rare when it comes to a took kit, not to mention activist interventions), the text may first appear odd because it conceives of an addressee that could be anyone and everyone: "This guidebook is meant for anyone who can utilize its content and recommendations for the creation, facilitation, production or commissioning of art in public spaces in Lebanon. It aims at minimizing some of the administrative challenges artists and cultural organizers usually face when applying for the permits necessary to carry out their projects. Furthermore, the guidebook is intended to sensitize authorities and administrations to the different aesthetics, practices and needs essential for these types of projects to happen" (Abi Khalil et al. 2016: 4). The neutral appeal of this fragment, its lack of confrontation, may be understood as a synonym of political indifference or bureaucratic aspiration. However, a quick look at the conditions that prompted the writing of this guide reveal that the opposite is actually true. In this chapter I argue that the main lesson we can learn from *A Few Things* is that art activist ecosystems cannot be measured by universal notions of agency, public relevance, or revolutionary/reformist intentions. My reading of *A Few Things* is moved by two main questions: First, to what extent can we identify a guidebook as an art activist intervention? Second, if the guide's main objective is to pave the way for Lebanese artists wishing to operate in the public sphere, should we identify the project as driven by a secular desire for consensus making? The first inquiry leads to challenging habitual assumptions about art activism and the public sphere. The second, to unthinking modernist notions of agency and collaboration uncritically associated with a secular project. For the first question, I borrow on Asef Bayat's monumental body of work on activism and social change. More specifically, I draw on Bayat to explain the capacity of Lebanese artists to learn from the practical experience of former public art initiatives as a form of "street politics" (1997) and "an art of presence" (2010). The analysis of agency and the politics of sectarianism presented as an attempt to answer the second question will be grounded on Talal Asad's lucid deconstruction of the secular-modern (see Scott and Hirschkind 2006).

Through an examination of *A Few Things*, I attempt to demonstrate how the unsettling potential of public art should not be related with its capacity to shock, nor limited to a series of formulas that artists can apply anywhere. Rather, that potential is linked to the process of creating a new vocabulary for public engagement while also leaving enough room for the unforeseeable to happen. *A Few Things* provides fertile ground to examine the main contradictions in the fractured and threatened public sphere of Beirut. More than this, through the recognition that agency is after all possible despite all the bureaucratic obstacles, sectarian hatred, and rampant privatization, the guide shifts the debate on postwar visual art practices in Lebanon, placing emphasis on the limited but real possibilities for public engagement that a new generation of artists is exploring as a way of complementing (much more than overcoming) the concerns on loss, conflicting memories, and the impossibility of historical record of a previous generation. These artists rely on the adoption of a "disciplined spontaneity," to borrow the words of the curator, archivist, and filmmaker Akram Zataari (Hojeij, Soueid, and Zaatari 2002: 83) concerning Lebanese video practices.

The work of the so-called postwar generation of Lebanese artists, including Rabih Mroué, Walid Raad/the Atlas Group, Walid Sadek, Akram Zaatari, Paola Yacoub, Ghassan Salhab, Lamia Joreige, Khalil Joreige, and Joana Hadjithomas, was traditionally associated with certain common interests: the impossibility of a historical common ground, the life of ruins;[2] the uselessness of traditional versions of historical record when remembering the internecine conflict that devastated Lebanon from 1975 to 1990; and the potential of archival and documentary technologies (in the form of video or photograph) to challenge the distance between fact and fiction, truth and mediated representation, rendering that distance productive. Hence, for example, Raad's creation of the Atlas Group in 1999 "to research and document the contemporary history of Lebanon."[3] Drawing on a fragmented and multiple subjectivity in order to develop an impossible yet fruitful archive, the Atlas Group challenges both the amnesty following the end of the Lebanese Civil War[4] (which was seen for many as an interval amid an ongoing state of conflict, as an ongoing situation) and the neoliberal reconstruction of several areas of Beirut, especially its downtown area, during the 1990s. Similarly, Zaatari explores how mediation and postproduction were essential in the configuration of images of martyrdom and their use and circulation by religious and secular parties. In projects such as *In This House,* Zaatari excavates a house occupied by a resistance group in Ain el Mir, a village located at the borderline with the Israeli occupation forces in 1985. The objective of Zaatari's archeological search was a letter written by Ali Hashisho, a member of the Resistance. In the letter, Hashisho narrates his experience of the occupation. The missive was hidden inside a mortar and then buried in the house's garden, waiting for a future occupant to unearth it. Zaatari's project is as much about recovering lost memories as it is about making sense of the uncanniness of dealing with them in the present. *In This House* opposes "excavational" to archival practices, the former being less committed to power and authority and tending more toward revelation and knowledge production.[5] In installations such as *Love Is Blind* or *The Labour of Missing/The Wreck of Hope*, an installation that engages the work of the mid-twentieth-century painter Moustafa Farroukh, Walik Sadek explores alternative concepts of negativity and loss to those proposed by traditional theories of trauma, pointing out that in Lebanon, trauma (and the need to forget) works in tandem with the excesses of a postwar society also blocked by a parallel obsession with consumerism and moving forward (Sadek and Fattouh 2012).

At first, the efforts of this generation in exploring the weight of multiple and conflicting memories involved in the production of truth, history, and nostalgia, postcard-like images of a vibrant past, could be identified as a postmodern denial of reality in favor of mediation and representation.[6] However, Chad Elias warns about the danger of reading the practices of that generation as mainly concerned with trauma and with the problematization of historical records *in the past*. For him, "the impulse to analyze these practices through the framework of trauma risks evacuating them of their potential as a site of political agency within communities of witnessing" (Elias 2018: 15). He identifies instead a shared interest in action and civic transformation through their exploration of the afterlives of "wounded images," that is, visual and cinematic documents ("authentic" and fictive) reaching our present and enabling new utterances through their continuous, posthumous reproduction. Following Hito Steyerl's (2009) concern with the "poor image," for Elias, the main preoccupation of those artists is with exploring the extent to which war in Lebanon was also a war "waged with and over images" (Elias 2018: 16). He claims that Lebanese artists are central pieces in the reimagination of alternative futures.[7] Issues of agency and public relevance, therefore, would not be alien to this body of work despite the fact of their being expressed mainly in gallery spaces and cinemas.[8]

Agreeing with Elias that there is a public concern in the work of Raad and others, I am more interested in exploring a less-examined group of practices seeking to occupy open spaces and, more than that, to directly address the possibilities for existing groups and communities to resurface from the withdrawal into representation and mediation, and to hypothesize recovering a minimum yet operational level of agency. *A Few Things* moves beyond the need to criticize the unreachability of sectarian groups through the infinite set of mediations and the fragmentation of memory deriving from Beirut's more than questionable process of reconstruction and the absence of an agreed version of the past. *A Few Things* shares with the work of the so-called postwar generation an interest in turning social memory into a productive site of cultural and political imagination. However, in this case, more emphasis is put on the practical conditionings applying to those wishing to produce public art projects. The set of rules contained in *A Few Things* translates the successes and failures of a troubled past, but instead of focusing on the untranslatability or inaccessibility of that past (an absence that cannot be filled), it reveals how it can provide ground for contemporary experimentations.[9] Addressing this process means defining what counts as public in a place like Beirut.

When the Lebanese Civil War ended in 1990, the government of Rafic Hariri undertook a process of urban reconstruction that sought to lay the ground for a wider process of social reconciliation and democratic "normalization." The private conglomerate Solidere led the reconstruction, choosing which buildings should be preserved and which zones should be given priority. Downtown Beirut, with its monumental colonial architecture dating back to the French and Ottoman occupations of the city, emerged as the main priority in the task of restoration. In Samir Khalaf's words (2012: 85): "Time, space, movement and interaction all became enveloped with contingency and uncertainty. Nothing was taken for granted anymore. People lived, so to speak, situationally. Short-term expediency replaced long-term planning. Everything had to be negotiated on the spur of the moment."

Solidere's coordination of the reconstruction process was highly problematic for at least three reasons. First, it granted a private company the right to decide over how the fifteen years of conflict ought to be remembered (and forgotten). Second, Solidere's intervention consisted of erasing any sign of conflict from the walls, which meant destroying a great part of the city center's heritage, replacing it with perfect replicas from which both traumatic memories and conflicting uses of the past were absent. One experiences an odd and disturbing feeling when contemplating the material results of Solidere's project in downtown Beirut. Everything recalls a city of the past, yet at the same time none of the elements in this scenario demands that the viewer remember. The Beirut Central District became a postcard-like replica (or a recreation) of Beirut's golden age, a consumer-friendly exclusionary space. Through nostalgia, history was rendered "pure space, pure commodity, pure real estate" (Makdisi 1997: 692). For all intents and purposes, downtown Beirut became a theme park full of fancy hotels and restaurants oriented to the consumer habits of a wealthy minority of Lebanese and foreigners, a landscape severed from its previous history and also prohibited to its contemporary inhabitants, as the task of "reconstruction" entailed massive evictions. Finally, along with the privatization of property came the intensification of public and private technologies and practices of surveillance that replicated and reterritorialized previous processes of class exclusion and marginalization, turning public spaces into strongholds.[10] As a result of this process, the public "became centred on very small confines," as Sune Haugbolle (2010: 57) argued. It is worth noting that security and surveillance operated not as a set of straightforward measures affecting the totality of the population but rather on a much more complicated scale that takes into account religious, political, and economic elements: "High-end shoppers and political actors hide behind the same type of barbed wire while each claims protection from the other—without, again, excluding the possibility for a same actor to move regularly across categories" (Fawaz, Gharbieh, and Harb 2009: 3). In this context, nonwritten privileges and allegiances to place turned out to be as important as official regulations controlling the use of public areas, something that had a decisive impact on the possibilities and limitations of artistic collectives such as TAP.

For TAP, legal research arose as an unexplored and timely field of enormous dimensions where such concerns with place could be articulated. The collective realized that sociopolitical changes were taking place so rapidly that it was more necessary than ever for artists to keep apace with the conditions regulating public interactions in Lebanon. More than this, it discovered that many of the most important rules applying to that shifting landscape were not written. Things became even more complicated when the collective discovered that the regulation of the uses of public spaces was not clear, homogeneous, or up to date. Even worse, the last document directly addressing that question had been issued by the French mandate in 1925. That document, resulting from one of the many successive colonial occupations Lebanon underwent throughout the twentieth century, is hardly applicable to the present situation: first, it conceived public spaces to be administered by (colonial) public instances; second, it recognized those spaces as de facto opened to equitable and free-of-charge use. Consequently, the two driving forces threatening the contemporary public sphere (communalization and illegal privatization) were absent from the equation at play in the 1925 legal text (Abi Khalil et al. 2016: 9–10).

In addition to gathering existing regulations on the use of public spaces, TAP also focused on developing legal research on freedom of expression. Here as well there was a huge disparity between what the law stipulated and what Lebanese citizens were entitled to.[11] For example, the exhibition of banners and posters for artistic purposes is regulated as if these were advertising images. However, if the nature of the banners is declared to be "religious," specific conditions regarding temporality and content may apply as well (Abi Khalil et al. 2016: 17). Ambiguity and legal vagueness accordingly become the norm; for instance, among the examples provided by the guide is a collective performance by the Popular Front for the Liberation of Art in downtown Beirut in 2013. This action included the display of banners referring to art as "salvation," "faith," "martyrdom," etcetera. Although containing clear allusions to religious vocabulary and mimicking the language of protest, in this case no permit was required. The guide also mentions a site-specific installation by Nada Sehnaoui produced in the same area ten years earlier, in 2003. On that occasion, the artists collected the personal memories of the civil war from the inhabitants of downtown Beirut. Those memories were transcribed into different documents, which were piled up forming columns. Blank pages were also added to the installation, giving the sense of loss and incompleteness that other artists have also transmitted using similar dialogical strategies (Elias 2018). In this case, , even though the action took place in a public space, the installation required permission not only from the Beirut Municipality but also from Solidere, the private company in charge of reconstructing downtown Beirut (Abi Khalil et al. 2016: 18–19). Finally, a third body of examples is based on relocations and changes of plan following unsuccessful attempts to secure public and private permits. This is the case of Raafat Majzoub's public participative performance *Alo Shayefni?* (Hello, can you see me?), a project exploring the functionality of abandoned architecture originally designed for downtown Beirut and later applied to various abandoned buildings. In this situation, the guide registers how prior meetings with sectarian groups explaining the nature of the action were held as a way of ensuring the development of the project.

To understand how *A Few Things* works, it is necessary to understand the nature of the pubic in Lebanon. In this sense, one might refer to the continuous pressure of two seemingly antagonistic forces, that of communalism and that of commodification, which, despite their differences, manage to work together in reducing the spaces available for collective interaction. Talking about the public in a place like Beirut involves finding potential points of convergence against a backdrop of political closure and privatization, in the atmosphere of collective hatred and mistrust permeating Beirut civil society. It has to do with coping with an excess of proximity without expectations of reconciliation (Sadek 2015).

Here "proximity" refers to pluralism and sectarianism (which should not be confused with religious differences, but rather related to how those become politicized at the same time as "public" spaces of consumerism acquire a quasireligious status). Yet it should also encompass something else: the spatial and historical relocations of the political in relation to the multiple sensibilities inhabiting the public sphere, or to put it more simply, the different ideas about what the public is and who is entitled to define it. Against the Habermasian empty space made available to dissenting agents seeking to convince and negotiate without restraints (without history), the "public" in the Lebanese case can be thinkable only as the continuous renegotiation of heterogeneous definitions of the civic across a fractured and ever-shifting territory.

Lebanese art critic and curator Rasha Salti sees in the reemergence of graffiti in the aftermath of the civil war a reflection of "Lebanon's postwar reconfiguration of 'publicness.'" Writing in 2008, at the peak of conflict that followed the short-lived 2005 Cedar Revolution, Salti (2008: 623) identifies public art as a central platform used by artists to both "de-ghettois[e] 'vanguard' or unconventional artistic practices from the exclusive microcosm of an intellectual and economic elite group and releas[e] them into the street." She argues that Lebanese artists are claiming a space within civil society for the defense of basic rights for social safety, environmental livability, and sexual difference. This space is often overlooked by the politicized agenda of sectarian groups.[12] Since politics and religion have been a heightened space in Lebanon for several decades, colonizing almost every discussion, public art emerges as a central tool for pushing the publicness of art forward and for securing a place for a politics of the many. As in many other countries in the Middle East, when it comes to artistic initiatives, volatility is the norm and consolidation the exception (Kortun 2004). It comes as no surprise, then, that public art initiatives are even more fragile and unpredictable than gallery-based art practices. Artists have to navigate a complex space with limited "official" institutional support.[13] Dealing with the practicalities of funding and bureaucracy, but also with the consequences of the continuous processes of spatial redefinition resulting from the ongoing situation of protracted and undefined conflict characterizing recent Lebanese history, *A Few Things* shares Salti's concerns with the limitations of an artistic and cultural class and the opportunities to operate within the sphere of civil society.

Taking into account those determining factors and the varied range of situations, for TAP it turned out that the exposure that Lebanese artists often have to international trends, and their previous knowledge of site-specific and public art practices, were not enough when navigating the choppy waters of bureaucratic impediments, institutional indifference, poverty, postwar trauma, and the communalist customs and sensibilities that shape present-day Lebanese society. It was necessary to start from scratch, to define a new artistic language, and to learn from successful and unsuccessful recent examples.[14] The articulation of a basic grammar for public art had to manage both the contradictions and the opportunities brought about by the process of postwar "recovery." No predefined formula would work in that context. Rather, TAP's interventionist actions (like those of the groups and individuals preceding them) are grounded on the belief that only sustained experimentation and local engagement can provide efficient answers to constantly changing transforming needs.

Although not specifically focused on artistic practices and art activism, several elements of Asef Bayat's monumental work on "street politics" and collective social transformation in the Middle East and the Arab world are identifiable in *A Few Things*.[15] Bayat is concerned with producing a "history of agency in times of constraints," so as to give critical space to alternative forms of activism currently going under the radar because of the theoretical limitations of the Western-centered critical tools used to examine them. Bayat's Middle East is shaped by unusual forms of activist agency as they struggle against existing ideologies and institutional pressure. At least three elements of his approach to this topic are relevant to this chapter. First, Bayat conceives activist interventions in a cumulative sense, as "Stepping-stone[s] for further claims," operating through "cumulative encroaching" and "winning new position to move on" (1997: 17, 56).

In the same way, *A Few Things* borrows from previous experiences to articulate a new grammar for public art in Lebanon. Secondly, coincidences can also be found between Bayat's action- and practice-oriented understanding of activism and TAP's interest in moving beyond ideological discussions to focus on the practical constraints Lebanese face when attempting to recover public spaces through artistic interventions. In both cases, emphasis is put on the conditions of engagement to articulate a politics not of protest but of ordinary practice. Finally, Bayat highlights how collective, ordinary activist action is galvanized through solidarities forged in public spaces. His view challenges Michael Hardt and Antonio Negri's (2005) idea of *multitude,* based on a global mass of heterogeneous individuals coming together.

For Bayat (1997: 21), "collective action is a function of shared interests and identities within a single group," a group that nevertheless has the capacity for transcending its habitual sphere of intervention so as to reach wider interlocutors. In a similar way, the sense of disorientation and the need to invent a new language of public art became even clearer in the first public interventions produced in Beirut during the 1990s. The first pieces of site-specific intervention in Beirut in the 1990s were produced by the artists association Ashkal Alwan.[16] The association undertook the difficult task of defining a grammar of public art in a context in which the roles attributed to artists, curators, and cultural managers and what was expected from each of them are not well defined. The first initiative took place in 1995 in the central Sanayeh Park and worked as a way of resuming dormant traditions of operating in public (Sadek 2007: 38). After vigorous negotiations, Ashkal Alwan obtained permission to display site-specific installations and develop interactive performances. Thirty artists were invited to work in different locations within the garden. The artists were present for the opening of the exhibition, at which they interacted with the audience. Christine Tohme, who curated the intervention and coordinated the event, points out that the Sanayeh Project was beneficial in two different respects: first, because it fueled a tradition of public art interventions that involves reusing public spaces; and second, because it mixed the "usual suspects" of the art world with the broader audience enjoying the park.[17] Two more points should be highlighted. By setting the event in a public garden at night, it challenged the general climate of suspicion that had become common for many Lebanese after fifteen years of civil war. Furthermore, by including a vast number of artworks and making possible an exchange between artists and the audience, it became clear that a mode of intervention different from that of the megalomaniac "reconstruction" of Solidere (which can be identified as the main "interventionist" in 1990s Lebanon) was possible. Additional initiatives took this model further. In 1997 Ashkal Alwan coordinated the production of ten public sculptures at the Sioufi Gardens. Since the project was the result of a commission by the Ministry of Culture aiming at the production of public sculpture, the degree of autonomy granted to the artists was limited.

Much more interesting were the Corniche and Hamra Street Projects, developed in 1999 and 2000, respectively. The Corniche is the long coastal promenade surrounding Beirut, one of the city's main spaces for socialization. On this occasion, the project included site-specific sculptures and installations, as well as interactive performances and debates over the use of the public space. In the Hamra Street Project, the main artery of West Beirut was used as a living laboratory of vernacular culture and intercommunal exchange. The art projects resulted from dialogical exchanges with the inhabitants of Hamra (themselves a far more heterogeneous group in terms of class than the gentrified postcard may suggest, and which includes not only "formal" spaces of consumerism but also a great number of "informal" workers whose presence still very much shapes the neighborhood). The final display of each production also took place at the same location, reinforcing the need to insert public art into the city's social fabric (Wilson-Goldie 2009). Dealing with the Hamra Street Project, Akram Zaatari (2006) acknowledges, "The artists' responses to *Hamra Street Project* transformed the notion of site-specificity into an open forum, and changed its organizing body, Ashkal Alwan, into a commissioner." The crucial point in this interpretation is that it allows us to measure public art practices in a genealogical way, through the echo those practices produce in future initiatives. The four main events organized by Ashkal Alwan in the late 1990s were the result of testing and perfecting different strategies of public interaction, which were also adopted by other creators around the same years. For instance, consider the exhibitionary logic of Marwa Arsanios, who, although confined to a private apartment, responds to similar interests in expanding the reach of public art, seeking alternative forms of collective livability and using dialogical interaction to raise awareness about the colonization of the public space through economic privatization. Something similar can be said concerning the Ayloul Festival, an annual event created in 1996 with the intention of providing a hint of contemporary artistic experimentation that also included performance and public display of video works, as well as international collaborations.[18]

It is worth remembering that the initiatives of the 1990s were produced under the pernicious influence of Solidere's megalomaniac "reconstruction" project, in which the occupation of public space by the private conglomerate operating in partnership with the government was seen by many as a continuation of the state of war by other means. Elias Khoury, for example, recognizes a continuation of the war logic in Solidere's systematic destruction of heritage and privatization of downtown Beirut in defense of "history" a continuation of the war logic, a continuation in which "the struggle for recovering memory was not in its essence a nostalgic draw for the past. Rather, it was a drive to claim the present, because the present can only be grounded in a break from its past. In other words, collective memory has to remain living for the present to be free from the hold" (Khoury 2006: 4). Similarly, writing as early as 1997, Saree Makdisi identified a colonizing element in Solidere's attempt to provide a unique, conflict-free face for the neoliberal, developmental urban and political project that followed the civil war. He recognized in Harirism a living lab in which an infinite colonization over virtually everything that exists (and even nonexistent realities, past and to come) is tested:

What Solidere and Harirism seem to represent is precisely the withering away of the state, whatever one might have called a public sphere or civil society, and their final and decisive colonization by capital. And perhaps it is for this reason that the company avoids any discussion of Lebanese national identity except in terms of visual pastiche. Instead of a redemption of the competing narratives of collective memory or national identity, Solidere offers an emptying-out of those collective claims and memories and the substitution of a "collectivity" defined by a stock-offering, in which a strictly individualized form of participation is regulated and defined by the purchase of stocks rather than in terms of historic or communal/ national identities and uncommodified rights. (Makdisi 1997: 693)

The context of *Few Things*, which was publicly launched in 2015, one decade after the assassination of Prime Minister Rafic Hariri, is not that of the first interventions by Ashkal Alwan. The guide is produced in the aftermath of the Solidere era, with the echo of a new, harmful Israeli invasion and the reemergence of new sectarian strife in mind. Perhaps more strangely, conflict happened simultaneously with the frenetic impulse of urban development, the gentrification of neighborhoods, and the consolidation of Beirut's culture of escapism. If the Solidere era was clearly identifiable as the colonization of the public and the state through conflicting memories and private capitalism, the following decade witnessed the consolidation and normalization of this model through a rampant competition of increasingly taller skyscrapers, increasingly fancier nightclubs, and increasingly utopian urban interventions.[19] More than this, the last decade blurred the signs of sectarian hostility even more, making it more difficult (for artists as for everyone) to know how to navigate the shifting psychogeography of sectarianism. Dealing with the contemporary panorama of urban fragmentation in Beirut, Hiba Bou Akar (2018: 9) characterizes Beirut urbanism as a military strategy, a way of preparing for conflicts yet to come. War in times of peace, she argues, "is not fought with tanks, artillery, and rifles, but through a geopolitical territorial contest, where the fear of domination of one group by another is played out over such issues as land and apartment sales, the occupation of ruins, access to housing, zoning and planning regulations, and infrastructure projects." To this she adds a crucial emphasis on "everyday sectarianism," which she takes to be the continuous negotiation and transformation of sectarian strife through everyday practices (11). It is this panorama that artists wishing to produce pieces of public art have to face (see figures 7.3 and 7.4).

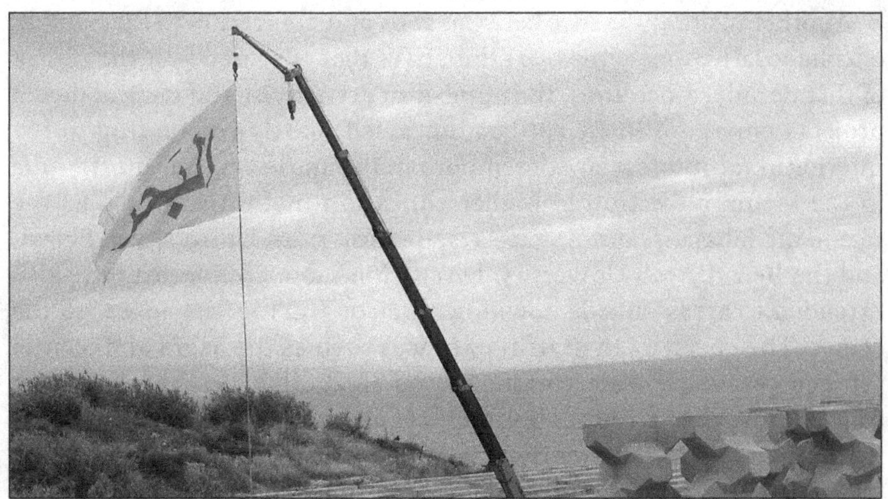

Figure 7.3. Omar Fakhoury, *The Flag*, a site-specific intervention in the framework of Art Interventions on Dalieh, 2017. *Source*: Courtesy of Temporary Art Platform.

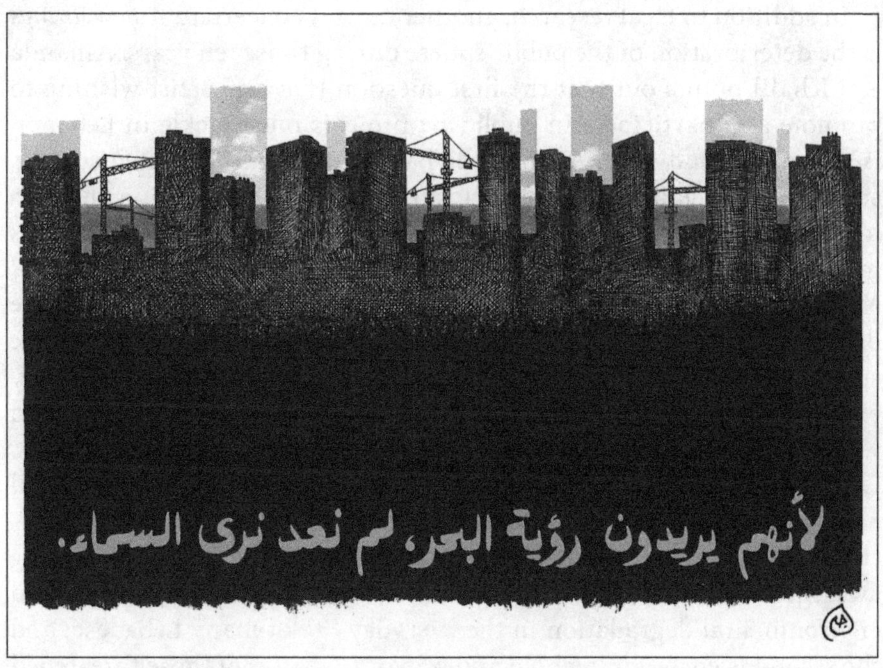

Figure 7.4. Jana Traboulsi, *Because They Want a View on the Sea, We Cannot See the Sky*, 2010. *Source*: Courtesy of Jana Traboulsi.

Another major difference between 2005 and 2015 relates to the number of collaborative and activist art initiatives that appeared over the course of that decade. Since 2005, the number of art activist and tactical media projects emerging in Beirut has increased, partly responding to the international interest in contemporary Lebanese art, but mostly due to the formative action of higher education institutions such as the Académie Libanaise des Beaux-Arts, the American University of Beirut, and the Beirut Arab University. Discussions about public art have also extended to areas outside downtown Beirut and the "art zones" in the center. The covering in graffiti of spaces such as the Sabra and Shatila refugee camps for Palestinians or the Hezbollah neighborhoods in south Beirut have attracted both critical attention and tourist curiosity. Although artistic interventions were not uncommon in those zones, what has changed is the general concern among the Lebanese mass of artists and critics about the impossibility of enclosing the debate about the public relevance of art within the comfort zone of central Beirut. This diversity informs the plurality of situations and the practical advice included in *A Few Things*.

In addition to legal research, another central concern in *A Few Things* is the deterioration of the public sphere during those ten years. Amanda Abi Khalil points out that the first question that any artist wishing to promote and participate in public art projects must tackle in Lebanon is that of the audience. Against the backdrop of a fragmented society, subjected to ongoing forms of enclosure and communalization and also to a continuous degradation of the public space, the question of "Who is my audience?" becomes more complicated than expected. The practical elements conditioning the strategies of public art artists, therefore, are directly marked by the distinctive qualities of the Lebanese postwar public sphere. As Abi Khalil explains, if the latter are not considered carefully enough, the project would run the risk of being unimportant or, even worse, counterproductive in relation to its communicational aspirations. One recurrent obstacle those projects faced had to do with how legal and illegal land use was limiting public areas. *A Few Things* performs two different tasks concerning those restrictions: the first is generating awareness about the impact of processes of privatization, enclosure, and environmental degradation in the everyday life of many Lebanese; and the second is encouraging bold and provocative uses of those threatened spaces as a way of harboring communicative and interactional processes and expanding their reach. In this context, the question of what can be done arises as central yet not self-evident. Projects such as *A Few Things* require us to consider agency anew.

Despite its centrality in explaining the saliency of activist and socially engaged practices, the concept of agency is often undertheorized. In many cases, a universal idea of activist agency is uncritically applied to multiple contexts. The critical success and widespread acceptance of (some) forms of socially engaged creativity by mainstream institutions is joined by the normalization of an unquestioned idea of agency uncritically attached to that ever-growing range of those creative practices. If socially engaged art practices are receiving increasing attention, the multiple forms agency can adopt in radical creative processes are subject to far less examination. In his seminal work on the secular, Talal Asad identifies agency as one of the main fractures of the modernist project hidden under the idea of the secular.[20] Asad recognizes a continuity of the modernist logic of progress in the universalization of a particular idea of agency based on an impersonal subject capable of transforming her/his reality through self-empowerment. The success of agency understood as the innate and unbound capacity of "active subjects" employing action and passion in "history-making" is grounded, so Asad (2003: 68) argues, in a "vindication of the secular," which is to be taken as a distorted, limited logic that silences alternative possibilities of acting and doing. That logic reinforces modernist notions of autonomy and individualism, for "to the extent that the task of confronting power is taken to be more than an individual one, it also defines a historical project whose aim is the increasing triumph of individual autonomy" (71). Against the normalization of that historical project, Asad conceives agency in a more complex sense, pointing out that "we should not assume that every act is the act of a competent agent with a clear intention. Nor should we assume that a proper understanding of agency requires us to place it within the framework of a secular history of freedom from all coercive control, a history in which everything can be made, and pleasure always innocently enjoyed—a framework that allegedly enables us to see ordinary life as distorted or incomplete" (72–73).

It is obvious that Asad is not interested in rejecting or denying agency but rather in acknowledging that the model of agency he criticizes is only one among many others, one nevertheless sanctioned by the historical project of secularism as unique and universally valid. His concern is with recognizing that agency acts as a complex notion encompassing multiple possibilities of action undertaken by a multiplicity of subjects by no means subsumable under the ideal figure of a "conscious agent-subject having both the capacity and the desire to move in a singular historical direction: that of increasing self-empowerment and decreasing pain" (2003: 79). The idea of pain is central in Asad's interest in expanding the concept of agency and detaching it from its appropriation by a limiting secular and modernist project of history making. Pain—traditionally attached to religious notions of self-sacrifice and restriction—allows him to explain how a certain notion of the secular (and the religious) makes possible a certain logic that explains and ultimately legitimizes the historical project of secularism.

I am less interested here in following Asad's identification of the secular and the religious as formations allowing and allocating form and meaning to specific practices and ideas, than in recognizing that a similar logic prevails when it comes to agency in socially engaged art practices. Many of the socially engaged art practices analyzed in this book are explainable only when a plurality of acting subjects is recognized. This becomes particularly evident in *A Few Things*. The nuanced and careful approach to action made by the guide reinforces Asad's concern with the limited horizon deriving from a universal (and secular) idea of agency. It also supports Bou Akar's idea of sectarianism as a continuously revised, multifaceted reality. Against the idea of a unique subject engaging without sociocultural constraints in processes of social transformation, *A Few Things* reveals the multiple and conflicting interests that often lie behind individual and collective (artistic) action. The interest behind the collection of norms and examples is not to provide a utopian image of a future freed from sectarian rivalries; rather, *A Few Things* shows that any consideration of agency must start out by taking into account how sectarian interests define competing modes of normativity, different definitions of and approaches to the public. Each of the examples analyzed in *A Few Things* arose out of particular agents responding to the precise circumstances, written and unwritten, of postwar Beirut. The public art initiatives resulting from those projects are modulated by diverse groups' sensibilities. Instead of seeing them merely as a limiting factor, thus rejecting the possibility of operating publicly, we can identify in the project's capacity to validate those conditioning elements a multiplicity of agencies seeking to cope with the shifting expectations of a society in transition. The correlation between action and normativity that follows from the advice given in the book reveals that public art is strongly grounded in specific sociocultural conventions. By taking account of these conventions, the group does not undermine the radical potential that public art can have; rather, it acknowledges how that potential is always fulfilled in contextual, located ways by contextual, located subjects.

It may well be that the current fortune of art activism and the reasons why it appeals to mainstream art institutions lie in the normalization (and henceforth loss of sociopolitical relevance, or at least, as we will see, critical heterogeneity) of the notion of agency itself. If that is the case, we will be facing a paradoxical situation: the more practices claim to be socially relevant, the more standardized and therefore the more rigid, the less applicable the idea of creative social relevance becomes. The importance of institutional explanations for this uniformization cannot be dismissed. However, the hypothesis that the presumed loss of radicality of socially engaged art practices lies also in the domestication and reduction of our grammar of agency is also plausible. Causes and consequences should not be confused (in other words, criticism is not to be blamed for the capitulation of activist practice). Resorting to a pessimistic identification of socially engaged art with a(n already defunct or at least moribund) artistic style is not the point either. The matter is much simpler and touches on the need to give more thought to the relations between agency and interpretation, theory and practice.

A first step in that direction would include conceiving agency as a complex concept subject to different conceptual formations. This means understanding that what we can and cannot do is not only dependent on our will as free, homogeneous subjects. Nor should agency be constrained by our cultural conditioning. When we act (and the kind of acting socially engaged art brings to the scene emerges as particularly interesting), the interplay between desire and constraints is tested. What is crucial is that each notion of agency (and the success of civil society theorizations has but multiplied the number of ways in which we can understand the concept!) involves a whole different set of possibilities. Conceiving (art) activist agency as a universal, human attribute that is always available to all subjects not only limits our capacity to understand how and when we act; it also conditions our real capacity to do so. The consequences of accepting an unquestioned, universal notion of agency in any context has disastrous consequences for our understanding of how art works. It also normalizes the limiting horizon of Western-centered avant-gardist aesthetics, reducing the relevance of different activist forms as if they were only gradually perfected forms of a unique, Western model of social relevance. By contrast, provincializing agency means not only challenging the idea that we all have the same prerogatives as civic subjects (as individual beings) but also that acting can mean disparate things even when similar in appearance. Reading agency, as Asad does, as integrated into a variety of contingent and conflicting sets of formations enriches our capacity to assess the multiple ways in which art works.

A Few Things raises important questions about the limitations and possibilities of cultural criticism dealing with public art. First, it pushes to its limits the idea that art should operate in connecting individual agencies within previously defined and largely neutral, universal, public spheres. Contrary to that image, the guide reveals how public art projects are often the result of a careful consideration of multiple options. That consideration, it should not be forgotten, can always bring unforeseeable (positive or negative) results. Second, *A Few Things* challenges the idea that art activism operates publicly by moving individual wills that decide to freely associate and gather around shared causes, as if the private life and identity of those individual agencies happens on equal terms. Rather, the guide reveals that action is more often than not the result of not-predetermined decisions and desires. Third, *A Few Things* further complicates the very idea of the public, glimpsing a looming future of rampant modernization (the scars of past and ongoing conflicts, the landscape of permanent war so commonly referred to after 9/11, being flattened out by hyperbolic development *a la Dubai*). The project concentrates the collective experience of fighting long-lasting sources of harm: consumerism and communalism, oblivion and sectarian memory.

Yet something else can be identified in the advice given to those artists adventurous enough to exchange the shelter of top-of-the-range gallery spaces for the crowded public areas of Beirut. The apparent neutrality of the book sharply contrasts with the urgency of the histories informing it. The recommendations contained in *A Few Things* set out to be sufficiently uncontroversial as to leave space to individual creativity (itself a way of avoiding overt politicization of sectarian values). However, that neutrality also evokes how public art can become a threshold of collective imagination. The apparent apolitical and "bureaucratic" tone of the guide should not be confused with ideological escapism. *A Few Things* works in opening a common ground where difference and untranslatability are not minimized. At the same time, it allows enough space for artists to learn from previous experience in order to define an alternative vocabulary of the public. "The political" in *A Few Things* involves giving space to possibilities left aside amid the noise of the exacerbated tensions existing in the country. The action of public artists and activists opens up a space for a different politics beyond war and sectarianism, a politics that I nevertheless have some qualms in considering simply as secular or nonsectarian.[21] For *A Few Things* does not dismiss religion and sectarian politics; it points out how to best dialogue with these. Indeed, the careful consideration of nonwritten normativity we find in *A Few Things* reveals that the context of public art is in negotiation with, not in complete opposition to, personal and collective desires and expectations.

◆ ◆ ◆

Part Four

ENCLOSURES, APERTURES, AND THE PERFORMATIVE

8

◆ ◆ ◆

UTILITY, MULTISPECIES AGENCY, AND SPECULATIVE STUDY

On Ensayos

Introduction

In writing about *arte útil*, Tania Bruguera establishes a distinction with representational creativity. *Arte útil* would be committed to "imagin[ing], create[ing], develop[ing] and implement[ing] something that, produced in artistic practice, offers the people a clearly beneficial result" (Bruguera 2011). Bruguera first put *arte útil* into practice in her home country between 1985 and 1996 by restaging Ana Mendieta's actions and in 2002 creating the Cátedra Arte de Conducta (Behavior Art School), a forum for alternative education and a platform for public (art) interventions that revolved around the specificities of the civic in Cuban society.[1] Finally, in 2011 the artist initiated the Immigrant Movement International in partnership with the Queens Museum of Art, a creative and political think tank aimed at promoting migrants' rights.

The replacement of "authors with initiators and spectators with users" (Bruguera 2011) (a movement that owes much to the theorist Stephen Wright's book *Lexicon of Usership*, and which borrows from Wright's idea that art should adopt a one-to-one scale) acquires a programmatic tone in the last iteration of Bruguera's notion of *arte útil*, the Museum of Arte Útil, created in the Old Building of the Van Abbemuseum in Eindhoven, the museum now directed by Charles Esche.[2] As the project's website summarizes, to be useful, art must meet eight criteria:

221

1. Propose new uses for art within society
2. Challenge the field within which it operates (civic, legislative, pedagogical, scientific, economic, etc.)
3. Be "timing specific," responding to current urgent needs
4. Be implemented and function in real situations
5. Replace authors with initiators and spectators with users
6. Have practical, beneficial outcomes for its users
7. Pursue sustainability while adapting to changing conditions
8. Reestablish aesthetics as a system of transformation.[3]

Although the validity of each criterion as well as of the quasidecalogue they form when grouped together is undeniable, several questions arise: who would be in the position of determining that a particular project has practical, beneficial outcomes for its users? Could it be the case that a single project might be used in different ways? What happens when sustainability is not desired or programmed? Who establishes the sense of urgency motivating a specific art project?

For Bruguera, art should be a tool for producing a better society that does not yet exist, for experimenting with more democratic social relations even when those relations are put into practice in an experimental way. Such art will allow creators to go "from the state of proposal to that of application in reality" (2012). In this sense, the materialization of each artistic initiative will be more a matter of transference or translation than one of individual creative genius: since the effectiveness of *arte útil* is defined by its collective, social applicability, and success, the way of leveraging each initiative derives directly from its capacity to transform the viewer into a user. Since failure is not a possibility (as Bruguera herself states in the *arte útil* manifesto), a positive project would be, then, a useful one. On the contrary, a project that fails will do so twice: first, socially, because of its inability to become useful, but also aesthetically, because of its inability to transcend the formalistic and representational paradigms of art's autonomy.

Is there any alternative to this contradiction? Could an artistic initiative "fail" and nevertheless remain useful? Could it be useless and yet socially meaningful? Since the notion of *arte útil* gained public recognition (in 2013 the *New York Times* dedicated an article to welcoming social practice art as a thriving and increasingly familiar creative manifestation), those two questions have fostered a heated debate, and much has been written both in favor of and against Bruguera's concept of *arte útil* (see, for example, Aikens 2015). More interestingly, to continue that debate is to acknowledge that the categories of usefulness and uselessness are concepts shaped by coloniality and rampant neoliberalism in the Americas. The project analyzed in this chapter, Ensayos Tierra del Fuego, compels us to redefine usefulness and uselessness from the relation between nature and use-value in the Americas. In adopting that optic, my intention is not to criticize Bruguera's notion of the useful but rather to historicize some of the most common meanings *and uses* of utility itself through the lens of colonizing and emancipative epistemologies in the Americas. What does utility look like when framed through those two conflicting perspectives, and how could an emancipative and decolonial approach to utility be helpful in challenging the utilitarian paradigm that holds sway over every facet of human life nowadays, art included?

Ensayos

Ensayos is a nomadic educational and research platform located in the southernmost part of Chile. Ensayos was initiated in 2010 through the collaboration of curator Camila Marambio and the scientists and conservationists working at the Wildlife Conservation Society's Karukinka Natural Park in the Chilean part of Tierra del Fuego. One year earlier, Marambio visited Tierra del Fuego for the first time and became fascinated by the wildness of the region. The untamed landscape of Tierra del Fuego stood, for Marambio, as a major exception challenging the Anthropocene's universalist scope. In Tierra del Fuego, humankind emerges not as a dominant species but rather as part of an always adaptive ecosystem struggling to respond to "extreme" conditions. For Marambio, the remoteness and the feral character of Tierra del Fuego sparked a vast range of possibilities and inspired her to contact the person in charge of the park's conservational program, the biologist Bárbara Saavedra. Ensayos was initially conceived of as an artistic residency, although the original scope of the project changed and expanded soon after.

Marambio and Saavedra designed and organized a dialogical model of conversation and cooperation among artists and scientists based on sustained exchange and open-ended, extradisciplinary investigation. In the first iteration of Ensayos, which took place in February 2011, a group of twelve, persons artists and scientists, traveled across Karukinka Natural Park raising questions about the meaning and relevance of natural conservation, about the importance of nonhuman species in Tierra del Fuego's history of resilience, and about the best way of inserting artistic creativity as a central part of the scientific initiatives taking place in the area.[4] For Marambio, this first trip provided three main guidelines. First, that collaboration should emerge from the sustained engagement with the locality of Tierra del Fuego; nothing should be brought and produced in advance. Second, inquiry should prevail over production and obtaining results. And finally, artists were invited to think along with scientists on already existing matters. In Marambio's words, "Important issues had already been determined beforehand by people who had been there for a long time, much longer than ourselves. We would not discover new issues to be addressed, there were already several pressing issues that we could tackle from a fresh perspective."[5] (See figures 8.1 and 8.2.)

As a result of this first experience, the different topics of Ensayos were chosen.[6] The second iteration was dedicated to the topic of alien species and was centered around the introduction of the North American beaver (*Castor canadensis*) in Tierra del Fuego. It included performances, academic and artistic research, and exhibitions. The third iteration, which began in 2016, dealt with the importance of nature and nonhuman agency in the history of resistance of Tierra del Fuego. The main result in this case was *Distancia*, a TV and online documentary series on the region made by a video artist, a curator, and several collaborators. The fourth iteration began in 2018 and deals with issues of animal and interspecies maritime cooperation. Finally, a fifth iteration is ongoing and focuses on indigenous sovereignty in the region.

The successive iterations of Ensayos have something else in common: they allow for an engagement with Chilean and Argentinian history from the point of view of the successive attempts at colonization of the

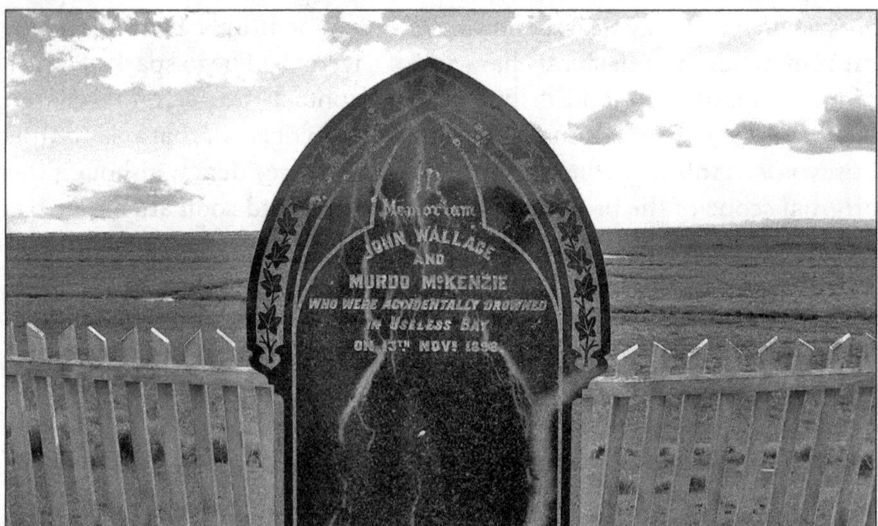

Figure 8.1. Ensayos, drowned in Useless Bay, 2011. *Source*: Courtesy of Christy Gast.

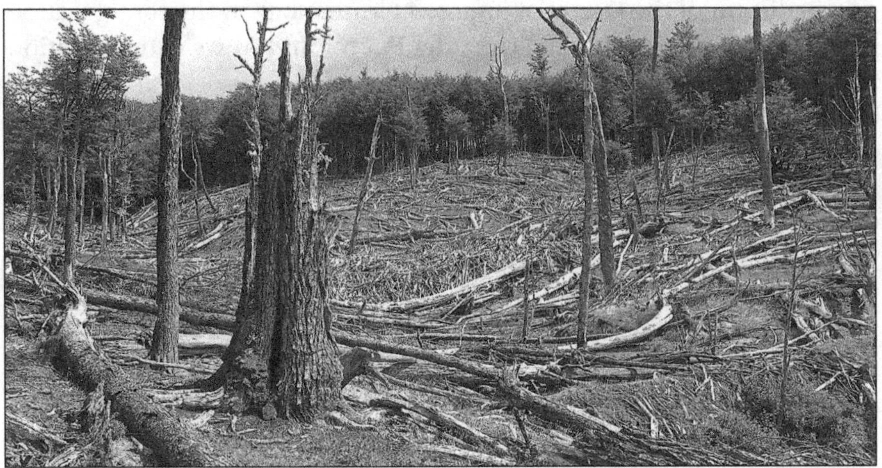

Figure 8.2. Ensayos, abandoned beaver dam at Karukinka, 2016. *Source*: Courtesy of Christy Gast.

Southern part of the Americas. Incorporated into the European imaginary in 1520 after Ferdinand Magellan's expedition, Tierra del Fuego would be associated with extreme natural conditions. The region was called *"el último confín de la tierra"* (the last edge of the earth) by the English explorer and settler Lucas Bridges (1952). Considering Tierra del Fuego as the edge of the earth is not merely rhetorical; on the contrary, it alludes to the expansion of settler and extractive colonialism. In this sense, the region occupied a privileged place as a synonym of exotic wilderness, an image also projected into the minds of many Chileans. Its proximity to the Antarctic also reinforces whiteness and "Europeanness" as markers of Chilean identity, while rejecting the impact of indigenous groups and normalizing acts of violence and silencing against those communities in the past and in the present.[7] The continuity and pervasiveness of this logic is evident in recent episodes of Chilean history, such as when the country chose an iceberg as the main attraction of the Chilean Pavilion at the 1992 Universal Exhibition in Seville.[8]

When I first interviewed Marambio, she mentioned that she had an exotic image of Tierra del Fuego before travellng to Karukinka (the Selk'nam name of Isla Grande) for the first time. The existence of toponyms such as Bahía Inútil, Porvenir, and Buen Suceso (Useless Bay, Future, and Good Fortune) still speaks to how that image derives from the viewpoint imposed by the logic of discovery and colonization. The case of Bahía Inútil, a bay that received its name because of the colonizers' inability to establish a port in it, remained for Marambio a clear indicator of the weight of imposed terminology in the configuration of the psychogeography of Tierra del Fuego, and in its categorization as a remote space resisting, but also calling for, colonization. By highlighting the colonial categorization of nature in the way in which Tierra del Fuego is perceived, this nomenclature proved to be a key tool for redefining inherited notions of utility in the light of art's potential to encourage and repurpose human and nonhuman interrelations. This becomes clear, for example, if we pay attention to the positive impression that Marambio provides while crossing Bahía Inútil: "I fell in love with the rough landscape of Tierra del Fuego, knowing also that the region has quite a violent colonial history behind it, one that the scientists were not fully addressing. Suddenly I found this term, *Bahía Inútil*. I thought: there is something here that has to do with the ways in which this land renders every great human project useless."[9] If Tierra del Fuego reveals the pervasiveness of coloniality in the Americas through a centuries-long process of extermination of indigenous populations by settlers or *estancieros* investing in sheep farming, in its feral character it also presents an inexhaustible capacity for resistance and inventiveness. For Carla Macchiavello (2015), who has dedicated an essay to the project, "Tierra del Fuego has a long history of attempts at colonization, 'ensayos' at taming, civilizing, owning the so-called wild." The usefulness and uselessness of the territory were mobilized for different purposes under the logic of colonization, naturalizing the extermination of indigenous communities under the guise of progress and productivity, and justifying the inclusion of certain so-called alien animal species (sheep, but not beavers) as part of the landscape for the very same reasons. Importantly enough, the vastness and remoteness appeared to be a valuable resource for the Chilean military dictatorship of Augusto Pinochet, who, as Macchiavello (2015: 8) explains, placed a concentration camp on Dawson Island as part of the attempts to "recolonize" the territory Macchiavello (figures 8.3 and 8.4).[10]

What is remarkable about that history is that many of those "ensayos" were unproductive and ended up being unsuccessful. In approaching the resilient character of the landscape of Tierra del Fuego and the possibility of alternative ecosystems resisting imposed categorizations, Ensayos identifies in nature a powerful ally for epistemological and active decolonization and recognizes the natural conditions of the region as a perfect example of the existence of portions of the Americas actively resisting colonization and proposing alternative relationships between humans and nonhumans and alternative understandings of utility.

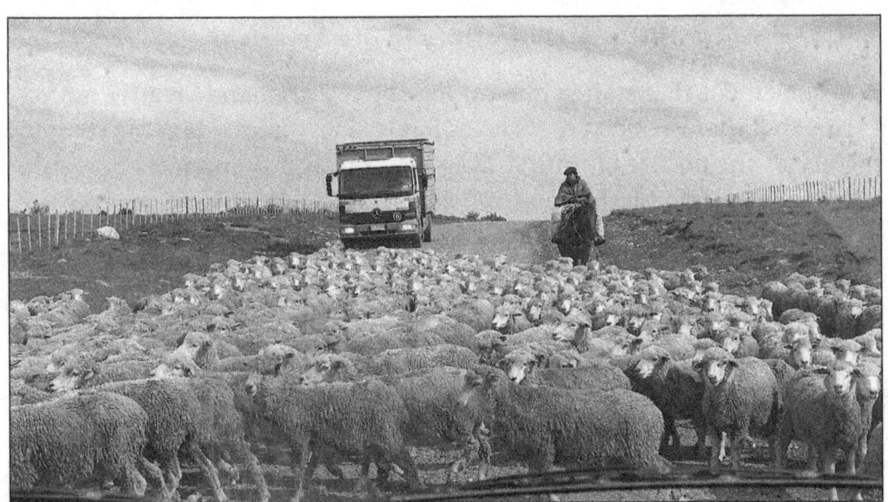

Figure 8.3. Ensayos, on the road to Estancia Vicuña, 2016. *Source*: Courtesy of Christy Gast.

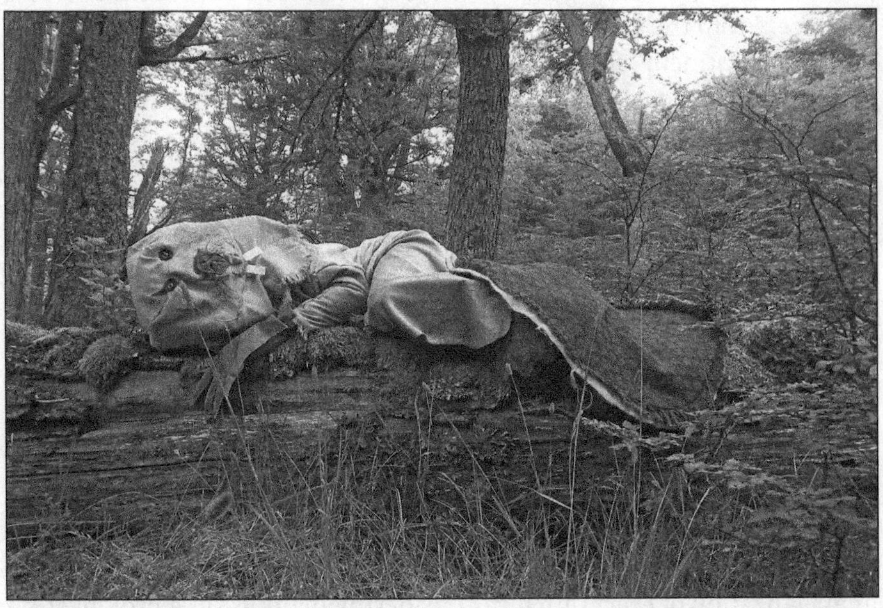

Figure 8.4. Ensayos, *Being*, Camila Marambio, Isla Navarino, 2014. *Source*: Courtesy of Christy Gast.

Historicizing Utility in the Americas

A first element that stands out among the research and creative actions carried out in the context of Ensayos has to do with revealing the complex history of the notion of utility. The project also demonstrates how difficult it is to define (within and outside art) what is *útil* and what is not. If the history of the (European ongoing colonization of the) Americas is framed from the perspective of the history of the exploitation of the continent, then it is crucial that exploitation go hand in hand with the redefinition of the American territory as a fertile *terra nullius* that can be seized and made productive. Colonization imposed on the Americas a normative and normalized way of looking at and inhabiting the landscape, one shaped by profitability and excess. For centuries, productivity and unproductivity regulated the relationship between power, landscape, and economic transformation on the continent. The act of symbolically naming and categorizing the land according to the resources that could best benefit the economic interests of European colonizers played a central role in preceding and justifying acts of physical and coercive violence. From the very first moment when Columbus seized the land of the "new continent" for the Castilian crown, the act of conquering was directly associated with the act of organizing and administering the lands of the Americas. Tzvetan Todorov (1987) explains that, for Columbus, the exoticism of the people he encounters is noteworthy in his diaries simply because it can be incorporated into the description of the landscape he prepares for the Reyes Católicos of Castilla and Aragón (Catholic Monarchs), being this description that ultimately lies at the end (or the beginning) of his journey. The depictions of men and women appearing in the diaries resemble the same utilitarian criteria applied to the newly "discovered" flora and fauna, thus comparing wealthy individuals and succulent roots, or acknowledging, already in 1492, that the humans and the rest of the species that the expedition was finding along the journey were of "superior" quality.

The first steps of the Spanish colonization of the Americas offer an early and eloquent example of what Randy Martin (2002) called the financialization of everything. In considering mankind as a prolongation of nature, Columbus not only dehumanizes the native inhabitants; perhaps more subtly, he also imposes on them the same quantitative logic he applied to the landscape of the continent, which was grounded on early extractive and capitalist utilitarianism. The equivalence of humanity and nature in Columbus's diaries portrays the Caribbean territories in which he travels as a tabula rasa ready to be conquered, transformed, and made productive, preceding and preparing the way for the act of conquest itself (Todorov 1987: 41). In presenting the lands of the Caribbean as easy and available for conquest and the indigenous population as naturally productive and generous, Columbus introduces a mythical conception of the noble savage that is entirely based on the notions of use value and utilitarian exchange. In the first entries of his 1492 diary, Columbus is surprised at the indifference to material possessions he believes he identifies in the indigenous populations he meets. Although this generosity is presented as a sign of moral purity and noble character, it is also conceived of as a lack of civilization, a sign of backwardness that the passing of time and the labor of colonization would at least partially amend.

At this point it is worth remembering that the first exchanges between Europeans and indigenous communities took the form of dispossession and established an uneven power relation, in which valuable metals were extracted and shipped back to Europe in exchange for cheap trinkets. If we accept that this exchange initiated a sustained act of dispossession, debt, and collective subordination that impoverished the native populations of the continents in favor of the colonizers, then we can consider it to be the cornerstone upon which the coloniality of power was sustained and reproduced before and after the independence of American nations. Columbus's failure to perceive the existence of a completely different value system determining the natives' behavior is not just a problem of communication. On the contrary, the projection of the image of the noble savage (which always comes attached to its counterpart of the "bad," violent, and mischievous savage) fulfills in itself a utilitarian role: that of imposing, and later normalizing, a capitalist logic of use value as the degree zero of any exchange, as the only possibility of progress. The exchange of trinkets for gold in 1492 inaugurated in the Americas a centuries-old tradition of uneven development that reaches up to the exchanges explored by Ensayos in Tierra del Fuego. In fact, the formal independence of Latin American nations starting in the nineteenth century did not interrupt the prevalence of this logic but rather consolidated it. Key to the reproduction of the logic of unevenness and dispossession is the normalization of a specific notion of usefulness dominated by a colonial, and later on by neoliberal rationality. From this perspective, it becomes easy to understand how uneven exchange continues to be sustained and prolonged in the name of development and progress, how the onslaught against indigenous and Black populations continues to be backed by the liberal governmentality of Latin American nation-states. In both cases, usefulness and the supposed improvement in the living conditions of the many are presented as the main justification for neocolonial and neoliberal interventions. Suffice it to mention here that the logic of development was linked to the defense of modernization as the only way of achieving the well-being of the many, thus justifying the dispossession of those ecosystems and human groups whose presence contradicted and slowed progress.[11]

If we go back to Bruguera's manifesto of *arte útil*, we will see that within the text utility is synonymous with transforming affection into effectiveness. In relation to this argument, perhaps it is worth remembering that affection and effectiveness are not incompatible with the logic imposed by the Spanish colonizers. The complex intertwining of use value, coloniality, and artistic production in the Americas becomes evident by looking at how artistic objects were produced, displayed, and socialized. The history of Latin American visual creativity in early colonial times is full of examples of subtle acts of mobilizing individual and collective affection to consolidate epistemic and physical acts of colonial violence while making them seem normal and invisible. The channeling of precolonial religious habits with the purpose of imposing and naturalizing Catholicism, as for example in the use of open spaces for ecumenical gatherings or in the assimilation of indigenous iconography as part of the educational device employed in the task of "civilizing" the native, played a central role in the conquest and colonization of the Americas. This is the case, for example, of numerous convents erected in Mexico in the sixteenth century, including those of Huejotzingo, Acolman, and Actopan, where the space dedicated to the atrium was expanded and provided with a carefully chosen iconography. The images displayed in the atriums of those convents were conceived with the purpose of appearing as familiar as possible to the indigenous populations that were to be catechized. The use of public spaces fulfilled two different purposes: on one hand, it continued the tradition of indigenous public gatherings; on the other, it transformed the experience of "education" and "evangelization" into a collective spectacle full of theatrical and "performative" elements oriented toward the progressive transformation of the "spectators" into "active" believers. Something similar applies to more material features of art making: the production of colonial artistic objects for provision to churches in the Viceroyalty of Peru can be closely linked to the extraction of silver in the Potosí or Huancavelica mines, for example. It is undeniable that in both cases art was used by the colonizers for the purpose of winning over the American populations and securing the conquest. Essentially, in neither case does affect replace effectiveness; rather, individual and collective affections are ideologically repurposed and utilized as ways of making colonial governmentality more pervasive and easier to assimilate.[12]

Collaborative Art and/as Multispecies Entanglements

Ensayos subverts progress-driven approaches to and mappings of the Americas by exploring feral resilience of localized, small-scale, multispecies entanglements. This becomes evident in the second iteration of Ensayos, which lasted for three years. The introduction of the *Castor canadensis* was part of an unsuccessful experiment that attempted to turn the beaver's fur into a profitable resource, an experience of colonization of nature partially independent of human settlement. Without the threat of predators, the beavers proliferated and intensified their presence in the ecosystem, which had important consequences for the conservation of the local flora. The presence of the beavers in Tierra del Fuego bears important symbolic connotations that exemplify the logic of utilitarian and extractive reason lying behind coloniality. The introduction of the "exotic" species bears witness to the inefficient and selfish management of natural resources, in which a complete ecosystem can be jeopardized for the sake of immediate profit. Grounded in a binary distinction between "we" and "they," the identification of the beaver as a foreign "other" that does not "belong" reproduces the same logic that the colonizers and the Chilean state implemented concerning indigenous populations and multispecies ecosystems. As the social scientist Macarena Gómez-Barris explains, the selective incorporation of certain foreign elements has been the base of settler colonialism in Chile, in which suitable species (both human and nonhuman) are accepted as a valuable contribution to the nation's self while others are rendered illegal, unproductive, and alien.[13] This is the case even in those moments when humanitarian and philanthropic arguments are used to justify settlement and dispossession. What is interesting here is that the history of settler colonialism cannot be reduced to its human side; on the contrary, it forces us to look at coloniality as a set of uneven forces targeting and threatening human and nonhuman life in equal terms (Gómez-Barris 2017: 84).

It should also be remembered, following Gómez-Barris, that those forces were incapable of completely suppressing "sites of differentiated and inexhaustible potential" across the continent, "complex Afro-Indigenous spaces of coexistence with the nonhuman world that have been formed in relation to the colonial Encounter" (2017: 3). Dealing with 18eighteenth-century landscape visual representation, and more particularly with slave gardens in the Caribbean, Jill H. Casid also demonstrates the importance of nature in the naturalization of imperial power, arguing that "empire reformulated itself as its opposite, an anti-empire, by putting botany in the central place. Landscaping functioned to introduce and naturalize empire's transplantations within the idiom of the local or the 'place'" (Casid 2005: 240). At the same time, however, she agrees with Gómez-Barris in recognizing the resistive botanical potential of subverting and queering spatial and species normativity, turning landscaping and gardening into productive zones of contact and contestation, and producing interspecies histories of resilience and mutual care (xxi). Here Casid echoes W. J. T. Mitchell's conception of landscape as simultaneously an imposed tradition of land (and world) picturing expanded as part of the colonial episteme *and* a contested terrain where alternative understandings of nature proliferate and speak back (Mitchell 2002). By acknowledging the visual technology of landscaping as a contested terrain, those three authors recognize a nonhuman agency in the attitudes of resistance and subversion adopted by indigenous populations in the Americas, while also warning about the negative consequences of erasing those episodes of resistance from the genealogies of colonial and imperial violence.

For the artists and scientists joining forces in the second iteration of Ensayos,[14] one possibility would have been to target the beavers as an invasive threat to the local ecosystem. Instead, they chose to look at the complex relationship between human and nonhuman. By asking which consequences would have to adopt the perspective of the beavers,[15] the group challenges simplistic differentiations between native and foreign. First, this shift in the way of looking exposes the complex ways in which extractive and neocolonial interests operate. In this case, the adoption of a nonhuman perspective emphasizes the similarities in the episodes of human and "natural" violence at play in the region, pointing out how economic profit, unnatural selection, and dispossession appear as recurring terms in both cases. More importantly, by looking at the beavers as unassimilable "others" that nevertheless have become "locals" and therefore have played a central part in the history of Tierra del Fuego, the Ensayo makes us think issues of normality, normativity, and identification in alternative terms. At the same time, it challenges the possibility of understanding the history of the multispecies interrelationships taking place in Tierra del Fuego from an exclusively human point of view.

Linked to this, the second reason that renders Ensayos interesting for expanding notions of artistic utility relates to its exploration of a nonhuman-centered vision of agency. Ensayos is concerned with decentering agency in order to cover a wider range of human and nonhuman interactions. As we saw with Beirut in chapter 7, agency and usefulness have long been the main instrument for leveraging the success of socially engaged art projects. If a community achieves their expected outcomes, a project could be considered positive in social terms. On the contrary, if the artistic project is incapable of empowering audiences or achieving the goals drawn by the artists (which are two very different, even potentially contradictory things in themselves), its social relevance is called into question. What artists and communities can and cannot do, in sum, determines how the whole project is conceptualized. Agency, in any case, is always located in human hands, either those of the artists or an amalgam of the artist and the community.

Within the last decade, several voices have urged us to look at agency from a less reductive, multispecies point of view. Debates on environmentalism and new materialism have shown how nonhumans condition human agency in decisive ways, forcing us to redefine intentionality and effect in radically new terms (see, in particular, Haraway 2015; Shiva 1993; Heise 2016). From this standpoint, when humans act (and this, of course, would include art), this "acting" forms part of a longer chain of alliances that decisively includes natural forces. Framing socially engaged art projects that put into practice alternative forms of agency would imply redefining the "collective" behind those projects, while also exploring artistic collaboration not simply as the formation of a community but also as the articulation of alternative multispecies interrelationships. This logic becomes evident throughout all the iterations of Ensayos, from the interaction with beavers as a way of decolonizing the naturalization of human and natural species linked to settler colonialism in the second Ensayo to the exploration of cultural responses toward whales and coastal ecosystems in the fourth.

In a recent essay, Camila Marambio (n.d.) started linking the sonic research on animal species with the recordings of the Selk'nam natives of Tierra del Fuego. In her view, those voices constitute an alternative sonic archive of Tierra del Fuego, one unavoidably linked to the region's history of exploration and extermination of native populations, but also one whose sounds haunt the prevailing logic of usefulness and uselessness determining present-day ecosystem relations in the territory. By exploring the history of extinction and resilience of the Selk'nam side by side with that of animal species, Marambio's deconstructive analysis of ethnomusicology sets out the hidden links between indigenous dispossession, the taking over of the territory by foreign specialists and "experts," and the productive logic of natural exploitation. Without romanticizing animal agency or indigenous resilience, Marambio retools her own position as a researcher and ultimately as a "foreigner," paying attention and listening to alternative voices without claiming any right to speak on their behalf (Marambio, n.d.). In this sense, by adopting an alternative, multispecies take on agency, Ensayos reveals subversive histories of cohabitation between humans and nonhumans,[16] forcing us to interpret issues of success or failure with new eyes.

Ensayos as Study Ecosystems

In Ensayos, the medium is not a passive landscape where humans operate. Rather, the environment conditions the results of each project, adopting an active role alongside artists and scientists in the research and creative processes. For the artists involved in each Ensayo (Chilean as well as transnational), the main objective is to test new potential approaches to nature unmarked by the scientific aspiration of categorizing nature in order to take possession of it. Study in Ensayos implies a decisive move away from the logic of classification proper to modern science. The project stands for the idea that learning with(in) and from nature provides a good way of thinking differently about the researchers' position of privilege. Instead of conceiving research as a specialized task of categorizing reality sustained on the grounds of disciplinary authority imposed on the native land and population, the program compels different practitioners to challenge their disciplinary boundaries while inventing alternative modes of collaboration.[17] In this context, nature is not a passive entity waiting to be researched but rather an active agent conditioning and modifying the outcomes of human cooperation.

The recognition of artists as an added value in research processes is far from self-evident. When I interviewed Camila Marambio, she outlined the difficulties of convincing environmental scientists about the potential of art to challenge assumed ideas on nature and the role of humans within a given ecosystem. For Marambio, the collaboration with the scientist community at Karukinka Natural Park posed two different challenges. The first involved communicability, with the need to bridge the diversity of languages, methodologies, and expectations of scientists and artists. Related to this, the second was concerned with claiming a middle ground in which art would not be subordinated as a purely ornamental or speculative appendix. If true collaboration was to be achieved, then artists would have to tune their sense of utility in close dialogue with the universally accepted notion of usefulness commonly associated with science. For Marambio, dealing with the inherited expectations about what artists and scientists could do meant insisting on the creative potential of the speculative capacity associated with artistic research.

In Santiago I met with the director of Karukinka Natural Park and proposed a collaboration with her. I would bring artists and have them collaborate within the research teams. I tried to make it clear that the artists would not decorate already existing projects, nor embellish the landscape. On the contrary, they would apply fieldwork methodologies to understand the place and raise questions from that perspective. The entire project should unfold from the dialogue between artists and scientists. I contemplated the possibility of those exchanges leading nowhere. I held on to the idea of the useless. From that viewpoint, I highlighted the idea that we were not aiming at anything utilitarian. There was a strong emphasis on the question itself, and on the fact that this question could perhaps reveal complexity or disorder. I told her that we would call into question many of the principles she had worked on for so long.[18]

It could seem that by claiming uselessness as art's territory, Marambio is opposing *arte útil*'s commitment to ground art as a socially transformative tool while reifying art by restaging "old" modernist models of artistic autonomy. Following her argumentation, however, she conveyed the completely opposite idea to me. In conceiving research as an unforeseeable collaborative activity that in order to produce results must challenge its own enclosure within disciplinary categories, I understood Marambio's words as a call to undiscipline the normative space in which knowledge takes place. The speculative tone she adopted ("I contemplated the possibility of those exchanges leading nowhere") does not give up on knowledge production but rather claims that it could come only from a different place, a yet to be recognized space of cooperation in which creative and rational methodologies stand on equal terms. For Marambio, artistic collaboration cannot be understood as separate from the task of defining an alternative framework in which dialogue and professionalization could be thought anew.

Dealing with the context of the US university, Stefano Harney and Fred Moten conceptualize professionalization as concomitant with the colonial logic of enclosure that lifts certain individuals up while promoting generic dispossession for many others. By linking professionalization with social (and racial) segregation and the ongoing privatization of everything existing,[19] Harney and Moten outline how the act of demarcating epistemological categories and establishing norms for these is central to the definition and performance of professional competence and the exerting of authority. In this regard, they pose the question "What would be outside this act of the conquest circle, what kind of ghostly labored world escapes in the circling act, an act like a kind of broken phenomenology where the brackets never come back off and what is experienced as knowledge is the absolute horizon of knowledge whose name is banned by the banishment of the absolute?" (Harney and Moten 2013: 34). As a way of answering this question, Harney and Moten propose an alternative understanding of knowledge sharing: study. Study is shaped by the possibilities opened by places of refuge (public institutions made private but nevertheless still providing spaces for collective conspiracy) for indebted students and knowledge seekers transforming debt into an unpayable mutual dependency.[20] Study, then, would be equivalent to shared knowledge and interest presided over by a nonutilitarian notion of utility, by a speculative and experimental logic that sneaks into institutional space and privilege to create something new, that relies as much on mutual engagement as on "fugitive planning."

In Ensayos, study appears to be a recurrent principle manifest in the privileging of conversations and negotiations over final production. As Carla Macchiavello points out (2015: 3), the project could be easily read in terms of both utility and uselessness, a great part of its potential being dependent on sustained attention and apparently impractical derivations from normative, disciplinary observation. This becomes evident in the way that the participants in these conversations relinquish their disciplinary specialization to engage the group from undefined positions. Finally, the logic of study conditions the choosing of a specific ecosystem as the main objective determining each iteration as well as the means of transforming those objectives into practical results. This becomes evident in Ensayos 4, which started in December 2018 and focuses on whale pods. The group enrolling in the artistic and scientific program, which included artists, marine biologists, educators, and sociologists, analyzed the movements and collaborative techniques of groups of migrating whales as an indicator of the impact of climate change on the coastal territory of Tierra del Fuego. The project conceives of whale pods as both part of the ongoing transformation of complex multispecies ecosystems *and* as a potential source of alternative methods of cooperation that can be applied elsewhere. Furthermore, on this occasion the area of study was widened through comparative cases with other "peripheral" coastal territories, such as the Lofoten Islands and Tasmania, all areas shaped by different forms of colonization. By claiming a plural perspective as the only way of gaining sight of the complex consequences of past and ongoing processes of colonization and extractivism in the studied areas, Ensayos redefines human and nonhuman grouping as a speculative yet productive collaborative logic. By adopting a comparative logic, the project challenges the fallacy of continentalism, putting into practice Nelson Maldonado-Torres's understanding of postcontinentality as "an expression of the idea that continents are not natural spaces, but projects that rely on specific notions of spatiality" (2011: 5).[21] By exploring nonhuman acts of migration and insubordination, it reveals intimate and unexpected connections taking place within and across continents and going below the lens of official colonial histories (Lowe 2105). Finally, by challenging the centrality of human and scientific perspectives, the project manages to keep a local focus while rethinking intercontinental relations anew.

The methodology employed in the fourth iteration of Ensayos has enormous implications for envisaging alternative uses of collaborative and socially engaged art outside of the commercial and utilitarian needs imposed by educational and skilling institutions. The undefined, horizontal relationship between nonhuman agents, scientists, and artists challenges the idea of artists as specialized, particularly fitted "experts" that work by identifying a problem and providing a tailored solution. That logic has become inefficient for two main reasons. First, because it is grounded in the colonial paradigm of expertise, which lies in the assumption that having an (increasingly expensive) background in social practice makes someone more capable of detecting the problems of any human group. And second, because this mode of thought foregrounds utility within utilitarianism (*lo útil en lo utilitario*), thus condemning artists to the task of counseling and providing prototype versions of a better reality.

Conclusions: Redefining Utility
after the Privatization of Everything

If *arte útil* is to be understood only from the point of view of the replacement of spectators by users and from art's specific goal of providing potentially beneficial outcomes from and to those users, then it becomes impossible to critically analyze the harmful ways in which capitalism and coloniality are deploying utilitarianism along with flexibility to create new forms of social control and economic profitability. When reduced to this extreme, our society would be easily understood by referring to another paradigm, that of the beta tester, rather than to that of the user. The beta tester is that subject who receives initial privileges in the use of a product with the counterpart of her use being monitored, counted, and rendered into data to benefit the company. In this asymmetric exchange, (nonpaid) labor and precarity are the ghosts haunting free use and social exchange. In this context, the personal is rendered extractive through data mining; each singularity is transformed into intelligence. In a

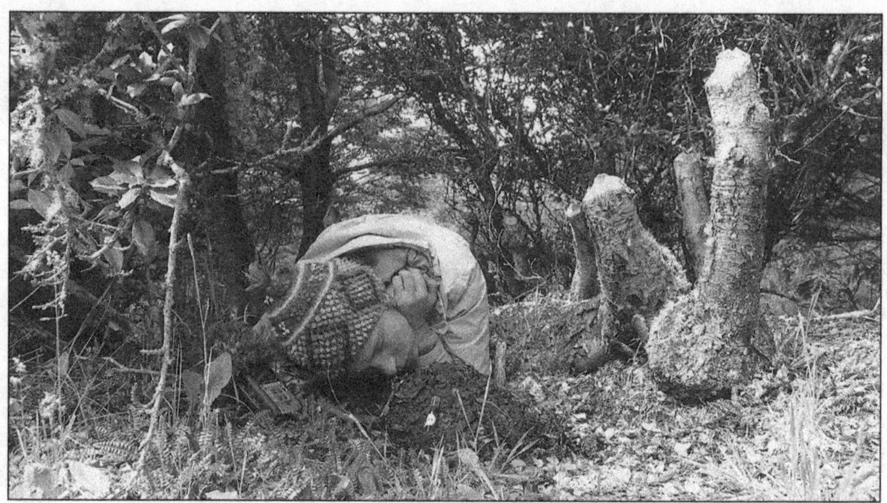

Figure 8.5. Ensayos, Camila Marambio testing scent mounds at Rio Calavera, 2016. *Source*: Courtesy of Christy Gast.

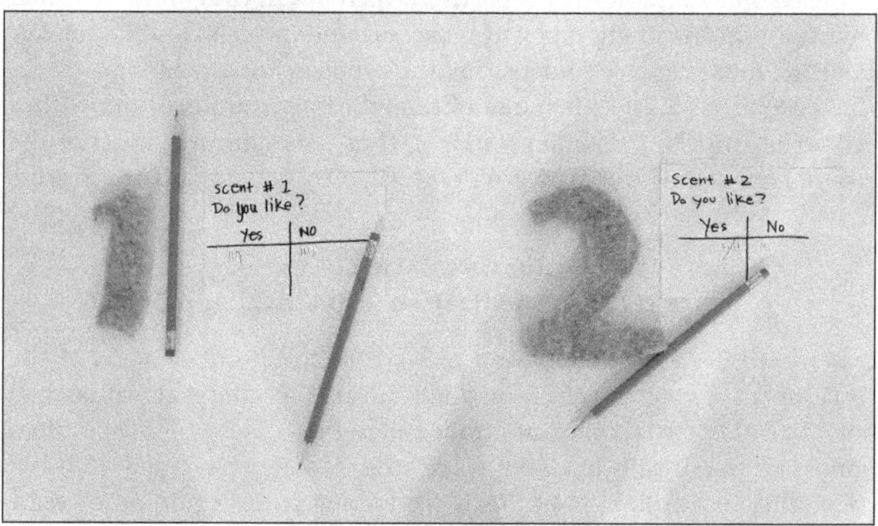

Figure 8.6. Ensayos, testing scents at New York's Freest Art School, 2015. *Source*: Courtesy of Christy Gast.

process that constitutes the nightmarish reverse of the optimism around the Internet in its earliest days, the figure of the beta tester exposes the limits of networking society and challenges.[22] (See figures 8.5 and 8.6.)

Ensayos expands the notion of utility in two different ways. First, by revealing how the colonial genealogy of utility in the Americas was carved out its abnormal, ideological normalization. And second, by echoing past and present speculative, multispecies entanglements as potential alternatives to the rationality lying behind the identification of Tierra del Fuego with a useless (or useful) land. In Ensayos, the systemic relations between human and nonhumans in Tierra del Fuego do not stand as a consequence of the geography on the edge of the southernmost territory of the Americas; rather, this remoteness is used to reveal the cracks surfacing amid the all-pervasive landscape of emptiness with which the region has been historically associated.

9

◆ ◆ ◆

ACTIVISM AND PERFORMANCE IN THE AGE OF INTELLECTUAL AND ARTISTIC WITCH HUNTING

This chapter analyzes the influence and impact of art activism at a time when its cultural appropriation by alt-right forces is becoming more ubiquitous at a global level. My interest lies in exploring the continuities of colonial modes of subjection affecting racialized and gendered bodies. It seems to me that those continuities raise crucial questions about accessibility to and ownership of the public space. Performance is central for displaying, consolidating, and making public restrictive and exclusionary notions of citizenship. Borrowing from recent debates on performativity and the public sphere, this chapter focuses on the ways in which alt-right groups in Brazil and Portugal appropriate, disseminate, and normalize celebratory and nostalgic gestures with a colonial genealogy. By so doing, it attempts to inscribe the emergence of conservative performativity in relation to the occupation and enclosure of the public space in Portuguese-speaking contexts within broader debates on the social relevance of art activism as a response to the consolidation of post-truth governmentality and the emotional politics linked to the increasing securitization of everything after 9/11. Those transformations are particularly evident in the two contexts analyzed here, as becomes clear from the onslaught on basic civic freedoms and the prosecution of activists and, more generally, of any force opposing neoliberal expansion during the Jair Bolsonaro era in Brazil, or the reemergence of borders in Europe associated with the articulation of images of the continent as a stronghold under siege in the context of the so-called Syrian refugee crisis. This chapter will therefore argue that both processes ultimately derive

241

from deeper contradictions related to Portugal's and Brazil's partially shared (yet, as is obvious, from different positions) colonial logic.

Central to the view presented in this chapter is the increasing importance of performativity and public exposure against the backdrop of the strengthening of reactive, conservative nationalism. If alter-globalization, post-Seattle and, later on, postoccupy turns in contemporary activism seemed to define activism as potentially benefitting from the global expansion of immaterial labor and the consolidation of networked culture, more recent events, including Brexit and the presidencies of Donald J. Trump and Jair Bolsonaro, force us to reconsider the role of the national as horizon and conditioning force of activist imagination. At the same time, digital conservatism is consolidating material, urban processes of marginalization on the grounds of selective biopolitical categorizations and more overt forms of institutional and populist exclusion. The emergence of alt-right groups is substantially challenging the transnational dimension within which those debates were inscribed, forcing us to reconsider the role of national alliances in relation to the securitization of borders and the increased public hold on exclusionary notions of citizenship disseminated through populist means.

The reinforcement of neoconservative movements worldwide poses serious threats to transnational progressive activism, but in no way does it mean the complete interruption of post-Seattle creative insurgence. In 2018 I took part in one of the most exciting academic exchanges I can remember.[1] Around thirty-five creators, activists, and scholars (among whom I had the luck to be included) were asked to produce live coverage of the current fortune of art activism against the neoconservative nationalist wave. If the 2018 report evidences anything, it is the idea that despite the generic threat we face nowadays and the encroachment of defensive nationalisms, there is still fertile ground for the forging of alliances. Continuing this collective debate and expanding through close analysis of two recent and interrelated acts of public confrontation spanning both sides of the Atlantic, this chapter asks whether activism, and whether performativity, are needed to challenge the exclusionary assault on the public sphere that lies behind the proliferation of alt-right nationalisms.

Some Facts . . . and Fictions

On October 5, 2017, an alt-right group surrounded the statue of Padre António Vieira located in Lisbon, Portugal. This action responded to a call launched by the activist and antiracist group Descolonizando to gather around the statue with flowers, candles, and posters in memory of the Amerindian and African populations that were victims of Portuguese colonialism in Brazil. Vieira was a Portuguese Jesuit who played a central role in the evangelization of Brazil in the seventeenth century. Considered one of the main literary figures of the Portuguese canon, he was a strong defender of the rights of Amerindian populations. Vieira's position toward slavery, however, was more ambivalent, this fact being the main issue at play in the call. This ambivalence, in any case, is not apparent in the statue installed in downtown Lisbon, which represents Vieira standing alongside three "indigenous" children in a rather paternalistic way (see figure 9.1).

This location was chosen for the demonstration for various reasons. First, it was the most recent public urban intervention by the Lisbon City Council, which installed the statue in the central location of the Largo Trindade Coelho in June 2017.[2] Furthermore, the city council had justified the need to publicly recognize Vieira as a central figure in the definition of Portuguese culture. Against this view stood a group who perceived the sculpture to be an incomplete and partisan homage to a historical figure of "Lusophone" letters such as Vieira.[3] What finally took place resembles similar events worldwide, including in Charlottesville, where the alt-right protesters impeded any approach to the statue, gathering in a circle around it in order to "protect" it from defacement.[4] Police forces intervened by dispersing both groups with the excuse of avoiding further riots, thus putting an end to the performance.

The events of October 5 were followed by a heated debate in social and print media in which the organizers of the demonstration remained silent. Twelve days later, Descolonizando offered a detailed explanation of the reasons behind the call. In this document, the group affirmed no allegiance to any political party, and no intention to damage the statue nor to protest against the figure of Padre António Vieira. The issue was the way in which Vieira is publicly represented and discussed. This monument is ethically and aesthetically questionable. Since form is content, and content is form, this statue emerges as a colonial specter in the public space, enacting a Luso-tropicalist vision of history that, on its turn, describes Portuguese colonialism as a benevolent project. Such a vision obscures the complexity of the historical figure of Padre Vieira, who defended the systematic enslavement of Africans and the forced conversion of South American indigenous populations (see Cohen 1998; *Luso-Brazilian Review* 2003). In this sense, this idealized representation also contributes to obliterating the legacies of slavery and colonialism in the Portuguese public sphere and contemporary society.[5]

For the activists of Descolonizando, the recent confrontation with alt-right groups restaged a way of understanding Portuguese identity

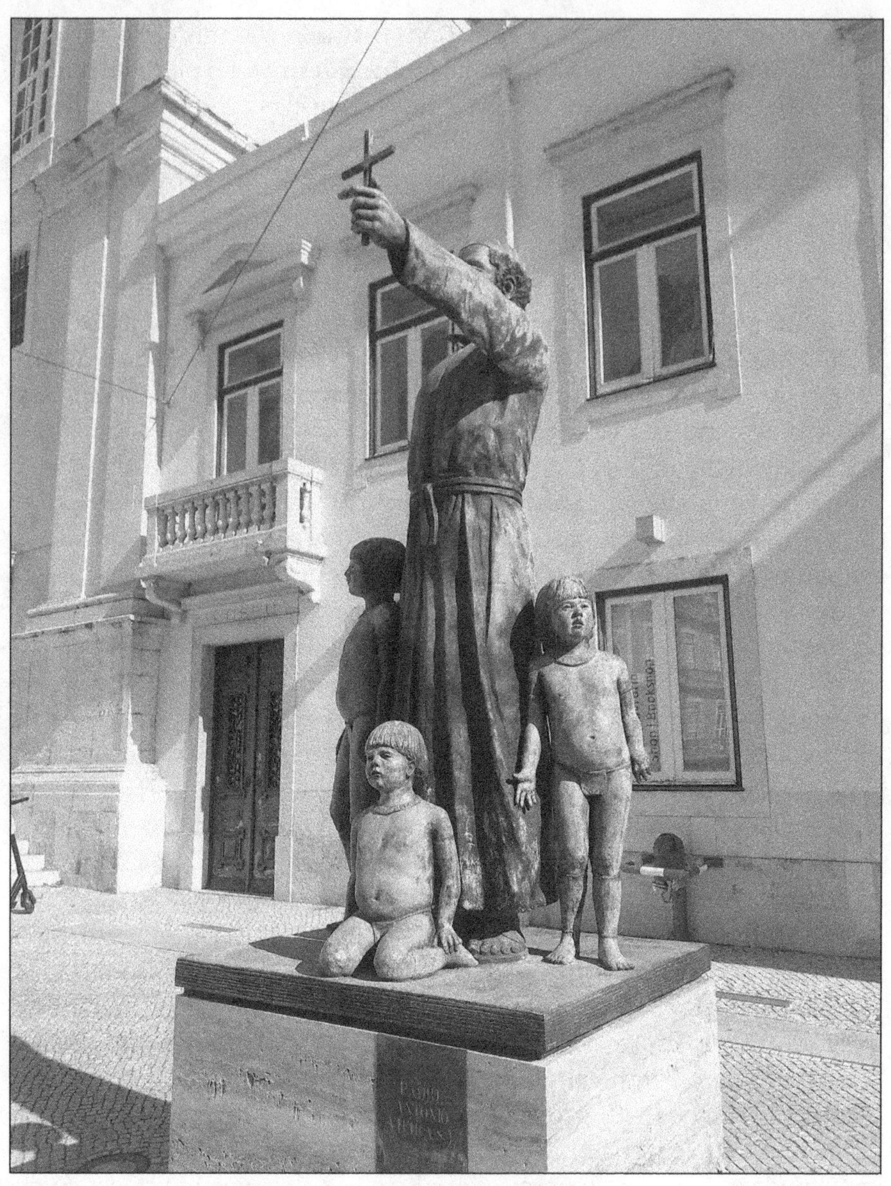

Figure 9.1. Padre António Vieira statue, Largo Trindade Coelho, Lisbon. *Source*: Courtesy of Carlos Garrido Castellano.

grounded in the silencing of the most troubling aspects of Portuguese colonialism and in the public commemoration of specific episodes of the Portuguese imperial past. In this respect, the attitude of the persons supposedly "protecting" the sculpture of Vieira was only the result of a more widespread defensive nationalism that despite the articulation of new iterations of *portugalidade* remains alive and well in broader segments of present-day Portuguese society.

Descolonizando's criticism of the supposedly benevolent side of Portuguese colonialism echoes an ongoing interest in Portuguese postcolonial debates in laying bare the legacy of Luso-tropicalist approaches to Portuguese colonialism. Margarida Calafate Ribeiro and Ana Paula Ferreira (2003) categorize coloniality as both a *fantasma* and a *fantasia* (a ghost and a fantasy) relentlessly haunting Portugal's cultural and social imagination. The endurance of this double *fantasma* and *fantasia* is demonstrated through the continuous public attempts by Portuguese authorities to whitewash colonial memories, which are conceived of as either something belonging to a remote and distant past, and/or justified as "softer" versions of the processes of colonization and imperialism imposed by other European nations.[6] The continuities mapped by Calafate Ribeiro and Ferreira are also visible through the unproblematic silencing of the consequences of imperialism in the creation of multiethnic societies in Europe, as for example when racialized bodies are biopolitically categorized and surveyed or when those bodies are stigmatized as migrant bodies even when born on European soil (see Mata 2006; Ferreira 2014; Peixe Dias and Dias 2012). Finally, as explored in the discussion of Amílcar Cabral in chapter 3, those imperial *fantasmas* and *fantasias* are reproduced through the banishing of the sites and memories of decolonization outside, but also inside, Europe (see figure 9.2).

The collective reading convoked by Descolonizando attempted to confront these elements. By pointing out the inadequacy of the iconographic and ideological project lying behind the protective and paternalist sculpture of Vieira, the group revealed the links between present-day tourist iterations of Lisbon as a global, multicultural city and nostalgic memories of Portugal's colonial past,[7] a relationship publicly sanctioned by the participation of official entities in commemorative acts and their problematic role in the configuration of places of memory. Giving space to performative responses in relation to the Vieira statue revealed that for many Portuguese, coloniality is still a living presence conditioning the situations of exclusion and marginalization that racialized Portuguese, and particularly Afro-descendant Portuguese, still face. Finally, by claiming that Vieira cannot fully account for the

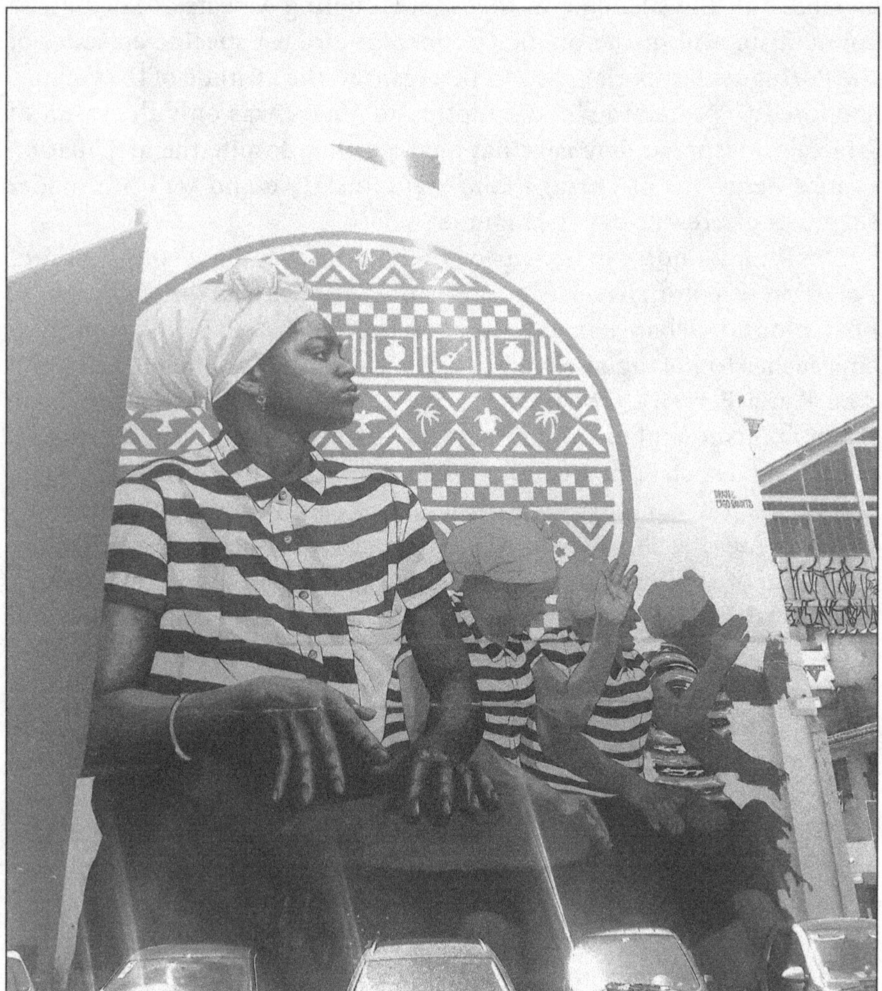

Figure 9.2. Public art piece by Frederico Draw and Ergo Bandits made on the occasion of the opening of the Casa da Cultura de Cabo Verde, Lisbon. *Source*: Carlos Garrido Castellano.

complexities of Portuguese society, the group demanded an alternative relationship between memory and space, one that could decolonize Lisbon's imperial past while at the same time revealing its role in the configuration of decolonial potential.

In the discussions that followed the confrontation around the Vieira sculpture, the political and cultural situation of contemporary Brazil gained the attention of many Portuguese. Some tragic episodes, such as the assassination of the feminist activist Marielle Franco and the disappearance of Rosiney Trindade de Oliveira, were publicly discussed and fueled enraged protests in many Portuguese cities. As many Brazilians decided to move to Portugal in response to the escalating violence linked to the political turmoil that preceded the election of Bolsonaro, the feeling spread among the population that Portugal could be facing a less obvious but equally harmful process in which specific individuals or groups would face increasing vulnerability. In the same way, the emergence of alt-right and populist groups and the normalization of acts of violence against women, environmental activists, and racialized Brazilians provided a clear example of what was wrong in the celebratory vision proposed by the sculpture of Vieira. Not for nothing do the figures of "indigenous" children converge under the priest's patronizing figure supposed to represent Brazilian society. The whole sculptural ensemble stands for, enacts, and reproduces a view of the Portuguese metropolis educating, forming, and shaping the colonial subject/nation (see figures 9.3 and 9.4).

One month after the events of October 5, in November 2017, Judith Butler faced several attacks when invited to lecture at the University of São Paulo. In one of her lectures, Butler was accused of encouraging pedophilic and zoophilic attitudes. Prior to that moment, ultraconservative groups had been asking for the events to be cancelled, while a collective document demanding that Butler not be allowed to enter the country circulated online. In the last lecture, Butler's effigy in the form of a witch was burnt in the street amid several expressions of hate enacted against the philosopher. These expressions equated Butler's ideas with her presence and the supposed social acceptance of a so-called *ideologia de gênero* (gender ideology) in Brazil. Whereas the topics addressed by Butler were not directly related to gender (rather, they focus on democracy and populism), as in Portugal the attacks targeted a *fantasma* inasmuch as they targeted a "fantasy" (in Butler's [2017] own words, "an imaginary talk acting as underside of a real seminar"), an imaginary intervention against which discourses of hate were articulated.

Ideologia de gênero became one of the most used expressions in the 2018 elections that raised Jair Bolsonaro to the Brazilian presidency. Frequently employed by alt-right and ultraconservative groups, *ideologia de gênero* is supposed to imply a conspiracy involving attacks against the *família tradicional*, religious marriage, and the biological correlation between sex and gender. Crucial to this interpretation is the belief that gender debates express an ideology and therefore serve covert political and social interests. Furthermore, the supposed effect of *ideologia de gênero* is strongly linked to the proliferation of fake news and populist arguments. By calling attention to possible threats affecting the whole of Brazilian society, supposed attacks against traditional gender values

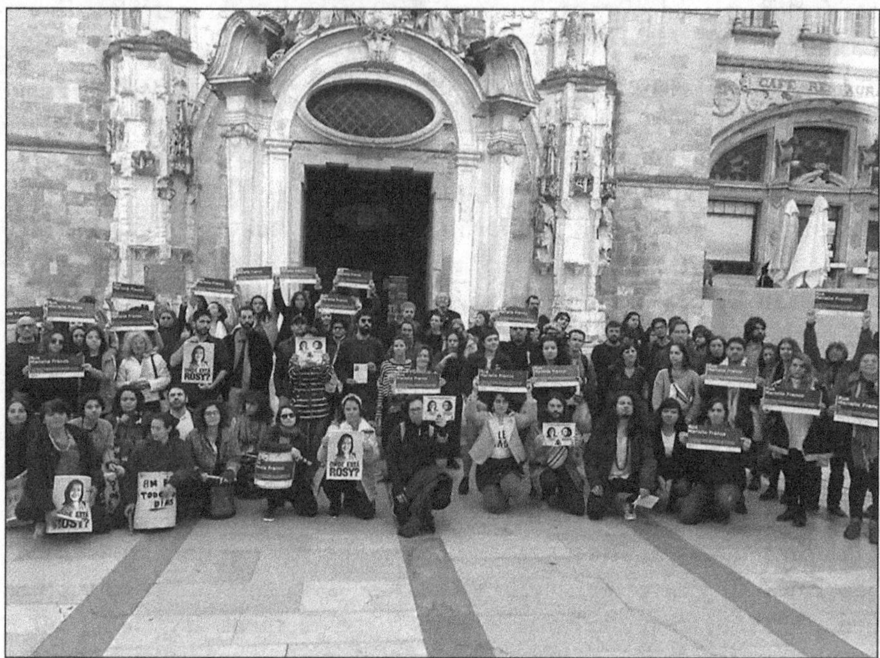

Figure 9.3. Strike in Portugal against violence against women in Brazil, Coimbra, Portugal. Photograph by Bárbara Lobo. *Source*: Courtesy of Luiza Beloti Abi Saab.

were used to polarize broader debates on gender inequality and violence against women and LGTBQ+ individuals and communities. In this process, crucial political and economic issues are framed through a moral dimension. It is worth noting that the debates on *ideologia de gênero* involve continuity with a continuing onslaught on the Brazilian working class carried out under the banner of neoliberal aspirations. In the exaggeratedly grandiloquent movement that expelled the Brazilian Partido dos Trabalhadores (PT) and Dilma Rousseff from government we can also find a similar moralization of political debates (in this case, any alternative to neoliberal expansion and the accumulation of power and wealth is equated with corruption). As Alfredo Saad and Lecio Morais (2018: 164) explain, on the occasion of the impeachment against Rousseff, the PT and the Brazilian left became the target of massive hate simply because both were identified as obstacles to a neoliberal expansion that until then could remain alive and well without giving up its democratic façade.

The debates arising as a result of the attacks on Butler continued in the following days, remaining alive in the memories of many Portuguese

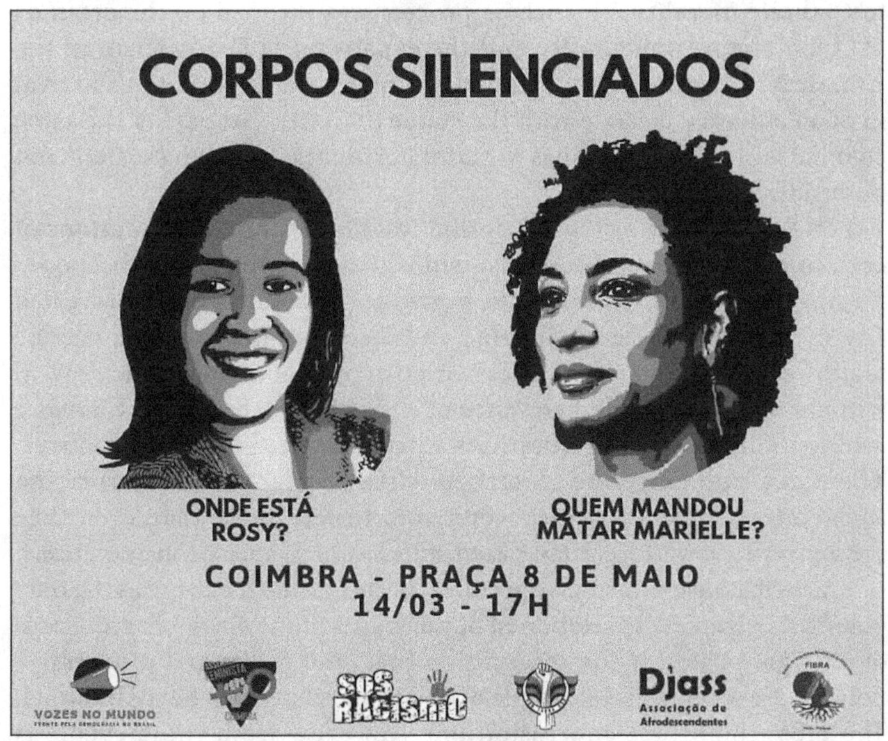

Figure 9.4. Online banner mobilized as part of the strike in Portugal against violence against women in Brazil, Coimbra, Portugal. *Source*: Courtesy of Luiza Beloti Abi Saab.

and Brazilian colleagues while I was writing this chapter years later. In the weeks spanning September through November 2017, the distance between fact and fiction blurred. The burning of Butler's effigy and the "defense" of Vieira's sculpture can be read as evidence of a disquieting trend reaching across the Atlantic: the "protection" of Vieira by alt-right groups in Lisbon was predicated under the plea of recognizing a universalized and expansive idea of *portugalidade* within the values that the figure of the Portuguese *homem de letras* is meant to represent. On the other side of the equation, the attack on Butler can be read as more than a regressive movement reacting against feminism. It is also the enactment of a particular ideology that reproduces colonial acts of social cleansing while restaging exclusionary corporeal categorizations. The act of burning Butler's effigy resonates with previous acts of iconophobia and iconophilia brought to Brazil by Portuguese colonialism, which implied the destruction of "pagan idols" and the subduing of indigenous communities to Catholic morality. This whole process was justified on the grounds of colonial governmentality and the expansion of Catholicism in the Americas. If the legacy of colonialism reverberated in Butler's arrival in São Paulo, the episode with the statue of Vieira was part of the same colonial legacy that continues to haunt Portuguese-speaking societies on both sides of the Atlantic.

Performativity offers a standpoint for addressing the limitations of certain postcolonial aspirations, while also revealing potential nodes for unexpected solidarities. If the events of the autumn of 2017 revealed anything, it is that intersectionality and decolonization can no longer be identified as "mainstream gender or postcolonial theory." They reveal without doubt the public relevance of emancipative practices, therefore asking a different set of questions when confronting these practices. Theory can no longer be identified with the practice of interpreting social and cultural processes from ivory towers; more than ever, they are a privileged-yet-everyday-based standpoint of social contradictions.

Emancipative performative gestures, in this context, emerge as the only possible horizon of expectation in our day. One of the major consequences of alt-right protest is the recognition that civil rights and progressive policies are a valuable yet fragile achievement that must be maintained. The most important conclusion one can draw from these events is that they are continuously reinventing and updating our emancipative vocabulary. One can only look with nostalgia to those moments when the debates over radical criticism and activist creative practices were articulated around (and against) the capacity of cultural institutions and capitalism to appropriate them. Although these forces are still very much at play, a more complex situation has emerged, one primarily (but not exclusively) shaped by the verification of certain limitations in the discursive concatenation of bodies and causes, and the appropriation of art activism by conservative forces.

Ours is a temporality of open forms and undefined agencies. Coloniality enters that temporality not in the form of nostalgia but rather in the very material form marked by the repositioning of ideology, bodies, loves, and hatreds. In 2016, Hito Steyerl proposed that gaming culture was essential in the construction of a sense of future, of a tomorrow: "To play," she affirms, "is to re-actualize the rules as one goes along. Or to create rules that demand new actualization every time." For Steyerl, the act of playing appears as a medium of social creativity, which allows us to "re-creat[e] not only the city, but society itself" (2016). In this reinvention, intersectionality is a must. Under this view, the attacks on Butler seemed to be fraught, not because of their lack of approximation to reality (far right violence can be too real), but rather because they target a blurred objective. They can attack Butler for her gender theory, her criticism of the modern-day State of Israel, or her support of civil rights. But epitomizing her as the embodiment of evil, in the form of a witch, dismantles the pretensions of democracy insinuated in the 2017 protests. This does not mean that they shouldn't be taken seriously. Passions are important when it comes to activism. But this lack of coherence posits a question of a different genre. The events analyzed in this chapter force us to look at the position from which emancipative futures and alliances are built in order to redefine them from scratch.

Fantasmagorias do Império (Imperial Ghosting) and the Making of Exclusionary Public Spaces

The public relevance that the attacks against Butler and the "defense" of the Vieira statue acquired in broad segments of the population derives from the way in which both events touch the most sensitive fibers of Portuguese and Brazilian nationalism. To understand why both events drew so much attention, it is useful to inscribe them within a wider genealogy of privatization, reduction, and securitization of the public space that is directly linked with the perpetuation of coloniality through acts of enclosure and marginalization in both Brazil and Portugal. This section considers the reactions against Butler and the Descolonizando group in relation to a deeper colonial genealogy that normalizes situations of exclusion and turns those situations invisible. More than this, I believe there is a correlation between the creation of sanitized and exclusionary monuments and sites oriented toward the selective and unproblematic public commemoration of colonialism, and the ways in which neoconservative groups appropriate and make use of the public space.

The performative poetic reading organized around the sculpture of Vieira reveals the opposition between two tendencies in postcolonial Portugal. On one hand, the erection of the sculpture can be seen as a symptom of the public enactment of a problem-free image of Portugal as a multicultural and cosmopolitan society, an image that implies a conscious forgetting of the traumatic consequences of colonialism as well as a continuity with a nostalgic definition of Portuguese identity in relation to the "glories" of its imperial past. On the other, the occupation of the Largo Trindade Coelho recalls previous occupations in which memory places were turned into sites of insurgent and intersectional performativity. A quick glance at landmark areas of the Portuguese capital reveal that the legacy of colonialism remains visible and, what is more problematic, very much unquestioned in critical terms.

A clear example of this is Belém, which Elsa Peralta conceives as one of the most paradigmatic places where a triumphant memory of Portugal as imperialist power is still exalted and oriented toward tourist ends, a cornerstone for the enactment of selective memories, "the configuration of conflictive narratives as part of a seemingly coherent and univocal discourse" (2013: 362).[8] Belém is a landmark cultural reference for the entire country. It is a space that brings together the most iconic symbols of Lisbon history and Portuguese nationalism, such as the Belém Tower or the Mosteiro dos Jerónimos (Hieronymite Monastery), two jewels of the Portuguese Gothic historically linked to the country's "expansion" from the fourteenth century. In Belém the visitor will also find some of the most visited museums in the city, including the contemporary art space Belém Cultural Center and the National Archaeology Museum (based in the Mosteiro dos Jerónimos), and the so-called Jardim Botânico Tropical (Tropical Botanical Garden). Finally, the current shape of Belém is very much indebted to the process of ideological resignification undertaken by the Portuguese Estado Novo, which included the erection of iconic monuments such as the Padrão dos Descobrimentos, a gigantic *caravela* (carabel ship) built in 1958 that sought to commemorate the so-called maritime vocation of the Portuguese. The fact that many of those monuments and spaces still bear names that clearly allude to an unproblematic idea of the "discoveries" reveals to what extent the ideological project of the dictatorship is still disguised under the touristic façade of contemporary Lisbon.

Comparing Belém with other memory complexes, Peralta reveals how the present appearance of Belém as a touristic complex rearticulates many of the contradictions and silences at play in the contemporary memorial and museum complex by inscribing an unproblematic image of the imperial past within an abstract notion of Portuguese national identity. She identifies a tradition reaching back to the nineteenth century by referring to examples such as the Museu Etnográfico Português, created in 1893, in which the public educational action of such institutions justifies the presence of colonial objects and narratives as part of an unproblematic explanation of the Portuguese "expansion." The concealing of the thorniest sides of Portuguese colonialism and the "nationalization" of the overseas "experience" as quintessentially characteristic of the Portuguese people will be reproduced by the Portuguese Estado Novo. From the 1940s, as Peralta highlights, the Salazar regime placed great emphasis on transforming Belém into a symbolic area inscribed within a glorified and supposedly uninterrupted past but paradoxically deprived of contemporary inhabitants (see Sapega 2008a,

2008b). Belém became then what it is now, a monumental scenario frozen in time and oriented toward commemorating a problem-free image of *portugalidade* nationally and internationally. Turning Belém into a memory space frozen in time, the Estado Novo attempted to naturalize the presence of the empire by fixing that presence and inscribing it into the DNA of every Portuguese: "At the end of Portuguese colonial rule, Belém enshrines a representation of national identity focused on two main themes: the people, distant and present, as a 'natural' entity inherited from tradition and custom; and the maritime saga, disseminating the image of an empire without colonies, ecumenical, humanist and universal, central in Portugal's self-representation as the country of the 'discoveries' and not as the center of colonial power" (Peralta 2013: 387).[9] Belém is not unique, yet it stands as one of the most important examples of the way in which memorial spaces serve the social reproduction of an amnesiac view of the Portuguese past. In this case, the same space ultimately remains complicit with more recent processes of urban transformation and gentrification. We must not forget, in any case, that Lisbon (like many other cities) also conveys a powerful genealogy and a hidden landscape of contestation. For many decades, the city served as meeting point for anticolonial leaders and creators (including Amílcar Cabral) who succeeded in finding a platform to articulate subversive alliances beneath the dull surface of the Estado Novista metropolitan space. Fast-forwarding to the present, those alliances are continued by racialized groups that occupy public spaces and turn them into sites of revolt, as happened in the controversy around the Vieira statue.

Within the last decade, a decisive transformation has taken place in contemporary Portugal, one related to the increasing importance conceded to the *lugar de fala* (place of speech) implicit in processes of cultural creativity. Many racialized activists and creators are increasingly pointing out the shortcomings of a postcolonial approach that criticizes the amnesia toward Portugal's imperial past but at the same time avoids addressing the ongoing processes of precarization and the systemic racism that affects the lives of many whose presence in Portugal is a direct consequence of the Portuguese expansion (see Peixe Dias and Dias 2012; Gorjão Henriques 2017). This renewed debate has been fueled by the organization of strikes against police violence and racism in so-called *bairros periféricos* (peripheral areas) in Lisbon and Oporto (see Ferro and Raposo 2016; Raposo and Varela 2017). It is striking that the organization of collaborative projects by Afro-descendant activists living in those areas has shifted public perceptions of them while also raising increased public awareness:

Colonialism is increasingly becoming a public matter for many Portuguese citizens, one associated with how Portuguese identity should be defined. Importantly, there is a growing response to a collective desire to integrate more voices and agencies into decolonizing Portuguese society. In [those processes of collaborative creativity], memory and history relate to accessibility in public space. Accessibility in turn relates to infrastructure: public service, urban planning and education. The elementary curriculum continues to enforce a celebratory view of Portugal's colonial expansion, with updates met with delay. Small gestures in cultural activities fostering shared spaces challenge notions of associated with whiteness and "locality". Such discussion spaces draw attention to Afro-Portuguese communities' creative role in shaping today's Lisbon. (Garrido Castellano and Paulo 2019)

The public gathering around the sculpture of Vieira is a direct consequence of the two projects examined here: on one hand, it makes evident the celebratory vision of colonialism proposed by official figures and its suitability for touristic and neoliberal privatization. On the other, it accounts for a process of occupation of the public space in which racialized subjects approach specific monuments or areas as places of contestation and decolonization.

In the case of Brazil, the systemic exclusion and policing of racialized bodies reveals how intertwined the enclosure and privatization of the public space is with the survival of coloniality. As groups such as the São Paulo–based collective Frente 3 de Fevereiro have clearly demonstrated, institutional racism and selective police violence are part of a deeper process of biopolitical governmentality that chastises and ostracizes Black bodies and identities while symbolically and physically relocating their presence. This strategic process of confinement and policing that turns the Black body into a symbol of violence, the collective argues, is ideologically charged and conveys impeding any effective discussion of racism under the argument that Brazilian society is a supposedly racism-free society. As the collective stresses, this negation becomes particularly violent since it does not even offer the possibility of calling racism by its name.

Many of the actions of Frente 3 de Fevereiro have been oriented toward dismantling the myth of racial democracy (the idea of all Brazilians being equal as a result of the process of miscegenation initiated by Portuguese colonialism). The group has also pursued making explicit the way in which many public spaces remain banned to racialized Brazilians. In one of their most famous initiatives, the group asked *"Onde estão os negros?"*

(Where are the Blacks?), urging a public debate on the invisibilization and criminalization of Black bodies in modern-day Brazil. Frente operates in "cultural" contexts, as in the last staging of *Onde estão os negros?* that took place in the last months of 2018, when a banner with that slogan was displayed in front of the Museu de Arte de São Paulo as part of an exhibition attempting to decolonize Brazilian museums organized by the Brazilian activist and academic André Mesquita in collaboration with *Afterall* journal. At the same time, however, their area of research and direct action goes far beyond the contemporary art medium, as when they addressed the militarization of urban surveillance and police in the context of the 2014 World Cup that took place in the country.

The Frente's activities served as a preamble for more recent occupations (such as those mentioned in the introduction to this chapter) of the public space in major Brazilian cities in response to the political and social crisis that revolved around the impeachment of the PT and the coming to power of Bolsonaro. At the same time, they explain why artists and visual activists are being increasingly targeted by neoconservative groups as potential threats: through their capacity to visualize the material and tangible ways in which present-day Brazilian society reproduces patterns of racial and gender-based exclusion, they reveal the fallacy behind the colonial myth of racial democracy. The burning of Butler's effigy and the activist interventions of Frente 3 de Fevereiro (among many other examples) can be directly related to and were preceded by escalating episodes of violence against left-wing activists and contemporary creators throughout Brazil. They also form part of an ongoing campaign that saw cultural creators as dangerous agitators undermining *brasilidade.*

The attacks against Butler were not unique. In September 2017, a performative reinterpretation of Lygia Clark's *O Bicho* by Wagner Schwartz was accused of inciting "inappropriate" sexual behavior and pederasty. The debate, proceeding from a moment when a child touches the foot of the naked performer, quickly transcended the boundaries of the "art world" and triggered enraged comments in national and international social networks as well as protests in São Paulo. Weeks earlier, in Rio Grande do Sul, the exhibition *Queermuseu—Cartografias da diferença da arte brasileira* was cancelled in response to the protests also accusing the curator of encouraging allegedly "inappropriate" sexual behaviors. As in the case of Portugal, cultural processes that years before would have passed unnoticed (an academic lecture, an artistic performance, an art exhibition) became the center of enormous public attention and controversy. Each of those actions (the controversy surrounding Schwartz's performance, the closing of *Queermuseu*, the attacks on Butler) also operated in a fictional way. The accusations Schwartz faced were grounded on a sexual intention that neither the artist nor the museum ever expressed. The closing of *Queermuseu* also relied on hypothetical effects the exhibition could have on Brazilian society.

The attacks on Butler were based, then, on a lecture she never gave. A similar logic applies in the case of the "protection" of the Vieira sculpture in Lisbon. This act relied on a threat that never materialized, one that was not present in the original call that organized the protest. The next section explores this threat in relation to the competing performative acts arising in both processes.

Acting, the Enclosed, and the Unforeseeable

So far, we have seen how alt-right activism borrows the tactics of left-wing and art activism to enact exclusionary views on the (racialized and sexualized) body of the nation. We also traced the relation between those views and broader exclusionary processes targeting the public space. Now it's time to analyze what capacity of response for emancipative agendas both episodes leave open. What does the performative act of burning Butler's likeness as a witch tell us about our bond with emancipative, activist creative agency? What sort of transference can lead to embodying Butler as an object of mass concern and as a potential threat to national security? How can the hugging of a sculpture be associated with alleged attacks on the body of the Portuguese nation? What moral and symbolic economy makes it possible to disguise such acts of hate as protective gestures? What affect and effects are articulated in and through both events?

Responding to two very different conjunctures, the actions against Butler and the act of hugging Vieira's sculpture respond to similar ideals, and ultimately work in a similar way. Both strive to build a common cause based on the existence of a threatened nation whose values are under attack by intellectual ideas and politically committed nonconformist creative actions. A singular transformation takes place here: objects (Butler's "witch" effigy and the statue of Vieira) are turned into symbols that must be destroyed or protected at all costs to ensure the safety of the nation's citizens. However, words and specific bodies, academic lectures, poems, and works of contemporary art, are understood as potentially threatening, as specifically targeting the body of the nation. In both cases, the right to represent that body is claimed by a reduced group as an exclusive good, materialized, through strange forms of iconophilia and iconophobia, in the form of an artistic object. In both cases, however, each action takes the form of a confrontation with unforeseen consequences. In both Brazil and Portugal the conflicts around images analyzed in this chapter participate in the open-endedness that Bruno Latour confers on "iconoclash."[10] Indeed, the performative horizon of the position that acts to exclude any other position at play in both the attacks on Butler and the "hugging" of Padre Vieira's statue is determined by two principles: closure and exposure. Attempting to have a public impact, they end up enclosing reality (burning Butler's figure and surrounding a statue) as if these acts could eradicate competing, alternative views of reality. In the case of Butler's replica, her figure incarnates all the elements that are considered harmful for a specific segment of the citizenry, a segment, nevertheless, claiming the right of standing for the entire community. Butler is caricaturized through the figure of the witch, a historically loaded symbol charged in the popular imagination (as Silvia Federici [2004] has explained) with primitive fears of economic and gender equality menacing the capitalist horizon of the modern age. It is revealing that this popular imagination came into being in the same modern age in which figures such as Vieira normalized exclusionary gender and racial policies through religion.

The identification of Butler as a supposed witch was possible because of the colonial genealogy of so-called abnormal bodies and behaviors naturalized by Vieira, among others, including the public sanctioning of certain customs, practices, and attitudes concerning the female body while declaring others to be anomalous. In this case, any other alternatives are denied when personal acts of mourning are excluded from the public sphere. The scene ends with the intervention of the police and the cancelation of the event. The final result of the October 2017 events evokes Nancy Fraser's idea of abnormal justice, which she understands as an unstructured situation grounded on mutual disagreement and the inexistence of a shared grammar that could lead to the resolution of the conflict. For Fraser, the point is not to long for past forms of "more syntactic" justice but rather to expose the "historically specific" basis of contemporary paradigms (Fraser 2008: 396). This reasoning fully applies to the activist intervention around the Vieira statue. In this case, not only did the right-wing alleged defense impede any other public expression about what Vieira represented; the fact that the "performers" were surrounded by a second circle of policemen created a strange situation: the fear that any potential conflict might arise resulted in the protection of a group whose motivations were in turn driven by a similar fear that (pacifist) discourses and actions might cause harm to the exposed and vulnerable body of the sculpture, which, as we argued before, sought to incarnate a broad notion of *portugalidade*.[11]

Inasmuch as this protective, phantasmagoric dimension is present in both actions, they become violent in a basic way: both actions transform the emergence of sociopolitical alternatives epitomized by Butler in Brazil and the debates on coloniality in Portugal into fictional threads directed at the entire nation in order to close these alternatives down and ban them from the public sphere. By interrupting the openness that both critical theory and visual creativity bring, the performances preclude and impose a particular reaction, that of rejection. Both performative actions we are dealing with here iterate an exclusion of the unpredictability that is always associated with performative sociopolitical gestures. It is in this basic way that we can define the symbolic violence at play in both events, and it is this act of closure that introduces a basic difference from emancipative performativity, driven by unpredictability and bodily interdependence.

The witchcraft performance in Brazil and the hugging of Vieira's statue in Lisbon affirm exclusive ownership of national history while preventing any alternative view or action from emerging within the same public space. In both cases, the adoption of a point of view and the enunciation of that positioning are expressed through publicly enacted actions. These actions, nevertheless, are of a very peculiar kind, since they shut down any competing action by arguing that this act of foreclosure is indispensable for ensuring personal and collective safety. Since both the witch-burning and statue-hugging performances bind individual or group identity with national identity, "safety" here adopts a contradictory form, representing a totality that nevertheless excludes any opposing view, a totality based on reductive exclusivism. A strange situation emerges, in which violence and closure are claimed by two different and unconnected groups, operating in two different countries, as the only ways of ensuring peace.

When I first came to know about both events, an unpleasant feeling of déjà vu took shape in my mind. There are strong precedents for each situation. They respond to a crescendo of extreme attacks on culture and difference that have gained public ground. As early as 2004, Butler herself identified a similar fear turned into public hatred in the anti-intellectual and anti-artistic climate that originated in the post-9/11 era. Dealing with the same chronology, Sara Ahmed mapped the cultural politics of hate, especially when addressing migrant or nonwhite bodies, as crucial in the configuration of territorialities and identities in the early 2000s. To some extent, then, none of this is new; yet, one can but wonder about the magnified dimensions of both events. Whereas Butler's name has been associated with activism for many decades, the way her physical presence (for it was that presence, and not any particular "deconstructive" words) compounded far-right hate and triggered its performative enactment in the public space demands a closer examination.

Beyond Control, Hopefully

The events of October 2017 in Portugal and November 2017 in Brazil revealed how entangled discussions about art are within central nodes of our public sphere. The performances organized in Brazil, which involved striking against cultural and social conservatism but also against cuts in culture budgets, as well as the actions around Butler's conferences, and in Portugal around Vieira and slavery, reveal the extent to which "art matters" can constitute "social matters." Seen for a long time as an exclusionary field for a small group of initiates, art emerges here as challenging the economic and biopolitical contradictions of our reality.[12] And the good news is that that reality is contagiously adopting not only art's flexibility and precarity-based organizational mode but also its open-endedness and critical belief in the capacity of using creativity in the configuration of alternative futures.

The immediate responses to both controversies might be characterized as "cultural wars" (see Phillips 2017; Ferreira and Louro 2017). From the perspective outlined here, I consider this approach to be incomplete. Although a rapid glance at both contexts can identify in them two sides struggling for public recognition, presenting antagonistic arguments, what these public events actually reveal is how exclusion is not limited to economic forms alone. In the two alt-right performances commented on here, culture appears as a battlefield where the objective is not to "win a war" but to eradicate any potential alternative. The two sides of these debates are not merely marking out different ideological positions; they are also configuring two very different sets of rules. The point, then, is to think whether culture takes the shape of an interdependent, open-ended human totality, or instead portrays itself as an exclusionary reduction. The fact that academic and artistic events are being targeted reveals a fear of the potential of both platforms to devise alternative horizons. Fear operates here by introducing a fictional thread that makes the acts of (real) injury justifiable and bearable. The attacks on artists, activists, and academics in Brazil and the "defense of *portugalidade*" therefore cannot be understood as cultural wars, as interventions into what Stuart Hall denominated a "war of positions," but as symptoms, as the ultimate consequences of a process of expulsion attempting to close down the open-endedness of these wars once and for all.

Any utterance of violence and injury, Butler argues, opens up a possibility to respond. By violently interpellating a person, that person gains a name, which is to say a space of enunciation. Condensed in time, the act of utterance nevertheless contains an unpredictable future that, as Butler explains, "exceeds itself in past and future directions, an effect of prior and future invocations that constitute and escape the instance of utterance" (Butler 2013: 3). That possibility of escape allows alternative, noninjurious answers to injurious utterances. This idea, which informs the base of Butler's *Excitable Speech: A Politics of the Performative*, sheds new light on what happened in Brazil and Portugal in 2017, illuminating fertile paths for understanding how acting configures the contours of our spaces of coexistence. These spaces are not a given thing but rather something produced *through* our capacity to perform publicly. In that sense, in both Portugal and Brazil what one could at first identify as culture wars brought the contradictions of both nations' racialized bodies into public debate. Discussing art became attached to raising urgent questions about who can speak, where, and to whom. Art matters became national matters, yet in a sort of undefined, fragmented, and intersectional way.

The performance of witchcraft that took place in Brazil in 2017 is better understood when compared to another act of identification, that of Damien Hirst's ultraexpensive sculpture *For the Love of God* with the 1 percent by the Occupy Wall Street movement. At the time, Gregory Sholette recognized in this identification a serious limitation of the emancipative potential of contemporary art, at least of a contemporary art system grounded in grandiloquent and spectacular gestures. In this sense, he argued that "to many, the art world is the primary symptom of the 1% economy" and that, ultimately, the failure and collapse of the art world parallels the field of "real" economy and social relations. Against this backdrop, Sholette describes what he calls "bare art," a postautonomous production that nonetheless still has a paradoxical capacity to "point to new forms of potential solidarity within, but also beyond our art world" (Sholette 2017: 32).

Less than a decade later, the attacks on Butler and the visual arts scene in Brazil are meant to represent a whole different set of values, where critical thinking and visual creativity are no longer identified with a privileged zone but are rather intertwined within sociopolitical matters (and even within biopolitics!) in such a way as to be considered a serious threat to the entire nation. Are the images of Hirst's *For the Love of God* and of Butler's replica comparable? In what ways does the transition between the two represent the eloquent demise of emancipative perspectives in our present moment? Why, and how, does a progressive academic lecture raise such digital and bodily opposition? What turns a public sculpture (at least temporarily) into the center of a debate around the fractures of postcolonial Portugal? What grants these forces such virulence, making them transcend the digital realm in order to then acquire a physical appearance?

One can easily recognize that the public performativity of hate is fraught in both cases, since it targets fictions, not facts. Yet both attacks had a performative appeal, one that materialized and embodied emotions, to the point of becoming contagious. It is evident that what is at stake in this case exceeds Butler's feminist criticism and the figure of Vieira (or his statue). These processes are symptoms of a globally recognizable panorama in which the lexicon and the horizon of activism are being taken over by alt-right forces. Butler's lectures mobilized sympathizers and conservatives outside academic spaces at a time when gender politics and the achievements of two centuries of gender rights are more questioned than ever. In the case of Lisbon, coloniality stopped being the subject matter of social sciences and academics and became the center of collective discussions about the symbolic landscape of Lisbon neighborhoods. If these events reveal anything, it is that the belief that art and progressive criticism are socially irrelevant can no longer be sustained. After decades of social indifference, for conservative movements the "enemy" has come to be located within culture, in the "minority" contexts of academia and the artistic avant-garde. Yet, paradoxically, conservatism seems to be taking the potential impact of emancipative creative and critical practice more seriously than progressive politics, in Brazil, Portugal, and elsewhere.

It seems that nowadays, activist creativity and critical thought have come to be identified as a public enemy. For a long time, socially and politically engaged artists, activists, and thinkers found either (minority) critical appraisal or indifference, and were either marginalized or engulfed by cultural institutions to serve economic ends. Now the situation seems to have changed. While the separation between art and life seems to be thinner than ever, this transformation has become a nightmare version of the aspirations of progressive, socially committed aesthetics: artists and intellectuals have become public figures and confirmed the relevance of a politically engaged artistic and critical approach to reality, but this recognition of the contemporaneity of emancipative horizons has come from an unexpected side, that of right-wing violence. When a mob decides to strike a burning witch-like replica of Judith Butler, one can only wonder how these matters have become such a pressing public concern. A few years ago, indifference and social irrelevance were the threat to the aspirations of socially committed art and criticism. The violent response that Butler's visit to Brazil elicited demonstrates that "cultural matters" are at the center of Brazil's racialized national body, something that reveals without any doubt the relevance of emancipative praxis and thought in our supposedly postideological present.

In the Portuguese case, the activists and intellectuals that approached the statue on October 5 were not trying to express any specific reading on Vieira. The act did not simply take the form of an overt criticism directed against the official cultural politics of postcolonialism in Lisbon, based on many occasions on the public enactment of a celebratory image of the city as a conflict-free multicultural creative hub that had succeeded in getting rid of the contradictions of its past as a metropolis. Their objective was, rather, to underscore the importance of leaving some definitions, some debates, open. The countering act operated by alt-right protesters attempted to eliminate, in both discursive and formal ways, the openness of such an act. The fact that the demonstration was cancelled can be seen as an achievement of that goal. The discussion that ensued in the following days, however, clearly exceeded the repercussions of the event, extending its consequences in time and space and illustrating the survivability of certain affects and effects beyond the immediate act in which they are conceived.

In this case, the "afterlives" of an exchange that had art at its core greatly transgressed the boundaries of aesthetics. This expansion proved to be useful if for no other reason than inscribing antiracist performativity as deeply embedded in the configuration of the supposedly multicultural landscape of Lisbon. Since the 1990s, the city has portrayed an image of itself as more attentive to racial difference than many other European capital cities. In this context, art operates as a sort of specialized realm where discourses about racism and decolonization are frequent, something that does not mean, however, that certain bodies and voices are allowed to occupy certain positions. On the contrary, these bodies and voices are still spoken for, defined from outside. It is from this limitation that authors such as Jota Mombaça argue that focusing on Vieira's postcolonial afterlife is not enough. Instead, Mombaça argues that "the political work of these Euro-white artists and intellectuals whose discourses aim to challenge the obstinacy of racism in present day Portuguese culture has to go necessarily beyond the critique of the statue, whose solid inscription in the Lisbon landscape can over-evidence the density of colonial mentality in the present as much as hide the much more discreet mechanism under which this mentality is affirmed in the relational texture of life between the world of white people and the persons systematically marginalized by it" (Mombaça 2017; translation mine). As many voices have stressed, the contemporary dimension of present-day Lisbon as a touristic, multicultural European capital has been achieved through a selective interpretation of the role of colonialism in the configuration of postcolonial and postdictatorial Portugal. The main question arising here is how far cultural producers have been complicit with or have even fostered that banishment. In the previous quotation we can detect a warning against the incompleteness of Portuguese visual production in addressing the situation of exclusions and the continuity of racism in present-day Portuguese society. That incompleteness would take place despite the consolidation in academia and the visual arts of a debate on the contradictions arising out of Portugal's incapacity to deal with the most troublesome aspects of its former imperial identity. Postcolonial debates gained momentum in the Portuguese academic world by the end of the 1990s, matching a long process of identity redefinition related to Portugal's joining the European Union. A cornerstone of this process was the organization in 1998of the World Trade Exhibition in Lisbon as part of the five hundredth anniversary of the "Portuguese discoveries."[13] The 1998 World Exhibition was seen by many as a missed opportunity for the country to come to terms with its contemporary peripheral role in Europe while definitively setting aside nostalgic memories of Portugal's imperial past. In any case, the social, political, and cultural transformations the country was experiencing provided the basis for a renewed debate on the continuities of colonialism in contemporary Portugal. Boaventura de Sousa Santos, Miguel Vale de Almeida, Cláudia Castelo, Francisco Bethencourt, and Margarida Calafate Ribeiro stand among the initiators of a debate that from a very early moment emphasized a wide multiplicity of disciplinary approaches and cultural manifestations. Those debates started a little later in the visual art medium around the installations and public art interventions of Ângela Ferreira and Vasco Araújo, and the curatorial activity of spaces such as Culturgest and the Calouste Gulbenkian Foundation in Lisbon, or the Serralves Foundation in Oporto.

The gathering around Vieira's statue expresses the need felt by many racialized activists to transcend the exclusionary areas of academia and the art medium while at the same time connecting their objectives with those of broader segments of the population. The performative side of the confrontation added to the role that social networks played in disseminating the events and providing a space for exchange, evidence of the increasingly central role that debates on agency and exclusion in relation to racialized presence in public spaces are acquiring at the heart of Portuguese society.

Conclusion: Exposing Ourselves to Others

Performance is the clearest proof that our agency means exposing others to ourselves and exposing ourselves to others. Although deeply connected with the politics of love and hate channeled through the Internet, performance still appears to be a central node in delimiting the contours of civil society. Whereas the processes we are analyzing took social media as their battlefield, they also needed to materialize and publicly embody the politics of hate.

In our two examples, expressing hate through social media did not suffice; also necessary was an embodiment of hate and physical approximation to the hated bodies. This approximation reveals a deep connection between progressive discourses and the capacity to perform these in the public sphere. This connection has important consequences, for it banishes the idea that intellectuals and socially committed artists operate in closed fields with no public relevance. Yet if the attacks on Butler and the defense of *portugalidade* through the act of surrounding and embracing the sculpture of Vieira reveal how a material and physical excess always remains when social and political causes are mobilized, they are also outnumbered by a range of actions in which progressive activism and emancipatory action and thought take advantage of this bodily approximation.

The removal of the Confederate flag in Charleston South, Carolina, in 2015 by artist and activist Bree Newsome offers an interesting parallel and can be seen as one such action (see Sholette 2017). In this case, the action was conceived in a performative way, outlining the public relevance of undertaking certain actions in certain places. At the same time, it countered straightforward associations among national identity, belonging, and flags. We live in a time when flags have become symbols standing for closuring totalities. Associated for a long time with the "constructed" character of nationalisms, they have come to be repoliticized as symbols of "with us or against us" identities. Newsome's action cannot be seen as taking sides within a war of position. Rather, and more importantly, her action points to a radical reopening of the discursive and *performative* fields that determine whether mutual acceptance and respect or hatred, exclusion, and racial violence shape the

American public sphere. In this case, the act of removing the flag asserted that public life should be organized around egalitarian interdependence but also around repositioned and redefined citizenship. In the two performances analyzed in this chapter, citizenship is framed under the urgency of expanding the realm of the sayable and the doable against the threat of exclusionary configurations of the public. As I have attempted to demonstrate, exposure (understood in the sense of being affected by something and affecting that reality in turn, of occupying an external, public space, and collectively being without protection from harm) emerges not only as a symptom of vulnerability but also as a powerful place of enunciation and emergence, one simultaneously shaped by and shaping decolonial genealogies and possibilities.

BLACK LIVES MATTER AND/FOR THE GENEALOGIES OF SUBVERSIVE ARTISTIC CREATIVITY

I rewrote the first part of this coda in 2020, while President Donald Trump was running for reelection and pandemic capitalism placed many cultural activists such as the ones appearing in this book in situations of confinement and risk that I could not foresee when I originally wrote it back in 2017. No matter how you look at things, and without the need of any magic ball to predict the future, it became clear that the kind of hope for the future that many art activist projects seem to bring is being subjected to unprecedented threat. I guess this is why one chooses to write a book like this. This ain't a time for happy endings. In fact, any such thing as an ending (the closure of something and the productive hesitations leading to the beginning of something new, something other) looks more and more uncertain. The obnoxious "new normality" contains a great deal of "good ole" normality as we always knew it. That includes the cultural sector, where the demand for constant self-actualization and flexibility-as-precarization have been accepted as a new normal necessary in times of pandemic capitalism. It would be naive to believe that this "Netflix" way of making culture is something temporary and that things will go back to normal as soon as the circumstances change.

All the projects discussed in this book, and many others, are investments in future making. They conceive of cultural agency as an unforeseeable collective tool. It is precisely because of this that we need to consider art activism seriously. One of the events that inspired me to write this book was Judith Butler's visit to Brazil in 2017. That visit was revealing in many senses, as it marked the clash between the rise of neoconservative politics globally and the concatenation of progressive feminist and antiracist forces. I wrote the chapter on Butler and Padre António Vieira at that time. That first version went under the title "Beyond Control, Hopefully." As with the whole book, it included a great deal of optimism about art's potential for occupying the streets in progressive ways. I did not know then that art activism was soon to be declared a national threat in Brazil or that activists were to be chased and hit and run over by the army in the United States. In 2017 a handful of neoconservatives "defended" the statue of Padre Vieira; in 2020, a Portuguese far-right party campaigned for the creation of "a police dedicated to protecting statues and monuments." The only good thing about this unfolding of events is that it shows that art remains a frontline of progressive mobilization.

I do not know whether Black Lives Matter will reach Cork, where I write these final lines. In Ireland, the assassination of George Floyd on May 25, 2020, was met with incredulity and anger. It immediately brings to mind Direct Provision, a system of "hospitality" for asylum seekers that regularizes segregation and systemic racism. In Cork, the protestors painted a mural that links Black Lives Matter and the strike against Direct Provision and remains in place as of March 2021. Every time I look at it, I force myself to remember that neoconservative political backlash and pandemic capitalism make art activism more necessary than ever. I was caught off guard by the events of recent years. That's no bad thing. On the contrary: a book on popular mobilization can work only if it is surprised and overtaken by circumstances. That's the best of symptoms.

If one of the two main concerns of this book has dealt with the loss of transformative purchase deriving from the appropriation of art activism, the other has to do with the inexhaustible renovative potential of cultural creativity when put to the task of progressive mobilization. Striking and critically thinking about that striking are long-term endeavors. Looking backward and looking anew are powerful allies and useful tools for that purpose. The idea is not to suggest that time hasn't passed or that we should wait for better times; rather, the point is to historicize the current circumstances in ways that are simultaneously accurate and open-ended, which is why I opted to leave the remaining part of this coda as it was at the end of 2017.

◆　◆　◆

When Black Lives Matter first appeared in 2013, it seized an opportunity arising out of necessity. For many, as Ruth Wilson Gilmore (2017) reminds us, to matter implied to materialize, to expand and make visible an emancipative geography. The actions following the deaths of Michael Brown, Eric Garner, and many others demanded accountability for the systemic and sustained violence racialized subjects have historically undergone. But there was something else. The need for justice was turned into a space of possibility where an alternative redrawing of the public became temporarily possible. It may be true that Black Lives Matter created "a new way of seeing" (and being seen in public), as Nicholas Mirzoeff aptly puts it. But the mo(ve)ment emerging around and after the hashtag also rebranded our very vocabulary of being in common. "Seeing," for Mirzoeff, represents not just seeing (the naturalized-yet-historical point of privilege of the observer) but rather "the point of intersection between what we know, what we perceive, and what we feel— using all our senses." For him, the movement is about "seeing what there is to be seen, in defiance of the police who say 'move on, there's nothing to see here,' and then giving the visible a sayable name" (Mirzoeff 2017: 17–18). From that perspective (from the expanding nature of words when activated through moments of activist sharing), if creative collaboration is about collectively investing time, then it might be useful to ask how that time looks when radically materialized. If the success (aesthetic as well as social) of art as a collaborative tool depends on the outcomes resulting from experience (from the materialization of collectively invested time), then it might be useful to ask how our grounds of collaboration (our collaborative futures) look when framed thought the lens of Black Lives Matter.

A first clarification: Black Lives Matter is not just a mo(ve)ment. It is also a genealogy. The voices that have pinpointed the deep roots linking contemporary and past acts of resistance and insubordination against racialized violence and exclusion are many. Suffice it to mention here Michelle Alexander's (2012) identification of mass incarceration as a new Jim Crow; Sohail Daulatzai's (2012) capacity to relate post-9/11 anti-Muslim feelings to the silencing of the role of the Nation of Islam and Black Muslim radicalism in the configuration of transnational subversive alliances; Lewis Gordon's (2015) rooting the experience of nonbeing of African Americans in the Fanonian imagery of hell and nonexistence; Nikhil Pal Singh's (2005, 2017) ability to insert the contemporary antiracist actions of Black activists into "a long civil rights era"; Fred Moten's (2013) recognition of Black aesthetics as (subversive) action; and Christina Sharpe's (2016) identification of Blackness with being awakened to injustices both locally and transnationally. Those are just some examples of the interest in recent scholarship in grounding contemporary acts of insurgence within a deeper Black radical tradition that challenges and goes far beyond any US-centrism.

Black Lives Matter reinvented our activist vocabulary by producing a subversive symbolic order that puts together code and flow, information and reaction, surplus and collective imagination. Black Lives Matter challenges the preponderance of netactivism and clicktivism by showing its codependence with physical, collective acts of appearance and affirmation. At the same time, the movement exemplified the need to read previous theories *and* practices of the commons (such as Occupy Wall Street's identification with the 99 percent) from the point of view of the deep fracture that racial discrimination represents in US society. From the unruly yet genealogic temporality of Black Lives Matter appears a first lesson of interest for the issues dealt with in this book: our activist futures will be decolonial or simply will not be. Black Lives Matter grew out of alternative alliances created through the time of necessity imposed on racialized subjects by racial capitalism. Resisting necessity (which is the same as publicly emerging as a subject) always implies breaking away from the divisible, from the logic of speciation and/as specialization that determines what counts as a grievable life and what does not. Racialization, as Stefano Harney and Fred Moten argue, "is present in the very idea of dominion over the earth; in the very idea and enactment of the exception" (2017: 85). In contrast, appearing together is for both authors a matter of recognizing that we all live in different degrees of "common dispossession."[1] Assuming resistance as a matter of appearing together (of materializing) new collectivities can be quite productive in determining the guiding principles through which we measure our (artistic) radicality. If racial capitalism works through common dispossession (which never means being equally dispossessed), then struggling against it would forcefully mean instantiating the public in such a way as to allow the encounters forbidden by specia(liz)ation.

Crucial to challenging the coloniality of the logic that depicts violence as episodic events taking place in neutral spaces is to understand that "people are being killed in racialized spaces" (Mirzoeff 2017: 18). Against the idea that space is a neutral landscape, we might instead see interhuman agency operating against the grain of "socially assigned disposability" and its reverse, our critical capacity for "spacing appearance," to borrow from Athena Athanasiou's apt formulations (Butler and Athanasiou 2013: 194), constrained yet not limited by that disposability. The task might be to recognize that we create space even in those circumstances where place is made normative to such an extent as to annul most instances of personal and collective affirmation. Rejecting the idea that violence is casual and rooting it into deeper and thicker genealogies of institutional and institutionalized specia(liz)ation and normative specialization, the challenge lies in acknowledging spaces prefiguring and materializing unthinkable alliances. Following Michel Rolph Trouillot's brilliant approximation of the improbability of the Haitian Revolution, "unthinkable" here stands for the imminence of processes about to happen and yet without a clear name, collectively and affirmatively undefined, so to speak. Trouillot reframed the unthinkable as critical common sense acting against normalized and normalizing monotony: "When reality does not coincide with deeply held beliefs, human beings tend to phrase interpretations that force reality within the scope of these beliefs. They devise formulas to repress the unthinkable and to bring it back within the realm of accepted discourse" (1995: 72). Is not this a beautiful metaphor of the logic presiding over conservative interpretations of activism and (art-channeled) social transformation? For Trouillot, the unthinkable stands in opposition to the utopian. Whereas the latter suggests transformation not yet produced, the former implies that our critical capacity to apprehend that transformation always lags in relation to the praxis that ought to be captured and designed. The crucial point lies in the fact that there is always a resistance to nominalism (to our capacity to delimit the frontiers between [art] activism and the return to order subjacent to its institutionalization).

In this book I conceive that resistance (the organic ways in which praxis slips between our fingers when we try to seize it) as a fertile point of departure for rethinking art's politics. I have also attempted to enlist socially engaged art in a broad genealogy of subversive place making. In this sense, I fully share Ruth Wilson Gilmore's idea that "abolition geography starts from the homely premise that freedom is a place. Place making is normal human activity" (2017: 227). As different as art is in relation to reality (which can be a lot or not that much), the artistic practices analyzed here share with activism a genuine interest in investing time in exchange for and at the service of the decolonization of the spaces of racial capitalism. I see in those spaces a living genealogy of struggle expanding and contracting across boundaries and time, breathing through history and breathing silenced voices and bodies into history. When motivated by a wish to decolonize, socially engaged art becomes situated in action, localized-yet-exportable subversive thought.

What Mirzoeff demonstrates in his analysis of Black Lives Matter is how powerful an artistic and visual imagination can be when applied to dismantling the spaces and logic of white supremacism and racial capitalism. The experience of Black Lives Matter is significant here mainly because it can hardly be limited to any national context. Rather, it should be situated as part of the *longue durée* of emancipative practices (many of them emerging from the Global South) analyzed in this book. Mirzoeff is right in linking Black Lives Matter to the history of racial emancipation in the Americas, a history that has in the Haitian Revolution a central (albeit not unique) chapter. From this perspective, it is possible to recognize in Black Lives Matter the productivity of a decolonial, collective practice of space making. But focusing on this movement would leave the question on the relevance of a socially engaged art untouched. Instead, we should ask: What can activists learn from socially committed artists? Shall we identify in those the enemy, a tool for cultural gentrification and other forms of expulsion? I am aware of the difficulty of maintaining the division between "art and reality" to begin with: as Gregory Sholette demonstrates, artists-qua-precarious can also be activists, joining the ranks of broader mobilizations, sometimes as their avant-garde but much more often as active and attentive listeners. Yet, the question remains: if more imaginative insurgent futures reverberate through Black Lives Matter, in which ways does art articulate with those?

A first challenge that both activism and collaborative art may share is the fact that both are particularly useful for revealing the ways in which the governmental logic of capitalism lies in colonial and racialized divisions. It turns out that capitalism's capacity to co-opt socially ameliorative intentions and practices is one of the lessons it takes from its racial component. As Frantz Fanon clearly explained, colonialism works as a sort of a world turned upside down, where social betterment is intended to mean social exclusion; help, dispossession; the public, the exclusionary; and so on. In this sense, the need to articulate a different vocabulary for socially engaged art (or for any kind of radical, decolonial creativity) intersects with the need to undo the grammar of ongoing colonization. Unsettling the latter, exposing its unfair, unnatural logic, would necessarily mean reinventing the former.

Another possible answer to the question may lie in the fact that socially engaged art practice speaks to the way in which different rationalities—specific combinations of race, class, and gender—can and do emerge through creative praxis. For example, a paradigm of art politics based on the idea that the only possibility for artists is to be co-opted by the system will benefit a particular kind of audience and foreclose a particular set of possibilities. Inversely, a focus on the unpredictability of experimentation will frame the terms of the debate in a wholly different way. This why experience—and not content, intentions, or expertise—emerges as the central feature of radical creativity. For the purposes of this book, experience has been conceptualized as situated logic action, that is, as a way of collective thinking *through,* or while doing. In highlighting the performative nature of thinking and its situatedness, we must not forget the fact that our intentions might not be materialized in the way we expect them to be. Dealing with the role of experience in African American philosophy, Lewis Gordon argues that "the interpretation of experience is not . . . a private affair. It is part of the complex world of communication and sociality" (2006: 31). The consequence of this is that experience should not be straightforwardly identified as something good. On the contrary, an excessive and exclusionary focus on experience could lead to reenacting the colonial divide between mind and body, praxis and theory. As Gordon further clarifies, the danger lies in perpetuating the assumption that "colored folks offer experience that white folks interpret" (31). Challenging that assumption should be a cornerstone of a decolonized radical creativity. Learning from the practical actions of other (racialized) bodies would also pose important challenges to the methodologies applied to analyze that creativity. The fact that more often than not the discipline has been grounded on "white folks' interpretation of colored folks' experience" speaks volumes on the magnitude of what is to be done. Yet, throughout this book, I have tried to show that our genealogies of radical creativity would look completely different if framed through the lens of the collective actions and thought seeking to dismantle the normativity of racial capitalism. At the same time, it is crucial to recognize that those actions and thoughts are more than neutral elements awaiting analysis. Rather, they demand a different methodological approach. They also provide valuable analytical tools for tackling the main question behind this book: if (art) activism is being taken to new frontiers by racialized subjects attempting to decolonize our spaces of negotiation and exchange, then why is it that the critical vocabulary we employ to deal with such practices is still subject to a universalist Western rationality?

Finally, both collaborative art and activism demonstrate that the articulation of an emancipative politics is based on contributive, nonpredetermined sociability. Black Lives Matter is redefining our activist vocabulary for many reasons, one of which lies in its capacity to open correlative spaces in which subversion circulates and passes on to other struggles. The challenge will be to insert (our critical appreciation of) socially engaged art into that emancipative continuum, remaining attentive to the dangers deriving from its institutionalization and specialization, but also to the fractures and conspiracies opened by specific creative practices.

NOTES

Notes to the Introduction

1. Tsang Tak "Kith" Ping, conversation with author, 2017. Kith was involved in the protests for the preservation of Queen's Pier in Hong Kong, one of the symbols of the city's colonial history but also a recognizable and charismatic landmark for many Hong Kongese. The pier was slated to be demolished to give way to an ambitious program of urban remodeling that finally took place. Kith participated in many other actions against the gentrification of the city in which he had been born, which happens to be one of the most expensive and ravaged urban environments in the world. In 2020 Kith lectured and developed new performative actions.

2. Tsang Tak "Kith" Ping, conversation with author, 2017.

3. At the same time, however, many voices have warned about the increasing frequency with which the verb "decolonize" has been uncritically applied to a never-ending range of sociocultural initiatives (see especially Tuck and Wayne Yang 2012). While the term "decolonization" is used throughout this book, I share both authors' concern about the need to ground in and derive decolonial thought from specific, praxis-based initiatives.

Notes to Chapter 1

1. "The third current cannot be named as a style, a period, or a tendency. It proliferates below the radar of generalization. It results from the great increase in the number of artists worldwide and the opportunities offered by new informational and communicative technologies to millions of users. These changes have led to the viral spread of small-scale, interactive, DIY art

(and art-like output) that is concerned less with high art style or confrontational politics and more with tentative explorations of temporality, place, affiliation, and affect—the ever-more-uncertain conditions of living within contemporaneity on a fragile planet" (T. Smith 2012: 34).

2. The first current is concerned with "expanding the white cube," whereas the third has to do with "domesticating the gallery space" (T. Smith 2012: 32).

3. Nowhere is this clearer than in *Documenta 11*'s emphasis on the transient, transnational and ever-shifting nature of the mega-exhibition as site of experimentation and cultural translation. The conception of the event as a succession of platforms displayed on different continents, however, reinforced art's dependency on a kind of spectator capable of displacing herself from one location to the next one. See Philipsen (2010, especially chapter 7).

4. I will not attempt to add anything here about what the best definition of "postcolonialism" might be. Rather, embracing the vagueness and polysemy implicit in both its theoretical definition and its indiscriminate application in the field of contemporary art, I will use the term here to refer to three different things that are somehow commonly confused: a certain trend within contemporary art, an academic discipline concentrated in the United States and Europe, and a mode of criticism concerned with the afterlives of colonial power in a supposedly postcolonial world. In none of those meanings, however, can we find a unique interpretation. I am more interested in seeing what a certain "postcolonial inflection" in contemporary art adds to the relation between socially engaged art and other artistic practices, especially exhibition making. For an already classic discussion on the meaning of postcolonialism, see Shohat (1992); McClintock (1992); Dirlik (1994).

5. Indeed, the bond between postcolonialism and globalization, as Simon During (2010: 402) well argued, is a long-lasting one, the second implying a rearticulation of colonial power relations.

6. This topic has been the object of vast attention in the last few years. See, for example, Harris (2017); Osborne (2013, 2018).

7. Hito Steyerl (2017) identifies freeport art storage as both the underside and the condition of possibility of art biennials.

8. Ellipsis in the original.

9. As this book seeks to argue, however, not all socially engaged projects go through this process of representation, nor do they pursue representation in exhibition form.

10. Bennett's emphasis on ideology and concealment within the exhibitionary complex brings to mind Foucault's claim (1989: 33) that "the presence of the law is in its concealment."

11. The editors argue, emphatically: "In the art context, the global turn is best documented in controversial but influential exhibitions whose significance to make history or mark history on their own only

became apparent in the years that followed" (Belting, Buddensieg, and Weibel 2013: 60).

12. For instance, among the "global" spaces for art included in the exhibition appears the Brazilian Instituto Cultural Inhotim, described in the *Global Contemporary* catalog in the following terms: "There the environment lives in harmony with art, and both are the basis of wide-reaching educational initiatives of social nature." Located in the Minas Gerais region, an area with a dense history of colonial economic exploitation, the Instituto was built to display the private collection of a wealthy local businessman. The Instituto spans several hectares and includes a botanical garden and large-scale public art interventions by landmark Brazilian and international artists. Whereas the Instituto has developed educational activities, those have been restricted to a reduced audience capable of reaching the space. As the Instituto's owner was condemned in 2017 for corruption and money laundering, issues of sustainability, accessibility, ownership, and art's public relevance immediately emerge. Does not the Instituto respond to an age-old use of art by the wealthy 1 percent of the population? Can we find anything new in a project that blatantly reproduces the dynamics of power of colonial Brazil through using art and nature to build a refuge from the "troubled reality" of everyday life? The point, of course, is not to criticize *The Global Contemporary* for not having anticipated what would happen in this case. What is at stake is more complex and more general and has to do with asking what histories of art arise when we take projects such as the Instituto as models of a globalized art system.

13. In the book's online presentation, the editors argue, significantly, "The internet does not exist. Maybe it did exist only a short time ago, but now it only remains as a blur, a cloud, a friend, a deadline, a redirect, or a 404" (Bratton 2015).

14. In this essay Gardner's main concern is with "what kind of afterlife, if any, postcolonialism may have amid the battle of wills, and the will to hegemony, between the national and the global" (2011: 148). This question will remain a direct preoccupation of my own exploration throughout this book of the transformative potential of socially engaged art practices emerging in postcolonial societies.

15. To return to Dimitrikaki (2012: 317), "The exhibition form can be seen as a dissemination mechanism for radical work—executed first in the wider field of socio-economic relations—that can broaden the public's exposure to this work's intentions and outcomes. Yet this dissemination mechanism also facilitates the collapse of pedagogy into the consumption of 'outputs', which is of course a ubiquitous feature of the post-Fordist knowledge economy. [. . .] In doing so [the exhibition] becomes complicit in making peripheral the complex cooperative production of the experiential knowledge it stands for."

16. As Aijaz Ahmad (1995: 9) puts it, "We have a *globalised condition of postcoloniality* that can be *described* by the 'postcolonial critic' but never fixed as a determinate structure of power against which determinate forms of struggle may be possible outside the domains of discourse and pedagogy."

17. In Neil Lazarus's words (2005: 423), Marxist-infused postcolonialism implies a reaction against the following assumptions: "A constitutive anti-Marxism; an undifferentiating disavowal of all forms of nationalism and a corresponding exaltation of migrancy, liminality, hybridity, and multicultur-ality; a hostility toward [. . .] totality and systematic analysis [. . .]; an aversion to dialectics; and a refusal of an antagonistic or struggle-based model of politics." Although Lazarus's criticism toward mainstream postcolonialism could be nuanced, what interests me in this case is how those theoretical assumptions could be easily translated into artistic terms following the logic of the argumentation presented in the first section of this chapter. A second point of Lazarus's perspective that is useful for my interests here, and that is easily understandable through this book's main goal, has to do with his idea that those assumptions limited not only the range of positions within postcolonial studies but also the practical examples analyzed by them.

18. Parry refers at this point to the usage of Frantz Fanon by central figures such as Homi Bhabha, whom she faults for subduing Fanonian thought to a theoretical "lifting" in order to make it more ambivalent and less ideological. Under her view, "Bhabha proffers Fanon as a premature poststructuralist," expunging the material dialectics of power between colonizer and colonized (Parry 2004: 16). As a consequence, "in place of the permanently embattled colonial situation constructed by anti-colonialist theory, installs either a silent place laid waste by imperialism's epistemic violence, or an agonistic space within which unequally placed contestants negotiate an imbalance of power" (14).

19. "The liberal-humanist orthodoxy placed great literature 'above' politics and society; new criticism privileged words-on-the-page, and even some recent approaches such as deconstruction can continue to think about literary texts in isolation from their contexts. [. . .] And so we have a some-what paradoxical situation: on the one hand, we can see the power of texts, and read power as a text; on the other hand, colonialism-as-text can be shrunk to a sphere away from the economic and the historical, thus repeating the conservative and humanist isolation of the literary text from the contexts in which it was produced and circulated" (Loomba 2015: 96–97).

20. It is important to note that not all the voices of postcolonial critics will agree on this. Arif Dirlik (1998: 180), for example, identifies a radical shift in the way postcolonialism deals with revolution through erasing antico-lonial modes of cultural and political resistance. In this sense, he proposes "postrevolutionary" as an alternative to the blurred historicity implicit in

postcolonialism. While I agree about the fact of postcolonialism having erased anticolonial memories and modes of resistance (many of which are still at play in socially engaged art today), two caveats might be made to this argumentation. First, as the next section will argue, the active purchase in the present of anticolonial ideas of radicalism and creativity forces us to understand decoloniality as a process still active in our present. Second, the artistic forms discussed in this book, which happen in a time posterior to the colonial but at the same time keep a revolutionary ethos, complicate this discussion even further.

21. The most relevant of those is undoubtedly the 1966 World Festival of Black Arts organized in Dakar as part of Senghor's cultural politics. The responses to the festival, including the antiessentialist creativity of groups such as the Laboratoire Agit'Art, should also be taken into account. For an in-depth discussion of both projects, see Harney (2004).

22. The way Araeen attempts to deal with the history of *Third Text* is revealing of the journal's original scope. For Araeen (2000: 3), *Third Text* was unusual in emerging "to explore, expose and analyse what has been excluded and repressed by institutional power." He adds that the point was not that institutional racism was shaping the 1980s art scene, but rather that the incorporation of "non-white artists" into curatorial and art historical narratives was often complicit with the "ignorance and suppression of the whole history of their contribution to mainstream developments" (Araeen 2000: 3).

23. It is important to understand here that "Third World" is not perceived here as a geographical reality but rather as a space of possibility, a way of mobilizing "South" solidarities across art.

24. "[Art] can innovate and set up structures, both symbolic and material at the same time and within the same space, that can empower people without whose revolutionary struggle things cannot change" (Araeen 2010: 86).

25. Stephen Wright (2013a) puts it in the following terms: "The *idea of art* brings about a minimal shift within sameness."

26. This section borrows from my last book, *Beyond Representation in Contemporary Caribbean Art*, where I deal in detail with socially engaged and collaborative artistic practices. I have developed a similar focus in previous essays, among them Garrido Castellano (2016), (2017a), and (2017b).

27. The Havana Biennial began in 1984 with a clear Third World focus. The Caribbean Biennial was originally promoted by UNESCO at the end of the 1980s, although it took form only in Santo Domingo in 1992. After three editions it evolved into a triennial, although it was organized under this form only once.

28. These include *Caribe Insular: Exclusión, Fragmentación, y Paraíso* (Spain, 1998); *Kréyol Factory* (France, 2010); *Westling with the Image: Caribbean Interventions* (United States, 2011); *Caribbean: Crossroads of the World*

(United States, 2012); and *Relational Undercurrents: Contemporary Art of the Caribbean Archipelago* (United States, 2017). These attempts to represent the Caribbean owe much to initiatives organized in the Caribbean region from the 1980s onward. I have dealt with the history of Caribbean exhibitional practices in detail in Garrido Castellano and Brébion (2012).

29. Here we can mention Beta-Local and Área in Puerto Rico, Espacio Aglutinador and Lasa in Cuba, Instituto Buena Bista in Curação, and L'Artocarpe in Guadeloupe, to name just a few projects still active.

30. Lind adds (2009: 103) that "curating is not so much the product of curators as it is the fruit of the labor of a network of agents."

31. For instance, the journal has dealt with decolonizing practices and art institutions (2017), artistic collaboration within biennials and feminist curating (2016), alternative institutionalism (2014), and institutional critique (2012).

32. *The Interventionist* consisted of an exhibition and a book. Nato Thompson curated the exhibition and coedited the book in collaboration with Gregory Sholette.

33. These include Douglas Masamuna (video artist), Sammy Baloji (photographer), Gulda El Magambo (photographer), and Patrick Mudekereza.

34. It is highly telling that the last edition of *Condition Report*, which came out in 2018, centered its attention in African art histories.

35. See http://www.panicplatform.net/about.html.

Notes to Chapter 2

1. In recognizing the existence of more than one art world, I am following the lucid insights of Stephen Wright (2013b) and Gregory Sholette (2010). Both recognize "1:1 scale" and activist art as operating within a different set of parameters and in complex relation with representational, spectacle-based art worlds. Wright recognizes that the problem is not that the mainstream art world denies the existence of alternative possibilities, but rather that its ecosystem downplays these possibilities in order to swallow them. Borrowing from this debate, in this chapter I wonder what remains at the margins of socially engaged and activist art ecosystems after their recently acquired positive, global purchase.

2. "The phenomenon of 'political modernity'—namely, the rule by modern institutions of the state, bureaucracy, and capitalist enterprise—is impossible to think of anywhere in the world without invoking certain categories and concepts, the genealogies of which go deep into the intellectual and even theological traditions of Europe. Concepts such as citizenship, the state, civil society, public sphere, human rights, equality before the law, the individual, distinctions between public and private, the idea of the subject, democracy, popular sovereignty, social justice, scientific rationality, and so on all bear

the burden of European thought and history" (Chakrabarty 2009: 4). This affirmation fully applies to socially engaged art.

3. Chakrabarty (2009: 16) defined European thought as being "at once both indispensable and inadequate in helping us to think through the experiences of political modernity in non-Western nations, and provincializing Europe becomes the task of exploring how this thought—which is now everybody's heritage and which affect us all—may be renewed from and for the margins." To produce a similar task within the field of socially engaged art (with its praxis and its thought on praxis) arises as a perfect definition of this book's main goal.

4. Ahluwalia borrows here from Robert Young's sharp grounding of post-structuralism (Young 2004: 1): "If 'so-called post-structuralism' is the product of a single historical moment, then that moment is probably not May 1968 but rather the Algerian War of Independence."

5. To be sure, postcolonial studies also undertook its own way toward discourse analysis, eschewing alternative forms of creative engagement with the continuities of colonial power (for a critical revision of this process, see Ahmad 1992; Dirlik 1994; Lazarus 1999; Young 2001). As I will show in the following chapter, this positioning is fortunately being critically rethought.

6. In 2016, while doing research in the University of California in San Diego, I discussed the failures and successes of social practice with Grant Kester. Acknowledging that the problem was much more complex than a matter of nomenclature, Kester identified a sign of transgression in the impossibility of comprehending the different kinds of art practices with transformative aspirations into a single categorization. Against the rapid professionalization of the field, Kester insisted on the subversive potential of diglossia: in his view, the many names we use to refer to these kinds of practices are a good symptom of their present relevance.

7. In Sholette's words (2017: 212), "This is not a simple matter of good intentions being coopted by evil institutions. We are well beyond that point."

8. Of course, "walls" here does not stand for physical boundaries but rather the instrumental reason regulating cultural policies, as Andrea Fraser (2005), among others, aptly recognized.

9. Sholette (2017: 218) also points out that "if anything, the focus on socially engaged art by the mainstream art world has actually eclipsed, rather than illuminated[,] the many individuals still active in community arts, turning long-simmering resentments once directed at the art world establishment into charges of appropriation and colonization."

10. The paradigm of this mode of conceiving artistic participation is undeniably Santiago Sierra, whom Bishop quintessentially identifies as paradigmatic of the mode of participative aesthetics she purposes. This critical interpretation is dependent on Sierra's self-definition as a "minimalist with

a guilt complex" (minimalista con complejo de culpa)." Recent social practice criticism has focused on discussing Bishop's positive valorization of the shock caused by Sierra, which would in turn derive from his insertion into an artistic avant-garde. It is less common to frame Sierra's work under alternative visual genealogies. For instance, María Íñigo Clavo (2011) connects Sierra with a genealogy of imperial imagination, comparing his *250 cm Line Tattooed on 6 Paid People, Havana* with a historical photograph found at the Liverpool International Slavery Museum, in which the workers of a plantation stand with the letters of a "Merry Christmas" message painted on their bodies. If we follow Íñigo Clavo and see in Sierra's work not only an opportunistic revamping of minimalism but also an exploitation of global poverty without acknowledging its colonial roots, the originality of his antagonistic aesthetics is called into question. By looking at the continuities between Sierra's anthropomorphic Minimal forms and a tradition of colonial image, a different framework for aesthetic criticism emerges. If Sierra is often faulted for the amoral exploitation of disenfranchised subjects to expose the conditions which these subjects often inhabit, then its connection with a genealogy of colonialist imagination dismantles much of the shock and novelty of his social sculptures. This connection, it is important to note, is not only ethical; it is also formal. Under this view, Sierra's work manifests a desire for extracting universal values and messages out of homogenized situations. Those situations (often taking place in Third World countries) are intended to illustrate and awaken an audience that has the privilege of visiting art galleries or joining international biennials.

11. See González (2011). This interest in laying bare the infrastructural nature of social discrimination was evident, for example, in the selection of the 1993 edition of the WhitneyBiennial. The forms and strategies used to combat that discrimination, however, cannot be limited to poststudio, biennial-based practices, such as installation or video art, for they significantly repurposed the language of art activism from former decades. The cases of Group Material, ACT UP, and REPOHistory are paradigmatic in this sense, which indeed also attempted to counter the limitations in reach and social repercussion of representational forms of politically engaged art.

12. Bryan-Wilson (2011: 19) points out how the Art Workers' Coalition "used their conceptual toolbox to hammer out activist, interventionist objects." This intention was pursued despite the existence of "structural inequalities—including racism and sexism" (25) at the heart of the coalition, inequalities that eventually led to its end. Indeed, many of the art activist and collaborative projects developed by racialized subjects in the following decades attempted to complement the Art Workers' Coalition's interest in standing for a community of art practitioners through a critique of exclusionary politics at play in institutional and public cultural infrastructures.

13. Among the precedents of *Mapping the Terrain* we can mention Lippard's *The Lure of the Local* (1997), Arlene Raven's *Art in the Public Interest* (1989), and Suzi Gablik's *The Reenchantment of Art* (1992).

14. David Scott rightfully recognized in the Grenada Revolution the last attempt to overturn the hegemonic dominance of the United States and the Cold War governmentality from a Marxist- and Bandung-infused revolutionary positioning. Scott sees in Bishop's death "not merely the beginning of the end of the particular story of the Grenada Revolution itself . . . but the beginning of the end of a whole *era* of revolutionary socialist expectation—indeed, of revolutionary socialist possibility" (2013: 4). The Grenada Revolution, however, had a deep impact in shaping emancipatory horizons in the Americas and beyond, as the centrality it occupies in Sankara's speeches corroborates. And although both actions belong to a particular epoch, that of the preamble of the 1980s conservative backlash, their consequences cannot be limited to those particular historical circumstances.

15. Malini Johar Schueller (2009: 4) categorizes similar processes of local-global resistances along the US framework as "resistance postcolonialism."

16. By "racialized" I mean not only having a racial background other than "white" but also to cast and perform an identity in racial terms.

17. Joseph Henry (2014) rightfully notes how antiracist protests arising after curatorial, sensationalistic provocations are often dismissed as censorship, thus reinforcing an idea of aesthetic privilege still falling on the side of the institution. Binding together these three polemics, Henry argues that "this has always been the painful reality of the contemporary, especially non-profit, artworld, which for the most part remains committed to a liberal project of 'critique' or 'ideas' or the 'public' while absorbing any matter of inequalities, from the elite capitalist pedigree of its management to its acutely skewed membership demographics."

18. This act of disappearance does not only imply repressing memories of past projects pursuing social transformation through art; its disappearance from the most common histories of socially engaged art also affects how we receive and conceptualize the utopian potential of these practices, which in turn makes the current devaluation of "radical," non-mainstream-oriented forms of artistic practice easier.

19. The term "Nuyorican" refers to people with Puerto Rican ancestry living in New York.

20. The origins of the Museo del Barrio are also useful for their capacity for making us rethink the role that cultural institutions could play in fueling activist causes.

21. Again, looking at the current debates from the point of view of those initiatives would prove revealing. After his "conceptual action," Irizarry was incarcerated for four years. It was the second time he went through an

experience of incarceration. Irizarry always conceived of his work as political action—not a performance, but a body of "real-symbolic" actions charged with political significance. Would, then, his work fall under Bishop's idea of the social turn as "what avant-garde we have today: artists using social situations to produce dematerialized, antimarket, politically engaged projects that carry on the modernist call to blur art and life" (Bishop 2006b, 179)? Irizarry's 1979 action was (fortunately) "dematerialized"; but was it so in the sense that we commonly associate with (a certain criticism of) collaborative practices?

22. More recent episodes of this tradition, also inscribed under the problematic coloniality of US sovereignty under Puerto Rican territory, must include the brilliant responses by a younger generation of Puerto Rican artists to the assassination of Filiberto Ojeda Ríos by the CIA in 2005 and to the ecological crisis of Vieques island.

23. A different interpretation of this episode is offered by Ahearn himself in an interview with Tom Finkelpearl. See Finkelpearl (2001).

24. Indeed, this interest in exploring productive articulations of art and politics while taking racial difference into account already shaped Lippard's earlier work. Take, for example, *Color Scheming,* a short text published in 1981 in which Lippard interprets the politics of spectatorship of Black and Third World artists under the lens of art funding and institutional racism. Reproduced in Lippard (1984: 242–45).

25. Put another way, "The idea of community arts, then, can be at once more humble and more ambitious than most contemporary art that is about but not of a place" (Lippard 1997: 283).

26. It is not by chance that Tom Finkelpearl alludes to this book in his reconstruction of 1980s and 1990s genealogy of socially engaged art.

27. It is curious how the social interaction produced around Biggers's murals is rarely recognized, despite Lowe's insistence in claiming the figure of Biggers as a precedent. A valuable discussion of the collaborative nature of Biggers's work can be found in Jensen Theisen (2010).

28. "Lowe's perception of his own function as an artist began to change" (Kester 2012: 216).

29. Richard Powell (2002: 15) argues that "black diasporal cultures are characterized by forms that are not only alternative to mainstream counterparts, but proactive and aggressive in their desire to articulate, testify, and bear witness to that cultural difference." Powell also traces the debates over individual and collective identities in Black art to the first experiences of art criticism by African Americans at the beginning of the twentieth century, noting that Black subjectivity always relied on a sense of community to speak a white supremacist and racist gaze back.

30. What is more interesting in Gilroy's oft-quoted formulation is the way

he grants an active agency to Black struggles in the construction of modern (English-speaking) transnational alliances. For Gilroy, some cultural manifestations produced by Black subjects across the Atlantic (especially music) have redefined literacy-centered modernist aesthetics, "provid[ing] a model of performance which can supplement and partially displace concern with textuality" (1993: 36).

31. Piper's background is in philosophy.

32. Kester's dialogical model as expressed in *Conversation Pieces*, nevertheless, does not fully explore the theoretical roots of those alternative aesthetic traditions. Significantly enough, the first chapter of the book emphatically discusses a pervasive lineage of analytical obscurity at play in Clement Greenberg, Michael Fried, and Jean-François Lyotard, but leaves unexplored how cultural theorists within and outside Europe and the United States offered alternative, positive interpretations of the radical role of cultural dialogue. Similarly, the analysis of Dawn Dedeaux's collaborative intervention in New Orleans prisons draws not from Africana theory but from Pierre Bourdieu and Jean-Luc Nancy.

33. In the meantime, the practice of public art has also been reconceptualized. See Cartiere and Willis (2008); Cartiere and Zebracki (2015); Doherty (2015).

34. This tendency to forget was brilliantly explored already in 1961 by Basil Davidson in *The Black Man's Burden: Africa and the Curse of the Nation-State*.

35. In *The Return of the Real*, Foster famously criticized a mode of artistic intervention based on the identification of cultural alterity as a potential site for political transformation available to the artistic community. Under these circumstances, Foster reminds that "identity is not the same as identification," while warning against the "ideological patronage" that artistic immersion could bring (1996: 174). Acknowledging Foster's advice, it is worth remembering also that patronage and alterity are not unavoidable outcomes of artistic collaboration; they are just one possibility among many others. Artistic collaboration, furthermore, often does much more than portray or represent communities. Further explorations of the relation between artistic participation and the ethnographic method can be found in Downey (2009) and Sansi Roca (2014).

Notes to Chapter 3

1. See Deckard and Schapiro (2019); Nilges (2015); Nilges and D'Arcy (2016). On the normalization of a neoliberal, futureless understanding of the contemporary, see Peck (2010); Brown (2015).

2. In that sense, Benita Parry (2004: 66) justifies the appeal of the anticolonial legacy in the following terms: "Proposals on how resistance is to be theorized display within the discussion that rehearse questions about

subjectivity, identity, agency and the status of the reverse-discourse as an oppositional practice, posing problems about the appropriate models for contemporary counter-hegemonic work." Socially engaged art's agenda being directly embedded in the task of providing practical, effective ways of addressing "contemporary counter-hegemonic work" and looking actively for answers for those questions, its revision appears more than justified.

3. Cape Verde and Guinea-Bissau had quite different colonial histories, deriving both from the role Portuguese colonialism conceded to each territory, and also from the specificities of the process of colonization itself. Cape Verdeans were for a long time a sort of "first-class colonized subjects" who were even in charge of the management of Guiné, at least until 1879, when that territory became a colony separated from the insular administration. The official relation between both territories does not mean an absence of contact or the sharing of a historical past. Cabral's interest in binding both territories by overcoming their differences may be seen both as a political project and, as António Tomás recognizes, a "biographical" desire deriving from his personal trajectory as Guinean-born of Cape Verdean parents. See Tomás (2007); Rabaka (2010b, 2014); Medeiros (2012).

4. All the authors who dealt with Cabral's aftermath coincide in pointing out the lack of successors his thought found, and the fragility of the process of unification between Guinea-Bissau and Cape Verde. Although the declaration of independence of both territories in 1973 brought a unified national government, soon both countries would take separate paths. Luis Cabral, Amílcar's brother, was the first president of Guinea, governing from 1973 to 1980, when he was put down by a military strike. In Cape Verde, Arístides Maria Pereira assumed the leadership of the country from 1975 to 1991, when his successor was chosen in democratic elections.

5. Cabral insisted on the idea that nationalism could be useful only when it challenges the legacies of colonialism in the colonized subjects. He stressed the need for continuing the collective process of self-criticism and social bettering that for him shaped cultural agency beyond the moment of formal independence.

6. The debates held at the Casa were essential in the shaping of the Portuguese postcolonial present, because of the temporal overlapping of the anticolonial and antidictatorship movements. Much of the issues framing the evolution of Portuguese society—among them the existence of racism, the specificities of Portuguese colonialism, the importance of migration in the definition of a multiracial society and the ways in which a "Lusotropical" discourse invisibilized racism within that society, the marginalization of Black subjects and the role of Lisbon as a meeting point for clandestine, emancipative movements—found a preamble in the discussions taking place at the Casa. Many of those issues related to the "colonial question" still remain

largely unanswered despite the fact that Portugal "normalized" its democratic, postcolonial identity and entered the European Union in 1985, and they have reappeared in multiple ways throughout the last decades of the twentieth century and the first decades of the twenty-first. This debate has produced a fertile discussion in the last decade. See, for example, Mata (2006); Arenas (2016); Calafate Ribeiro and Ferreira (2003); Vale de Almeida (2002, 2004).

7. It is worth remembering that what the Portuguese called the "Colonial War" and the articulation of critical voices against the dictatorship of Salazar were interconnected processes. Framed for a long time as exceptional due to the confluence with the dictatorship and the length of Portuguese colonialism, the anticolonial struggles in the Lusophone world and the constitution of postcolonial, postdictatorship Portugal have to be inserted within a wider, transnational framework. See de Sousa Santos (2002); Sousa Ribeiro and Calafate Ribeiro (2016).

8. On the value of this experience for Cabral's revolutionary action, see de Andrade (1980); Fobanjong and Ranuga (2006).

9. "Da capacidade de saber aliar, na transformação de cada factor principal e no conjunto, a teoria à prática e esta àquela" (translation mine).

10. "Áqueles que verão nela (na luta) um carácter teórico, temos que lembrar que toda a prática fecunda uma teoria. E que, se é verdade que uma revolução pode falhar, mesmo que seja nutrida por teorias perfeitamente concebidas, ainda ninguém praticou vitoriosamente uma Revolução sem teoria revolucionária" (translation mine).

11. Reiland Rabaka's attempts to identify Cabral as a "materialist" and not as a Marxist can be included in this line of thought. For Rabaka (2014: 241–58), Cabral detached himself from Marxism, which is understood as a Eurocentric, universalizing set of formulas. Although it is clear that Cabral rejected orthodox Marxism by virtue of his interest in grounding theory out of the specificities of Africa, and even pointing out that "Marx was never in Africa," his interest in social transformation cannot be explained outside the strong tradition of Black, anticolonial Marxism that was at its height in the 1960s and 1970s. The erasure of that tradition and the identification of Marxism only as a product of the West often obliterates the existence of that tradition. The fact of Rabaka being interested in reassessing the influence of a radical tradition of Africana theory makes the absence of Black Marxism even more drastic. Marxism was, for Cabral, a decisive influence whose potential, of course, should always be tested. See also Parry (2004).

12. "A interpretação de Chabal procede a uma divisão excessivamente rígida entre ciência e ideologia, como se replicasse a distinção entre coisas e palavras no interior do domínio das próprias palavras, supondo que a terminologia científica fará transparecer a realidade e que as categorias ideológicas a iludirão" (translation mine).

13. "Situar os trabalhos científicos de Cabral no quadro tanto de uma história da ciência como de uma história das ideologias políticas" (translation mine).

14. "A nossa resistência cultural consiste no seguinte: enquanto lutamos contra a cultura colonial e os aspectos negativos da nossa própria cultura, quer na nossa personalidade, quer no nosso meio, temos de criar uma nova cultura, também baseada nas nossas tradições, mas respeitando todas as conquistas do mundo actual para bem da humanidade" (translation mine).

15. "A única camada social capaz, tanto de consciencializar em primeiro lugar a realidade da dominação imperialista, como de manipular o aparelho do Estado, herdado dessa dominação" (translation mine).

16. "O essencial do secundário, o positivo do negativo, o progressista do reacionário, para caracterizar a linha mestra da definição progressiva de uma cultura nacional" (translation mine).

17. "Constitui, tanto localmente como no seio das diásporas implantadas na metrópole colonialista, o drama socio-cultural das elites coloniais ou da pequena burguesia indígena, vivido mais ou menos intensamente segundo as circunstâncias materiais e o nível de aculturação, mas sempre no plano individual, não colectivo" (translation mine).

18. Cabral's words against elitist aesthetics anticipate the crisis of governance and nationalist emancipation that will lead to the emergence, in the 1980s, of Afropessimism, an explanation highlighting the current economic and political constraints of African countries. As we will see in subsequent chapters, Afropessimism has significantly marked the way agency is conceived in cultural debates on the continent. It has also been used as a point of departure for a kind of foreign glance at Africa by hand of art collectives such as Superflex and European artists such as Renzo Martens, which justify a sort of realistic approximation to the situation of poverty and the supposedly endemic problems of the continent as effects of global capitalism, rejecting any alternative, action-based position against those predicaments.

19. "Parte dessa minoria, integrada no movimento de pré-independência, utiliza dados culturais estrangeiros para exprimir, recorrendo principalmente à literatura e às artes, mais a descoberta da sua identidade do que as aspirações e os sofrimentos das massas populares que lhe servem de tema. E como utiliza precisamente para essa expressão a linguagem e a língua da potência colonial, só excepcionalmente consegue influenciar as massas populares, em geral iletradas e familiarizadas com outras formas de expressão artística" (translation mine).

20. "Os elogios não selectivos; a exaltação sistemática das virtudes sem considerar os defeitos; a cega aceitação dos valores da cultura sem considerar o que ela tem ou pode ter de negativo, de reacionário ou de regressivo,

a confusão entre a que é a expressão de uma realidade histórica objectiva e material e o que parece ser uma criação do espírito ou o resultado de uma natureza específica; a ligação absurda das criações artísticas, sejam válidas ou não, a pretensas características de uma raça" (translation mine).

21. On Fanon's ambiguous relation with negritude, see Parry (1998); Filostrat (2008).

22. On this concern, see Rabaka (2010b).

23. "A negação, pela pequena burguesia indígena, da pretensa supremacia da cultura da potência dominante sobre a do povo dominado, com o qual tem necessidade de se identificar para resolver o conflito sócio-cultural em que se debate, procurando uma identidade" (translation mine).

24. "Quando o "retorno às fontes" ultrapassa o caso individual para se exprimir através de "grupos" ou de "movimentos," os factores que condicionam, tanto interna como externamente, a evolução político-económica da sociedade, atingiram já o nível em que esta contradição se transforma em conflito (velado ou aberto), prelúdio do movimento de pré-independência ou da luta pela libertação do jugo estrangeiro. Assim, o "retorno às fontes" só é historicamente consequente se implica não apenas um comprometimento real na luta pela independência, mas também uma identificação total e definitiva com as aspirações das massas populares, que não contestam somente a cultura do estrangeiro mas ainda, globalmente, o domínio estrangeiro" (translation mine).

25. See San Juan (2002); Parry (2002). I acknowledge here the comments of Kristian van Haesendonck, who pointed me in this direction concerning both texts.

26. "A libertação nacional e a revolução social não são mercadorias de exportação. São (e sê-lo-ão cada dia mais) um produto de elaboração local—nacional—[. . .] determinado e condicionado essencialmente pela realidade histórica de cada povo, e apenas assegurado pela vitória ou a resolução adequada das contradições internas de vária ordem que caracterizam essa realidade" (translation mine).

27. Some of the issues pointed out by the Angolan thinker are extremely relevant to a discussion of Cabral's idea of agency. Tomás acknowledges the mobilizing potential of nationalism and national culture, although he states that, in this case, it did not take sufficient account of the cultural diversity of Guinea-Bissau and Cape Verde. Furthermore, he mentions that the fact of the political party being in charge of determining the "caminhos ascendentes," the paths of improvements that each cultural manifestation should follow, renders the resistance of those who refuse those decisions unintelligible and empty of meaning. That last point is particularly relevant, since it forces us to understand cultural resistance as a complex positioning act.

28. Against this logic, we should recall Cabral's interest in stressing the

irreducible heterogeneity and the plurality of cultures existing in the African space.

29. On the lacunae of anticolonial nationalism, see Lazarus (1999); Chatterjee (1993); Loomba (2015).

30. John Fobanjong and Thomas K. Ranuga have stressed how Cabral's emancipative aspirations cannot be understood outside a broader, Lusophone, and also pan-African context. See Fobanjong and Ranuga (2006).

Notes to Chapter 4

1. This missed encounter between Adorno and James has been read in different terms. Brian Alleyne (1999: 363), for example, acknowledges that both thinkers recognize in cultural criticism an "engagement in politics." In the case of James, he notes that this recognition led to a more positive appraisal of mass culture, "an insufficiently critical appraisal of these forms and of the structures and institutions that produced and disseminated them" being the "negative side" deriving from Jamesian proximity to popular culture (366). As I will try to argue in this chapter, this argument repeats one of the main accusations against James's cultural criticism, that it partially ignored the ways in which US popular cultural forms could be used as instruments of governmentality, to use Foucault's term. Here I will try to show how an alternative reading of James's criticism is possible.

2. Sylvia Wynter (1996: 69) rightfully identifies in James a multifaceted personality, categorizing him as "a Negro yet British, a colonial native yet culturally a part of the public school code, attached to the cause of the proletariat yet a member of the middle class, a Marxian yet a Puritan, an intellectual who plays cricket, of African descent yet Western, a Trotskyist and Pan-Africanist, a Marxist yet a supporter of black studies, a West Indian majority black yet an American minority black." It is this complexity that is missing in such readings of the conversations between Adorno and James.

3. See Osborne (2013, 2018).

4. James's interest in popular cultural forms has been the main focus of much of what has been written about the Trinidadian author after his death in 1989. The following years saw an effervescence of critical texts dealing with several facets of James's life and work, as well as unpublished material (especially *American Civilization*) coming to light. Concerning aesthetics, a first issue that any recognition of an aesthetic side in James must grapple with, is the claim made by cultural studies to ownership of his legacy. James's recognition of sport and mass culture as art, as well as his interest in capturing an active agency amid the spectators of cinema, for example, made him a more than suitable candidate for any genealogy of the discipline. The attractive formulations of James's writings (as in titles such as "Every cook can govern"

[1977a]) have favored uncritical interpretations of his work. James, however, always insisted on producing critical judgments of the aesthetic value of any cultural product he analyzed, "popular" or otherwise. Critical readings on the dangers of cultural studies' "appropriation" of James can be found in N. Nielsen (1996); A. L. Nielsen (1997); A. Smith (2006a, 2016); St. Louis (2007).

5. It is highly significant that Jamesian aesthetics was developed within a landscape marked by the collapse of the New Deal aspirations and the consolidation of New York as world leading intellectual and artistic center after the arrival of European migrants fleeing the Second World War. As I will try to demonstrate, the main lineaments of James's aesthetics gain special relevance when considered with this context in mind, since they stand for potential alternatives to US modernism at the very moment of its foundation.

6. On James's interpretation of the figure of the intellectual and his articulation of alternative, radical forms of conceiving research, see Bogues (1997); Farred (1994); Glaberman (1999); Hall (1996). An appraisal of James's "activist" side can be found in Clennon (2017); Maldonado-Torres (2005).

7. James's and Adorno's approaches to popular culture were not just evolving in opposite directions; they also arose from very different perspectives. Besides being a historian and intellectual, James took part as an activist in the trenches of social and racial issues from his youth to his last days. In 1935 he organized a movement of protest against the Italian invasion of Abyssinia. In the years he spent in the United Kingdom, he not only took part in party politics, but also joined bottom-up Marxist movements. While in the United States, he created with Grace Lee Boggs and Raya Dunayevskaya the Johnson-Forest Tendency, a Marxist branch independent from Trotskyism. Some of the texts published under the banner of the Tendency were collectively authored, and arose out of a process of collective exchange that often included US workers.

8. The use of "men" here does not stand for a generic. As observed by James himself, the recognition of women's agency in shaping social causes was one of the weakest points of the Jamesian critical apparatus, despite the recognition of feminism by the early 1950s as a central force for social transformation. Only in his later years did James attempt to correct this position.

9. Later on, he also compares cricket with visual arts, pointing out the importance of figure and form, movement and pauses, as the medium through which the player expresses himself to extract "the significance of movements" (James 1990: 197).

10. This section draws heavily on Smith's books and articles on James.

11. A. Smith (2010: 159) points out that "James also offers a warning to a socially or historically minded criticism which, whatever its admirable intentions, too often seems willing to treat culture as simply the stuff with which politics gets done."

12. Smith is concerned in this article with determining where the adherence of both Bourdieu and James to "the ethics of a field" (literature and art in the case of the first, and cricket in the second) contradicts the interest that both have in revealing the "social contaminations" to which these fields were exposed and, therefore, in pointing out the impossibility of conceiving them as autonomous from the contradictions of market economy and British colonial interest, respectively. Smith responds to this problem by pointing out the inevitable two-dimensionality of intellectuals, compelled to operate within the realm of academia but also committed to engaging in sociopolitical struggle in order to survive. Both James's work and his own life provide good examples of this.

13. James's astute readings of the social significance of the trajectories of the Trinidadian cricket player Wilton St. Hill are good examples of this. For James, St. Hill represented the best of West Indian cricket talent, originality, and audacity. James praised him for his capacity for improvising and inventing solutions in the form of strikes. St. Hill, who "played his own game" (1990: 94) became a national symbol: when he batted, "it was the instinct of an oppressed man that spoke" (97). This, however, meant nothing in coming to terms with his failure as a professional cricketer in the United Kingdom. There, James admits, "he was a horrible, a disastrous, an incredible failure, the greatest failure who ever came out of the West Indies" (101). Avoiding any uncritical praise of St. Hill for his West Indian popularity, but also strongly rejecting those British critics who identified in him an "exotic fancy" (103), James produced a critical appreciation that recognized St. Hill's sociocultural significance but was realistic enough to make any judgment dependent on practice itself.

14. "The only thing that keeps me quiet is the movies. So at all hours of the day or night I go where there is a picture, often the nearest. That is why I see some over and over again" (James 1992: 128).

15. This includes imprisoned communists, with whom James developed a close relationship despite their ideological divergences.

16. As Richard King (2006: 108) argues, both James and Arendt shared the condition of exiled intellectuals "forced constantly to renegotiate the tension between universalism and particularism" and showing a similar out-of-the-box, humanist interest in self-activity and spontaneous agency, as in crucial events such as the Hungarian Revolution of 1956. One cannot but question, however, how far that comparison can be pursued if James's enthusiasm for new subjects of agents of transformation is compared with the tone with which Arendt embraced the emergence of student insurgence.

17. Here it is worth noting Said's response to the state of indecision deriving from the image of the intellectual depicted by Adorno's disengaged

aesthetics. For Said, the existence of some privileges, of some pleasures, cannot be detached from the experience of exiled intellectuals. Among those, Said mentions the development of a comparative eye, focused on the enlightening juxtapositions of old and new experiences, and the understanding of situations as historically contingent (and, therefore, mutable). It is not surprising, then, that after mentioning the name of Giambattista Vico, "who has long been a hero of mine" (2012: 61) and who approached human society with "respect, but not reverence," as paradigmatic of this intellectual model, the next model that comes to Said's mind would be James.

18. This is not the first time James recurs to alternative temporalities. A similar case must be made of *The Black Jacobins*, in which, according to Natalie Melas (2014: 65), "James's noncontemporaneity finds in the Haitian past a precocious, unresolved modernity." Melas goes further to assert, with Christopher Taylor, a concatenation of alternative historical times precluding future forms of emancipation by virtue of what she calls "a revolutionary simultaneity or contemporaneity that in effect gives on to a noncontemporaneity of the future" (67).

19. James thus makes the Black sharecroppers irreducible to any broader adscription to more general agrarian or working classes in the United States: "These southeast Missouri Negroes are unique. All the statistics of the Bureau of Commerce will be useless unless we understand what type of people they are and the conditions which have shaped them" (McLemee 1996: 26).

20. "His writing on the sharecroppers marks a moment of epistemological sharing between the postemancipation Caribbean and the South" (Taylor 2012: 78). In this and other episodes of his career, James achieved a productive balance between close engagement with the context of struggle, and an acute transnational interest in the concatenation and translation of social and activist causes. This transnational, global dimension also adds something to the relevance of James as a critic of popular, collaborative, engaged forms of creativity.

21. "The sharecroppers' refusal to become wage laborers cuts a 'narrative fissure' into the script of development, opening a way of imagining anticapitalist futures different than those narratives of futurity available to urban proletariats" (Taylor 2012: 78).

22. Anthony Bogues (1997: 61) explains these features, and particularly James's capacities for listening to ordinary men and making sense of their everyday lives, to his early literary ambitions in Trinidad: "This ability to listen for hours and absorb the 'stories' of working people, a feature of James's early literary career, was now transposed to the political domain. It marked his political methodology and was the essence of his political imagination and style."

23. Cynthia Hamilton (1992: 434) rightly argues that James's interest in

everyday struggle is coupled with a recognition of an aspiration to totality and a rejection of fragmentation at play in these acts of transgression. Her point, that "the cultural expressions of Africans in the New World are manifestations of the methods and tools of survival, as well as a critique of what they found. For this reason, culture is central to James's work" (436), speaks well of the impossibility of detaching the interest James had in popular culture from his political aspirations. James understood that it is *through* culture that many important social and political battles are waged. His subtlety in dealing with these battles represents a central part of his legacy for any genealogy of radical aesthetics.

24. This point was the central reason behind his rejection of Stalinist Russia and, later on, of Trotsky's idea of the Soviet Union as the avant-garde of world revolution. Unlike Trotsky, James recognized the potential of spaces of everyday collective creative action worldwide, identifying in them a transformative potential that lay at the core of his understanding of revolutionary politics.

25. *Facing Reality* was James's response to the events of 1956, in which he saw confirmed his earlier mistrust of the USSR as the sole avant-garde of world revolution. More importantly, the years around 1956 were particularly eloquent for James concerning the potential of self-organization in fueling social revolt. It is crucial to note that the image of that potential always acquired a global tone for James: one year later, in 1957, he traveled to Ghana to meet Kwame Nkrumah. His writings on Africa (James 1977c) are closely related to *Facing Reality*. On James's response to the years around 1956, see Høgsbjerg (2006a).

26. It is remarkable that this lecture was given one year after the creation of the West Indies Federation, a political confluence that sought to develop a progressive social and political agenda beyond national boundaries. The West Indies Federation ended a few years later, in 1962, due to internal contradictions. In writing about Caribbean artists, therefore, James was looking at a future that was already fading. Remarkably, the text refuses to essentialize a transformative potential in art or literature (or in any other creative manifestation, for that matter). It also rejects attributing any social significance in virtue of the content of art and literary forms. Rather, by stressing how art's social relevance is contingent, depending on the capacity of practitioners to provide useful aesthetic responses, James confronted a situation that remains more than timely for dealing with contemporary Caribbean visual culture. See Paget and Buhle (1992).

27. It is common to begin any genealogy of US social transformation art in the 1960s. For example, Tom Finkelpearl (2013: 7), who dedicates a lengthy essay to exploring the roots of collaborative artistic practice in the United States, mentions the social movements arising in this decade, among

them the civil rights movement, the counterculture, and feminism, as the direct precedents of contemporary forms of collaborative, socially engaged art. By "rescuing" the figure of James, I do not intend to counter historical perspectives such as Finkelpearl's. I see in James much more than a (Marxist-infused) precursor to these movements, one operating at a time when the contradictions that would lay the ground for the 1960s movements were being established.

Notes to Chapter 5

1. In addition to 32° East, the organizing institutions included Makerere University, AKA Gallery, Nommo Gallery, the Ugandan Museum, Alliance Française Kampala, and the Goethe-Zentrum Kampala. The partnership worked together not only at raising funds but at curating and decision making.

2. The chosen artists were Bwambala Ivan Allan, Emma Wolukau-Wanambwa, Eria Nsubuga "Sane," Eric Mukalazi, Lilian Nabulime, Ronex, Ruganzu Bruno, Sanaa Gateja, Stella Atal, Waswad, Xenson, and Sue Crozier Thorburn (a British artist living in Uganda and the only foreigner in the show).

3. The oldest art institutions in Uganda are the Makerere University, the Uganda Museum, and the Nommo Gallery, the last two being state-controlled. In the last ten years, this panorama has been completed through the emergence of a large number of private art galleries. To that we have to add 32° East, Ugandan Art Trust, an alternative space created in 2012.

4. The station was closed in 1992, and KLA ART reclaimed it for public use.

5. This series of visits was new to Ugandan art. Besides "putting the artists on the map," it served to encourage a climate of dialogue among the community of creators and the festival's audience.

6. Here it is essential to mention the existence of a strong tradition of customizing and diversifying *boda bodas, matatus* (four-wheeled public transport), and other vehicles dedicated to informal transport. KLA ART 014 seconds this phenomenon, using art to channel some of the—again—already existing aspirations for social recognition and improvements in the security conditions of the sector, while benefitting from the vibrant visual inventiveness of Kampala's vernacular scene; it in no way initiates it.

7. The Boda Boda Project was not exempt from a surprising and flashy effect. For many, the intervened *boda bodas* might have been perceived as crazy objects amid the crowd of vehicles populating Kampala. While that gimmicky dimension was present in the relations among artists, drivers, and audiences, it cannot account for the diversity of experiences and exchanges comprised by the initiative.

8. The beginning of the presidency of Yoweri Museveni in 1986 marked

the end of the "dictatorial period" that included the governments of Idi Amin between 1971 and 1979 and the second rule of Milton Obote between 1980 and 1985.

9. It is important to note, however, that some of the most complex concerns the project will touch on in the following years, such as concealment, public identification, and the connection between HIV and care issues, had already appeared in an embryonic form at this stage.

10. A first experiment took place in 2005 in Katikamu, Luwero. Since then, several experiments in different regions of Uganda have completed this original research.

11. "It was noted that revealing the symbolism of the objects in the soap influenced the audience's response. It was important for the audience to observe the sculptures for themselves, then to respond to the soap and the objects embedded in them" (Nabulime 2007: 158). The illiteracy of the communities of participants is also behind this choice.

12. On the impact of Mudimbe's book, see Fraiture (2013).

13. In this case, the use of art as a means of protesting and producing awareness redefines artistic exchanges.

14. Trowell quoted in Kyeyune (2003: 55).

15. This process was framed in a very nuanced and fertile way. This is especially evident in the "Letters to the Editor" section. For example, in a moment as significant as 1961, the journal addressed in a direct way the transformations taking place in Uganda and East Africa that were linked to the process of independence. Issues of race, religion, and economics were framed and discussed together, not only with reference to the immediate environment where the journal was being published but also in relation to a broader panorama.

16. This is especially evident in the reconfiguration of the Ugandan academic landscape. In 2006, Kizito Maria Kasule, an artist, scholar, and current dean of the Makerere Art School, opened the Nagenda International Academy of Art and Design, a private institution of higher education. The controversy arose in relation to the Makerere's social relevance and its public condition in relation to the suitability and profitability of this new school, which was more oriented toward teaching practical skills and preparing students for a market-driven art scene.

17. As Nabulime and Cheryl McEwan (2011: 291) point out, "The soap sculptures generated discussions in workshops and public exhibitions, but there is clearly scope for participants to take these into domestic spaces to precipitate discussion about sexuality. Translating what can be discussed in public venues into the spaces of the home is notoriously difficult in patriarchal societies, but this is essential in HIV/AIDS prevention. As relatively inexpensive and easily understood works of art, soap sculptures could

provide an effective bridge between these spaces that changes personal consciousness and in turn leads to social change."

18. See also Comaroff and Comaroff (2009).

19. See also Stoler (2013).

20. On the importance of activism in decentering the sphere of politics and spreading the realm of power, see Zibechi (2010).

21. As Margaret Nagawa explains (2008: 155), "For a long time, formal art training was only offered at Makerere University," something that determined its centrality in the debates on artistic modernity and aesthetics, while also shaping the composition in terms of gender of the Ugandan artistic community. In that text, Nagawa outlines in detail how the cultural economy of women artists in Uganda is highly influenced by family relations, formal education, conceptions of modern art and indigeneity, and, finally, by the Ugandan institutional milieu (Nagawa 2008). See also Tumusiime (2012).

22. This is especially evident in the ways both projects "articulate" themselves in order to apply for external funding. However, as I have attempted to show, this articulation is not essential, nor does it condition the rest of the initiatives and negotiations at play in each project.

Notes to Chapter 6

1. Sen and Hill (2011: 4) highlight this continuity, pointing out the fact that neither Soeharto nor his army companions have been brought to justice. See also Lindsay and Liem (2012).

2. The coupling here (and throughout this chapter and some other sections of this book) of dictatorship and colonialism attempts to capture the complexities of Asian relations with Europe. In many Asian countries, as John Clark (1998) famously observed, modern Asian art is not the result of the interaction with Western culture, nor is modernization simply the result of European colonialism. Rather, it resulted from a denser intertwining of cultural and political relations between "local" and "foreign" cultures. This is the case in the Indonesian context, where three and one half centuries of Dutch control never succeeded in suppressing the cultural influences and power relations among the plurality of "local" cultures inhabiting the archipelago. On a more practical level, this occupation was preceded and followed by others.

3. Collectivism was not the only form of politically conscious art employed by Indonesian artists during the Reformasi. However, it became increasingly popular by the late 1990s. On alternative forms of "political" and "activist" art under the Reformasi, see Museum Nusantara (n.d.); Sumartono (2001).

4. Jim Supangkat (2005: 220) characterizes this process as quintessentially ambivalent, pointing out that after the 1990s Indonesian artists had more opportunities of showing (and selling) their work abroad, but that opportunity did not necessarily become associated with artistic innovation. On the contrary, a market was consolidated for "master painters," whereas more experimental work was rejected under the excuse of its (lack of) saleability. Agreeing with this interpretation, I would complete it by saying that biennials and art fairs somehow provided a parallel scenario for riskier "contemporary" artworks, and that this trend was not beneficial for the impact of long-term, bottom-up creativity in the country either.

5. Yogyakarta is famous for having one of the most eclectic cultural scenes in all of Java. Dealing with "popular culture" in the city forcefully implies addressing this diversity of "local" and "foreign" influences, which does not mean that tensions are nonexistent. See Richter (2008); see also Warsono (2012).

6. Caroline Turner (2005: 197) maintains that the Indonesian concept of *merdeka*, freedom (but also autonomy), "combined with the ideal of transforming society for the better through artistic action, has been of great significance in Indonesian contemporary art."

7. The recognition of art collectives as an alternative source of contemporary, practice-based aesthetics in Indonesia counters the master narrative that posits medium innovation, individual creativity, and internationalization as the birth of the contemporary in the country. Thomas J. Berghuis (2011: 399–400) has recently exposed the limitations of this approach by looking at the activity of ruangrupa in Jakarta.

8. In this sense, although I speak from the limitations of not belonging to the context, I would argue that some of the collaborative strategies examined here did have an impact on larger sectors of the Indonesian society, directly addressing the skepticism expressed by Supangkat (2005: 226) when saying, "In fact, it is difficult to judge whether the works had an impact or whether they simply became political. Politicians did not really care whether the protests were artistic or not; meanwhile, art critics did not see anything significant—politically or aesthetically—behind the political buzzwords."

9. The city of Yogyakarta was always a Javanese religious and cultural capital and holds strong links with the anticolonial movement. The city is also home to an effervescent student movement, which makes contemporary artists from Yogyakarta more prone to social engagement. Traditionally, the city was opposed to Bandung, where formal artistic education had a more liberal, Western approach. Although the Yogyakarta-Bandung division is still commonly referred to in Indonesian art criticism, in practice Bandung was also the hub of important progressive student movements and gathered artists with a strong educational and social vocation, such as Arin Dwihartanto Sunaryo and Tisna Sanjaya.

10. The collective process of production is well explained by Heidi Arbuckle in her thesis on Taring Padi. See Arbuckle (2000: 51–54).

11. A good example is provided by Heri Dono's *Looking at the Marginal People* installation, a mechanical assembly of humanoid faces grotesquely chatting. In this case, the *rakyat* emerges as an obsessive yet caricaturized entity modulated with irony by the artist.

12. Taring Padi's interest in propaganda art and 1920s social realism can also be understood as a way to oppose the proliferation of electoral posters that by 1999 populated Yogyakarta and other Javanese cities.

13. See Kuss (2000). Alexandra Kuss's text belongs to a landmark exhibition of contemporary Indonesian art, *AWAS! Recent Art from Indonesia*, that toured in the Netherlands, Germany, Australia, and Japan. The show was organized by Cemeti, another collective initiative in Yogyakarta. Taring Padi's absence from the show points to the complex relation between both groups.

14. The problem of individualism has been a common failing of Indonesian art history and criticism since early modern times. For example, Sudjojono's famously referenced orientation to the everyday life of ordinary Indonesians was never just an individual aesthetic decision; rather, it lay behind the creation of collective alliances such as PERSAGI and LEKRA, of which Sudjojono himself was an important part. In short, debates about aesthetics should never be interpreted as abstract theoretical elucubrations driven by a handful of "modernist masters." They were *lived* contradictions that had an impact on the lives and labors of artists.

15. The counterpart of this collaboration, although it was not at play in all *sanggars*, was the hierarchical organization of the artistic learning process through the master-student binary. See Rath 2005: 23.

16. The main cultural institutions dealing with visual arts were created soon after the country's independence. This is the case of the Bandung Institute of Technology, created in 1947, and the ASRI, which was founded in 1950.

17. "It is difficult to determine, however, if the LEKRA delegations' trips were a result of government support or of party recommendations" (Isabella 2018: 96). This policy would indeed equate the practical side the nonalignment policy of Soekarno, who, according to Isabella, "was able to exploit the rivalry between the United States and the Soviet Union, ultimately obtaining a huge amount of aid for Indonesia from both sides" (95).

18. This strategic approach to cultural matters is evident in Sudjojono's texts from the 1950s, as evidenced in fragments such as this one: "We will not blame our European colleagues for their mistakes. We will honour them, for they have worked sincerely, even sacrificing their lives for a great aspiration. We will use their works as a landmark, like a shipwreck in the ocean, of our people's struggle in this world and in our revolution in Indonesia, not

only to enable artists to become artistic, but also to make the whole society become artistic, to become artistically conscious as Indonesia was before [in the past]" (Sudjojono and Isabella 2017: 164).

19. This view counters interpretations such as that of Yvonne Spielman (2017: 52), who argues that the emergence of socially engaged art initiatives during the Sukarno government was the consequence of the state's interest in promoting "a revolutionary art." State interests notwithstanding, the action of Indonesian collectives reveals a complex game of positioning that in turn involved both taking advantage of and criticizing the state.

20. This also applies to LEKRA's literary and theatrical production. Thus Michael Bodden (2010: 30–32) explains how social realism always coexisted with other creative sources in the plays created by members of the group.

21. Abstract art and recovering cultural and religious traditional symbols was useful for this purpose.

22. Agung Hujatnikajennong, interview with author, August 2018.

23. The first national television network, Televisi Republik Indonesia, and the launching of a communications satellite were the product of Soeharto's interest in extending the control of the regime over the Indonesian archipelago (Kunci and EngageMedia 2009: 16).

24. A more traditional exhibition called "Video In" took place in the National Gallery. The rest of the festival, under the title "Video Out," was placed in public spaces throughout Java.

25. For instance, Jürriens (2013b) sees similarities between the sustained engagement that some community media groups develop and LEKRA's theatrical strategies. This connection is all the more interesting since it helps reduce the apparent breach existing between media and digital activist groups and collectives relying on more "conventional" artistic expressive forms.

26. On the role of media in the shaping of Indonesian democracy, see Sen and Hill (2007, 2011).

27. Indonesia frequently ranks among the world's top five users of social networks such as Facebook, Twitter, and Instagram.

28. Sen and Hill (2007). See also Kunci and EngageMedia (2009: 19).

29. The most famous critique of relational aesthetics in this sense is still provided by Claire Bishop's "Antagonism and Relational Aesthetics" (2004). New critical views have also explored other equally problematic facets of relational aesthetics, such as the fact that many of the activities Bourriaud's movement recognized as quintessentially contemporary were already a common part of the vocabulary of feminist art from previous decades (see Reckitt 2013). The case of ruangrupa is also interesting in this sense, because it challenges the leading role that art spaces could play in the redefinition of everyday life.

30. Available at http://ruangrupa.org/15/15-years/.

31. Available at http://ruangrupa.org/15/15-years/.

32. Vanhoe (2016: 45) adds, "The collective is not really rooted in the actual neighbourhood where the [ruangrupa] house is located." This might change in the near future, when ruangrupa completes its transformation into an educational platform and starts operating in its new location.

33. Wok the Rock, interview with author, August 2018.

34. Wok the Rock interview.

35. Farid Rakun, conversation with author, August 2018.

36. As on other occasions, Kunci made use of foreign collaboration in the first stages of the initiative, in this case partnering with the international Wasteland Twinning Network.

37. Bon Suwung project description, last accessed March 5, 2021, http://space.kunci.or.id/bon-suwung/.

38. Megamix Militia project description, last accessed March 5, 2021, http://megamixmilitia.kunci.or.id/about/.

Notes to Chapter 7

1. "Sectarianism" has become a catchall constantly applied to postwar Lebanon. Roughly speaking, it refers to both the division of the Lebanese society into religious groups and the sanctioning of this system through the coexistence in the government of representatives of each sectarian group by constitutional law. As we will see, in reality sectarianism responds to a much more complex structure in which class and social divisions coexist with economic interests, where communal struggles are often repurposed and redefined as "external" or "internal" according to competing interests and alliances. On top of this, the sectarian surface of the Lebanese government does not, as Rasha Salti (2002: 85) argues, impede the ruling class from being "a stellar example of collaboration and solidarity" despite religious differences. See also Salloukh et al. (2015).

2. On the importance of ruins in the 1990s visual landscape of Beirut, see Seigneurie (2011); Gumpert and Toufic (2010).

3. The Atlas Group website, last accessed March 5, 2021, http://www.theatlasgroup.org/.

4. Although the Ta'if Accord, signed in November 1989, marked an end to the civil war, many authors highlight how the absence of victors and vanquished implied the prolongation of the conflict under other guises. The Lebanese Civil War is often described as a long-term civil strife mixed up with proxy wars and regional economic and military interests. On the "multitemporality" of conflict and violence in contemporary Lebanon, see Hermez (2017).

5. *In This House* is a single-channeled video in which two stories overlap: the military experiences of photojournalist and Communist Ali Hashiso,

and the excavation of a garden in Southern Lebanon where Hashiso buried a letter of gratitude destined for an unidentified future reader (Feldman 2009: 311). See also Elias (2018).

6. "The Real," as Catherine David (Dagher et al. 2007: 104) points out, has little weight in contemporary Lebanese art.

7. "The problem is, I argue, not so much about how to give a voice to mute witnesses and traumatized survivors. Instead, it is about how in respeaking testimonies and reenacting events, artists in Lebanon can provide the grounds for the radical remembering of the past and the reimagining of futures in a present haunted by the specter of failed leftist political projects and the defeat of multicultural and secular forms of nationalism in the region" (Elias 2018: 18).

8. Similarly, Kaelen Wilson-Goldie (2007: 86) argues that the work of this generation appeared while broader debates on the public space were gaining momentum. These debates are often forgotten when the work of the artists of this generation is looked at from the point of view of their international success.

9. Jalal Toufic (2009) uses the metaphor of a mirror in vampire films to refer to Lebanese artistic practices. For a partially critical view on Toufic, see Naeff (2014).

10. The counterpart of this process had private places becoming social spaces. See Monroe (2016); Naeff (2018).

11. Religious offense is a clear example of the limitations of any well-intentioned view of freedom of expression. Samir Khalaf (2012) describes Beirut society as an excitable cauldron where the slightest expression is taken as a major offense turning into escalating forms of violence and outrage. Allowing for those sensibilities becomes as important for Lebanese public artists as dealing with official regulations concerning freedom of expression. The practice-based nature of *A Few Things* arises as a consequence of this predicament.

12. Hence the choosing of "artistic," "less problematic" environments (such as Hamra or Mar Mikhael) for graffiti and public interventions. In March 2018, I attended a symposium on city walls as sites of protest and activism organized by Salti at the Sursock Museum. All the interlocutors (which included artists Hatem Imam, Hamed Sino, and Jana Traboulsi) reinforced the idea that choosing a particular neighborhood predetermines the "translatability" of the activist message and its reach. Hamra as a site of activism, however, should not be dismissed, as Miriyam Aouragh (2016: 128) argues. Although nurtured by a middle-class, educated, and Internet-savvy class, the protests articulated a third option between war and sectarianism. Both online and offline activist are "ignoring ghosts and constructing their own present" (Aouragh 2016: 130).

13. In a conversation with Stephen Wright (2007: 59), Walik Sadek points out that the main problem affecting the art scene in Lebanon is not the lack of institutions but rather the intermittent and self-managed character of those. In turn, Wright finds the activity of Lebanese artists as operating within an extradisciplinary dimension replacing the fenced space of political activism.

14. Curiously, *A Few Things* does not take account of the rich tradition of political posters from at least the beginning of the civil war, a time when, in Zeina Maasri's words (2009: 3), the "military engagement on the battlefronts was coupled with a relentless battle of signs and symbolic appropriation of territory through extensive poster production and distribution."

15. I will borrow mostly from Bayat's *Life as Politics: How Ordinary People Change the Middle East*, which was first published in 2010. Despite the distance in time, I believe that many of Bayat's arguments are still relevant for analyzing recent processes of social transformation. Besides this, Bayat's ideas on activism as a possible yet constrained form of agency reappear in his most recent *Revolution without Revolutionaries: Making Sense of the Arab Spring* (2017). In both works, the focus is on ordinary actions carried out by subaltern groups as a central political field, an interest that can be in tune with the creative projects examined in this book despite the fact that the position of socially engaged artists and creatives is not strictly comparable to that of the groups examined by Bayat.

16. Created in 1993 by Christine Tohme, Ashkal Alwan first functioned as a mobile platform for researching and archiving experimental artistic practices in postwar Lebanon. Like other alternative institutions examined in this book, the project gradually consolidated its presence within the Lebanese cultural scene by turning to educational activities and settling down in a permanent location. Ashkal Alwan's two main initiatives have been Home Works, a public forum on cultural practices in the Middle East, and Video Works, an event that commissioned and displayed hundreds of video artistic productions. On Ashkal Alwan's educational program, see Sholette (2016).

17. Ashkal Alwan's Sayaneh project, last accessed March 5, 2021, https://arteeast.org/wp-content/uploads/2015/04/Sanayeh-Project.pdf?x83780.

18. As with many other alterinstitutional practices examined in this book, Ashkal Alwan and the Ayloul Festival relied on international funding, which was received by the organizers of both initiatives as a mixed blessing that allowed a certain strategic midterm planning but also brought economic dependence in its wake. This dependence, in any case, did not involve bowing to international expectations.

19. Katarzyna Puzon (2016: 270) describes contemporary Lebanese practices as "sites of memory." Although I agree that memory still remains a major concern for Lebanese artists operating in the public sphere, I argue that collaborative initiatives such as *A Few Things* move beyond memory to

interrogate the conditions for possible new uses of the public space in Beirut. See also Mashaa Collective (2013).

20. In Asad's words (2003: 25), "I take the secular to be a concept that brings together certain behaviors, knowledges, and sensibilities in modern life."

21. John Nagle (2018a, 2018b) identifies feminist, LGTB, and victims as paradigmatic examples of nonsectarian activism in Lebanon, which he recognizes as "articulat[ing] powerful forms of protest and opposition to particular aspects of power-sharing identified as particularly harmful to wider society" (2018a: 18). Although *A Few Things* can be seen as operating in a similar sense, the guidebook also dismantles the idea of sectarianism as being synonym with top-to-bottom, consociational government. Rather, through focusing on the intersections between written and unwritten norms, the project challenges rigid definitions of sectarianism and secularism, revealing the importance for Lebanese art activists to understand the subtle and continuous articulations of both ideas.

Notes to Chapter 8

1. The results can be found at *Field Issue 12/13: Art, Anti-Globalism, and the Neo-Authoritarian Turn,* last accessed March 5, 2021, http://field-journal. com/issue-12?cat=30.

2. The chosen location constitutes one of the most transited and gentrified area of Lisbon, standing in between the major tourist destinations of the Praça do Príncipe Real and Baixa/Chiado, right by the popular Miradouro de São Pedro de Alcântara. The choice of this *largo*, or square, conferred a ceremonial tone on the official act of commemoration, highlighting its symbolic meaning by placing the statue in front of the iconic Church of São Roque. The greater concentration of tourists and the abundance of hotels and Airbnbs in the zone ensured participation in the public reading, since for many inhabitants of the peripheries of Lisbon the area would appear remote and disconnected from their interests.

3. The use of the word "Lusophone" here is intended as ironic and alludes to the idea of "Lusofonia" (the Lusophone world), an ideologically and politically charged concept that attempts to give the idea of a shared Portuguese-speaking community. The main problem with this concept is that it keeps Portugal at the center of that community while sanitizing and concealing the negative consequences of the Portuguese imperial expansion. See Vale de Almeida (2004); de Sousa Santos (1990, 2013).

4. In June 2020 André Ventura, the leader of the far-right political party Chega, went one step further by asking for the creation of a "special police force" committed to the task of fighting against "statue vandalism."

5. Descolonizando Facebook website, last accessed March 5,

2021, https://pt-pt.facebook.com/pages/category/Community/Descolonizando-1948301182079309/.

The statement is available at Descolonizando's Facebook account (consulted February 2019). Luso-tropicalism is a well-known, much-discussed concept in Portugal. It borrows (if loosely) from Gilberto Freyre's insights on Portuguese colonialism, yet under the Estado Novo the concept was instrumentalized so as to allude to the exceptionally gentle character—the "brandos costumes"—of the Portuguese people, as well as to their innate capacity to "adapt" to any specific climate or context. Both arguments were used to defend the idea that Portuguese colonialism was somehow an attenuated and more benign form of colonialism than those imposed by other European powers. See Castelo (1998).

6. Recent iterations of this trope can be found in the Portuguese Prime Minister Marcelo Rebelo de Sousa's visit to Gorée Island in 2017. Although acknowledging the participation of Portugal in the slave trade across the Atlantic, Rebelo de Sousa also emphasized the "singularity" of Portuguese colonialism, provoking a vivid debate. Another recent controversy pointing in the same direction is related to the construction of a (still unmaterialized) museum of slavery in Lisbon and the name that such museum would receive.

7. The writings of Eduardo Lourenço are a classic reference in this sense. See in particular Lourenço (1988, 1999, 2001).

8. "A conformação de narrativas conflituais numa narrativa aparentemente coerente e unívoca" (translation mine).

9. "No fim do domínio colonial português, Belém encerra uma representação da identidade nacional focada em duas temáticas principais: o povo, remoto e presente, enquanto entidade 'natural' herdada da tradição e do costume; e a saga marítima, veiculando a imagem de um império sem colónias, ecuménico, humanista e universal, central na auto-representação de Portugal enquanto país dos 'descobrimentos' e não como centro de poder colonial" (translation mine).

10. Latour distinguishes "iconoclash" from "iconoclasm" in the following terms: "Icono*clasm* is when we know what is happening in the act of breaking and what the motivations for what appears as a clear project of destruction are; icono*clash*, on the other hand, is when one does not know, one hesitates, one is troubled by an action for which there is no way to know, without further enquiry, whether it is destructive or constructive" (Latour 2002: 16).

11. Vieira's protectiveness toward the "indigenous" children eloquently counters this enactment.

12. Strictly speaking, the social relevance of contemporary "art matters" can be traced back many decades, as, for example, W. J. T. Mitchell in his genealogy of "offending images," a discussion that clearly resembles the topics I address in this chapter. See Mitchell (2013).

13. The events commemorated were the first journey around the world by Vasco da Gama and the "discovery" of Brazil.

Notes to Coda

1. "Tomorrow the cops could come back, or the bank, bringing the violence of speciation, against which there is just this constant and general economy of friendship—not the improvement that will have been given in one-to-one relation but the militant preservation of what you (understood as we) got, in common dispossession, which is the only possible form of possession, of having in excess of anyone who has" (Harney and Moten 2017: 86).

BIBLIOGRAPHY

Abi Khalil, Amanda, Nayla Geagea, Sasha Ussef, and Amahl Khoury, eds. 2016. *A Few Things You Need to Know When Creating an Art Project in a Public Space in Lebanon*. Beirut: Temporary Art Platform.

Ahluwalia, Pal. 2010. *Out of Africa: Post-Structuralism's Colonial Roots*. London: Routledge.

Ahmad, Aijaz. 1992. *In Theory: Classes, Nations, Literatures*. London: Verso.

Ahmad, Aijaz. 1995. "The Politics of Literary Postcoloniality." *Race & Class* 36 (1): 1–20.

Ahmed, Sara. 2014. *The Cultural Politics of Emotion*. London: Routledge.

Aikens, Nick. 2015. "The Use of History and the Histories of Use: Museum of Arte Útil and Really Useful Knowledge." Last accessed March 5, 2021. http://www.arte-util.org/the-use-of-history-and-the-histories-of-use-museum-of-arte-util-and-really-useful-knowledge-author-nick-aikens/.

Alexander, Michelle. 2012. *The New Jim Crow: Mass Incarceration in the Age of Colorblindness*. New York: The New Press.

Alleyne, Brian W. 1999. "Cultural Politics and Globalized Infomedia: C. L. R. James, Theodor Adorno and Mass Culture Criticism." *Interventions* 1 (3): 361–72.

Appiah, Kwame Anthony. 1991. "Is the Post- in Postmodernism the Post-in Postcolonial?" *Critical Inquiry* 17 (2): 336–57.

Araeen, Rasheed. 2000. "A New Beginning." *Third Text* 14 (50): 3–20.

Araeen, Rasheed. 2010. *Art beyond Art: Ecoaesthetics: A Manifesto for the 21st Century*. London: Third Text.

Aranda, Julieta, Brian Kuan Wood, and Anton Vidokle, eds. 2015. *The Internet Does Not Exist*. Berlin: Stenberg.

Arbuckle, Heidi Leanne. 2000. *Taring Padi and the Politics of Radical Cultural Practice in Contemporary Indonesia.* PhD thesis presented at the Curtin University of Technology.

Aouragh, Miriyam. 2016. "Online Politics and Grassroots Activism in Lebanon: Negotiating Sectarian Gloom and Revolutionary Hope." *Contemporary Levant* 1 (2): 125–41.

Arenas, Fernando. 2016. "Migrations and the Rise of African Lisbon: Time-Space of Portuguese (Post)coloniality." *Postcolonial Studies* 18 (4): 353–66.

Asad, Talal. 2003. *Formations of the Secular: Christianity, Islam, Modernity.* Stanford, CA: Stanford University Press.

Bartolovich, Crystal. 2004. "Introduction: Marxism, Modernity, and Postcolonial Studies." In *Marxism, Modernity and Postcolonial Studies,* edited by Neil Lazarus and Crystal Bartolovich, 1–21. Cambridge: Cambridge University Press.

Basualdo, Carlos. 2010. "The Unstable Institution." In *The Biennial Reader,* edited by Elena Filipovic, Marieke Van Hal, and Solveig Ovstebo, 124–36.

Bayat, Asef. 1997. *Street Politics: Poor People Movements in Iran.* New York: Columbia University Press.

Bayat, Asef. 2010. *Life as Politics: How Ordinary People Change the Middle East.* Amsterdam: Amsterdam University Press.

Bayat, Asef. 2017. *Revolution without Revolutionaries: Making Sense of the Arab Spring.* Stanford, CA: Stanford University Press.

Biehl, João. 2001. "Vita: Life in a Zone of Social Abandonment." *Social Text* 68 19 (3): 131–49.

Belting, Hans, Andrea Buddensieg, and Peter Weibel. 2013. "Documents: Exhibitions and the Global Turn." In *The Global Contemporary and the Rise of New Art Worlds,* edited by Hans Belting, Andrea Buddensieg, and Peter Weibel, 60–74. Karlsruhe, Germany: ZKM.

Bennett, Tony. 1996. "The Exhibitionary Complex." In *Thinking about Exhibitions,* edited by R. Greenberg et al., 58–81. New York: Routledge.

Berghuis, Thomas J. 2011. "ruangrupa: What Could Be 'Art to Come.'" *Third Text* 25 (4): 395–407.

Bignall, Simone. 2010. *Postcolonial Agency: Critique and Constructivism.* Edinburgh: Edinburgh University Press.

Bilbao Yarto, Ana. 2019. "From the Global to the Local (and Back): Curatorial Strategies in Biennials and Small Visual Arts Organisations." *Third Text* 33 (2): 179–94.

Billig, Johannes, Maria Lind, and Lars Nilsson, eds. 2007. *Taking the Matter into Common Hands: On Contemporary Art and Collaborative Practices.* London: Black Dog Publishing.

Bishop, Claire. 2004. "Antagonism and Relational Aesthetics." *October* 110:51–79.

Bishop, Claire. 2006a. *Participation*. London: Whitechapel.

Bishop, Claire. 2006b. "The Social Turn: Collaboration and Its Discontents." *Artforum*: 178–83.

Bishop, Claire. 2012. *Artificial Hells: Participatory Art and the Politics of Spectatorship*. London: Verso.

Bodden, Michael. 2010. *Resistance on the National Stage: Modern Theatre and Politics in Late New Order Indonesia*. Athens: Ohio University Press.

Bogues, Anthony. 1997. *Caliban's Freedom: The Early Political Thought of C. L. R. James*. London: Pluto Press.

Boltanski, Luc, and Eve Chiapello. 2005. *The New Spirit of Capitalism*. London: Verso.

Bou Akar, Hiba. 2018. *For the War Yet to Come: Planning Beirut's Frontiers*. Stanford, CA: Stanford University Press.

Bratton, Benjamin H. 2015. "The Internet Does Not Exist." *E-Flux*. Last accessed March 5, 2021. https://www.e-flux.com/books/66665/the-internet-does-not-exist/.

Bridges, Lucas E. 1952. *El último confín de la tierra*. Buenos Aires: Emecé Editores.

Brown, Wendy. 2015. *Undoing the Demos: Neoliberalism's Stealth Revolution*. New York: Zone.

Bruguera, Tania. 2012. "Reflexions on Arte Útil (Useful Art)." In *Arte actual: Lecturas para un espectador inquieto,* edited by Yayo Aznar and Pablo Martínez, 194–97. Madrid: Centro de Arte 2 de Mayo. Last accessed March 5, 2021. http://www.taniabruguera.com/cms/592-0-Reflexions+on+Arte+til+Useful+Art.html.

Bryan-Wilson, Julia. 2011. *Art Workers: Radical Practice in the Vietnam War Era*. Berkeley: University of California Press.

Buhle, Paul. 2017. *C. L. R. James: The Artist as Revolutionary*. London: Verso.

Busch, Annett, and Anselm Franke, eds. 2015. *After Year Zero: Geographies of Collaboration*. Chicago, IL: Chicago University Press.

Butler, Judith. 2006. *Precarious Life: The Powers of Mourning and Violence*. London: Verso.

Butler, Judith. 2013. *Excitable Speech: A Politics of the Performative*. New York: Routledge.

Butler, Judith. 2017. "Judith Butler escreve sobre sua teoria de gênero e o ataque sofrido no Brasil." *Folha de São Paulo*, November 19, 2017. Last accessed March 5, 2021. http://www1.folha.uol.com.br/ilustrissima/2017/11/1936103-judith-butler-escreve-sobre-o-fantasma-do-genero-e-o-ataque-sofrido-no-brasil.shtml#article-aside.

Butler, Judith, and Athena Athanasiou. 2013. *Dispossession: The Performative in the Political*. Cambridge: Polity Press.

Cabral, Amílcar. 1976. *A arma da teoria: Unidade e luta*. Lisbon: Seara Nova.

Cabral, Amílcar. 1979. *Análise de alguns tipos de resistência.* Bolama: PAIGC.

Cabral, Amílcar. 1999. *Nacionalismo e cultura.* Santiago de Compostela, Spain: Laiovento.

Calafate Ribeiro, Margarida, and Ana Paula Ferreira, (organizers). 2003. *Fantasmas e fantasias imperiais no imaginário português contemporâneo.* Porto, Portugal: Campo das Letras.

Camnitzer, Luis. 2007. *Conceptualism in Latin American Art: Didactics of Liberation.* Austin: University of Texas Press.

Cartiere, Cameron, and Shelly Willis, eds. 2008. *The Practice of Public Art.* London: Routledge.

Cartiere, Cameron, and Martin Zebracki. 2015. *The Everyday Practice of Public Art: Art, Space, and Social Inclusion.* Durham, NC: Duke University Press.

Casid, Jill H. 2005. *Sowing Empire: Landscape and Colonization.* Minneapolis: University of Minnesota Press.

Castelo, Cláudia. 1998. *"O modo português de estar no mundo": O luso-tropicalismo e a ideologia colonial portuguesa, 1933–1961.* Porto, Portugal: Afrontamento.

Castro-Gómez, Santiago. 2005. *La hybris del punto cero: Ciencia, raza, e ilustración en la Nueva Granada, 1750–1816.* Bogotá: Editorial Pontificia Universidad Javeriana.

Chabal, Patrick. 1983. *Amílcar Cabral: Revolutionary Leadership and People's War.* Cambridge: Cambridge University Press.

Chakrabarty, Dipesh. 2009. *Provincializing Europe: Postcolonial Thought and Historical Difference.* Princeton, NJ: Princeton University Press.

Chatterjee, Partha. 1993. *The Nation and Its Fragments: Colonial and Postcolonial Histories.* Princeton, NJ: Princeton University Press.

Cheah, Pheng. 2016. *What Is a World? On Postcolonial Literature as World Literature.* Durham, NC: Duke University Press.

Clark, John. 1998. *Modern Asian Art.* Honolulu: University of Hawaii Press.

Clennon, Ornette. 2017. *The Polemics of C. L. R. James and Contemporary Black Activism.* London: Palgrave.

Cohen, Thomas M. 1998. *The Fire of Tongues: António Vieira and the Missionary Church in Brazil and Portugal.* Stanford, CA: Stanford University Press.

Comaroff, Jean, and John Comaroff. 2009. *Ethnicity, INC.* Chicago, IL: Chicago University Press.

Comaroff, Jean, and John Comaroff. 2012. *Theory from the South: Or, How Euro-America Is Evolving toward Africa.* Boulder, CO: Paradigm.

Cooper, Frederick. 1994. "Conflict and Connection: Rethinking Colonial African History." *American Historical Review* 99 (5): 1516–45.

Cozier, Christopher. 2011. "Notes on Wrestling with the Image." In *Wrestling with the Image: Caribbean Interventions,* edited by Christopher Cozier and Tatiana Flores, 6–15. Washington, DC: The World Bank.

Crow, Joanna. 2014. *The Mapuche in Modern Chile: A Cultural History.* Miami: University Press of Florida.

Dagher, Sandra, Catherine David, Rasha Salti, Christine Tohme, and T. J. Demos. 2014. "Curating Beirut: A Conversation on the Politics of Representation." *Art Journal* 66 (2): 98–119.

Daulatzai, Sohail. 2012. *Black Star, Crescent Moon: The Muslim International and Black Freedom beyond America.* Minneapolis: University of Minnesota Press.

Davidson, Basil. 1992. *The Black Man's Burden: Africa and the Curse of the Nation-State.* New York: Times Book.

Davis, Mike. 2001. *Magical Urbanism: Latinos Reinvent the U.S. City.* London: Verso.

de Andrade, Mário. 1980. *Amílcar Cabral: Essai de biographie politique.* Paris: François Maspero.

de Sousa Santos, Boaventura. 1990. "11/1992 (Onze teses por ocasião de mais uma descoberta de Portugal)." Last accessed March 5, 2021. https://estudogeral.sib.uc.pt/handle/10316/10930.

de Sousa Santos, Boaventura. 2002. "Between Prospero and Caliban: Colonialism, Postcolonialism, and Inter-Identity." *Luso-Brazilian Review* 39 (2): 9–43.

de Sousa Santos, Boaventura. 2013. *Pela mão de Alice: O social e o político na Pós-modernidade.* Lisbon: Almedina.

Deckard, Sharae, and Stephen Shapiro, eds. 2019. *World Literature, Neoliberalism, and the Culture of Discontent.* London: Palgrave.

Dimitrikaki, Angela. 2012. "Art, Globalisation and the Exhibition Form: What Is the Case, What Is the Challenge?" *Third Text* 26 (3): 305–19.

Dirlik, Arif. 1994. "The Postcolonial Aura: Third World Criticism in the Age of Global Capitalism." *Critical Inquiry* 20:328–56.

Dirlik, Arif. 1998. *The Postcolonial Aura: Third World Criticism in the Age of Global Capitalism.* Boulder, CO: Westview Press.

Doherty, Claire. 2004. *Contemporary Art: From Studio to Situation.* London: Black Dog Publishing.

Doherty, Claire. 2015. *Public Art (Now): Out of Time, Out of Place.* London: Art Books.

Downey, Anthony. 2009. "An Ethics of Engagement: Collaborative Art Practices and the Return of the Ethnographer." *Third Text* 23 (5): 593–603.

During, Simon. 2000. "Postcolonialism and Globalization: Towards a Historicization of Their Inter-Relation." *Cultural Studies* 14 (3–4): 385–404.

Dussel, Enrique. 1973. *América Latina: Dependencia y liberación.* Buenos Aires: García Cambeiro.

Elam, J. David, and Kama Maclean, eds. 2014. *Revolutionary Lives in South Asia: Acts and Afterlives of Anticolonial Political Action*. London: Routledge.

Elias, Chad. 2018. *Posthumous Images: Contemporary Art and Memory Politics in Post-Civil War Lebanon*. Durham, NC: Duke University Press.

el-Malik, Shiera, and Isaac A. Kamola, eds. 2017. *Politics of African Anticolonial Archive*. Lanham, MD: Rowman & Littlefield.

Enwezor, Okwui. 2008. "The Postcolonial Constellation: Contemporary Art in a State of Permanent Transition." In *Antinomies of Art and Culture: Modernity, Postmodernity, Contemporaneity*, edited by Terry Smith, Okwui Enwezor, and Nancy Condee, 207–35. Durham, NC: Duke University Press.

Farred, Grant. 1994. "'Victorian with the Rebel Seed': C. L. R. James, Postcolonial Intellectual." *Social Text* 38:21–38.

Fawaz, Mona, Ahmad Gharbieh, and Mona Harb, eds. 2009. *Beirut: Mapping Security*. Stuttgart, Germany: Diwan.

Federici, Silvia. 2004. *Caliban and the Witch: Women, the Body, and Primitive Accumulation*. New York: Autonomedia.

Feldman, Hannah. 2009. "Excavating Images on the Border." *Third Text* 23 (3): 309–22.

Felshin, Nina. 1995. *But This Is Art? The Spirit of Art as Activism*. Seattle, WA: Bay Press.

Ferreira, Ana Paula. 2014. "Lusotropicalist Entanglements: Colonial Racisms in the Postcolonial Metropolis." In *Gender, Empire, and Postcolony: Luso-Brazilian Intersections*, edited by H. Owen and A. M. Klobucka, 49–69. New York: Palgrave Macmillan.

Ferreira, Ana Paula, and Margarida Calafate Ribeiro, eds. 2003. *Fantasmas e fantasias imperiais no imaginário português contemporâneo*. Lisbon: Campo das Letras.

Ferreira, Nicolau, and Manuel Louro. 2017. "Estátua do padre António Vieira guardada por 'neonazis.'" Público, October 5, 2017. Last accessed March 5, 2021. https://www.publico.pt/2017/10/05/sociedade/noticia/accao-de-protesto-contra-a-estatua-do-padre-antonio-vieira-barrada-por-neonazis-1787874/amp.

Ferro, Ligia, and Otávio Raposo, eds. 2016. *O trabalho da arte e a arte do trabalho: Circuitos criativos de artistas imigrantes em Portugal*. Lisbon: Observatório das Migrações.

Filipovic, Elena. 2005. "The Global White Cube." In *The Manifesta Decade: Debates on Contemporary Art Exhibitions and Biennials in Post-Wall Europe*, edited by Barbara Vanderlinden and Elena Filipovic, 63–84. Cambridge, MA: MIT Press.

Filostrat, Christian. 2008. *Negritude Agonistes, Assimilation against Nationalism in the French-speaking Caribbean and Guyane.* Cherry Hill, NJ: Africana Homestead Legacy.

Finkelpearl, Tom. 2000. "Interview: John Ahearn on the Bronx Bronzes and Happier Tales." In *Dialogues in Public Art,* edited by T. Finkelpearl, 80–102. Cambridge, MA: MIT Press.

Finkelpearl, Tom, ed. 2001. *Dialogues in Public Art.* Cambridge, MA: MIT Press.

Finkelpearl, Tom, ed. 2013. *What We Made: Conversations on Art and Social Cooperation.* Durham, NC: Duke University Press.

Fisher, Jean. 2009. "The Other Story and the Past Imperfect." *Tate Papers* 12. Last accessed March 5, 2021. http://www.tate.org.uk/research/publications/tate-papers/no-12/the-other-story-and-the-past-imperfect.

Fobanjong, John, and Thomas K. Ranuga, eds. 2006. *The Life, Thought, and Legacy of Cape Verde Freedom Fighter Amilcar Cabral.* Lewistown, NY: Edwin Mellen Press.

Forsdick, Charles, and Christian Høgsbjerg, eds. 2017. *The Black Jacobins Reader.* Durham, NC: Duke University Press.

Foster, Hal. 1996. *The Return of the Real: The Avant-Garde and the End of the Century.* Cambridge, MA: MIT Press.

Foucault, Michel. 1989. *Maurice Blanchot: The Thought from Outside.* Cambridge, MA: Zone.

Foulcher, Keith. 1987. "Politics and Literature in Independent Indonesia: The View from the Left." *Source: Southeast Asian Journal of Social Science* 15 (1): 83–103.

Fraiture, Pierre-Philippe. 2013. *V. Y. Mudimbe: Undisciplined Africanism.* Liverpool, UK: Liverpool University Press.

Fraser, Andrea. 2005. "From the Critique of Institutions to an Institution of Critique." *Artforum* 44 (1): 278–86.

Fraser, Nancy. 2008. "Abnormal Justice." *Critical Inquiry* 34 (3): 393–422.

Gablik, Suzi. 1992. *The Reenchantment of Art.* London: Thames & Hudson.

Galimberti, Jacopo. 2017. *Individuals against Individualism: Art Collectives in Western Europe, 1956–1969.* Liverpool, UK: Liverpool University Press.

García Canclini, Néstor. 2014. *Imagined Globalization.* Durham, NC: Duke University Press.

Gardner, Anthony. 2011. "Whither the Postcolonial?" In *Global Studies: Mapping Contemporary Art and Culture,* edited by Hans Belting, Jacob Birken, Andrea Buddensieg, and Peter Weibel, 142–57. Ostfildern, Germany: Hatje Cantz.

Garrido Castellano, Carlos. 2016. "Caribbean Curatorial Agencie:. A Cultural Object's Unruliness and Its Affective Aftermaths." *Cultural Dynamics* 28 (3): 249–65.

Garrido Castellano, Carlos. 2017a. "Artistic Autonomy in Non-Autonomous Contexts: Reframing Collective Agency and Insurgence from Caribbean Artist-Managed Spaces." *Social Identities: Journal for the Study of Race, Nation and Culture* 23 (4): 1–21.

Garrido Castellano, Carlos. 2017b. "Caribbean Artistic Genealogies of Withdrawal: Rethinking Caribbean Visuality beyond Objecthood." *Interventions: International Journal of Postcolonial Studies* 19 (8): 1153–72.

Garrido Castellano, Carlos. 2018. "Activism against Nostalgia and Self-Defeatism." *Afterall*. Last accessed March 5, 2021. https://www.afterall. org/online/activism-against-nostalgia-and-self-defeatism-gregory-sholette-delirium-and-resistance-activist-art-#.WvGmcExFw2y.

Garrido Castellano, Carlos. 2019. *Beyond Representation in Contemporary Caribbean Art: Space, Politics, and the Public Sphere.* New Brunswick, NJ: Rutgers University Press.

Garrido Castellano, Carlos, and Dominique Brébion, eds. 2012. *De los últimos creadores de mapas: Pensamiento crítico y exposiciones colectivas de arte caribeño contemporáneo, 1990–2011.* Madrid: La Discreta.

Garrido Castellano, Carlos, and Jerssi Paulo. 2019. "Unapologetic Soundings of Afro-Portuguese Creativity." *Afterall* 47:126–35.

Gilmore, Ruth Wilson. 2017. "Abolition Geography and the Problem of Innocence." In *Futures of Black Radicalism,* edited by G. T. Johnson and A. Lubin, 225–41. London: Verso.

Gilroy, Paul. 1993. *The Black Atlantic: Modernity and Double Consciousness.* London: Verso.

Giunta, Andrea. 2007. *Avant-Garde, Internationalism, and Politics: Argentine Art in the Sixties.* Durham, NC: Duke University Press.

Glaberman, Martin. 1999. *Marxism for our Times: C. L. R. James on Revolutionary Organization.* Jackson: University Press of Mississippi.

Green, Charles, and Anthony Gardner. 2016. *Biennials, Triennials, and Documenta: The Exhibitions that Created Contemporary Art.* Oxford: Willey Blackwell.

Gómez-Barris, Macarena. 2017. *The Extractive Zone: Social Ecologies and Decolonial Perspectives.* Durham, NC: Duke University Press.

González, Jennifer A. 2011. *Subject to Display: Reframing Race in Contemporary Installation Art.* Cambridge, MA: MIT Press.

Gordon, Lewis R. 2006. "African-American Philosophy, Race, and the Geography of Reason." In *Not Only the Master's Tools: African American Studies in Theory and Practice,* edited by L. R. Gordon and J. A. Gordon, 3–51. London: Routledge.

Gordon, Lewis R. 2013. "Thoughts for Today, Inspired by Amílcar Cabral." In *Claim No Easy Victory: The Legacy of Amílcar Cabral,* edited by Firoze

Manji and Bill Fletcher Jr., 183–89. Cantley, UK: Council for the Development of Social Science Research in Africa and Daraja Press.

Gordon, Lewis R. 2015. *What Fanon Said: A Philosophical Introduction to His Life and Thought*. New York: Fordham University Press.

Gorjão Henriques, Joana. 2017. *Racismo em Português: O lado esquecido do colonialismo*. Lisbon: Tinta-da-China.

Grimshaw, Anna. 1993. "*American Civilization*: An Introduction." In *American Civilization*, by C. L. R. James. New York: Blackwell, 1–26.

Grosfóguel, Ramón. 2011. "Decolonizing Post-Colonial Studies and Paradigms of Political-Economy: Transmodernity, Decolonial Thinking, and Global Coloniality." *Transmodernity: Journal of Peripheral Cultural Production of the Luso-Hispanic World* 1 (1). Last accessed March 5, 2021. https://escholarship.org/uc/item/21k6t3fq.

Gumpert, Matthew, and Jalal Toufic, eds. 2010. *Thinking the Ruin*. Istanbul: Istanbul Studies Center.

Hall, Stuart. 1996. "A Conversation with C. L. R. James." In *Rethinking C. L. R. James*, edited by Grant Farred, 15–45. Cambridge: Blackwell.

Hall, Stuart. 2005. "Cultural Identity and Diaspora." Last accessed March 5, 2021. https://sites.middlebury.edu/nydiasporaworkshop/files/2011/04/D-OA-HallStuart-CulturalIdentityandDiaspora.pdf.

Hamilton, Cynthia. 1992. "A Way of Seeing: Culture as Political Expression in the Works of C. L. R. James." *Journal of Black Studies* 22 (3): 429–43.

Hanchard, Michael. 2001. "Afro-Modernity: Temporality, Politics, and the African Diaspora." In *Alternative Modernities*, edited by D. Parameshwar Gaonkar, 272–99. Durham, NC: Duke University Press.

Haraway, Donna. 2015. "Anthropocene, Capitalocene, Plantationocene, Chthulucene: Making Kin." *Environmental Humanities* 6:159–65.

Hardt, Michael, and Toni Negri. 2005. *Multitude: War and Democracy in the Age of Empire*. New York: Penguin Random House.

Harney, Elizabeth. 2004. *In Senghor's Shadow: Art, Politics, and the Avant-Garde in Senegal, 1960–1996*. Durham, NC: Duke University Press.

Harney, Stefano and Fred Moten. 2013. *The Undercommons: Fugitive Planning and Black Study*. New York: Autonomedia.

Harney, Stefano, and Fred Moten. 2017. "Improvement and Preservation: Or, Usufruct and Use." In *Futures of Black Radicalism*, edited by G. T. Johnson and A. Lubin, 83–95. London: Verso.

Harris, Jonathan P. 2017. *The Global Contemporary Art World*. Oxford: Willey Blackwell.

Haugbolle, Sune. 2010. *War and Memory in Lebanon*. Cambridge: Cambridge University Press.

Heise, Ursula. 2016. *Imagining Extinction: The Cultural Lives of Endangered Species*. Chicago, IL: The University of Chicago Press.

Helguera, Pablo. 2011. *Education for Socially Engaged Art*. New York: Jorge Pinto.

Henry, Joseph. 2014. "Sources of Harm: Notes on the Alternative Artworld." *Hyperallergic*. Last accessed March 5, 2021. https://hyperallergic.com/147841/sources-of-harm-notes-on-the-alternative-artworld/.

Henry, Paget, and Paul Buhle. 1992. *C. L. R. James's Caribbean*. Durham, NC: Duke University Press.

Hermez, Sami. 2017. *War Is Coming: Between Past and Future Violence in Lebanon*. Philadelphia: University of Pennsylvania Press.

Høgsbjerg, Christian. 2006a. "Beyond the Boundary of Leninism? C. L. R. James and 1956." *Revolutionary History* 9 (3): 144–59.

Høgsbjerg, Christian. 2006b. "C. L. R. James: The Revolutionary as Artist." *International Socialism* 112. Last accessed March 5, 2021. http://isj.org.uk/clr-james-the-revolutionary-as-artist/.

Hojeij, Mahmoud, Mohamad Soueid, and Akram Zaatari. 2002. "'Disciplined Spontaneity': A Conversation on Video Production in Beirut." *Parachute* 108:80–91.

Holmes, Brian. 2007. "Do-It-Yourself Geopolitics: Global Protest and Artistic Process." Last accessed March 5, 2021. https://brianholmes.wordpress.com/2007/04/27/do-it-yourself-geopolitics/.

Holmes, Brian. 2012. "Eventwork: The Fourfold Matrix of Contemporary Social Movements." In *Living as Form: Socially-Engaged Art from 1991 to 2011*, edited by Nato Thompson, 72–86. Cambridge, MA: MIT Press and Creative Time.

Holt, Claire. 1967. *Art in Indonesia: Continuities and Change*. Ithaca: Cornell University Press.

Hujatnikajennong, Agung. 2007. "Video as a Social Device." In *Ok Video: Militia*, edited by Hafiz, 26–30. Jakarta: ruangrupa.

Hujatnikajennong, Agung. 2009. "Turning Points in Contemporary Art: The Indonesian Art World and the Impact of the 1980s." In *Beyond the Dutch: Indonesia, the Netherlands, and the Fine Arts from 1900 until Now* [in Dutch], edited by M. Knol, R. Raben, and K. Zijlmans, 139–45. Amsterdam: KIT Publisher and Centraal Museum.

Hujatnikajennong, Agung. 2010. "For Those Who Are (So Much) in Love with the City (of Jakarta)." In *Decompression #1: Expanding the Space and Public: Ruangrupa's 10th Anniversary*, edited by ruangrupa, 11–14. Jakarta: ruangrupa.

Hujatnikajennong, Agung. 2014. "Trajectories/Contingencies: Indonesian Contemporary Art and the Regional Context." In *Concept, Context, Contestation: Art and the Collective in Southeast Asia*, edited by I. Renzi, 26–32. Bangkok: Bangkok Art and Culture Centre.

Íñigo Clavo, María. 2011. "Rumors, Representations, Revolutions." Paper presented at Tate Gallery.

Isabella, Brigitta. 2018. "The Politics of Friendship: Modern Art in Indonesia's Cultural Diplomacy, 1950–65." In *Ambitious Alignments: New Histories of Southeast Asian Art, 1945–1990*, edited by S. H. Whiteman, S. Abdullah, Y. Low, and P. Scott, 83–107. Singapore: Power Publications and National Gallery Singapore.

Jackson, Shannon. 2011. *Social Works: Performing Art, Supporting Publics.* New York: Routledge.

James, C. L. R. 1977a. *The Future in the Present: Selected Essays.* Elmhurst, NY: L. Hill.

James, C. L. R. 1977b. *Nkrumah and the Ghana Revolution.* London: Allison & Busby.

James, C. L. R. 1977c. "The Artist in the Caribbean." In *The Future in the Present: Selected Essays,* 183–90. Elmhurst, NY: L. Hill.

James, C. L. R. 1990. *Beyond a Boundary.* London: Stanley Paul.

James, C. L. R. 1992. "Letters to Constance Webb." In *The C. L. R. James Reader,* edited by Anna Grimshaw, 127–53. Oxford: Blackwell.

James, C. L. R. 1993. *American Civilization.* Edited and introduced by Anna Grimshaw and Keith Hart. New York: Blackwell.

James, C. L. R. 2001. *Mariners, Renegades, and Castaways: The Story of Herman Melville and the World We Live In.* Hanover, NH: Dartmouth College.Jensen Theisen, Olive. 2010. *Walls that Speak: The Murals of John Thomas Biggers.* Denton: University of North Texas Press.

Johar Schueller, Malini. 2009. *Locating Race: Global Sites of Post-Colonial Citizenship.* New York: State University of New York Press.

Jones, Caroline. 2010. "Biennial Culture: A Longer History." In *The Biennial Reader,* edited by Elena Filipovic, Marieke Van Hal, and Solveig Ovstebo, 66–88. Berlin: Hatje Kantz Verlag.

Jones, Caroline. 2017. *The Global Work of Art: World's Fairs, Biennials, and the Aesthetics of Experience.* Chicago, IL: Chicago University Press.

Jürriens, Edwin. 2013a. "Between Utopia and Real World: Indonesia's Avant-Garde New Media Art." *Indonesia and the Malay World* 41 (119): 48–75.

Jürriens, Edwin. 2013b. "Social Participation in Indonesian Media and Art: Echoes from the Past, Visions for the Future." *Bijdragen tot de Taal-, Land- en Volkenkunde* 169 (1): 7–36.

Jürriens, Edwin. 2015. "Shaping Spaces: Video Art Communities in Indonesia." In *Performing Contemporary Indonesia: Celebrating Identity, Constructing Community,* edited by B. Hatley and B. Hough, 98–120. Leiden: Brill.

Jürriens, Edwin. 2017. *Visual Media in Indonesia: Video Vanguard.* London: Routledge.

Kakande, Angelo. 2016. "Art and the 'Ghost' of 'Military Dictatorship': Expressions of Dictatorship in Post-1986 Contemporary Ugandan Art." *Start: Journal of Arts and Culture* (Kampala), December 14. Last accessed

March 5, 2021. http://startjournal.org/2016/12/art-and-the-ghost-of-military-dictatorship-expressions-of-dictatorship-in-post-1986-contemporary-ugandan-art/.

Kala, Euridice. 2014. "Introduction." in Euridice Kala (ed.) *Boda Boda Lounge Project. From Space (Scope) to Place (Position).* (Troyeville, South Africa, Vansa,), 8.

Kapur, Geeta. 2007. *When Was Modernism: Essays on Contemporary Cultural Practice in India.* New Delhi: Tulika.

Kasfir, Sydney Littlefield, and Till Förster, eds. 2013. *African Art and Agency in the Workshop.* Bloomington: Indiana University Press.

Kester, Grant. 2004. *Conversation Pieces: Community and Communication in Modern Art.* Berkeley: University of California Press.

Kester, Grant. 2011. *The One and the Many: Contemporary Collaborative Art in a Global Context.* Durham, NC: Duke University Press.

Kester, Grant. 2013. "The Device Laid Bare: On Some Limitations in Current Art Criticism." *E-Flux* 50. Last accessed March 5, 2021. http://www.e-flux.com/journal/50/59990/the-device-laid-bare-on-some-limitations-in-current-art-criticism/.

Kester, Grant. 2015. "On the Relationship between Theory and Practice in Socially Engaged Art." *A Blade of Grass.* Last accessed March 5, 2021. http://www.abladeofgrass.org/fertile-ground/on-the-relationship-between-theory-and-practice-in-socially engaged-art/ Last accessed March 5, 2021.

Khalaf, Samir. 2012. *Lebanon Adrift: from Battleground to Playground.* London: Saqui.

Khoury, Elias. 2006. "The Novel, the Novelist, and the Lebanese Civil War." Last accessed March 5, 2021. https://nelc.washington.edu/sites/nelc/files/documents/events/2006lebanon-eliaskhoury.pdf.

King, Richard. 2006. "The Odd Couple: C. L. R. James, Hannah Arendt and the Return of Politics in the Cold War." In *Beyond Boundaries: C. L. R. James and Postnational Studies,* edited by Christopher Gair, 108–28. London: Pluto Press.

Koh, Jay. 2015. *Art-led Participative Processes: Dialogue and Subjectivity within Performances in the Everyday.* Helsinki: University of the Arts Helsinki.

Kortun, Vasif. 2004. "Going Public: The Development of Current Art Spaces in the Region." *Bidoun* 1. Last accessed March 5, 2021. https://bidoun.org/issues/1-we-are-spatial#going-public.

Kouoh, Koyo, ed. 2013. *Condition Report: Symposium on Building Art Institutions in Africa.* Ostfildern, Germany: Hatje Cantz Verlag.

Krauss, Rosalind. 1979. "Sculpture in the Expanded Field." *October* 8:30–44.

Kunci and EngageMedia. 2009. *VideoChronic: Video Activism and Video Distribution in Indonesia*. Pyrmont, Australia: EngageMedia.

Kunci and Para Site, eds. 2016. *Afterwork Readings*. Hong Kong: Kunci and Para Site.

Kuss, Alexandra. 2000. "Proximity and Distance—The Field of Tension between Individual and Society." In *AWAS! Recent Art in Indonesia*, 25–42. Yogyakarta, Indonesia: The Japan Foundation, HiVOS.

Kwon, Miwon. 2004. *One Place after Another: Site-Specific Art and Locational Identity*. Cambridge, MA: MIT Press.

Kyeyune, George. 2003. *Art in Uganda in the 20th Century*. PhD diss., London, SOAS.

Kyeyune, George. 2008. "Pioneer Makerere Masters." In *Art in Eastern Africa,* edited by Marion Arnold, 127–45. Dar Es Salaam, Tanzania: Mkuki na Nyota.

Lacy, Suzanne. 1995. *Mapping the Terrain: New Genre Public Art*. Seattle, WA: Bay Press.

Latour, Bruno. 2002. "What Is Iconoclash? Or Is There a World beyond the Image Wars?" In *Iconoclash: Beyond the Images Wars in Science, Religion, and Art,* edited by B. Latour and P. Weibel, 16–40. Cambridge, MA: MIT Press.

Léger, Marc James. 2012. *Brave New Avant-Garde: Essays on Contemporary Art and Politics*. Alresford, UK: Zero Books.

LEKRA. 1950. "The LEKRA Manifesto." Reproduced in Arbuckle 2000.

Lind, Maria. 2009. "Active Cultures. Maria Lind on the Curatorial." *Artforum* 48 (2): 102–3.

Lind, Maria. 2007. "The Collaborative Turn." In *Taking the Matter into Common Hands: On Contemporary Art and Collaborative Practices,* edited by J. Billig, M. Lind and L. Nilsson, 15–31. London: Black Dog Publishing.

Lindsay, Jennifer, and Maya H. T. Liem, eds. 2012 *Heirs to World Culture: Being Indonesian, 1950–1965*. Leiden: KITV Press.

Lippard, Lucy. 1984. "Color Scheming." In *Get the Message? A Decade of Art for Social Change*, 242–45. Boston: E. P. Dutton.

Lippard, Lucy. 1997. *The Lure of the Local: Senses of Place in a Multicentered Society*. New York: New Press.

Lippard, Lucy. 2017. "Preface." In *Delirium and Resistance: Activist Art and the Crisis of Capitalism,* by Gregory Sholette, xvii–xxix. London: Pluto Press.

Lazarus, Neil. 1999. *Nationalism and Cultural Practice in the Postcolonial World*. Cambridge: Cambridge University Press.

Lazarus, Neil. 2005. "The Politics of Postcolonial Modernism." In *Postcolonial Studies and Beyond*, edited by Ania Loomba, Suvir Kaul, Matti

Bunzl, Antoinette Burton, and Jed Esty, 423–39. Durham, NC: Duke University Press.

Loomba, Ania. 2015. *Colonialism/Postcolonialism*. 3rd ed. London: Routledge.

Lourenço, Eduardo. 1988. *O Labirinto da Saudade: Psicanálise mítica do destino português*. Lisbon: Dom Quixote.

Lourenço, Eduardo. 1999. *Mitologia da saudade, seguido de Portugal como destino*. Lisbon: Companhia das Letras.

Lourenço, Eduardo. 2001. *A nau de Ícaro: Imagem e miragem da lusofonia*. Lisbon: Companhia das Letras.

Lowe, Lisa. 2015. *The Intimacies of Four Continents*. Durham, NC: Duke University Press.

Luso-Brazilian Review. 2003. Special issue, "António Vieira and the Luso-Brazilian Baroque" 40 (1).

Lynd, Staughton, and Andrej Grubačić. 2008. *Wobblies and Zapatistas: Conversations on Anarchism, Marxism, and Radical History*. Oakland, CA: PM Press.

Maasri, Zeina. 2009. *Off the Wall: Political Posters of the Lebanese Civil War*. London: IB Tauris.

Mabaso, Nkule. 2016. "Editorial Note. In This Context: Collaborations and Biennials." *OnCurating* 32. Last accessed March 5, 2021. https://www. on-curating.org/issue-32.html#.yeiwbwj7q2w.

Macchiavello, Carla. 2015. "Caring, Curiosity and Curating, beyond the End." *Seismopolite: Journal of Arts and Politics* 11. Last accessed March 5, 2021. https://www.seismopolite.com/artandpolitics.

Macchiavello, Carla. 2018. "El darwinismo chileno: Apropriaciones del sur del sur en el arte chileno de los noventa." In *A la intemperie: Recomposiciones del arte en los años 90 en Chile*, edited by M. Dardel, C. Macchiavello, S. Salinero Rates, and M. Cárdenas Castro. Vol. 6. Santiago, Chile: LOM Ediciones.

Maharaj, Sarat. 2008. "'Sublimated with Mineral Fury': Prelim Notes on Sounding Pandemonium Asia." In *Farewell to Post-colonialism: The Third Guangzhou Triennial Reader*, edited by Gao Shiming, Sarat Maharaj, and Chang Tsong-zung, 66–97. Guangzhou, China: Guangzhou Triennial.

Makdisi, Saree. 1997. "Laying Claim to Beirut: Urban Narrative and Spatial Identity in the Age of Solidere." *Critical Inquiry* 23:661–705.

Maldonado-Torres, Nelson. 2005. "Frantz Fanon and C. L. R. James on Intellectualism and Enlightened Rationality." *Caribbean Studies* 33 (2): 149–94.

Maldonado-Torres, Nelson. 2008. *Against War: Views from the Underside of Modernity*. Durham, NC: Duke University Press.

Maldonado-Torres, Nelson. 2011. "Thinking through the Decolonial Turn: Post-continental Interventions in Theory, Philosophy, and Critique—An

Introduction." *Transmodernity: Journal of Peripheral Cultural Production of the Luso-Hispanic World* 1 (2).

Mamdani, Mahmood. 1996. *Citizen and Subject: Contemporary Africa and the Legacy of Late Colonialism.* Princeton, NJ: Princeton University Press.

Marambio, Camila. n.d. "Oda a Yvette." Unpublished essay.

Martin, Courtney J. 2010. "Rasheed Araeen, Live Art, and Radical Politics in Britain." *Getty Research Journal* 2:107–24.

Martin, Randy. 2002. *Financialization of Daily Life.* Philadelphia, PA: Temple University Press.

Mashaa Collective. 2013. "Reclaiming the Commons in Beirut." *ArteEast: The Global Platform for Middle East Art,* Fall 2013. http://arteeast.org/quarterly/reclaiming-the-seashore-through-art-and-activism/.

Mata, Inocência. 2006. "Estranhos em permanência: A negociação da identidade portuguesa na pós-colonialidade." In *Portugal não é um pais pequeno: Contar o Império na Pós-Colonialidade,* edited by M. Ribeiro Sanches, 285–317. Lisbon: Cotovia.

McClintock, Anne. 1992. "The Angel of Progress: Pitfalls of the Term 'Post-Colonialism.'" *Social Text* 31/32:84–98.

McKee, Yates. 2017. *Strike Art: Contemporary Art and the Post-Occupy Condition.* New York: Verso.

McLemee, Scott, ed. 1996. *C. L. R. James and the "Negro Question."* Jackson: University of Mississippi Press.

Medeiros, Tomás de. 2012. *A verdadeira morte de Amílcar Cabral.* Lisbon: Althum.

Melas, Natalie. 2007. *All the Difference in the World: Postcoloniality and the Ends of Comparison.* Stanford, CA: Stanford University Press.

Melas, Natalie. 2014. "Comparative Noncontemporaneities: C. L. R. James and Ernst Bloch." In *Theory Aside,* edited by Jason Potts and Daniel Stout, 56–78. Durham, NC: Duke University Press.

Mignolo, Walter. 2003. *The Darker Side of the Renaissance: Literacy, Territoriality, and Colonialization.* Ann Arbor: Michigan University Press.

Mignolo, Walter. 2009. *The Idea of Latin America.* Oxford: Blackwell.

Mills, Charles. 2017. *Black Rights / White Wrongs: The Critique of Racial Liberalism.* Oxford: Oxford University Press.

Mirzoeff, Nicholas. 2017. *The Appearance of Black Lives Matter.* Miami, FL: Name.

Mitchell, W. J. T. 2002. "Imperial Landscape." In *Landscape and Power,* edited by W. J. T. Mitchell, 5–35. Chicago, IL: University of Chicago Press.

Mitchell, W. J. T. 2013. *What Do Pictures Want? The Lives and Loves of Images.* Chicago, IL: University of Chicago Press.

Mombaça, Jota. 2017. "A coisa tá branca!" *Buala*. Last accessed March 5, 2021. http://www.buala.org/pt/mukanda/a-coisa-ta-branca.

Monroe, Kristin V. 2016. *The Insecure City: Space, Power, and Mobility in Beirut.* New Brunswick, NJ: Rutgers University Press.

Moon, Damon. 2000. "Guess Who's Coming to Dinner? Some Observation on Trans-cultural Curation." In *AWAS! Recent Art in Indonesia*, 63–74. Yogyakarta, Indonesia: The Japan Foundation, HiVOS.

Mosquera, Gerardo, ed. 1996. *Beyond the Fantastic: Contemporary Art Criticism from Latin America.* London: InIVA.

Moten, Fred. 2013. *In the Break: The Aesthetics of the Black Radical Tradition.* Minneapolis: University of Minnesota Press.

Mudimbe, Valentin-Yves. 1988. *The Invention of Africa: Gnosis, Philosophy, and the Order of Knowledge.* Bloomington, Indiana University Press.

Museum Nusantara. n.d. *Reformasi Indonesia! Protest in Bleed, 1995–2000.* Delft, Netherlands: Museum Nusantara.

Nabulime, Lillian Mary. 2007. *The Role of Sculptural Forms as a Communication Tool in Lives and Experiences of Women with HIV/AIDS in Uganda (PhD Dissertation).* Newcastle, UK: University of Newcastle.

Nabulime, Lilian, and Cheryl McEwan. 2011. "Art as Social Practice: Transforming Lives Using Sculpture in HIV/AIDS Awareness and Prevention in Uganda." *Cultural Geographies* 18 (3): 275–96.

Naeff, Judith. 2014. "Absence in the Mirror: Beirut's Urban Identity in the Aftermath of Civil War." *Contemporary French and Francophone Studies* 18 (5): 549–58.

Naeff, Judith. 2018. *Precarious Imaginaries of Beirut: A City's Suspended Now.* London: Palgrave.

Nagawa, Margaret. 2008. "The Challenges and Successes of Women Artists in Uganda." In *Art in Eastern Africa*, edited by Marion Arnold, 145–69. Dar Es Salaam, Tanzania: Mkuki na Nyota Publishers.

Nagle, John. 2018a. "Beyond Ethnic Entrenchment and Amelioration: an Analysis of Non-Sectarian Social Movements and Lebanon's Consociationalism." *Ethnic and Racial Studies* 41 (7): 1370–89.

Nagle, John. 2018b. "Defying State Amnesia and Memory Wars: Nonsectarian Memory Activism in Beirut and Belfast City Centres." *Social & Cultural Geography.* Last accessed March 5, 2021. https://www.tandfonline.com/doi/abs/10.1080/14649365.2018.1497191?journalCode=rscg20.

Namakula, Elizabeth. 2014. "Mapping Kampala with KLA ART 014." *Start: Journal of Arts and Culture* (Kampala), November 20. http://startjournal.org/2014/11/mapping-kampala-with-kla-art-014/.

Neves, José. 2017. "Ideologia, ciência e povo em Amílcar Cabral." *História, Ciências, Saúde-Manginhos* 24 (2). Last accessed March

5, 2021. https://www.scielo.br/scielo.php?script=sci_arttext&pid= S0104-59702017000200333&lng=pt&tlng=pt.

Neogy, Rajat. 1961. "Culture in Transition." *Transition* 1 (November): 2–5.

Nielsen, Neil. 1996. "Negativities of the Popular: C. L. R. James and the Limits of 'Cultural Studies'" In *Rethinking C. L. R. James,* edited by Grant Farred, 85–103. Cambridge: Blackwell.

Nielsen, Aldon Lynn. 1997. *C. L. R. James: A Critical Introduction.* Jackson: University Press of Mississippi.

Nilges, Mathias. 2015. "Neoliberalism and the Time of the Novel." *Textual Practice* 29 (2): 357–77.

Nilges, Mathias. 2019. *Right-Wing Culture in Contemporary Capitalism: Regression and Hope in a Time without Future.* London: Bloomsbury.

Nilges, Mathias, and Michael D'Arcy. 2016. *The Contemporaneity of Modernism: Literature, Media, Culture.* New York: Routledge.

Oguibe, Olu, and Okwui Enwezor, eds. 1999. *Reading the Contemporary: African Art from Theory to the Marketplace.* London, InIVA.

Okeke-Agulu, Chika. 2010. "Roundtable II: Contemporary African Art History and the Scholarship." *NKA* 26:80–151.

Okolloh, Ory. 2015. "Ory Okolloh Explains Why Africa Can't Entrepreneur Itself Out of Its Basic Problems" *Quartz Africa,* September 15. Last accessed March 5, 2021. https://qz.com/502149/video-ory-okolloh-explains-why-africa-cant-entrepreneur-itself-out-of-its-basic-problems/.

Osborne, Peter. 2013. *Anywhere or Not at All: Philosophy of Contemporary Art.* London: Verso.

Osborne, Peter. 2018. *The Postconceptual Condition: Critical Essays.* London: Verso.

Ose, Elvira Dyangani. 2013. "La poétique de l'Extra-ordinaire : L'esthétique de la Reconnaissance dans L'art Contemporain Africain." In *Condition Report: Symposium on Building Art Institutions in Africa,* edited by Koyo Kouoh, 109–21. Ostfildern, Germany: Hatje Cantz Verlag.

Pal Singh, Nikhil. 2005. *Black Is a Country: Race and the Unfinished Struggle for Democracy.* Cambridge, MA: Harvard University Press.

Pal Singh, Nikhil. 2017. *Race and America's Long War.* Berkeley: University of California Press.

Parry, Benita. 1998. "Resistance Theory / Theorizing Resistance." In *Modernism and Négritude: The Poetry and Poetics of Aimé Césaire,* edited by James Arnold. Cambridge, MA: Harvard University Press.

Parry, Benita. 2002. "Liberation Theory: Variations on Themes of Marxism and Modernity." In *Marxism, Modernity and Postcolonial Studies,* edited by Crystal Bartolovich and Neil Lazarus, 125–50. Cambridge: Cambridge University Press.

Parry, Benita. 2004. *Postcolonial Studies: A Materialist Critique*. London: Routledge.

Pease, Donald. 2001. "Introduction." In *Mariners, Renegades, and Castaways: The Story of Herman Melville and the World We Live In*, by C. L. R. James, vii–xxxiii. Hanover, NH: Darmouth College.

Peck, Jaime. 2010. *Constructions of Neoliberal Reason*. Oxford: Oxford University Press.

Peet, Roger. 2007. "Taring Padi: Under Siege in Indonesia." In *Realizing the Impossible: Art against Authority*, edited by J. MacPhee and E. Reuland, 120–30. Oakland, CA: PM Press.

Peixe Dias, Bruno, and Nuno Dias, eds. 2012. *Imigração e racismo em Portugal*. Lisbon: Edições 70 and Le Monde Diplomatique.

Peralta, Elsa. 2013. "A composição de um complexo de memória: O caso de Belém, Lisboa." In *Cidade e Império: Dinâmicas coloniais e reconfigurações pós-coloniais*, E. Peralta and N. Domingos (organizers). Lisbon: Edições 70, 361–415.

Peters-Klaphake, Katrin. 2014. "KLA ART Puts East African Art on the Map." *Contemporary And*. Last accessed March 5, 2021. http://contemporaryand.com/magazines/kla-art-puts-east-african-art-on-the-map/.

Petersen, Anne Ring. 2017. *Migration into Art: Transcultural Identities and Art-Making in a Globalised World*. Manchester, UK: Manchester University Press.

Philipsen, Lotta. 2010. *Globalizing Contemporary Art: The Art World's New Internationalism*. Aarhus, Denmark: Aarhus University Press.

Phillips, Don. 2017. "'This Exhibition Contains Nudity': The Front Line of Brazil's Culture Wars." *Guardian*, November 30, 2017. Last accessed March 5, 2021. https://www.theguardian.com/cities/2017/nov/30/exhibition-nudity-brazil-culture-wars-sao-paulo-mam-masp-modern-art.

Pieters, Katrin. 2015. "Art in Kampala at Work 012." In *New Spaces for Negotiating Art and Histories in Africa*, edited by Kerstin Pinther, Ugochukwu-Smooth C. Nzewi, and Berit Fischer, 52–72. Berlin: Lit Verlag.

Pincus, Robert L. 1995. "The Invisible Town Square: Artists' Collaborations and Media Dramas in America's Biggest Border Town." In *But Is It Art?: The Apirit of Art as Activism*, edited by Nina Felshin. Seattle, WA: Bay Press.

Pinther, Kerstin, Ugochukwu-Smooth Nzewi, and Berit Fischer, eds. 2015. *New Spaces for Negotiating Art and Histories in Africa*. Berlin: Lit Verlag.

Povinelli, Elizabeth. 2011. *Economies of Abandonment: Social Belonging and Endurance in Late Liberalism*. Durham, NC: Duke University Press.

Powell, Richard. 2002. *Black Art: A Cultural History*. London: Thames & Hudson.

Puzon, Katarzyna. 2016. "Memory and Artistic Production in a Post-War

Arab City." In *Post-Conflict Performance, Film, and Visual Arts,* edited by Des O'Rawe and Mark Phelan, 265–85. London: Palgrave.

Quijano, Aníbal. 2007. "Colonialidad del poder y clasificación social." In *El giro decolonial: Reflexiones para una diversidad epistémica más allá del capitalismo global,* edited by S. Castro-Gómez and R. Grosfóguel, 93–127. Bogotá: Siglo del Hombre Editores.

Rabaka, Reiland. 2010a. *Africana Critical Theory: Reconstructing the Black Radical Tradition, from W. E. B. Du Bois and C. L. R. James to Frantz Fanon and Amílcar Cabral.* Lanham, MD: Lexington Books.

Rabaka, Reiland. 2010b. *Forms of Fanonism: Frantz Fanon's Critical Theory and the Dialectics of Decolonization.* Lanham, MD: Rowman & Littlefield.

Rabaka, Reiland. 2014. *Concepts of Cabralism: Amílcar Cabral and Africana Critical Theory.* Lanham, MD: Lexington Books.

Ramnath, Maia. 2015. "No Gods, No Masters, No Brahmins: An Anarchist Inquiry on Caste, Race, and Indigeneity in India." In *No Gods, No Masters, No Peripheries: Global Anarchism,* edited by Barry Maxwell, 44–80. Oakland, CA: PM Press.

Rancière, Jacques. 2010. *Dissensus: On Politics and Aesthetics.* London: Continuum.

Raposo, Otávio, and Pedro Varela. 2017. "Faces do racismo nas periferias de Lisboa. Uma reflexão sobre a segregação e a violência policial na Cova da Moura." Paper presented at the 9th Portuguese Conference of Sociology.

Rath, Amanda Katherine. 2005. *Taboo and Transgression in Contemporary Indonesian Art.* Ithaca, NY: Cornell University, Herbert F. Johnson Museum of Art.

Raven, Arlene. 1989. *Art in the Public Interest.* Ann Arbor, MI: UMI Research Press.

Reckitt, Helena. 2013. "Forgotten Relations: Feminist Artists and Relational Aesthetics." In *Politics in a Glass Case: Feminism, Exhibition Cultures, and Curatorial Transgression,* edited by A. Dimitrikaki and L. Perry, 131–57. Liverpool, UK: Liverpool University Press.

Richter, Max M. 2008. "Other Worlds in Yogyakarta: From Jatilan to Electronic Music." In *Popular Culture in Indonesia: Fluid Identities in Post-Authoritarian Politics,* edited by A. Heryanto, 164–82. Abingdon, UK: Routledge.

Rivera Cusicanqui, Silvia. 2010. *Ch'ixinakax utxiwa: Una reflexión sobre prácticas y discursos descolonizadores.* Buenos Aires: Tinta Limón.

Robinson, Cedric. 2005. *Black Marxism: The Making of the Black Radical Tradition.* Chapel Hill: University of North Carolina Press.

Ross, Andrew. 1996. "Civilization in One Country? The American James." In *Rethinking C. L. R. James,* edited by Grant Farred, 75–85. Cambridge: Blackwell.

Saad Filho, Alfredo, and Lecio Morais. 2018. *Brazil: Neoliberalism versus Democracy*. London: Pluto Press.

Sadek, Walik. 2007. "Place at Last." *Art Journal* 66 (2): 34–47.

Sadek, Walik. 2015. "When Next We Meet: On the Figure of the Nonposthumous Survivor." *ArtMargins* 4 (2): 48–63.

Sadek, Walik, and Mayssa Fattouh. 2012. "Tranquility Is Made in Pictures." *Filip* 17. Last accessed March 5, 2021. https://fillip.ca/content/tranquility-is-made-in-pictures.

Said, Edward. 2012. *Representations of the Intellectual*. New York: Knopf Doubleday Publishing Group.

Salloukh, Bassel F., Rabie Barakat, Jinan S. Al-Habbal, Lara W. Khattab, and Shoghig Mikaelian, eds. 2015. *The Politics of Sectarianism in Postwar Lebanon*. London: Pluto Press.

Salti, Rasha. 2002. "Framing the Subversive in Post-War Beirut." In *Home Works: A Forum on Cultural Practices in the Region: Egypt, Iran, Iraq, Lebanon, Palestine, and Syria,* edited by Christine Tohme and Mona Abu Rayyan, 78–94. Beirut: Ashkal Alwan.

Salti, Rasha. 2008. "Urban Scrolls and Modern-Day Oracles: The Secret Life of Beirut's Walls." *Third Text* 22 (5): 615–27.

Sambrani, Chaitanya. 2016. "PERSAGI (Persecutan Ahli-Ahli Gambar Indonesia)." *Routledge Encyclopedia of Modernism*. Last accessed March 5, 2021. https://www.rem.routledge.com/articles/persagi-persatuan-ahli-ahli-gambar-indonesia.

San Juan, E. Jr. 2002. "Postcolonialism and the Problematic of Uneven Development." In *Marxism, Modernity, and Postcolonial Studies,* edited by Crystal Bartolovich and Neil Lazarus, 221–40. Cambridge: Cambridge University Press.

Sankara, Thomas. 2007. *Thomas Sankara Speaks: The Burkina Faso Revolution, 1983–1987*. London: Pathfinder.

Sansi Roca, Roger. 2014. *Art, Anthropology, and the Gift*. London: Palgrave.

Sapega, Ellen W. 2008a. *Consensus and Debate in Salazar's Portugal: Visual and Literary Negotiations of the National Text, 1933–1948*. University Park: Penn State University Press.

Sapega, Ellen W. 2008b. "Remembering Empire / Forgetting the Colonies: Accretions of Memory and the Limits of Commemoration in a Lisbon Neighborhood." *History and Memory* 20 (2): 18–38.

Schatzki, Theodore. 2001. "Introduction: Practice Theory." In *The Practice Turn in Contemporary Theory,* edited by T. Schatzki, K. N. Cetina and E. Von Savigny, 10–24. London: Routledge.

Schwarz, Bill. 2005. "C. L. R. James's *American Civilization*." *Atlantic Studies* 2 (1): 15–43.

Scott, David. 1999. *Refashioning Futures: Criticism after Postcoloniality.* Princeton, NJ: Princeton University Press.

Scott, David. 2004. *Conscripts of Modernity: The Tragedy of Colonial Enlightenment.* Durham, NC: Duke University Press.

Scott, David. 2013. *Omens of Adversity: Tragedy, Time, Memory, Justice.* Durham, NC: Duke University Press.

Scott, David, and Charles Hirschkind, eds. 2006. *Powers of the Secular Modern: Talal Asad and His Interlocutors.* Stanford, CA: Stanford University Press.

Seigneurie, Ken. 2011. *Standing in the Ruins: Elegiac Humanism in Wartime and Postwar Lebanon.* New York: Fordham University Press.

Sen, Krishna, and David T. Hill, eds. 2007. *Media, Culture, and Politics in Indonesia.* Jakarta and Kuala Lumpur, Equinox.

Sen, Krishna, and David T. Hill, eds. 2011. *Politics and the Media in Twenty-First Century Indonesia: Decade of Democracy.* London: Routledge.

Seo, Myengkyo. 2013. *State Management of Religion in Indonesia.* Abingdon, UK: Routledge.

Serubiri, Moses. 2016. "A Tree in Public Space." *Start: Journal of Arts and Culture* (Kampala), June 1. Last accessed March 5, 2021. http://start-journal.org/2015/06/a-tree-in-public-space/.

Sethi, Rumina. 2011. *The Politics of Postcolonialism: Empire, Nation, and Resistance.* London: Pluto Press.

Seto, Ario. 2017. *Netizenship, Activism, and Online Community Transformation in Indonesia.* London: Palgrave.

Sharpe, Christina. 2016. *In the Wake: On Blackness and Being.* Durham, NC: Duke University Press.

Shiming, Gao. 2008. "Observations and Presentiments on 'After Post-colonialism.'" In *Farewell to Post-colonialism: The Third Guangzhou Triennial Reader 3,* edited by Gao Shiming, Sarat Maharaj, and Chang Tsong-zung, 40–66. Guangzhou, China: Guangzhou Triennial.

Shiva, Vandana. 1993. *Monocultures of the Mind: Perspectives on Biodiversity and Biotechnology.* London: Zed.

Shohat, Ella. 1992. "Notes on the 'Post-Colonial.'" *Social Text* 31/32, 99–113.

Sholette, Gregory. 2010. *Dark Matter: Art and Politics in the Age of Enterprise Culture.* London: Pluto Press.

Sholette, Gregory. 2016. "Encountering the Counter-Institution: From the Proto-Academy to Home Workspace Beirut." In *Future Imperfect: Contemporary Art Practices and Cultural Institutions in the Middle East,* edited by Anthony Downey, 190–205. Berlin: Stenberg Press.

Sholette, Gregory. 2017. *Delirium and Resistance: Activist Art and the Crisis of Capitalism.* London: Pluto Press.

Shukaitis, Stephen. 2015. *The Composition of Movements to Come: Aesthetics and Cultural Labor after the Avant-Garde*. Lanham, MD: Rowman & Littlefield International.

Sinaga, Dolorosa. 2011. "Taring Padi: Not for the Sake of a Fine Arts Discourse." In *Taring Padi: Art Smashing Tyranny*, 23–41. Yogyakarta, Indonesia: Taring Padi.

Singh, Julietta. 2017. *Unthinking Mastery: Dehumanism and Decolonial Entanglements*. Durham, NC: Duke University Press.

Smith, Andrew. 2006a. "'A Conception of the Beautiful': C. L. R. James's *Glasgow Herald* Cricket Articles." *International Journal of the History of Sport* 23 (1): 46–66.

Smith, Andrew. 2006b. "Beyond a Boundary (of a Field of Cultural Production): Reading C. L. R. James with Bourdieu." *Theory, Culture and Society* 23 (4): 95–112.

Smith, Andrew. 2010. *C. L. R. James and the Study of Culture*. New York: Palgrave.

Smith, Andrew. 2016. "The Window and the Wardrobe: C. L. R. James and the Critical Reading of Sport and Literature." *Journal of Postcolonial Writing* 52 (3): 262–73.

Smith, Linda Tuhiwai. 2013. *Decolonizing Methodologies: Research and Indigenous People*. London: Zed.

Smith, Terry. 2009. *What Is Contemporary Art?* Chicago, IL: Chicago University Press.

Smith, Terry. 2011. *Contemporary Art: World Currents*. London: Lawrence King.

Smith, Terry. 2012. *Thinking Contemporary Curating*. New York: Independent Curators International.

Smith, Terry. 2016. *The Contemporary Composition*. Berlin: Stenberg Press.

Smith, Terry. 2019. *Art to Come: Histories of Contemporary Art*. Durham, NC: Duke University Press.

Sommer, Doris. 2014. *The Work of Art in the World: Civic Agency and Public Humanities*. Durham, NC: Duke University Press.

Sousa Ribeiro, António, and Margarida Calafate Ribeiro (organizers). 2016. *Geometrias da memória: Configurações pós-coloniais*. Porto, Portugal: Afrontamento.

Spielmann, Yvone. 2007. *Contemporary Indonesian Art: Artists, Art Spaces, and Collectors*. Singapore: National University of Singapore Press.

Spivak, Gayatri Chakravorty. 1999. *A Critique of Postcolonial Reason: Towards a History of the Vanishing Present*. Cambridge, MA: Harvard University Press.

Spivak, Gayatri Chakravorty. 2003. *Death of a Discipline*. New York: Columbia University Press.

St. Louis, Brett. 2007. *Rethinking Race, Politics, and Poetics: C. L. R. James's Critique of Modernity.* Oxford: Routledge.

Stavrides, Stavros. 2013. "Re-inventing Spaces of Commoning: Occupied Squares in Movement." *Quaderns-e,* 18 (2): 40–52.

Stavrides, Stavros. 2016. *Common Space: The City as Commons.* London, Zed.

Steyerl, Hito. 2009. "In Defense of the Poor Image." *E-Flux* 10 (November 2009). Last accessed March 5, 2021. https://www.e-flux.com/journal/10/61362/in-defense-of-the-poor-image/.

Steyerl, Hito. 2016. "A Tank on a Pedestal: Museums in an Age of Planetary Civil War." *E-Flux* 70. Last accessed March 5, 2021. http://www.e-flux.com/journal/70/60543/a-tank-on-a-pedestal-museums-in-an-age-of-planetary-civil-war/.

Steyerl, Hito. 2017. *Duty Free Art: Art in the Age of Planetary Civil War.* London: Verso.

Stoler, Ann Laura, ed. 2013. *Imperial Debris: On Ruins and Ruination.* Durham, NC: Duke University Press.

Sudjojono, Sindudarsono, and Brigitta Isabella. 2017. "'We Know Where We Will Be Taking Indonesian Art', 1948." *Southeast of Now: Directions in Contemporary and Modern Art in Asia* 1 (2): 159–64.

Sumartono. 2001. "The Role of Power in Contemporary Yogyakartan Art." In *Outlet: Yogyakarta within the Contemporary Indonesian Art Scene,* edited by M. Larner, 17–63. Yogyakarta, Indonesia: Cemeti Art Foundation.

Supangkat, Jim. 1997. *Indonesian Modern Art and Beyond.* Jakarta: The Indonesian Fine Arts Foundation.

Supangkat, Jim. 2005. "Art and Politics in Indonesia." In *Art and Social Change: Contemporary Art in Asia and the Pacific,* edited by C. Turner, 218–29. Canberra: Padanus Books, Research School of Pacific and Asian Studies and Australian National University.

Supriyanto, Eric. 2013. "Indonesian Contemporary Art: Becoming Contemporary, Becoming Global." In *SIP! Indonesian Art Today,* edited by M. Arndt, 8–16. Berlin: Distanz.

Taring Padi. 1998. "Manifesto: The Institute of People Oriented Culture, 'Taring Padi.'" Reproduced in Arbuckle. 2000.

Taring Padi. 2011. *Taring Padi: Art Smashing Tyranny.* Yogyakarta, Indonesia: Taring Padi.

Taylor, Christopher. 2012. "Sharing Time: C. L. R. James and Southern Agrarian Movements." *Social Text* 30 (2): 75–98.

Teh, David. 2012. "Who Cares a Lot? Ruangrupa as Curatorship." *Afterall* 30. Last accessed March 5, 2021. https://www.afterall.org/publications/journal/issue.30/who-cares-a-lot-ruangrupa-as-curatorship.

Thiong'o, Ngugi wa. 1993. *Moving the Center: The Struggle for Cultural Freedoms.* Oxford: James Currey.

Thompson, Clive. 2014. *Smarter Than You Think: How Technology Is Changing Our Minds for the Better*. New York, Penguin.

Thompson, Nato. 2015. *Art Activism in the 21st Century*. New York: Melville House.

Thompson, Nato. 2017. *Culture as Weapon: The Art of Influence in Everyday Life*. New York: Melville House.

Todorov, Zvetan. 1984. *The Conquest of the America: La conquista de América: El problema del otro*. Mexico: Siglo Veintiuno Editores.

Tomás, António. 2007. *O fazedor de utopias: Uma biografia de Amílcar Cabral*. Lisbon: Tinta da China.

Tomás, António. 2016. "Cabral and the Postcolony: Postcolonial Reading of Revolutionary Hopes." *Postcolonial Studies* 19 (1): 22–36.

Tomii, Reiko. 2018. *Radicalism in the Wilderness: International Contemporaneity and 1960s Art in Japan*. Cambridge, MA: MIT Press.

Tomii, Reiko, and Midori Yoshimoto, eds. 2013. *Collectivism in 20th-Century Japanese Art*. Durham, NC: Duke University Press.

Toufic, Jalal. 2009. *The Withdrawal of Tradition: Past a Surpassing Disaster*. Los Angeles: California Institute of the Arts.

Transnational Decolonial Institute. 2011. "Decolonial Aesthetics Manifesto." Last accessed March 5, 2021. https://transnationaldecolonialinstitute. wordpress.com/decolonial-aesthetics/.

Traverso, Enzo. 2016. *Left-Wing Melancholia: Marxism, History, and Memory*. New York: Columbia University Press.

Traverso, Enzo. 2017. *Left-Wing Melancholia: Marxism, History, and Memory*. New York: Columbia University Press.

Traverso, Enzo. 2019. *The New Faces of Fascism: Populism and the Far Right*. London: Verso.

Trouillot, Michel Rolph. 1995. *Silencing the Past: Power and the Production of History*. Boston: Beacon Press.

Tuck, Eve, and K. Wayne Yang. 2012. "Decolonization Is Not a Metaphor." *Decolonization: Indigeneity, Education and Society* 1 (1): 1–40.

Turner, Caroline. 2005. "Indonesia: Art, Freedom, Human Rights and Engagement with the West." In *Art and Social Change: Contemporary Art in Asia and the Pacific*, edited by C. Turner, 196–218. Canberra: Padanus Books, Research School of Pacific and Asian Studies and Australian National University.

Tumusiime, Amanda Evassy. 2012. *Art and Gender: Imag[in]ing the New Woman in Contemporary Ugandan Art*. PhD diss., University of South Africa.

Vale de Almeida, Miguel. 2002. "O Atlântico Pardo: Antropologia, pós-colonialismo e o caso "lusófono." In *Trânsitos coloniais: Diálogos críticos luso-brasileiros,* edited by C. Castelo, M. Vale de Almeida, and B. Feldman-Bianco, 23–37. Lisbon: Imprensa de Ciências Sociais.

Vale de Almeida, Miguel. 2004. *An Earth-Colored Sea: "Race," Culture and the Politics of Identity in the Post-Colonial Portuguese-Speaking World.* New York: Berghahn.

Vanhoe, Reinaart. 2016. *Also-Space, from Hot to Something Else: How Indonesian Art Initiatives Have Reinvented Networking.* Breda, Netherlands: Onomatopee.

Vincent, Cédric. 2013. "Transition: A Review Tested by Post-colonial Africa." *C&,* October 2. Last accessed March 5, 2021. http://www.contemporaryand. com/magazines/transition-a-review-tested-by-post-colonial-africa/.

Vicente, Mercedes, and Beck Jee-sook, eds. 2008. *Activating Korea: Tides of Collective Action.* Seoul: Govett-Brewster and Insa Art Space of the Art.

Viveiros de Castro, Eduardo. 2017. *A inconstância da alma selvagem.* São Paulo: Ubu Editora.

Young, Robert. 2001. *Postcolonialism: An Historical Introduction.* Oxford: Blackwell.

Young, Robert. 2004. *White Mythologies: Writing History and the West.* London: Routledge.

Wallerstein, Immanuel. 2004. *World-System Analysis: An Introduction.* Durham, NC: Duke University Press.

Warsono, Nano. 2012. *Jogja Agro Pop: Negosiasi Identitas Kultural Dalam Seni Visual.* Yogyakarta, Indonesia: Jogja Agro Pop.

Weibel, Peter. 2013. "Globalization and Contemporary Art." In *The Global Contemporary and the Rise of New Art Worlds,* edited by Hans Belting, Andrea Buddensieg, and Peter Weibel, 20–28. Karlsruhe, Germany: ZKM.

Wilson-Goldie, Kaelen. 2007. "Contemporary Art Practices in Post-War Lebanon: An Introduction." In *Out of Beirut,* edited by Simon Harvey, 81–90. Oxford: JRP Ringier.

Wilson-Goldie, Kaelen. 2009. "On the Politics of Art and Space in Beirut." *Nafas Art Magazine.* Last accessed March 5, 2021. https://universes.art/ en/nafas/articles/2009/kaelen-wilson-goldie/.

Wiryomartono, Bagoes. 2017. "Political Culture and Media in Post-Suharto Indonesia." *WaccGlobal.* Last accessed March 5, 2021. http://www.waccglobal. org/articles/political-culture-and-media-in-post-suharto-indonesia.

Wright, Stephen. 2007. "Territories of Difference: An E-Mail Exchange between Tony Chakar, Bilal Khbeiz and Walik Sadek." In *Out of Beirut,* edited by Simon Harvey, 57–81. Oxford: JRP Ringier.

Wright, Stephen. 2013a. "The Escapologist: Rasheed Araeen and the Transformative Potential of Art beyond Art." *Northeastwestsouth.* Last accessed

March 5, 2021. http://northeastwestsouth.net/escapologist-rasheed-araeen-and-transformative-potential-art-beyond-art.

Wright, Stephen. 2013b. *Towards a Lexicon of Usership*. Last accessed March 5, 2021. http://museumarteutil.net/wp-content/uploads/2013/12/Toward-a-lexicon-of-usership.pdf.

Wynter, Sylvia. 1996. "Beyond the Categories of the Master Conception: The Counterdoctrine of the Jamesian Poiesis." In *C. L. R. James's Caribbean*, edited by Paget Henry and Paul Buhle, 63–92. Durham, NC: Duke University Press.

Wynter, Sylvia. 2003. "Unsettling the Coloniality of Being/Power/Truth/Freedom: Towards the Human, after Man, Its Overrepresentation—An Argument." *CR: The New Centennial Review* 3 (3): 257–337.

Zaatari, Akram. 2006. "Terms Falling: Between Artist, Curator, and Entrepreneur." *Bidoun* 6. Last accessed March 5, 2021. https://bidoun.org/articles/terms-falling.

Zibechi, Raúl. 2010. *Dispersing Power: Social Movements as Anti-State Forces.* Oakland, CA: AK Press.